T0391947

SILIUS ITALICUS

General Editors

ANTONY AUGOUSTAKIS   FEDERICA BESSONE

CHRISTER HENRIKSÉN   R. JOY LITTLEWOOD

GESINE MANUWALD   RUTH PARKES

CHRISTIANE REITZ

OXFORD COMMENTARIES ON FLAVIAN POETRY

The Oxford Commentaries on Flavian Poetry series makes available authoritative yet accessible scholarly editions of Flavian literature, including the works of such authors as Statius, Valerius Flaccus, Silius Italicus, and Martial. Through publishing traditional philological commentaries on individual poetic books it aims to promote and stimulate further scholarship on this key epoch in the history of Roman literature.

Silius Italicus

Punica
Book 9

Edited with Introduction,
Translation, and Commentary

by
NEIL W. BERNSTEIN

OXFORD
UNIVERSITY PRESS

Great Clarendon Street, Oxford, OX2 6DP,
United Kingdom

Oxford University Press is a department of the University of Oxford.
It furthers the University's objective of excellence in research, scholarship,
and education by publishing worldwide. Oxford is a registered trade mark of
Oxford University Press in the UK and in certain other countries

© Neil W. Bernstein 2022

The moral rights of the author have been asserted

First Edition published in 2022

Impression: 1

All rights reserved. No part of this publication may be reproduced, stored in
a retrieval system, or transmitted, in any form or by any means, without the
prior permission in writing of Oxford University Press, or as expressly permitted
by law, by licence or under terms agreed with the appropriate reprographics
rights organization. Enquiries concerning reproduction outside the scope of the
above should be sent to the Rights Department, Oxford University Press, at the
address above

You must not circulate this work in any other form
and you must impose this same condition on any acquirer

Published in the United States of America by Oxford University Press
198 Madison Avenue, New York, NY 10016, United States of America

British Library Cataloguing in Publication Data
Data available

Library of Congress Control Number: 2022936278

ISBN 978–0–19–883816–6

Printed and bound in the UK by
Clays Ltd, Elcograf S.p.A.

Links to third party websites are provided by Oxford in good faith and
for information only. Oxford disclaims any responsibility for the materials
contained in any third party website referenced in this work.

In memoriam optimi patris
Leonard S. Bernstein (1941–2016) ז״ל

Carissimis amatissimisque feminis
Yi-Ting Wang, Danielle, Hannah, et Isabelle Bernstein

Acknowledgments

I'd like to thank the people who generously contributed their time and learning to this second foray into Silius' inexhaustible poem. Antony Augoustakis, Sergio Casali, Neil Coffee, Michael Dewar, William J. Dominik, Kyle Gervais, and Christiane Reitz kindly read drafts of the commentary (sometimes multiple) and provided invaluable suggestions. Kyle Gervais once more provided constant feedback on interpretation and contributed many improvements to the text. While I was at work on this commentary, Antony Augoustakis invited me to collaborate on a translation of the complete poem for Routledge (Augoustakis and Bernstein 2021). Considering how to bring Silius' poem to a contemporary audience and consulting with him on issues in the text improved the commentary immeasurably. Brian Baer, Françoise Massardier-Kenney, and the other participants of the 2017 NEH seminar "What Is Gained in Translation" further helped me think about translation as a mode of interpretation. Michael Sisson and Michael Skupin once more rescued the actual translation from frigidity. Mark Halliday and Jill Rosser, extraordinary poets and teachers, patiently guided me through the world of contemporary poetry. My research assistants, Miranda Christy, Nick Hughes, and Rachel Thomas, offered timely help in checking references.

I had completed a preliminary draft of the commentary when Silvia Zaia kindly shared her dissertation on book 9 in advance of publication. Her work has enriched this commentary in innumerable ways, and I remain profoundly grateful for her generosity. Audiences at Brock, British Columbia, McMaster, Ohio University, Toronto, and Western University gave invaluable feedback on several of the arguments advanced here. Hannah Bernstein has long since outgrown the *Hunger Games* series, yet still recalled Haymitch's narrow escape from death (173–4n.).

I would also like to thank Jessica Andruss, Paolo Asso, Bryan Baur, Brian Collins, Matt Cornish, Cory Crawford, Fred Drogula, Lavinia Galli Milić, Iratxe García Amutxastegi, Craig Gibson, Lauren Donovan Ginsberg, Alison Keith, Helen Lovatt, Loren Lybarger, Ray Marks, Damien Nelis, Carole Newlands, Bill Owens, Sophia Papaioannou, Ruth Palmer, Ruth Parkes, Claire Stocks, Michiel Van der Keur, the two anonymous referees, and many others who offered their judgment and guidance.

I am grateful to the Ohio University College of Arts and Sciences for granting me sabbatical leave for 2019–20. The Western University Department of Classical Studies granted me a collegial part-time academic home through the Distinguished Scholar in Residence Program. My thanks to Kyle Gervais, Randall Pogorzelski, and the rest of this extremely congenial department for their hospitality.

viii   *Acknowledgments*

The Oxford University Press team guided this book through an extraordinarily efficient, courteous, and professional review and publication process. My thanks to Cheryl Brant, Daniel Gill, Charlotte Loveridge, Georgina Leighton, Karen Raith, and Vicki Sunter. Donald Watt performed expert copyediting and offered many helpful suggestions. I am grateful to De Gruyter for permitting me to reproduce, with additions and variations, the text and apparatus criticus of Joseph Delz, *Silius Italicus Punica* (Stuttgart: B. G. Teubner, 1987).

My family's love and unyielding support throughout a seemingly endless pandemic has once more made another book possible, and I dedicate it to them with all my love and gratitude.

Contents

INTRODUCTION	1
1. Silius Italicus, Consular and Poet	3
2. The Historiographical and Rhetorical Tradition of Cannae	5
3. The Episodes of *Punica* 9	9
a. Paulus and Varro (1–65)	9
b. Solymus and Satricus (66–177)	10
c. The harangue and the disposition of the opposing forces (178–277)	14
d. The battle commences (278–410)	16
e. *Steigerung*: Hannibal and Scipio, Mars and Pallas, Vulturnus (411–555)	17
f. The elephants and Varro's flight (556–657)	20
4. Epic Tradition: The Inter- and Intratextuality of Cannae	21
a. Intratextual Cannae	21
b. Cannae as civil war: The conflict of the consuls and the names of the Roman characters	23
c. Silius' Cannae and Lucan's Pharsalus: Correspondences with Lucan, *Bellum Civile* 7	24
5. Language and Style	27
a. Diction and linguistic register	28
b. Figures	29
c. Metrics and prosody	30
6. Text and Translation	31
TEXT AND TRANSLATION	33
Sigla	34
COMMENTARY	91
Bibliography	263
Indexes	
Index Locorum	279
General Index	301
Latin Words	305

Introduction

Introduction

1. SILIUS ITALICUS, CONSULAR AND POET

Tiberius Catius Asconius Silius Italicus was born between AD 25 and 29 and began his long and successful public career, likely in the 40s, as an orator in the centumviral courts.[1] Pliny the Younger provides the fullest witness to his life in an obituary (*Epistles* 3.7). According to Pliny, Silius "damaged his reputation under Nero," as "he was believed to have pursued political prosecutions of his own volition." Silius became one of the consuls of 68, the last year of Nero's reign, and "then had conducted himself wisely and affably as a friend of Vitellius."[2] Tacitus records Silius' participation, near the conclusion of the civil war, as a member of Vitellius' entourage during the peace negotiations with Flavius Sabinus in December 69 (*Hist.* 3.65.2). Silius' career continued under Vespasian, as proconsul of Asia in 77/8.[3] He then entered a lengthy period of retirement, "spending his days in the most highly learned conversations" (Pliny *Ep.* 3.7.8 *doctissimis sermonibus dies transigebat*). His elder son, L. Silius Decianus, continued the family's political involvement as suffect consul under Domitian in AD 94.[4] In his seventies, after the accession of Trajan, Silius developed an incurable tumor and abstained from food to hasten his own death (Pliny *Ep.* 3.7.1).

Silius' long political career gave him a perspective not shared by the author of any other extant epic before him. Every detail of the sparse biographical testimonia has occasioned speculation attempting to link it to a feature of the *Punica*. The poet's personal experience of civil war, especially the fighting on the Capitol, may stand behind the references to Hannibal's menace to Rome and the Gallic capture of the city (Mezzanotte 1995: 360–1). The poet's apparent sympathies with Domitian have been inferred from Jupiter's encomium of the

---

[1] For general treatments of Silius' life, see Bernstein 2017: xii–xv, Littlewood 2011: xv–xix and Augoustakis 2010b: 3–6. For the political and social context of his work, see Augoustakis 2010b, Rutledge 2009, Coleman 1986, McDermott and Orentzel 1977, and White 1975.

[2] Pliny *Ep.* 3.7.3 *laeserat famam suam sub Nerone (credebatur sponte accusasse), sed in Vitelli amicitia sapienter se et comiter gesserat.* Rutledge 2002: 268–9 doubts that the consulship was a reward for Silius' prosecutorial activity.

[3] See Calder 1935; *RE* s.v. *Silius* 17 (Klotz), *PIR*[1] C 474, *CIL* 6.1984.9.

[4] *CIL* XV.7302, Pliny *Ep.* 3.7.2, Mart. 8.66. See Schöffel 2002: 553–62.

4 Introduction

Flavian dynasty (*Pun.* 3.594–629) and the praise of the emperor's restraint of rapacious governors (14.684–8). Yet we cannot determine how the *Punica* specifically reflects the poet's personal experiences or punctually link its episodes to specific contemporary events. More persuasive approaches have contextualized the references to the contemporary world as part of the poem's extended meditation on monarchal power.[5] Marks (2013, 2010c) has observed that Silius' choice of a historical subject constitutes a deliberate rejection of the mythological focus of his contemporaries' epics, Valerius' *Argonautica* and Statius' *Thebaid*. As a poet whose aesthetic sensibilities were formed in the Neronian era, Silius worked in the tradition of historical epic characteristic of that period, best represented to us by Lucan's *Bellum Civile* and Petronius' civil war parody (Wilson 2013). Through his choice of a Roman subject, here cast in the form of an epic poem, Silius also fulfilled the retired consular's traditional task of writing history.[6]

After his proconsulship, Silius appears to have withdrawn from direct political involvement and turned to poetic composition. In his fourth book of epigrams, around AD 88, Martial identifies his consular patron as an epic poet (*Epig.* 4.14) working on an epic about the war with Hannibal. This very general statement might suggest that episodes of the *Punica* were available to a wider public during this period. Statius was at work on the *Thebaid* during this time, and the two poets seem to have drawn on each other's work; Marks (2014: 137) speaks of "bi-directional influence."[7] Pliny observes that Silius "wrote poems with more care (*cura*) than inspiration (*ingenium*)."[8] Inspiration and care (*cura* is used here as a synonym of *ars*) represented a traditional complementarity for ancient literary critics. Poetic success depended on exercising both. Horace's dictum and Ovid's contrasting judgments of his predecessors are the best known examples of the critical polarity of *ars* and *ingenium*.[9] This commentary focuses primarily on Silius' *cura*. Most lemmata begin from the assumption that Silius is intimately familiar with the historiographical and rhetorical tradition of Cannae (see section 2), as well as the language and themes of a lengthy poetic tradition (see section 4). Like every Roman epic poet before him, he reworks and combines elements of these traditions into a new poem.

---

[5] Marks 2005a exemplifies such an approach in his reading of Scipio. Fucecchi 2014 examines the theme of monarchal power in the *Punica*. Mezzanotte 1995 argues that the poet's intention to praise the Flavian dynasty goes beyond Jupiter's prophecy.

[6] See Gibson 2010, Manuwald 2014.

[7] Potential examples of bidirectional influence in *Punica* 9 occur at 244–5n. and 307n.

[8] Pliny *Ep.* 3.7.5 *scribebat carmina maiore cura quam ingenio.* See Dominik 2010.

[9] See Hor. *AP* 408–11 *natura fieret laudabile carmen an arte, / quaesitum est: ego nec studium sine diuite uena / nec rude quid prosit uideo ingenium: alterius sic / altera poscit opem res et coniurat amice* with Brink's note; Ov. *Am.* 1.15.14 [*Battiades...*] *ingenio non ualet, arte ualet,* with McKeown's note; and Ov. *Trist.* 2.424 *Ennius ingenio maximus, arte rudis.*

2. THE HISTORIOGRAPHICAL AND RHETORICAL TRADITION OF CANNAE

non alias maiore uirum, maiore sub armis
agmine cornipedum concussa est Itala tellus.

Pun. 8.352–3

At no other time did a greater army of foot soldiers
and cavalry under arms shake the land of Italy.

The largest battle of the ancient Greco-Roman world occurred on August 2, 216 BC, when Hannibal's Carthaginian forces met the Romans outside the little town of Cannae on the Apulian plains. This battle occurred a little less than two years after Hannibal's forces had swept down from the Alps. On their way south to Cannae, the Carthaginians had smashed several Roman armies sent to stop them in a series of battles in northern and central Italy (see map). These include the battles of the Ticinus River (November 218), the Trebia River (December 218), and Lake Trasimene (21 June 217), which Silius narrates in *Punica* Books 4 and 5.[10]

By this point, nearly two years into the war, the Roman leadership had sufficient evidence that they could not fight a pitched battle on open ground against the Carthaginians. Hannibal's experienced troops were better disciplined than the raw Roman recruits, and their commanders were better at tactical combat. On the Apulian plains, Hannibal could use his larger and better-trained cavalry forces to greater effect. At Cannae, he tricked the Romans into breaking through his weak center and then trapped them in a double envelopment.

The ancient historians tended to exaggerate the slaughter that followed in order to make Rome's resurgence appear all the more remarkable. As Daly (2002: 23) observes, "The casualty figures which Polybius gives for the battle are more symbolic than factual." Modern estimates suggest that the Carthaginians slaughtered between 67,000 and 85,000 Romans and allies, while losing only 6,000 of their own forces. This battle fought with muscle power accordingly compares with the greatest modern battles fought with artillery and machine guns. For comparison, Napoleon's forces suffered 25,000 casualties at Waterloo, while the British lost 58,000 troops on the first day of the Somme.

In his remarkable synthesis, *The Allure of Battle,* the military historian Cathal Nolan has written of the dangerous illusion cast by Cannae, from antiquity right up through the Schlieffen Plan of World War I and Saddam Hussein's promised Mother of All Battles in the Iraq War.[11] Nolan speaks of a circumstance

---

[10] See Stocks 2014: 36–46 for comparison of the structures of Silius' narrative with Livy's.

[11] See Schlieffen 1931. Moltke aimed for a "second Cannae" at the battle of Königgrätz (1866); Nolan 2017: 283.

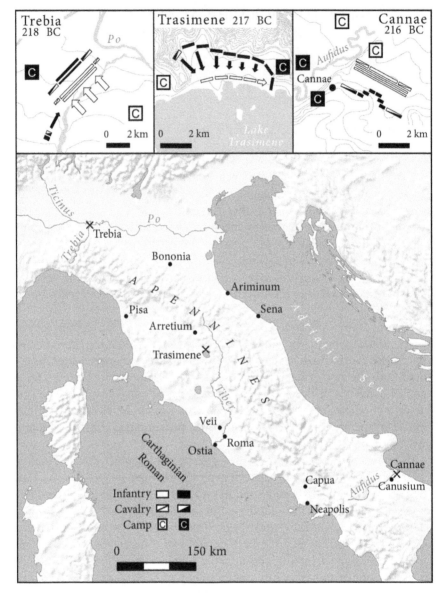

Map. Battles of Trebia, Trasimene, and Cannae

that occurred just often enough to deceive commanders into thinking that a massive battle could terminate a war. Roman epic tells its stories of battle in a similarly "alluring" vein. The poets focus on decisive battles, such as Actium in Virgil's *Aeneid*, Pharsalus in Lucan's *Civil War*,[12] or Theseus' swift victory at

---

[12] Section 4c details correspondences between Silius' Cannae narrative and Lucan's Pharsalus narrative.

2. *The Historiographical and Rhetorical Tradition of Cannae* 7

Thebes in Statius' *Thebaid*. Domitian's poem on the sacking of the Capitol (Mart. 5.5.7) may have adopted a similar approach. In Silius' day, the Flavian civil war similarly featured decisive battles, such as Bedriacum, which spelled the end for Otho, or Antonius Primus' assault on Rome, which brought down Vitellius.

But Cannae showed an important difference from these other decisive battles, real and mythical alike. Hannibal's overwhelming success in battle did not result in Carthaginian victory. As Nolan observes, this lesson was repeatedly forgotten throughout the history of Western warfare. Within a few years, the Romans recovered from the crushing defeat and forced their enemies to surrender. Silius accordingly gets to tell a story of defeat and swift recovery that neither Virgil nor Lucan chose to tell. The Cannae books, *Punica* 8–10, accordingly form an essential hinge in the epic, whether or not its author's original plan was to compose eighteen books.

For the Romans of the late Republic and early Empire, Cannae was one of Rome's greatest exemplary moments, an instance of hardship that inspired the ancestors to demonstrate their superior moral courage. Cicero (*Off.* 3.47) observes that "while suffering the disaster at Cannae, our Republic had greater courage than it ever did in prosperous times. There was no indication of fear, no talk of making peace."[13] Retelling episodes from the Second Punic War was a part of Roman education, and the Roman moralists would return again and again to Cannae as its central example.[14] In the tradition of these sources, the *Punica* represents Cannae as a moment of Roman moral greatness, spurred by military defeat.[15] Rome would go on to dominate the world, but suffer from moral decline as a consequence. Earlier critics accused Silius of indulging in nostalgia, as if writing about the Second Punic War were a means of looking away from the anxieties of his own times. But this perspective made sense to tradition-focused Romans; Cannae was also in the distant past for Cicero. Silius' narrative participates in a well-established Roman epic and rhetorical tradition.

The narrative of Roman generalship that leads to the disaster at Cannae forms a major theme in the first half of the *Punica*. Flaminius' failure at Trasimene leads Fabius to experiment with guerrilla warfare, which earns him the title of *Cunctator* ("Delayer") but keeps his troops alive. *Punica* Books 6 and 7 narrate Fabius' brief moment of success in the face of Hannibal's baiting and Minucius' insubordination. In Book 8, however, the newly elected consul Varro promises to end the war in a speedy victory, even though his consular colleague

---

[13] Cic. *Off.* 3.47: *nostra res publica ... quae Cannensi calamitate accepta maiores animos habuit quam umquam rebus secundis; nulla timoris significatio, nulla mentio pacis.*

[14] For education, see Kohl 1915: 92–6, who lists declamatory themes drawn from the Second Punic War. See also Juv. *Sat.* 7.160–4, with Courtney's note. For the moralists, see, e.g., Val. Max. 1.1.15–16, 6.4.1, 7.4.*ext.* 2, etc.; Tipping 2010: 36–9; Gallia 2012.

[15] See *Punica* 10.656–7, with Littlewood's note.

8   *Introduction*

Paulus attempts to restrain him. The earlier outcomes achieved by Flaminius and Fabius become their points of reference in their subsequent conflict.

For Paulus, Varro is another Flaminius who will bring on another defeat (55n.). For Varro, Paulus is as weak and cowardly as Fabius. Varro furthermore holds a trump card over Paulus. Paulus was earlier tried for malfeasance over his distribution of the war spoils from his Illyrian campaign during his consulship of 219 (see 25–7n. for sources). Had Paulus been convicted, he might have faced exile or even execution. As he gleefully abuses his colleague, Varro emphasizes Paulus' resulting unpopularity with the Roman people (23–37n.). Paulus' memory of the traumatic experience apparently leaves him less able to oppose Varro, and perhaps even predisposes him to make his suicidal charge in Book 10 rather than return home in further ignominy. As Marks (2005a) argues at length, the conflict between the consuls is one of Silius' many demonstrations of the ineffectiveness of republican government and the necessity of one-man rule.

The tragedy of Varro unfolds over Books 8–11 (Ariemma 2010). Silius characterizes him as "Varro, the source of all evil" (414n. *cuncti fons Varro mali*). Book 9 dramatizes his fateful decision to give battle at Cannae and its consequences. The consul repeatedly expresses contempt for negative omens and warnings from critics such as Fabius and Paulus. Fabius dubs Varro an *alter Flaminius* (8.310), and the new consul's behavior recapitulates crucial aspects of the previous one's. Both men rush into their consulship, experience mental disturbance, and express contempt for omens.[16] Unlike Varro, Flaminius at least has the experience of prior victories to contribute to his confidence. He dies in the battle he caused and thus becomes "no paltry example,"[17] where Varro incurs the additional shame of fleeing from Cannae.

Mental disturbance and inglorious retreat become Varro's leitmotifs throughout his tragedy. Before combat begins, Varro is *exsomnis* (5n.), *amens* (22n.), *turbidus* (23n., 36n.), *furens* (138n.), and *ardens* (262n.). The prophetic Roman soldier foretells his flight (8.666 *quo, Varro, fugis?*), while Solymus warns him *FVGE PROELIA VARRO* in a message written in his own blood (175n.). The narrator observes that Varro could have enjoyed a glorious death at Hannibal's hands, but for the gods' anger that sends Scipio to his rescue (424–30n.). In his apostrophe to Varro, the narrator observes that he will lament fleeing Hannibal's sword (427n.), and Varro contemplates suicide as he flees (649–50n.).

By contrast, the sole extended simile applied to Paulus in this book (38–43n.) compares him to a bereaved mother as he has a vision of the imminent death of his soldiers. The simile evokes a similar moment in Lucan (*BC* 2.297–304), where Cato compares himself to a father burying his child as he contemplates the imminent destruction of Caesar's invasion. As Ahl, Davis, and Pomeroy (1986: 2533–4) observe, the simile:

---

[16] Varro as an overeager charioteer (8.278–83); Flaminius as a bad helmsman (4.711–12). For mental disturbance, see 644n. ~ 5.54 *excussus consul fatorum turbine mentem*. Varro's contempt for omens: see 3–4n., 15–16n., 262n.; Flaminius' contempt (5.53–129).

[17] 5.638–9 *dabit exemplum non uile futuris / Flaminius*.

3. *The Episodes of* Punica 9

appears less grandiose and self-serving than Cato's and emphasizes the personal nature of Paulus's grief. The images of the great warrior and the mother are anti-thetical and paradoxical rather than mutually complementary as are those of the sage and father whose children represent, allegorically, the state. In Lucan, Cato's simile of the parent and child is a preamble to his wish to be the sacrificial offering for Rome's safety; in Silius the simile is a preamble to Paulus' speech begging Varro not to undertake the battle he knows will ruin Rome.

The contrast in characterization between the consuls continues into Book 10. Five more similes describe the doomed Paulus as he makes his suicidal charge, while Varro returns to Rome like a shipwrecked captain who should have gone down with his ship (10.608–14).

Comparison with the historiographical and rhetorical tradition shows that Silius has emphasized the tradition of hostility. Though critical of Varro, Livy offers a slightly more nuanced portrait of a commander who can remember Flaminius' example and respect certain omens. During the prelude to Cannae (Livy 22.42.9), Varro observes the sacred chickens' refusal to eat and does not give battle. After Cannae, the Senate preserves Varro's reputation by decreeing thanks to him and keeps him in various commands for the next decade.[18] The *Punica*, by contrast, emphasizes the differences between the reputations of Varro and Paulus. As he buries Paulus with extravagant honors, Hannibal gleefully exclaims: *'fuge, Varro'* (10.514), and Mago calls Varro "a coward who threw away his weapons" (11.524 *proiectis degener armis*) as he debriefs the Carthaginian Senate. Memory of a "consul shining the brighter in his purple" as he flees encourages the Capuans in their foolhardy opposition to Rome (11.154 *ut fugiat consul fulgentior ostro*). These contrasting models stand in the background during the final movement of the *Punica*, when the Senate debates Scipio's proposed invasion of North Africa (16.592–700). Against Fabius' opposition, Scipio justifies his aggression as more prudent than Varro's, and his success overturns the shame of Cannae.

3. THE EPISODES OF *PUNICA* 9

a. Paulus and Varro (1–65)

The initial episode of *Punica* 9 establishes the conflict between the consuls that continues throughout the book.[19] The narrator repeatedly characterizes Varro as hasty and hostile to good advice. The *proper-* ("hurry") stem serves as the consul's keyword (35n.). Like the youthful Hannibal, he is sleepless and wages fantasy battle in the dark (5n.). He ignores the omens that pervade Italy, in contrast to Paulus, who calls himself a *uates* as he delivers a prophecy of disaster

---

[18] See Clark 2014: 62–81; Rosenstein 1990: 32–3, 84–6.
[19] See Stocks 2014: 126–8, Ariemma 2010: 268–72, Niemann 1975: 164–74.

10   *Introduction*

(58n.). Viewing himself as a successor to Fabius, Paulus argues for continuing the strategy of guerrilla resistance (44–65n.).

Livy (22.41.1–3) reports an initial skirmish between the Romans and the Carthaginian raiders (cf. 10–12n.) and the subsequent disagreement between the consuls. Polybius (*Hist.* 3.110.3–5) reports the same conflicts more briefly. Livy's narrative continues by presenting a direct confrontation between the two consuls over the choice to give battle (Livy 22.44.5–7):

> inde rursus sollicitari seditione militari ac discordia consulum Romana castra, cum Paulus Sempronique et Flamini temeritatem Varroni, Varro Paulo speciosum timidis ac segnibus ducibus exemplum Fabium obiceret, testareturque deos hominesque hic, nullam penes se culpam esse, quod Hannibal iam uelut usu cepisset Italiam; se constrictum a collega teneri; ferrum atque arma iratis et pugnare cupientibus adimi militibus: ille, si quid proiectis ac proditis ad inconsultam atque improuidam pugnam legionibus accideret, se omnis culpae exsortem, omnis euentus participem fore diceret; uideret ut quibus lingua prompta ac temeraria aeque in pugna uigerent manus.

> This caused the camp of the Romans to be once more the scene of strife amongst the soldiers and dissension between the consuls. Paulus cast in Varro's teeth the recklessness of Sempronius and Flaminius; Varro retorted that Fabius was a specious example for timid and slothful generals, and called on gods and men to witness that it was through no fault of his that Hannibal had by now acquired as it were a prescriptive right to Italy, for he was kept in fetters by his colleague, and the soldiers, enraged as they were and eager to fight, were deprived of swords and arms. Paulus rejoined that if anything untoward should befall the legions, recklessly abandoned to an ill-advised and rash engagement, he would himself be guiltless of all blame, but would share in all the consequences; let Varro, he said, see to it, that where tongues were bold and ready, hands—when it came to fighting—were no less so.

> (tr. Yardley)

The terms of this conflict between the consuls help to structure the succeeding episodes of the book, as well as develop its civil war themes (see section 4b). When the corpses of Satricus and Solymus are discovered, Varro scornfully rejects Solymus' warning to flee the battle and claims such omens would only deter Paulus (262–6n.). This book's final moments (632–57n.) recapitulate the opening episode through ring composition. Varro ruefully concedes that Paulus was correct to issue his warning. Before the battle, only Paulus sees Varro as a madman (22 *amenti…uiro*); after the defeat, Varro accuses himself of *mentis…discordia* (648n.). The ring formed by the initial and concluding episodes defines the book as an integral unit within the larger three-book movement of Cannae.

b. Solymus and Satricus (66–177)

On the evening before the battle, Satricus, a Roman prisoner of war, escapes from the Carthaginian camp. He searches for armor amid the corpses of men

3. *The Episodes of* Punica *9*

who perished during the earlier skirmishing (66–89). Meanwhile, Satricus' son Solymus leaves his post and goes to look for the corpse of his brother Mancinus. He sees Satricus approaching from the direction of the Carthaginian camp, but does not recognize him in the darkness, and hurls his javelin (90–105). As Solymus approaches his victim, he sees him wearing his brother's armor and angrily promises to avenge him (106–19). His father Satricus identifies himself, absolves his son, and tells him to warn Varro not to give combat (120–51). Solymus ignores his father's absolution; after failing to keep his father alive, he stabs himself and writes "Varro, avoid the combat!" in his own blood (151–77). On the morning of the battle, the troops discover Solymus' warning and his corpse lying together with his father's. Varro insists that the omen would terrify a coward like Paulus, but not a brave patriot like him (262–6n.).[20]

This remarkable episode, one of the most effective in the *Punica*, recombines numerous type scenes into a new and original whole. One significant model is the epic night raid, whose primary exemplars are Homer's *Doloneia* and Virgil's Nisus and Euryalus episode. Elements such as the failed mission, the reflecting armor (106–9n.), and the address to the moon (168–72n.) evoke the Virgilian night raid. Silius' Flavian contemporaries developed the night raid in different directions from their Augustan predecessors. Valerius' night battle at Cyzicus stages the Ovidian theme of the mistaken encounter, this time on the battlefield (*Arg.* 3.1–261). The Argonauts unwittingly slaughter their former hosts in the dark, just as Solymus hurls a spear at his father on the assumption that he is a Carthaginian.

The multiple night raids in Statius' *Thebaid*, however, show that the type scene could be inspired by *pietas* rather than by *gloria* (Pollmann 2001). While Thiodamas leads a nighttime slaughter (Stat. *Theb.* 10.249–346), Hopleus and Dymas search for the corpses of their commanders Tydeus and Parthenopaeus (*Theb.* 10.347–448). At the epic's conclusion, Argia searches for her husband Polynices' body and unexpectedly encounters her sister-in-law Antigone engaged in the same quest (*Theb.* 12.349–408). Silius' men are similarly attempting to reunite their family: Satricus endeavors to return home, while Solymus is searching for his brother's corpse. Though their *pietas* is exemplary, tragic error leads them to destruction.

Some of the episode's tragic elements evoke Seneca's *Hercules Furens,* which Silius may have seen performed at the Neronian court. Amphitryon watches in horror as Hercules kills his family (*HF* 991–1031), but then forgives his son (*HF* 1200–57). Silius adapts the motifs of the parent's forgiveness of his murderous son's hands (125–6n.) and the murderer's address to his own hands (169n.).[21] He bends plausibility in assigning the ages of his characters to increase the pathos

---

[20] For discussions of the episode, see Ariemma 2010: 253–4, Marks 2010a: 137–8, Dominik 2006: 124–5, Fucecchi 1999: 315–22, 332–6, Mezzanotte 1995: 362–3, McGuire 1997: 134–5, Niemann 1975: 174–7.

[21] See Bernstein 2008: 132–59. Dominik 2006: 125 discusses the Solymus and Satricus episode as a recapitulation in miniature of the Saguntum episode. Dominik 2018 notes 169n. *pollutae*

12 *Introduction*

(70–1n.). The other Flavian epics make the extinction of family lines a major theme, as with the fall of Aeetes' house in the *Argonautica* and Oedipus' in the *Thebaid*. By contrast, Silius confines such tragic narratives to discrete episodes such as this one, the suicide at Saguntum (2.526–707), or the fall of the Syracusan monarchy (14.79–109).

The motif of mistaken identity recalls the Virgilian sack of Troy, during which the Trojans put on Greek armor (Verg. *Aen.* 2.395) and soon after draw their comrades' fire thanks to "the mistake of their crests" (*Aen.* 2.412 *errore iubarum*). Not all unwitting encounters occur on the battlefield, however. Bruère discusses allusion in the Satricus episode to three stories from Ovid's *Metamorphoses*, including Actaeon (66n.), Pyramus and Thisbe (81–2n., 98–9n., 108–9n.), and Cephalus and Procris (153–5n., 166–7n.).[22] Ovid's Pyramus and Thisbe story (*Met.* 4.55–166) similarly features a nighttime escape (81–2n.), hiding in a tomb when startled (98–9n.), and a mistaken recognition that results in the deaths of the principals.

Silius also drew on historiographical antecedents for this scene, which ranged more widely than the Second Punic War. In Livy's narrative, escapees from the Carthaginians bring a warning to the Romans not to give battle (Livy 22.42.10–12), but there is no nighttime drama of parricide and suicide. A popular story from Marius' capture of Rome, ultimately derived from the historian Sisenna, provides the motif of family murder. A soldier of Pompeius Strabo unwittingly killed his brother, who was fighting on the opposite side during the battle of the Janiculum in 87 BC.[23] Like Silius' Solymus, his response was to commit suicide out of *pietas*; he gave himself time first, however, to perform an elaborate funeral for his brother. The longest extant account is found in Valerius Maximus, who places it among stories of fraternal *caritas* (Val. Max. 5.5.4). Tacitus' version, included in his narrative of the later Flavian civil war as a comparison of past and present atrocities, ends with the pungent *sententia* "Just as glory in virtues was keener among our ancestors, so too was their shame in crimes."[24]

A less salutary historiographical narrative, but closer to the theme, comes from the Flavian civil war.[25] Vipstanus Messalla reported how a soldier in Galba's seventh legion killed his father, Julius Mansuetus. Like Silius' Solymus, he recognized his father as he plundered his corpse, and begged his forgiveness (160n.). Tacitus (*Hist.* 3.25) relates Messalla's account as follows:

---

dextrae as a programmatic evocation of Lucan's *Bellum Civile* (1.2–3 *populumque potentem / in sua uictrici conuersum uiscera dextra*) as a further analogy between parricide and civil war.

[22] See Bruère 1959. There are few significant verbal connections, however, between these episodes. Marks 2020 develops Bruère's discussion of Silius' dialogue with Ovid by examining the presence of motifs from the *Ibis* in the Cannae episode.

[23] Sisenna fr. 129 Peter; see Livy *Per.* 79, Val. Max. 5.5.4, Tac. *Hist.* 3.51, etc. The details of this battle remain confused; see Lovano 2002: 39–45.

[24] Tac. *Hist.* 3.51 *tanto acrior apud maiores, sicut uirtutibus gloria, ita flagitiis paenitentia fuit.*

[25] See most recently Dominik 2018: 284–6.

3. *The Episodes of* Punica 9 13

eo notabilior caedes fuit, quia filius patrem interfecit. rem nominaque auctore
Vipstano Messala tradam. Iulius Mansuetus ex Hispania, Rapaci legioni additus,
impubem filium domi liquerat. is mox adultus, inter septimanos a Galba conscrip-
tus, oblatum forte patrem et uulnere stratum dum semianimem scrutatur, agnitus
agnoscensque et exanguem amplexus, uoce flebili precabatur placatos patris
manis, neue se ut parricidam auersarentur: publicum id facinus; et unum militem
quotam ciuilium armorum partem? simul attollere corpus, aperire humum,
supremo erga parentem officio fungi. aduertere proximi, deinde plures: hinc per
omnem aciem miraculum et questus et saeuissimi belli execratio. nec eo segnius
propinquos adfinis fratres trucidant spoliant: factum esse scelus loquuntur
faciuntque.

The carnage was peculiarly marked by the fact that in it a son killed his own father.
The story and the names I shall give on the authority of Vipstanus Messala. Julius
Mansuetus of Spain, when enrolled with the legion known as Rapax, had left
behind him a young son. Later, when this son had grown up, he had been con-
scripted into the Seventh legion by Galba. Now he happened to meet his father,
whom he wounded and struck down; then, as he looked closely at the dying man,
the father and son recognized each other; the son embraced his expiring father
and prayed with tears in his voice that his father's spirit would forgive him and not
abhor him as a patricide. "The crime," he cried, "is the State's; and what does a
single soldier count for in civil war?" At the same time he lifted up the body and
began to dig a grave, performing the last duties toward a father. The soldiers near
first noticed it, presently more; then through the whole line were heard cries of
wonder, of pity, and of cursing against this most horrible war. Yet not one whit did
they slacken their murder of relatives, kinsmen, and brothers. They called the deed
a crime but did it.

(tr. Moore)

The Solymus episode contributes to the theme of family violence which per-
vades the first half of the *Punica*. The desperate Saguntines kill their own relatives to save them from Carthaginian capture (see *Pun.* 2.526–707 with my
commentary). Hanno demands Hannibal's son for ritual sacrifice; the commander views the choice as an honor, but claims that the boy has been reserved
for the greater fate of conquering the Romans (*Pun.* 4.763–829). Romans traditionally represented their consuls as the symbolic fathers of the state (Stevenson
1992), a motif that Silius employs in the initial series of battles. After Fabius
rescues his men from Hannibal's assault, they hail him as their father.[26] In the
present book, Paulus foresees the death of his men in the upcoming battle and
grieves like a mother bereaved of her son (40–3n). Solymus' vain efforts to
recover his brother's corpse and save his father's life, followed by suicide as
punishment for his error, provide a series of exempla for Varro beyond the
warning in blood (see further section 4b). The commander should have had

---

[26] *Pun.* 8.2–3; see Bernstein 2008: 139–56.

14   *Introduction*

concern for his symbolic children and not given battle. When the battle was lost, a suicidal charge like Paulus rather than inglorious flight may have been the more appropriate response to his failure, at least following the example of this episode.

c. The harangue and the disposition of the opposing forces (178–277)

The commander's inspiring speech before battle was a customary feature both of ancient historiography and of epic. By this point in Silius' narrative, there have been several examples of such "military harangues" (Villalba Álvarez 2008). Silius' Hannibal delivers a speech recalling his troops' accomplishments to date (184–91n.) and claims he needs no reward for himself except for glory (192–200n.). He offers Carthaginian troops rewards of land and allied forces grants of citizenship (200–11n.). The speech concludes with Hannibal's promise of a speedy end to the war; their next stop will be the Capitol (212–16n.).

Livy does not report a speech by either commander before Cannae. Silius has adapted in this harangue some elements of the speech given by Livy's Hannibal before Ticinus. These include the reminder of the troops' journey to date (185–6n; Livy 21.43.13) and the material offers of land and citizenship (200–11n.; Livy 21.45.5–6). Appian (*Hann.* 21) reports Hannibal's speech very briefly. Polybius is the only extant historiographical source to present a full speech for Hannibal at this moment (*Hist.* 3.111). The similarities between these speeches are not striking. Hannibal claims that his men have no need of inspiring words (Polyb. *Hist.* 3.111.5; cf. 184n.), a frequently employed topos. He claims that their victories have made them possessors of Italy and makes vague promises of Rome's wealth (*Hist.* 3.111.8–9), rather than enumerating their accomplishments and offering specific rewards.

Silius' Hannibal leads seasoned troops who have sacked Saguntum, crossed the Alps, and defeated Flaminius at Trasimene; yet he still regards it as his duty to inspire them before battle. There is an obvious contrast with Varro, a commander without previous military experience who leads raw recruits. It would have been helpful for him to offer them some encouragement and reminders to be wary of their formidable enemy. Instead, they have only heard on the previous day that each of them will be their own *dux* (33n.), possibly the worst thing to tell men facing a tactical genius like Hannibal. The absence of a harangue by Varro, whose *lingua procax* (*Pun.* 8.248) has supposedly benefited him heretofore, further testifies to his incompetence as a commander.

The opposed commanders then dispose their forces, beginning with Hannibal (217–43n.), who offers his troops a further exhortation (244–9n.). The Roman troops emerge from their rampart to discover the corpses of Satricus and Solymus. Varro shrugs off the terrible omen (249–66n.) and briefly

3. *The Episodes of* Punica 9

disposes his troops (267–77n.). The structure of the episode and its juxtapositions further emphasize the differences between the commanders. Hannibal's disposition of his troops occupies over twice as many lines as Varro's, which implies that he took far greater care over this essential tactical element. Meanwhile, he continues to inspire his men by offering to recognize their individual accomplishments, while Varro only presents a further denial of reality.

Though the narrator reports the disposition of forces omnisciently, it is evident that he does so from a Roman-centered perspective (Zaia 2016 *ad* 220–43). Livy places Hasdrubal on the left, Maharbal on the right, and Hannibal in the center (Livy 22.46.7); Silius similarly places Hannibal in the center (234–5n.), but Nealces on the left (226n.) and Mago on the right (227–9n.). The Roman commanders' disposition reflects the historiographical record somewhat more closely, possibly because these details were more fixed in the exemplary tradition. Silius describes each man as matched against a Carthaginian counterpart: Varro faces Nealces, Servilius Hannibal, and Paulus takes the right against Mago (267–74n.).[27]

The fiction of national unity forms another important component of the disposition narrative. Hannibal leads multiethnic forces who have followed him loyally from Africa, accompanied by others who have joined him along the way.[28] The enumeration of various North African peoples, followed by an array of Celtic and Spanish peoples (220–36n.), is an expansion of Livy's less specific designation of Africans, Gauls, and Spaniards (Livy 22.46.4). The miniature catalog further emphasizes Hannibal's ability to unite people who would otherwise have no connection by exerting personal charisma, offering material rewards, and activating their hatred of Roman domination. The Roman disposition narrative offers a briefer, but no less fictional account of Italian unity, a continuation of the fictions presented in the preceding book's catalog.[29] The narrative begins by specifying the participation of the Marsians and Samnites (269n.). The former would fight against Rome in the Social War; the latter had recently completed a series of bloody wars against the Roman invaders and would defect to Hannibal immediately after Cannae. As the contrast in matters of detail suggests, Silius' Cannae is no more the historiographers' version than Lucan's Pharsalus matches the accounts of Caesar or Appian. The poet's goal is to show Rome at its military nadir but moral zenith, with the entire peninsula united against a foreign enemy.[30]

---

[27] Cf. Livy 22.45.8 *consules cornua tenuerunt, Terentius laeuum, Aemilius dextrum*, Polyb. *Hist.* 3.113. See Bona 1998: 135, Cosack 1844: 33.

[28] See Dewar 2003, Auverlot 1992.

[29] *Pun.* 8.356–616; see Bernstein 2008: 189. Several of the populations that Silius lists in the Italian catalog either did not participate in the battle (such as the Praenestines, *Pun.* 8.365) or were supporters of Hannibal (the Ligurians, *Pun.* 8.605).

[30] Further divergences include the following: Silius is the only source to make the Aufidus River curve (219n.); Hannibal has elephant troops at his disposal (237–41n.), while Polybius indicates that he had none at this point (*Hist.* 3.74.11; see section 3f).

16   *Introduction*

d. The battle commences (278–410)

The initial phase of the battle[31] commences with an extended simile comparing the armies' advance to storm winds on the ocean (278–86n.). The simile marks the combat to come as Iliadic, and also prepares the reader for the subsequent interventions by the Vulturnus wind. *Discordia* then prompts the gods to descend to the battlefield (287–303n.). Virgil similarly sets Roman gods against a series of Egyptian gods at Actium, though naming only Anubis (*Aen.* 8.700–8), and Statius shows a confrontation between pro-Argive and pro-Theban gods (*Theb.* 10.883–98). At Cannae only one major Carthaginian god, Hammon, participates in support of his people, along with a crowd of minor divinities (298–9n.).

Beginning the catalog of deities who participate in the battle with *Discordia demens* (288n.) associates Cannae unmistakably with Roman civil conflict (see further section 4b). Ennius (*Ann.* 225 Skutsch) introduced *Discordia taetra*, who then enjoyed a long afterlife in Roman epic. She is one of the horrors resident in Virgil's Underworld, as well as one of the divine participants at Actium.[32] *Discordia* then appears seven times in Lucan's *Bellum Civile,* and Petronius includes her in his civil war parody. Statius involves her in his narrative of the Theban civil war, and Silius' Scipio encounters her during his descent to the Underworld.[33] In the *Argonautica*, Valerius drew the association between the *Discordia* of non-Roman peoples and Roman civil war. A simile compares the conflict between a pair of mythological Colchian brothers to warfare between Roman legions (*Arg.* 6.400–6). For Flavian readers, this simile inevitably recalls the recent war of AD 69 (Bernstein 2014). Silius' *Discordia,* then, is at once a component of a tradition that stretched back through Virgil to Ennius, as well as an immediately relevant reminder of the tenuousness of the present peace.

Juno's vendetta against the Romans is a familiar expectation by this stage of the *Punica*. From its opening lines, the narrative presents itself as a continuation of Virgil's mythological narrative, where the Romans are the successors to the Trojans (Bernstein 2018). Meanwhile, the participation of the minor Italian gods in defense of their homeland contributes to the fiction of Italian unity (Ripoll 2006: 249). The divine opposition accordingly reflects the Virgilian tradition quite closely; Juno and Minerva oppose the Romans, as they did throughout the *Aeneid*, and only one major foreign god receives a name. The

---

[31] I follow Niemann's division (1975: 184) for the phases of the battle: *Pun.* 9.278–410, 9.411–555, 9.566–657, 10.1–325.

[32] Verg. *Aen.* 6.280–1 *Discordia demens / uipereum crinem uittis innexa cruentis*; *Aen.* 8.702 *et scissa gaudens uadit Discordia palla.*

[33] Petr. *Sat.* 124.271–2 *ac scisso Discordia crine / extulit ad superos Stygium caput*; Stat. *Theb.* 2.288, with Gervais's note, *Theb.* 5.74, *Theb.* 7.50; Sil. *Pun.* 13.586–7 *Discordia gaudens / permiscere fretum caelo.*

3. *The Episodes of* Punica 9

motif emphasizes how Cannae has been represented throughout the epic as the high point of Juno's vengeance on the Romans (see further section 4a).

The beginning of combat showcases a series of familiar topoi, including Gigantomachic comparisons (304–9n.) and battle polyptoton (322–7n.). The opposing ranks are packed tight together (315–22n.), and the combatants fight with a variety of weapons (335–9n.) The invocation of the Muse (340–5n.), a motif that traditionally emphasizes the scale of the combat, is for once appropriate, as Cannae actually was the biggest battle of the ancient world. The address to Rome (346–53n.) develops the topos, familiar from Cicero (section 2), that adversity was morally beneficial for Rome, as its present prosperity has corrupted it (351–2n.). The conclusion of the Cannae episode employs the same motif, found throughout the historiographical and exemplary tradition. Fucecchi has aptly described Silius' "[invitation] to look at Cannae's tragic carnage as the first step of Rome's resurrection" as "an encomiastic paradox."[34]

After the initial volley, Nealces leads a successful breakthrough (354–69n.). Silius has drastically foreshortened the historiographical narrative of initial Roman breakthrough followed by double envelopment and slaughter.[35] His interest is not in verisimilitude but in *variatio* and exemplary narrative. The battle narration then proceeds through a series of individual vignettes. Scaevola vows to extend his fame through a heroic death, attacks numerous opponents, and is killed in turn by Nealces (370–400n.). The Carthaginian Symaethus then kills the friends Marius and Caper (401–10n.). Marius' name recalls the civil wars (see further section 4b), but Silius has carefully defused this association by making him one of a pair of idealized types who exemplify *concordia*.

e. *Steigerung*: Hannibal and Scipio, Mars and Pallas, Vulturnus (411–555)

After these duels between ordinary combatants, Silius elevates the narrative level by relating a series of extraordinary interventions. Hannibal pursues Varro (411–23n.), but Scipio intercepts him (424–37n.). A combat between the champions seems about to take place, both a rematch from Ticinus (430–3n.) and an evocation of the climactic duels of the *Iliad* or the *Aeneid*. An inconclusive result would risk bathos, while the death of one of the champions would have diverted the narrative impossibly from its historiographical frame. The passage accordingly shifts into a theomachy as Mars and Pallas each show concern for their favorites (438–85n.). This scene is the sole full-scale theomachy

---

[34] Fucecchi 2018: 33. See *Pun.* 10.656–7, with Littlewood's note.

[35] See Livy 22.47.5 *tandem Romani, diu ac saepe conisi, aequa fronte acieque densa impulere hostium cuneum nimis tenuem eoque parum ualidum, a cetera prominentem acie*; Polyb. 3.115.11–12.

18   *Introduction*

in Latin epic, in contrast to, for example, Apollo's briefer intervention at Virgil's Actium (Ripoll 2006: 238). Silius' model is the Homeric theomachy of Ares and Athene.[36] The Gigantomachic motifs introduced at the beginning of the combat continue: Mars offers Scipio a weapon forged in Aetna, like those carried by his father Jupiter (458–9n.), and Pallas tears away the side of a mountain to hurl at Mars (466–9n.).

Where Mars took no sides at Virgil's Actium (*Aen.* 8.700), here he has become a Roman patriot, while Minerva's support for Hannibal reflects her traditional opposition to the Trojans and thus by extension their descendants the Romans (Ripoll 2006: 250). The Budé editors put forth a related, but less likely hypothesis relating Minerva's support for Carthage to her putative African origins beside Lake Tritonis.[37] Marks's argument that Minerva's intervention in this scene should be read in limited terms is most persuasive. Her support of Hannibal "does not conflict or interfere with her long-term support of Rome: both loyalties can coexist" (Marks 2013: 300). Minerva's self-exculpation to Jupiter (530–4n.) is accordingly to be read sincerely.

After Minerva's departure, Mars rallies the Romans, and Aeolus responds by sending the Vulturnus wind at Juno's request (486–503n.). The prophetic soldier predicted this moment on the night before the battle: *Pun.* 8.663–4 *turbinibus furit insanis et proelia uentus / inque oculos inque ora rotat.* The wind devastates the Roman ranks (504–23n.). Meanwhile, Pallas and Juno complain to Jupiter about Mars's intervention (524–41n.). The supreme god reveals Fate to them: Scipio is destined to conquer the Carthaginians and win the title *Africanus,* while Hannibal will have to retreat from Italy (542–50n.). He sends Iris to recall Mars (551–5n.).

A divine narrative motivates the Vulturnus episode in the *Punica,* but it was also part of the historiographical tradition. Numerous sources blame the Roman defeat at Cannae partly on the Vulturnus wind. Livy observes what the Romans probably realized retrospectively, that Hannibal chose the site for his encampment in part to take advantage of the wind's direction.[38] The intense blast aided the Carthaginians in the battle by choking the Roman forces with dust (511–12n.):[39]

> uentus—Volturnum regionis incolae uocant—aduersus Romanis coortus multo
> puluere in ipsa ora uoluendo prospectum ademit.

> (Livy 22.46.9)

---

[36] Hom. *Il.* 5.846–63; see Juhnke 1972: 207–12. Ripoll 2006: 253 rather unfairly characterizes the episode as "une reprise plate et froide de topoi homériques."

[37] See *Pun.* 9.297n.; Volpilhac-Lenthéric 2003: 180 n.6.

[38] Livy 22.43.10–11 *prope eum uicum Hannibal castra posuerat auersa a Volturno uento, qui campis torridis siccitate nubes pulueris uehit. id cum ipsis castris percommodum fuit, tum salutare praecipue futurum erat cum aciem dirigerent, ipsi auersi terga tantum adflante uento in occaecatum puluere offuso hostem pugnaturi.*

[39] See also Sen. *NQ* 5.16.4, Florus *Epit.* 1.22, and Zonaras *Epit.* 9.1 καὶ ὁ ἄνεμος ὅ τε κονιορτὸς ἐς τὰς ὄψεις αὐτῶν βιαίως ἐμπίπτων ἐτάραττε καὶ τὸ ἆσθμα γινόμενον συνεχὲς ἐκ τοῦ καμάτου ἀπέφραττεν, ὥστ᾽ ἀπεστερημένοι μὲν τῆς ὄψεως, ἀπεστερημένοι δὲ καὶ φωνῆς, φύρδην καὶ ἐν οὐδενὶ κόσμῳ ἐφθείροντο.

3. *The Episodes of* Punica 9   19

The wind, locally known as the Volturnus, now rose in the direction of the Romans, rolling large clouds of dust right into their faces and obstructing their vision.

(tr. Yardley)

Some of the details, however, such as missiles sent backward by the wind (504–10n.), appear to derive from traditions not found in Livy. Venini ascribed this motif to poetic amplification; Lucarini observes, however, that the motif appears in Appian's account.[40] It is, therefore, likely that Silius adapted the motif from a historiographical or rhetorical tradition also used by Appian. In keeping with the *Steigerung* of this phase of the battle, the poet amplifies the wind's effects.

Hyperbolic description of the natural world is a typical feature of Roman epic. The *Punica* elsewhere exaggerates the effects of the tides at Gades (3.45–61), the Alps' sublimity (3.483–6), and the seismic violence of the Phlegraean Fields (12.113–57).[41] When Vulturnus returns to harass the Romans further at the climax of the battle, the wind even manages to push soldiers into the Aufidus River (10.205–7). Silius further embeds the wind's assault in a traditional epic narrative where the gods are ultimately responsible for disrupting normal conditions. Silius' gods characteristically call the natural world to their aid; for example, Juno asks the Trebia River to aid her in the battle, and Venus asks Neptune to end the storm (4.573–4) so Hannibal may be defeated militarily at Zama rather than ignominiously drowned (17.283–91).

Silius' contemporaries noticed his literary innovations in the Vulturnus episode, as well as his representation of the Campanian region. Statius makes the Vulturnus River one of the speakers of *Silvae* 4.3, his poem celebrating the completion in AD 95 of the *Via Domitiana* linking Sinuessa to Puteoli and Naples. As Fucecchi observes, this poem contains at least two unambiguous references to the Hannibalic invasion, which would seem irrelevant but for the existence of Silius' *Punica*.[42] These passages are likely not examples of what Marks has called "bi-directional influence" (see section 1), as we do not see evidence of Statius' influence on Silius here. Rather, Statius' shorter occasional poem tactfully celebrates the popularity of Silius' epic, which was likely nearing completion by AD 95.

---

[40] App. *Hann.* 22.99–100. See Lucarini 2004: 118–19, Nesselrath 1986: 216, and Venini 1972: 540–1.

[41] For Silius and the meteorological sublime, see Schrijvers 2006. For the Gades tides, see Manolaraki 2010. For the Alps, see Chaudhuri 2014: 234–43. For the Phlegraean Fields, see Muecke 2007.

[42] Examples include (a) Stat. *Silv.* 4.3.4–6 *certe non Libycae sonant catervae / nec dux advena peierante bello / Campanos quatit inquietus agros*; (b) Stat. *Silv.* 4.3.90–1 *qualis Cinyphius tacente ripa / Poenos Bagrada serpit inter agros*. See Fucecchi 2019: 191–3 for discussion.

20   *Introduction*

f. The elephants and Varro's flight (556–657)

After the gods depart the battlefield, Hannibal orders his elephant troops forward (556–60n.). He kills Minucius, Fabius' subordinate commander, whom he faced beforehand in *Punica* 7 (561–9n.). This conclusive rematch is a consolation prize for the combat with Scipio that he wanted. The elephants then advance (570–83n.) and kill individual Roman soldiers (584–98n.). Varro orders his men to assault the elephants with fire, which forces them to retreat to the river (599–619n.). Other Roman troops assault the elephants with missiles, and Mincius dies while fighting one single-handedly (620–31n.).

There were no elephants at the actual battle of Cannae. According to Polybius (*Hist.* 3.74.11), harsh winter weather after the Trebia killed all but one of them.[43] The Carthaginian Senate granted Hannibal elephant reinforcements only in 215 BC, after his success at Cannae (Livy 23.13.7). Silius is certainly aware of this tradition; Mago includes a request for more elephant troops when he debriefs the Carthaginian Senate after the battle (11.540 *defit iam belua*). Here as elsewhere, Silius' point in including the elephants is not historiographical verisimilitude, but to create further opportunities for his moralizing action story. His narrator admires the brave Roman soldiers who face an unfamiliar and overwhelming foe. As Burgeon (2016: 12) observes, the elephant is the allegorical emblem of Hannibal's army, and "malgré sa grandeur impressionante, voué à être vaincu par les vertueux Romains qui faisaient montre d'une grande *uirtus* et de *fides* à l'égard de l'*Vrbs*." Meanwhile, the Romans' efforts to bring down the beasts permit further variation in the battle narrative.

Although the Romans faced the elephants before at the Trebia (4.598–621), the new recruits at Cannae are presumably imagined to lack experience of them. The prophetic Roman soldier foresees the elephants' participation (8.670 *ac uictrix insultat belua campis*) as part of his catalog of frightening portents. The narrator admires the bravery of individual soldiers, such as Tadius, who fights back bravely after an elephant hoists him in the air (591–3n.), and Mincius, who suicidally fights one elephant single-handedly. Scholars have also seen connections between the Romans' assault with fire (599–619n.) and other combats.[44]

As the troops scatter, Paulus catches sight of Varro and rebukes him (632–57n.). The scene closes a ring with the book's opening; Paulus' warnings have come true, and Varro's bid to win re-election through a heroic victory turns into an ignominious flight from the battlefield. He contemplates suicide to avoid shame, a motif that evokes previous achieved and attempted suicides in the epic (644–51n.). The scene is the book's concluding instance of dialogue

---

[43] See also Livy 22.2.10; Livy 21.56.6 and 58.11 narrate the loss of the other elephants. See also Zonaras 8.24 (Dindorf 2.242.6–7).

[44] Burgeon 2016: 13 sees a prefiguration of the eventual burning of Carthage, as well as of Hannibal's attack on the Roman camp at Capua, which caused the Romans to retaliate with fire. See App. *Hann.* 7.41–2; Livy 26.5.10–26 does not mention the fire.

4. *Epic Tradition: The Inter- and Intratextuality of Cannae*   21

with Lucan's Pharsalus episode (see further section 4c). Lucan's Pompey has the choice to ride into battle like Paulus and die nobly: Luc. *BC* 7.669–70 *nec derat robur in enses / ire duci iuguloque pati uel pectore letum*. Instead the tradition reserves him, like Varro, for flight from the battlefield and the "ultimate fate" encoded by the historiographical record (Luc. *BC* 7.675–9). Where Varro thinks of no one but himself and his shame, Pompey is aware of his obligation to others. He thinks of sparing the lives of his soldiers, who may otherwise continue to fight over his body (*BC* 7.670–2), and of his wife Cornelia.

Lucan's narrator passes a different judgment on his *quondam* hero than Silius passes on Varro. This narrator speaks sympathetically to Pompey, where Silius allows Varro to condemn himself with his hesitant words. Pompey takes leave of Fate without care (Luc. *BC* 7.686–7 *iam pondere fati / deposito securus abis*), even though Fate has dictated that his body will be destroyed in shameful circumstances. Fortune has been the constant companion of his earlier career, and now he has superseded it: Luc. *BC* 7.686 *tam misero Fortuna minor*. In place of the fugitive, it is Caesar, like Varro, who will be the one judged by a hostile people when he enters Rome: Luc. *BC* 7.701–2 *quo pectore Romam / intrabit factus campis felicior istis?* In Lucan's conclusion to the Pharsalus episode, as Lovatt observes, "heroism and epic victory are utterly undermined by the civil war context" (2013: 117). Silius adapts the figure of the weak hero doomed to flight for his story of *bellum externum*.

4. EPIC TRADITION: THE INTER- AND INTRATEXTUALITY OF CANNAE

> Sometimes parts *don't* relate to each other in tidy and significant ways, but stick out like sore thumbs. Intratextuality is about how bits need to be read in the light of other bits, but it is also about the bittiness of literature, as uncomfortable squareness-in-round-(w)holeness.
>
> (Sharrock 2000: 7)

a. Intratextual Cannae

Sharrock's memorable formulation applies well to the Cannae episode's function within Silius' epic. It is the most significant "bit" of an epic that does not respect Romantic notions of organic unity. The three-book episode performs an important structural function as the hinge point of the seventeen-book epic, placed at the epic's center between Saguntum (Books 1 and 2) and Zama (Book 17). Repeated references to Cannae throughout the narrative forestall the epic's constant threat to disintegrate into bits. The battle serves as a reference point

22   *Introduction*

for the progress of Hannibal's invasion. Previous combats are preludes to Cannae, and subsequent ones fail to match its greatness. Silius embeds this event, like other key moments of the Second Punic War, within a mythological tradition that stretches from the Trojan War to his own day.

The epic's opening moments prefigure Cannae, as Juno foresees the battle and others share in the goddess's vision. Juno looks forward to seeing the field drenched in the blood of her Roman enemies: 1.50–1 *dum Cannas, tumulum Hesperiae, campumque cruore / Ausonio mersum sublimis Iapyga cernam.* Others who foresee Cannae include the Massylian priestess who delivers a prophecy as Hannibal takes his oath (1.125–6), the oracle of Ammon at Siwah (3.707 *inuade Aetoli ductoris Iapyga campum*), Proteus (7.481–4), and the prophetic Roman soldier (8.659–76). The narrator presents Cannae as the inevitable consequence of Varro's election as consul: 8.256–7 *Cannasque malum exitiale fouebat / ambitus.*

After the battle, the narrator and others refer to Cannae as the war's ultimate *comparandum*. As he concludes the narration of the battle, the narrator famously appeals to Cannae as the greatest moment for Roman mores and wishes Carthage remained to save Rome from moral decline: 10.657–8 *haec tum Roma fuit: post te cui uertere mores / si stabat fatis, potius, Carthago, maneres.* Victory emboldens Hannibal to make his theomachic assault on Rome (Chaudhuri 2014: 245–9). He cannot see why he should be deterred if Jupiter did not hurl his thunderbolt at Cannae (12.671–3).

The *Punica* presents the Second Punic War as a continuation of Juno's revenge on the Trojans. Within this larger frame, Silius figures Cannae as the revenge of two mythological opponents of Aeneas: the Greek hero Diomedes, who faced Aeneas at Troy; and Dido's sister, now the Italian goddess Anna Perenna. Cannae is located in the region supposedly once ruled by Diomedes, who took possession of south Italy after the Trojan War.[45] At *Aeneid* 11.252–93, the Greek hero rejects the Rutulian embassy and claims that he has suffered enough from his earlier war against the Trojans. Diomedes may not have fought the Trojans in Italy, but he will nevertheless get his revenge nine centuries later. Silius' Proteus informs the Nymphs that the Aetolian ghosts' vengeance has long been prophesied.[46]

As part of her preparations for Cannae, Juno summons Dido's sister Anna Perenna.[47] Though Anna purportedly supports the local Italians among whom she dwells, she remembers Aeneas' mistreatment of her sister and agrees to help Juno by encouraging Hannibal. Juno specifies that she and Hannibal are related through their common descent from Belus (8.30–1). For her part, Anna

---

[45] Silius' frequent references to Aetolia, the birthplace of Diomedes' father Tydeus, form part of his construction of Cannae's mythological narrative. Examples include 1.125 *Aetolos . . . campos*, 3.707, 7.483–4, 8.351, 99n., 495n., etc.

[46] 7.483–4 *damnatoque deum quondam per carmina campo / Aetolae rursus Teucris pugnabitis umbrae.*

[47] See McIntyre and McCallum 2019, Marks 2013.

4. *Epic Tradition: The Inter- and Intratextuality of Cannae* 23

agrees to assist the foreign invaders against the Romans who worship her, as a form of honor to her deceased sister Dido (8.39–43). Anna's conflict between her roles as an Italian goddess and a Carthaginian ancestor contributes to the Cannae episode's civil war theme (section 4b). Her hostility is limited spatially and temporally, however; she does not intervene after Cannae.

b. Cannae as civil war: The conflict of the consuls and the names of the Roman characters

The Cannae episode also presents the culmination of the narrative of Roman internal disunity. Earlier references to Roman discord begin with the epic's first meeting of the Roman Senate. Lentulus agitates for an immediate declaration of war on the Carthaginians, but Fabius prudently suggests trying diplomacy first (1.672–94). Flaminius' failure at Trasimene then provokes a conflict between proponents of opposed military strategies. After Trasimene, Fabius employs the delaying strategy that keeps his Roman troops alive. In doing so, however, he exposes himself to criticism from supporters of renewed attack and insubordination from his second in command, Minucius (see section 2 above). Hannibal's killing of Minucius at Cannae (563–7n.) provides a conclusion to this earlier episode of dissension. Fabius may have been able to rescue his subordinate once, but there is no keeping the Romans alive if they are determined to fight unwinnable battles.

In Book 8, Silius establishes Varro's election and the subsequent dissension between the consuls as a form of civil conflict that empowers the Carthaginians. For Fabius, Varro is a worse enemy than Hannibal waiting within his own camp (8.301 *teque hostis castris grauior manet*) and an *alter Flaminius* (8.310). Paulus agrees that Varro is the "other" consul given to the Carthaginians (8.332–3); for their conflict, see section 3a above. Further civil war motifs complement this conflict at the executive level. Solymus' parricide and suicide has been discussed above (see section 3b); the names of the Roman combatants provide a further example.

The catalog of individual combats is a standard narrative pattern in most ancient epics. However, Silius' Cannae establishes a contrast with Lucan's Pharsalus episode, which contains no narrative of combats between pairs of named warriors. Lucan's narrator explains that focusing on individuals would cause him shame when his subject is the collapse of the Republic (*BC* 7.617–19). Silius's Cannae narrative instead introduces several Roman characters who bear the family names of those who contributed most directly to the Republic's collapse. They have no known historiographical connection to the battle, and their names reflect subsequent periods of Roman civil strife (McGuire 1995). Key examples from book 9 include Marius (401–10n.) and Curio and Brutus (415n.); others from the neighboring books include Tullius (8.404) and Galba (10.194).

24 *Introduction*

The example of Curio demonstrates Silius' molding of historical narrative to produce an indirect commentary on his contemporaries' fear of renewed civil war. Other Scribonii may have been active at Cannae, though they had the cognomen Libo, not Curio.[48] Silius has changed the cognomen, a practice seen in other episodes,[49] to reflect C. Scribonius Curio, the praetor of 49 BC (*NP Scribonius* I.4). This Curio was a major figure in Caesar's civil war and receives a starring role in Lucan's *Bellum Civile* (Marks 2010b). As McGuire (1995: 111–12) observes:

> of the 84 historical and traceable [Roman] names, over half—47—have no known or presumable connection to the Second Punic War and have clear connections with the first centuries BCE and CE ... [The names] remind the reader that Rome's post-Cannae recovery will not necessarily be a permanent one.

For McGuire, the effect of the names was like a narrative where Washington crossed the Delaware with the Watergate conspirators. For this younger reader, born as the Watergate scandal was unfolding, it is more like reading a story of Gettysburg starring commanders named Reagan, Clinton, and Bush.

Though Silius tells the traditional story of Rome's greatest *bellum externum*, he complicates it by embedding unignorable reminders of its internal strife. Marks (2005: 283–8) reads the civil war elements of Cannae as a necessary precursor to Scipio's emergence, just as the civil wars of AD 69 were the precursor to the emergence of the Flavian dynasty. As Fucecchi (2018: 34) observes:

> by making Rome's worst defeat both the perturbing signal of the imminent crisis and the greatest victory of the Roman spirit of self-sacrifice, the *Punica* invites readers to look more confidently at the future ... Cannae's defeat provides the antidote which will allow Rome to survive the civil wars of the future, even those that Lucan could not forecast.

Silius' dialogue with Lucan's Pharsalus episode is another significant element of his civil war narrative, which I discuss in the next section.

c. Silius' Cannae and Lucan's Pharsalus: Correspondences with Lucan, *Bellum Civile* 7

As discussed above (section 2), Roman epic tells "alluring" stories of decisive battles. The *Punica* invites reading Cannae as an extended dialogue with Lucan's Pharsalus episode. The alignment between the two episodes begins with the

---

[48] Livy states that after Cannae, L. Scribonius appeared before the Senate as a delegate from the prisoners of war, and his relative L. Scribonius Libo, tribune of the plebs, made a motion for ransoming the prisoners. See Livy 22.61.6–7, 23.21.7. Schmitt argues that this story is "a mutation in the tradition and to be rejected" (*NP: Scribonius* I.5).

[49] For example, Tiberius Sempronius Longus (*NP: Sempronius* I.17) was the historiographically attested consul at Trebia. See Polyb. 3.71–4, Livy 21.52–6. Silius has assigned him the cognomen *Gracchus* (4.515 *degener haud Gracchis consul*) to evoke the Gracchi of the late second century BC.

4. Epic Tradition: The Inter- and Intratextuality of Cannae   25

initial conflict between Paulus and Varro over giving battle (see section 3a above). The scene evokes the similar moment immediately before Pharsalus, in which Lucan's Pompey responds to Cicero's urging to give battle (Luc. *BC* 7.87–123). Pompey expresses similar unwillingness to give battle on someone else's terms and points out that he has been successfully driving Caesar to defeat without bloodshed (*BC* 7.92–101). He characterizes a strategically appropriate decision to delay as bravery instead of cowardice: *BC* 7.105–7 *fortissimus ille est / qui, promptus metuenda pati, si comminus instent, / et differre potest*. In the end, Pompey reluctantly accedes, observing as he does that he risks destroying his troops (*BC* 7.107–23). Silius fills in his larger frame of Roman civil discord by introducing a Pompey figure at Cannae, headed for disaster as his peer pressures him to give battle.[50]

In the remainder of this section, I collect Silius' specific adaptations of passages of Lucan *BC* 7, and provide longer quotation to supplement the brief indications in the commentary.[51] Many of these passages are evidence of Silius' considerable effort to align his major battle scene specifically with Lucan's. Others, however, primarily represent the use of Lucan's verbal resources (e.g. 5n.) or both authors' participation in a common epic convention, such as 325–7n. (see further section 5a):

1–7n. Silius' gods send omens of defeat ~ Lucan's *Fortuna* sends omens of defeat:

- *BC* 7.151–2 *non tamen abstinuit uenturos prodere casus / per uarias Fortuna notas.*

- *BC* 7.205–6 *o summos hominum, quorum Fortuna per orbem / signa dedit, quorum fatis caelum omne uacauit!*

5n. *telumque manu uibrare* ~ Luc. *BC* 7.82 *uibrant tela manus.*

6n. Varro accuses Paulus of laziness ~ Pompey's soldiers accuse him of laziness: Luc. *BC* 7.52–3 *segnis pauidusque uocatur / ac nimium patiens soceri Pompeius.*

19–20n. Paulus hopes for one more day before the Romans are destroyed ~

- Lucan's narrator wishes the gods had given Pompey one more day: Luc. *BC* 7.30–1 *donassent utinam superi patriaeque tibique / unum, Magne, diem.*

- Pompey's wretched troops will not survive the whole day at Pharsalus: Luc. *BC* 7.47–8 *miseri pars maxima uolgi / non totum uisura diem tentoria,*

---

[50] See Marks 2010a: 138, Fucecchi 1999: 324.
[51] See the *index locorum* of Lanzarone 2016, as well as the full and sensitive discussions of Marks 2010a, Ariemma 2010, and Fucecchi 1999.

- Lucan's Lentulus looks back on the day of Pharsalus: Luc. *BC* 8.332 *una dies mundi damnauit fata?* See further 182–3n.

28–9n. Varro accuses Paulus of handing the soldiers' swords over to the enemy ~ Lucan's Pompey yields to Cicero and hands over *tam prospera rerum* to Fortune (Luc. *BC* 7.107–9).

30–4n. Varro tells his soldiers to ignore the *signum* for battle and be their own leaders ~
- Lucan's Cicero threatens Pompey with the troops' insubordination: Luc. *BC* 7.82–3 *uix signa morantia quisquam / expectat: propera, ne te tua classica linquant.*
- Each of Caesar's men follows *suum munus* and stands *ordine nullo*: Luc. *BC* 7.329–33.

44–65n. Paulus begs Varro not to give battle ~ Pompey expresses his reluctance to give battle (Luc. *BC* 7.87–123).

46n. *clade parce obuius ire* ~ Luc. *BC* 7.60 *cladibus inruimus nocituraque poscimus arma,* with Lanzarone's note.

52–3n. Paulus tries to persuade Varro that Fabius' delay did not mean cowardice (*cunctator et aeger, / ut rere, in pugnas Fabius*) ~ Pompey's forces similarly call him *segnis pauidusque* (Luc. *BC* 7.52) as he tries to persuade them *fortissimus ille est / qui, promptus metuenda pati, si comminus instent, / et differre potest* (Luc. *BC* 7.105–7).

66n. The narrator characterizes the killing of Satricus as *sceleratus…error* ~ Lucan's narrator asks the gods before Pharsalus: Luc. *BC* 7.58–9 *hoc placet, o superi, cum uobis uertere cuncta / propositum, nostris erroribus addere crimen?*

175n. Solymus writes in blood *FVGE PROELIA VARRO* ~ Lucan's narrator admonishes Pompey *fuge proelia dira* (Luc. *BC* 7.689), and earlier exhorts himself *hanc fuge, mens, partem belli tenebrisque relinque* (*BC* 7.552).

178–83n. The sun rises reluctantly at Cannae and Pharsalus: Luc. *BC* 7.1–2 *segnior, Oceano quam lex aeterna uocabat, / luctificus Titan.*

182–3n. Cannae was a unique day in history for the Carthaginians ~ Pharsalus was a unique day in Roman history that reversed all the preceding years of Rome's fate: Luc. *BC* 7.426–7 *sed retro tua fata tulit par omnibus annis / Emathiae funesta dies.*

210–11n. Hannibal offers his allied troops Carthaginian citizenship if they kill Romans (*ciuis…esto*) ~ Caesar orders his men to spare Pompeian fugitives and regard them as fellow citizens; Luc. *BC* 7.318–19 *uos tamen hoc oro, iuuenes, ne caedere quisquam / hostis terga uelit: ciuis qui fugerit esto.*

The disposition of forces: 217–43 (Carthaginian), 267–77 (Roman) ~ Luc. *BC* 7.214–34. Both Hannibal and Pompey lead multiethnic armies (Luc. *BC* 7.272–3 *mixtae dissona turbae / barbaries*).

217–18n. Hannibal throws over the *uallum* ~ Caesar does the same: Luc. *BC* 7.326 *sternite iam uallum fossasque implete ruina.*

244–51n. Hannibal promises to recognize his men's individual accomplishments ~ Caesar makes a similar promise: Luc. *BC* 7.287–9 *cuius non militis ensem / agnoscam? caelumque tremens cum lancea transit / dicere non fallar quo sit uibrata lacerto.*

259n. The Romans discover a father and son dead together (*et similes defuncto in corpore uultus*) and are aghast at the ill omen ~ Lucan's Sextus makes an ill-omened necromantic consultation immediately before Pharsalus: Luc. *BC* 6.631 *et uocem defuncto in corpore quaerit.* Soldiers also deliver prophecies before the major battle: Lucan's dead soldier at *BC* 6.776–820, the Roman soldier at *Pun.* 8.656–76.

304–9n. A simile compares Cannae to the Gigantomachy ~ Lucan similarly compares Pharsalus to the Gigantomachy: Luc. *BC* 7.144–50.

323–4n. "Battle polyptoton" ~ Luc. *BC* 7.573 *confractique ensibus enses.*

325–7n. Spears conceal the sky ~ Luc. *BC* 7.519–20 *ferro subtexitur aether / noxque super campos telis conserta pependit.*

333–4n. The soldiers shout ~ see Luc. *BC* 7.367–8 *plures tantum clamore cateruae / bella gerent,* with Lanzarone's note.

346–53n. The narrator addresses the Romans regarding their moral decline after Cannae ~ Lucan's narrator addresses the Romans regarding loss of liberty under the Caesars after Pharsalus (Luc. *BC* 7.205–13).

354–7n. Fortune varies in battle ~ Luc. *BC* 7.487–8 *rapit omnia casus / atque incerta facit quos uult Fortuna nocentes.*

5. LANGUAGE AND STYLE

Recent studies have examined general tendencies in Silius' uses of poetic language. This section accordingly focuses briefly on selected features specific to *Punica* 9.[52] In the Commentary, I use the formula "the phrasing is modeled on (Virgil, Ovid, Lucan, etc.)" to indicate that the poet used his predecessor's work as a verbal resource, without necessarily pointing to a strong thematic connection.

---

[52] For fuller discussion, see Bernstein 2017: xliii–xlvi, García Amutxastegi 2015: 27–34, Littlewood 2011: lxxx–lxxxvi, Santini 2008.

28 *Introduction*

a. Diction and linguistic register

Repetition with varied diction. Silius characteristically emphasizes an idea through repetition with varied diction. In terms of its frequency, "Silius' repetition is more abundant than Virgil's, yet far less so than Lucan's, and so retains its emphatic effect."[53] These effects are clearest in the book's opening episode, where the narrator foregrounds Varro's indifference to the omens and frantic desire to give an unwinnable battle. Five different words and phrases denote these omens: 1 *monstris*, 2 *signa*, 3 *omina*, 15 *pecudum fibras*, 16 *auspicia*. By contrast, variations on a single lexeme (*proper-*) characterize Varro's foolish haste: 8 *properi certaminis*, 18 *properanti in fata*, 35 *propere*. The repetition has been carefully spaced throughout the passage to avoid a sense of redundancy. Other examples of repetition with varied diction include 373n. *letum... mortem*, etc. In two places, the expectation of *variatio* may bear on the establishment of the text. See 399–400n. and 428–30n.

Original phrasing. García Amutxastegi (2015: 28) notes the following instances of original phrasing: 210n. *Ausonia...caede*, 334n. *Martis inops*, 574n. *Libycarum armenta ferarum*, 595n. *erectis...cruribus alte*. She further lists as "giros rebuscados e insólitos" (2015: 29) phrases including 61n. *crastina signa*, 295n. *mutato Castore*, 511n. *fauces praeclusus*, and 584n. *trepidos rerum*.

Graecisms. Like his Flavian contemporaries, Silius makes frequent use of Graecisms. In addition to proper names, he employs common nouns such as 220n. *barbaricus*, 444n. *cometen*, 497n. *barathro*, 587n. *thorax*.

Common words and their alternatives. Like the other epic poets, Silius often uses a common word, but will employ its more elevated synonym more frequently. Examination of the frequency of his choices reveals his poetic preferences. I give the following examples:

> *ductor* vs. *dux*. Servius on Verg. *Aen.* 2.14 observes DVCTORES *sonantius est quam 'duces'*; Silius uses *ductor* 199 times vs. *dux* 115 times; contrast *ductor* 23 times in Verg. *Aen.*, 8 times in Luc. *BC*.[54] See 24n.

> *ater* vs. *niger*. Bennardo (2021) quantifies and discusses the Flavian poets' uses of *ater* and *niger*; for the latter adjective, see 365n. Silius strongly prefers *ater* (96 times) to *niger* (20 times), as does Virgil ([*Aen.*] *ater* 71 times; *niger* 15 times); the other poets use both terms more equally. See 153–4n. and 365n.

> *senior* vs. *senex*. Silius uses *senior* more frequently (23 times) than *senex* in the singular (9 times). Statius' usage is comparable; see Stat. *Theb.* 2.94 with Gervais's note.

---

[53] Bernstein 2017: xliv. See also Spaltenstein 1986 on *Punica* 1.190.
[54] See Roche on Luc. *BC* 1.228, Harrison on Verg. *Aen.* 10.186, and Austin's note on Verg. *Aen.* 2.14.

5. Language and Style   29

ingens. Silius is more restrained in his use of the common epic adjective *ingens* than Virgil. *Ingens* appears 81 times in the *Punica* against 168 times in Verg. *Aen.,* 93 times in Stat. *Theb.*

b. Figures

Alliteration. Alliteration is very frequent. I give some notable examples of the figure:

> 152–3n. *non uerba uicesque / alloquio uocemue refert*: a plethora of "conversation" words, featuring alliteration of V-, emphasize Solymus' focus on attempting to save his father Satricus' life instead of responding to his pleas.

> 266n. *signauit moriens sceleratum sanguine carmen*: alliteration of S- emphasizes Varro's contempt for Solymus, whom he dismisses as an intentional parricide.

> 598n. *sternuntur subita, miserandum, mixta ruina*: alliteration and disrupted rhythm assist in describing an elephant's ungainly collapse.

Anaphora and gemination. Examples include 28–9 *tradant...tradant,* 290–2 *hinc Mauors, hinc Gradiuum.../ hinc Venus amens.../ hinc Vesta,* 515–16 *nunc...nunc,* etc. A run of geminations from 335–9 reflects the confusion of combat: see 335–6 *hi sude.../ hi pinu...hi pondere,* 338–9 *interdum...interdum.*

Chiasmus and synchysis. Flammini (1983) offers a lengthy (but not exhaustive) list of examples of chiasmus and synchysis, from which I select a few examples in Book 9. Simple examples include 406–7n. *sociataque toto / mens aeuo,* 625n. *digna uiro, fortuna digna.* An elegant example of chiasmus with variation in diction occurs at 150–1n. *absoluo...manum /...dextra, precor,* emphasizing the reference to Solymus' murderous hand. For an even more elaborate example of triple chiasmus, see 581–2n. *stat niueis longum stipata per agmina uallum / dentibus,* referring to the palisade formed by the elephants' tusks.

Figura etymologica. Like his Flavian contemporaries, Silius the *doctus poeta* displayed considerable learning throughout the *Punica* (Pomeroy 1990). Examples of *figurae etymologicae* in Book 9 include: 69n. *dono datus,* 75–6n. *Solymon...attrito nomine Sulmo,* 85–6 *exuuias...exutis,* 205n. *Cereri fruticantia culmis,* 222n. *Maurus atrox,* 223–4n. *ferro uiuere laetum / uulgus Adyrmachidae,* 242–3 *Numidis circumuolitare uagosque / ferre datur cursus,* 250–1n. *laetus...portitor* (Charon), 576n. *bellatrix...belua.*

Hyperbaton. Some examples of effective hyperbaton include the following:

30   *Introduction*

58–9n. *tuos…furores.* Hyperbaton emphasizes Paulus' accusation that Varro suffers from madness.

141–3n. *ultima…oscula.* Hyperbaton and enjambement heavily emphasize *oscula*, as the reader is kept wondering what final gift Satricus wishes from his son Solymus.

220–1n. *barbaricus…bellator*: both words start their respective lines and thus provide heavy emphasis to enjambed *bellator*.

Polyptoton. Punica 9 features what Wills (1996: 201) justly calls "the culmination of battle polyptoton" at 322–5n. *galea…galeae, clipeus…clipei, ensis…ense, pes pede uirque uiro.* Other examples include 158n. *nato natumque,*

"Golden" and "near golden" lines. A "golden" line consists of adjectives (aA) and nouns (nN) arranged around a verb (V) in the pattern aAVnN.[55] The only "golden" line of book 9 is 178 *talia uenturae mittebant omina pugnae.* "Near golden" arrangements of adjectives and nouns include aVNAn (99), aNnAV (256), VaANn (286, 463), aVANn (309), anAVN (512).[56] Arrangements that include prepositions or conjunctions include aVANn (51, with *quam*), nAVaN (225, with *ab*), VaANn (281, with *per*; 304, with *ad*), aAVnN (358, with *ceu* and *cum*), and VaAnN (583, with *ab*).

c. Metrics and prosody

When comparing Silius' metrical practices with those of Lucan and his Flavian contemporaries, Duckworth observed that "Silius Italicus is the most painstaking metrician of the four poets and displays more variety than any of the other three."[57] The *Punica* exceeds even Virgil's *Aeneid* in its preference for spondees over dactyls. Ceccarelli accordingly terms Silius' practice "decisamente arcaizzante," comparable to the styles of Ennius and Lucilius.[58] The three most common metrical patterns in Silius exemplify this preference for spondees: in descending order of frequency, they are DSSS (13.08%), SDSS (11.93%), and SSSS (9.68%).[59]

First foot. Silius is the only epic poet to begin the majority of his hexameters with a spondaic rather than dactylic first foot. In this regard, his practice more closely resembles Virgil and Lucan's, whereas his Flavian contemporaries follow Ovid's preference for an opening dactyl. Hexameter poets

[55] See Mayer 2002, Wilkinson 1963: 215–17.
[56] See Flammini 1983 on chiastic arrangement in the *Punica.*
[57] Duckworth 1967: 142. See also Ceccarelli 2008: 1.134.
[58] Ceccarelli 2008: 1.84.
[59] Seventy-two lines in *Punica* 9 feature the maximum number of spondees in the first four feet; seven lines feature the maximum number of dactyls: 14, 128, 226, 293, 546, 566, 597.

generally avoid initial spondaic disyllables in the first foot, as they slow down the line. They occur in the first foot 37 times in the 657 lines of *Punica* 9 (5.6%), a notably higher rate than *Punica* 2 (3.5%) or Virgil *Aeneid* 8 (2.6%); the rate is comparable to Lucan *BC* 2 (5.0%).

Fourth foot. After Lucretius, hexameter poets began to avoid spondaic disyllables in this position because the coincidence of ictus and accent in the last three feet of the line produces a monotonous rhythm. Nine lines in *Punica* 9 feature this pattern (223, 302, 369, 376, 387, 419, 474, 634, 637). This is comparable to Lucan *BC* 2 (8 lines), but notably lower than *Punica* 2 (15 lines) or Virgil *Aeneid* 8 (15 lines).

Clausulae. Arribas Hernáez (1990: 254) describes Silius' clausulae as "highly elaborated, almost baroque, in keeping with the tastes of his era." She identified 192 hexameters (1.57%) in the *Punica* which terminate in atypical clausulae, i.e. those which do not follow the pattern 3 syllables + 2 syllables (*Dardana puppis*), 2+3 (*iussa senatus*), or 2+1+2 (*mouit ab ira*). This is a considerably lower rate than Virgil's (3.69%). The majority of the atypical clausulae in *Punica* 9 are of the type 1+2+2 (128n. *haud tua, nate*, 151 *at miser, imo*, 291 *hinc Venus amens*, 306 *aut sator aeui*, 335 *hi sude pugnas*, 529 *non placet Irim*, 600 *et facis atrae*). The others are 3+1+1 (26n. *talia, qui te*, 35n. *ocius atque hunc*).

6. TEXT AND TRANSLATION

While attending the Council of Constance in 1417, Poggio Bracciolini rediscovered a manuscript of Silius' *Punica* and made a copy which has since been lost. This archetype served as the source of the extant manuscripts. In the sixteenth century, Ludovicus Carrio (1547–95) and Franciscus Modius (1556–97) examined a manuscript preserved in the cathedral library at Cologne (also now lost) and published readings from it which remain valuable for establishing the text.[60]

I adopt the base text of *Punica* 9 and sigla employed in the apparatus criticus from Delz's well-regarded Teubner edition (1987). I depart from Delz's text in only a handful of places, in each case anticipated by an earlier critic:

	Delz	Bernstein
193	uero ω	magna *Watt (1984) 155*
228	ripas *codd.*	campos *Liberman (2006) 21*
429	incepta *Bauer*	excepta *Shackleton Bailey (1959) 174, prob. Delz*
649	Parcarumque *codd.*	Parcarumne *Lefebvre*

[60] See Littlewood 2011: xci–xcii, Delz 1987: v–lxix, McGushin 1985.

32   *Introduction*

As I prepared this commentary, Antony Augoustakis and I collaborated on a translation of the *Punica*.[61] We noted that each book of Silius' epic employs a wide range of linguistic and emotional registers. *Punica* 9 features a remarkable diversity of registers in a comparatively short space. The initial conflict between the consuls alternates between Varro's abuse and Paulus' mournful irony (1–65). The pathos that follows in the Satricus and Solymus episode creates a strong contrast (66–177). Irony is still present, but it has turned tragic. After a comparatively neutral passage—the harangue and disposition of forces (178–277)—the battle episodes (278–end) feature extravagant, hyperbolic language to render such extraordinary events as the theomachy, the assault of the Vulturnus wind, and the elephant charge. My translation aims to provide a preliminary interpretation of the text and also to capture some of its linguistic diversity. I have divided Silius' lengthy periods in the interests of readability and simplified kennings and periphrases (e.g. "war" for Mars).

---

[61] Augoustakis and Bernstein 2021. This translation is for a general audience and so includes more explicitation in the text (e.g. "Mars the war god") than the translation presented to accompany this commentary.

Text and Translation

Sigla

The following sigla are adopted from Delz 1987.

Primary manuscripts:

ω   consensus stirpium α et β

α   consensus codicum F et L

β   consensus codicis G cum γ

γ   consensus codicis O cum δ, V cum δ

δ   consensus codicum V et Γ, O et Γ

F   Firenze, Bibl. Laur., Aed. 196, c.1474–83

L   Firenze, Bibl. Laur., Laur. 37, 16, a. 1457

G   Firenze, Bibl. Laur., Laur. (Gadd.) 91 sub. 35, c.1440–50

O   Oxford, Queen's College 314, s. xv med.

V   Città del Vaticano, Bibl. Vat., Vat. lat. 1652, s. xv

Γ   Città del Vaticano, Bibl. Vat., Ottob. lat. 1258, a. 1426

Secondary manuscripts:

A   Firenze, Bibl. Laur., Acquisti e Doni 361, c.1470–80

B   Oxford, Bodleian Library, Canon. class. lat. 116, a. 1468

H   London, British Library, Harl. 4863, c.1470

J   Firenze, Bibl. Laur., Laur. 37, 17, a Bartholomaeo Fontio scriptus post a. 1471

P   Paris, Bibliothèque Nationale, Lat. 8066, a. 1461

Q   Città del Vaticano, Bibl. Vat., Vat. lat. 1652, a. 1470

R   Città del Vaticano, Bibl. Vat., Vat. lat. 3300

T   Paris, Bibliothèque Nationale, Lat. 8065, a. 1474/5 (?)

W   Città del Vaticano, Bibl. Vat., Vat. lat. 2779, c.1460

Sigla

X	Città del Vaticano, Bibl. Vat., Vat. lat. 3301, *c.*1475
Y	Città del Vaticano, Bibl. Vat., Vat. lat. 3302, a Pomponio Laeto scriptus
Z	Città del Vaticano, Bibl. Vat., Vat. lat. 2778, ante a. 1470
Λ	Budapest, EK Cod. lat. 8
Ξ	Cesena, Bibl. Malatestiana, Cod. Mal. S XII 3, a. 1464/5
ς	codices deteriores aut pars eorum
C	codex deperditus Coloniensis
Cc	lectio codicis Coloniensis a Carrione prolata
Cd	lectio codicis Coloniensis ab Arnoldo Drakenborch prolata
Ch	lectio codicis Coloniensis a Nicolao Heinsio prolata
Cm	lectio codicis Coloniensis a Francisco Modio prolata
Cm *Ep.*	Modius (1584)

Early printed editions cited in the apparatus:

b1	editio Basilensis prior 1522
b2	editio Basilensis secunda 1543
g	editio Lugduni 1547 apud Seb. Gryphium
j	editio Juntina ab Ambrosio Nicandro castigata Florentiae 1515
l	editio Damiani Benessae Rhacusei Lugduni 1514
m	editio Mediolanensis 1481
p	editio Parmensis, a. 1481
r1	editio Romana a. 1471 prior
r2	editio Romana a. 1471 posterior, a Pomponio Laeto recognita
v	editiones Venetae, aa. 1483, 1492, 1493

Abbreviations and notes:

corr.	correxit, correctum
edd. recc.	editors of the seventeenth to twenty-first centuries
edd. vett.	editors of the fifteenth and sixteenth centuries
F^2, etc.	a correction made either by the scribe himself or another hand
ins.	inseruit, insertum
om.	omisit
m.	manus
marg.	a reading in the margin

36 *Sigla*

Editions and critical studies:

Baehrens	Baehrens, Emil. 1872. "Kritische Satura." *Neue Jahrbücher für Philologie und Pädagogik* 105: 621–38.
Bauer	Bauer, Ludovicus. 1890–2. *Sili Italici Punica.* Leipzig: B.G. Teubner.
Bauer 1893	Bauer, Ludwig. 1893. *Handschriftliche und kritisch-exegetische Erörterungen zu den Punica des Silius Italicus.* Augsburg: Pfeiffer.
Bentley	Bentley, Richard. 1811. "Ricardi Bentleii emendationes ineditae in Silium Italicum." *The Classical Journal* 3: 381–6.
Blomgren	Blomgren, S. 1938. *Siliana: De Silii Italici Punicis Quaestiones Criticae et Interpretatoriae.* Uppsala: A.-B. Lundequistska Bokhandeln.
Bothe	Bothe, F. H. 1855–7. *Des Cajus Silius Italicus punischer Krieg: Oder, Hannibal.* Stuttgart: J. B. Metzler.
Damsté	Damsté, P. H. 1911. "Notulae criticae ad Silium Italicum." *Mnemosyne* 39: 113–34.
Delz 1997	Delz, Josef. 1997. "Nachlese zu Silius Italicus." *MH* 54: 163–74.
Frassinetti	Frassinetti, Paolo. 1988. "Contributi al testo di Silio Italico." *CCC* 9/2: 143–53.
Gärtner	Gärtner, Thomas. 2009. "Kritische Bemerkungen zu den *Punica* des Silius Italicus." *Exemplaria classica* 13: 71–94.
Heinsius	*apud* Drakenborch, Arnold. 1717. *Caji Silii Italici Punicorum Libri Septemdecim.* Trajecti ad Rhenum: Guilielmum Van de Water.
Lefebvre	Lefebvre de Villebrune, I. B. 1781. *C. Silii Italici de bello Punico secundo.* Parisiis: Via et Aedibus Serpentinis.
Liberman	Liberman, Gauthier. 2006. "What Future for the Text of Silius Italicus after Josef Delz?" *Aevum Antiquum* 6: 19–38.
Owen	Owen, S. G. 1909. "On Silius Italicus." *CQ* 3/4: 254–7.
Rossbach 1890	Rossbach, Otto. 1890. Review of Bauer 1890. *Deutsche Litteraturzeitung* 1890, nr. 51: 1869–71.
Rossbach 1892	Rossbach, Otto. 1892. Review of Bauer 1892. *Deutsche Litteraturzeitung* 1892, nr. 22: 720–2.

Shackleton Bailey	Shackleton Bailey, D. R. 1959. "Siliana." *CQ* 9: 173–80.
Van Veen	van Veen, J. S. 1893. "Notulae criticae ad Silium Italicum." *Mnemosyne* 21: 264–7.
Volpilhac-Lenthéric	Volpilhac-Lenthéric, Josée, ed. 2003. *Silius Italicus: La Guerre punique: Tome III: Livres IX et X*. Paris: Les Belles Lettres. [Josée Volpilhac-Lenthéric, *Livres IX–X*; Michael Martin, *Livres XI–XII*; Pierre Miniconi et Georges Devallet, *Livre XIII*]
Watt 1984	Watt, W. S. 1984. "Notes on Latin Epic Poetry." *BICS* 31: 153–70.
Watt 1985	Watt, W. S. 1985. "Siliana." *ICS* 10/2: 275–80.
Watt 1988	Watt, W. S. 1988. "Siliana." *MH* 45/3: 170–81.
Zaia	Zaia, Silvia. 2016. "*Sili Italici Punicorum Liber Nonus*: Introduzione e commento." Diss. Padua.

Sili Italici Punicorum Liber Nonus

Turbato monstris Latio cladisque futurae
signa per Ausoniam prodentibus irrita diuis,
haud secus ac si fausta forent et prospera pugnae
omina uenturae, consul traducere noctem
exsomnis telumque manu uibrare per umbras   5
ac modo segnitiae Paulum increpitare, modo acres
exercere tubas nocturnaque classica uelle.
nec minor in Poeno properi certaminis ardor.
erumpunt uallo fortuna urgente sinistra
consertaeque manus. nam sparsi ad pabula campis   10
uicinis raptanda Macae fudere uolucrem
telorum nubem. ante omnes inuadere bella
Mancinus gaudens hostilique unguere primus
tela cruore cadit, cadit et numerosa iuuentus.
     nec pecudum fibras Varro et contraria Paulo   15
auspicia incusante deum compesceret arma,
ni sors alterni iuris, quo castra reguntur,
arbitrium pugnae properanti in fata negasset.
quae tamen haud ualuit perituris milibus una
plus donasse die. rediere in castra, gemente   20
haud dubie Paulo, qui crastina iura uideret
amenti cessura uiro frustraque suorum
seruatas a caede animas. nam turbidus ira
infensusque morae dilata ob proelia ductor

3 forent $aV^2\varGamma^2$: foret β et $a\varGamma$: ac β **4** omnia O$_5$r2 *edd. a* v   **5** ex(s)omnis $L\varGamma$O : ex somnis FGV : e somnis *edd. a* rl   **6** segnitie α : segniciae O : segnitiae V 7 uelle] bello *uel* uallo *Heinsius*   **10** iam OBQ *Dausqueius*   **11** uolucrum *van Veen* 13 hostilem O   **15** contraria $aG^2V^2\varGamma$: contria β

SILIUS ITALICUS PUNICA, BOOK 9

These portents troubled Latium. In vain throughout Italy, the gods put forth the signs of the future disaster. Varro, the consul, passed the night without sleeping, just as if the omens of the upcoming battle had been lucky and fortunate. [5] In the dark, he brandished his weapon in his hand. Now he rebuked Paulus for his inactivity. At another time, though it was still night, he wanted to sound the shrill battle trumpets and war horns. Hannibal had no less eagerness to hurry on the contest. They broke out from the rampart as malign Fortune pushed them onward, and warbands began the combat. [10] The Macae had scattered all over the neighboring fields to plunder the grain. They poured forth a cloud of winged missiles. Before all others, Mancinus rejoiced to enter combat and to be the first to wet his spears with enemy blood. He fell, and a great number of young men fell as well. [15] Nor would Varro have held back his troops (though Paulus blamed the sacrificial animals' entrails and the gods' opposing omens), if the luck of alternating command which ruled the camps had not denied him the choice of giving battle, eager as he was to meet his fate. Yet this alternation was unable to give more than a single day to the thousands who would die. [20] Paulus wept as they returned to the camps. He saw without doubt that command would pass tomorrow to a man who was out of his mind. The lives of his soldiers had been saved in vain from slaughter. Rage unbalanced Varro, the new leader, and he opposed the delay caused by the deferred battle.

40   *Sili Italici Punicorum Liber Nonus*

'sicine, sic' inquit 'grates pretiumque rependis,   25
Paule, tui capitis? meruerunt talia, qui te
legibus atque urnae dira eripuere minanti?
tradant immo hosti reuocatos ilicet enses,
tradant arma iube aut pugnantum deripe dextris.
sed uos, quorum oculos atque ora umentia uidi,   30
uertere cum consul terga et remeare iuberet,
ne morem et pugnae signum expectate petendae.
dux sibi quisque uiam rapito, cum spargere primis
incipiet radiis Gargana cacumina Phoebus.
pandam egomet propere portas. ruite ocius atque hunc   35
ereptum reuocate diem.' sic turbidus aegra
pestifero pugnae castra incendebat amore.
      At Paulus, iam non idem nec mente nec ore,
sed qualis stratis deleto milite campis
post pugnam stetit, ante oculos atque ora futuro   40
obuersante malo, ceu iam spe lucis adempta
cum stupet exanimata parens natique tepentes
nequiquam fouet extremis amplexibus artus,
'per totiens' inquit 'concussae moenia Romae
perque has, nox Stygia quas iam circumuolat umbra,   45
insontes animas, cladi parce obuius ire.
dum transit diuum furor et consumitur ira
Fortunae, nouus Hannibalis, sat, nomina ferre
si discit miles nec frigidus aspicit hostem.'

25 sic Ch : nunc ω *fort. recte*   29   aut] et *Livineius* diripe ς *edd. vett.* dextris *Heinsius* : dextras ω, *Volpilhac-Lenthéric*   30 (h)umentia αGr2 : uiuencia O : liuentia V : luētia Γ : uuentia *Heinsius*   32 ne morem v : me morem αGΓ : memorem VO Martem *Heinsius* expectare Γ(*corr.*) O   33 rapito Cm *Ep.* 86 : sapito ω : capito $\Gamma\varsigma$ primis ωCm : primus B *edd. a* rl   35 pandam $\alpha\Gamma\varsigma$: pangam β propere ωCh : prope rlmpv : primus *edd. a* j   38 at FGδ : ac L : ut O   39 deleto Fβ : delecto L : dilecto $\Gamma\varsigma$: deiecto *Heinsius*   46 parce F^{2}LΓ^2 : parte Fβ : pte Γ 49 si Γ^2rl : sic ω

Silius Italicus *Punica, Book 9* 41

[25] "Is this the way, Paulus," he said, "is this how you repay thanks and the price of your head? Do the people deserve such rewards, those who rescued you from the laws and the urn that made dire threats? No, they should straight away hand over to the enemy the swords that you called back from battle! Order them to hand over their weapons or seize them yourself from the soldiers' fighting hands. [30] But you soldiers, I saw your eyes and faces were wet with tears when the consul ordered you to turn your backs and retreat. Don't wait for the customary signal for beginning combat. Each man should seize the way for himself as his own leader, as soon as the Sun begins to spread its first rays over the peak of Mount Garganus. [35] I myself will quickly throw open the gates. Rush swiftly and get back this lost day." Thus Varro, disturbed in his mind, set the sick troops on fire with deadly passion for combat. But Paulus was no longer the same, in either his thoughts or his expression. He was like a man who stands after the battle on the field strewn with dead soldiers. [40] He saw the future evil coming before his face, as if he were a mother who gapes stunned as her hope for her son's life is taken from her. With her final embraces, she pointlessly cherishes his limbs, still warm. "By the walls of Rome that has been so often stricken," he said, [45] "by these innocent souls whom night already enshrouds in Stygian darkness, spare us! Don't go to meet destruction. Until the gods' rage passes and Fortune uses up its anger, it is enough if the new soldiers merely learn to endure Hannibal's name and aren't cold with fear when they see the enemy."

42   *Sili Italici Punicorum Liber Nonus*

nonne uides, cum uicinis auditur in aruis,   50
quam subitus linquat pallentia corpora sanguis,
quamque fluant arma ante tubas? cunctator et aeger,
ut rere, in pugnas Fabius quotcumque sub illis
culpatis duxit signis, nunc arma capessunt.
at quos Flaminius—sed dira auertite, diui!   55
sin nostris animus monitis precibusque repugnat,
aures pande deo. cecinit Cymaea per orbem
haec olim uates et te praesaga tuosque
uulgauit terris proauorum aetate furores.
iamque alter tibi, nec perplexo carmine, coram   60
fata cano uates: sistis ni crastina signa,
firmabis nostro Phoebeae dicta Sibyllae
sanguine. nec Graio posthac Diomede ferentur,
sed te, si perstas, insignes consule campi.'
haec Paulus, lacrimaeque oculis ardentibus ortae.   65
       Necnon et noctem sceleratus polluit error.
Xanthippo captus Libycis tolerarat in oris
seruitium Satricus, mox inter praemia regi
Autololum dono datus ob uirtutis honorem.
huic domus et gemini fuerant Sulmone relicti   70
matris in uberibus nati, Mancinus et una
nomine Rhoeteo Solymus. nam Dardana origo
et Phrygio genus a proauo, qui sceptra secutus
Aeneae claram muris fundauerat urbem

---

50 aruis rl : armis *ω*   51 segnis L   53 quotcumque *Postgate* : quoscumque *ω*, *Zaia*   54 non *Baehrens (1872) 631* capessunt? *Rossbach (1892)*   55 at FCh : aut F²L*β* : haud *Γς* diui F(*corr. ex* duue)LV²(*in lac.*) *Γ²*rl : fata ~~duj~~ G : fata diui O : dira *Γ* : fata *Ξ*BJ   56 animus *αGΓ²* : aninnis O : animis *δ*   57 cymea L : Cumaea Ch : crinea F*β* : grynea *Γ²ς*   59 (a)etate *αΓς* : ertate *β*   61 ni *Γ²*Br2 : in *ω*   63 posthac F²Lrl : post haec F*β*   64 praestas O   66 palluit O   67 xantippo *αVς* : zantippo *β* cretus *Scaliger*   69 autololum *αΓ²* : ant(h)ololum *β* (-loum G)   70 huic *Γς* : hinc *ω*   72 rh(o)eteo *Γς* : th(o)eteo *ω* solymus LG² : solrinus *β* : solimus F*Γς*Ch *α*

Silius Italicus *Punica, Book 9* 43

[50] "When his forces are heard in nearby fields, don't you see how quickly the blood leaves their pale bodies, how their weapons drop before the battle trumpets? Yet you think Fabius is a delayer and weak in battle; however many men he led under these standards you blame, they still wield their weapons. [55] But those whom Flaminius—but gods, turn aside terrible omens! But if your spirit resists our warnings and entreaties, open your ears to the god. Long ago the Sibyl of Cumae sang of these events throughout the world. Back in the age of our ancestors, she foresaw you and your madness and spread it to the lands. [60] And now, I sing of fate before you as a second prophet, nor is my prediction hard to decipher. Unless you halt your battle standards tomorrow, you will confirm the words of Apollo's Sibyl with our blood. After this, these fields will not be named by Greek Diomedes, but they will be famous for you, the consul, if you persist." [65] As Paulus said these things, tears sprang up in his burning eyes.

In addition, a criminal mistake polluted that night. Satricus had endured slavery on the Libyan shores after Xanthippus had captured him. Soon after, he was given amid other offerings as a gift to the king of the Autololes, out of respect for his courage.

[70] He had left behind his house at Sulmo and twin sons at their mother's breast, Mancinus and Solymus; the latter had a Trojan name. For Satricus was Trojan in his origin and descent from a Phrygian ancestor who had followed Aeneas's scepter and founded a city with famous walls

44   *Sili Italici Punicorum Liber Nonus*

ex sese dictam Solymon. celebrata colonis   75
mox Italis paulatim attrito nomine Sulmo.
at tum barbaricis Satricus cum rege cateruis
aduectus, quo non spretum, si posceret usus,
noscere Gaetulis Latias interprete uoces,
postquam posse datum Paeligna reuisere tecta   80
et patrium sperare larem, ad conamina noctem
aduocat ac furtim castris euadit iniquis.
sed fuga nuda uiri. sumpto nam prodere coepta
uitabat clipeo et dextra remeabat inermi.
exuuias igitur prostrataque corpora campo   85
lustrat et exutis Mancini cingitur armis.
iamque metus leuior. uerum, cui dempta ferebat
exsangui spolia et cuius nudauerat artus,
natus erat, paulo ante Mace prostratus ab hoste.
      Ecce sub aduentum noctis primumque soporem   90
alter natorum, Solymus, uestigia uallo
Ausonio uigil extulerat, dum sorte uicissim
alternat portae excubias, fratrisque petebat
Mancini stratum sparsa inter funera corpus,
furtiua cupiens miserum componere terra.   95
nec longum celerarat iter, cum tendere in armis
aggere Sidonio uenientem conspicit hostem,
quodque dabat fors in subitis necopina, sepulcro
Aetoli condit membra occultata Thoantis.
inde, ubi nulla sequi propius pone arma uirumque   100
incomitata uidet uestigia ferre per umbras,
prosiliens tumulo contorquet nuda parentis

---

75 solymon r1 : solimon ω 77 at ω : ac r2v cum O : tum <in> *Watt (1988)* barbaricae…cateruae *Summers*   78 aduectus $\alpha\delta$: aductus G : adductus G^{2}O : adiunctus *Thilo
(1891) 622*   80 reuisere αG$^2\Gamma^2$O : reuiscere β 81 spectare *Liberman*   83 nam]
quia *Nicander*   86 exutis Γs : exutus ω 89 *om.* F *add. m.2 marg.* mace ω : Macae
Ch : Maca p, *edd. recc.*   91 solymus α : solimus β 96 celerarat Γ^2s : celebrarat ω
98 necopina *Cellarius* : nec opina ω 99 contendit…occulta O   100 propius $\alpha\Gamma$:
proprius β

Silius Italicus *Punica, Book 9*

[75] and called it Solymos after himself. Soon Italian settlers crowded in and little by little it became Sulmo as its name shortened. But now Satricus had come to Italy with the king and his barbarian band. The king did not disdain using him as an interpreter to know the meaning of Latin speech in Gaetulian if he had the need. [80] After Satricus was given the chance to see the buildings of Paelignia again and hope for his ancestral home, he called on the night as an aid to his endeavor and slipped secretly out of the brutal camp. But the man fled without his gear. For he avoided taking a shield that would give away his plan, and he made for home without a weapon in his hand. [85] And so he searched the corpses sprawled on the battlefield and the spoils. He girded himself with Mancinus' cast-off armor. And now his fear was lighter. But it was his son, laid low a little before this by an enemy Maca, whose limbs he stripped, whose spoils he carried from his bloodless corpse.

[90] Look! At the coming of night and the beginning of sleep, Satricus' other son, Solymus, made his way across the Roman rampart as a watchman. While he alternated the watches assigned by lot at the gate, he looked for his brother Mancinus' corpse laid out amid the scattered dead. [95] He yearned to bury the wretched man secretly in the ground. He had not hurried far along his path when he saw an enemy coming, heading in arms from the Carthaginian rampart. Unexpected luck gave him a sudden opportunity: he concealed himself, hiding away his limbs in Aetolian Thoas' tomb. [100] Then he saw that no armed soldiers followed close behind and that the man had made his way unaccompanied through the shadows. He leapt up from the tomb and hurled his javelin unerringly

46 *Sili Italici Punicorum Liber Nonus*

in terga haud frustra iaculum, Tyriamque sequentum
Satricus esse manum et Sidonia uulnera credens,
auctorem caeci trepidus circumspicit ictus.   105
uerum ubi uictorem iuuenili robore cursus
attulit et notis fulsit lux tristis ab armis
fraternusque procul luna prodente retexit
ante oculos sese et radiauit comminus umbo,
exclamat iuuenis subita flammatus ab ira: 110
'non sim equidem Sulmone satus tua, Satrice, proles
nec frater, Mancine, tuus fatearque nepotem
Pergameo indignum Solymo, si euadere detur
huic nostras impune manus. tu nobile gestes
germani spolium ante oculos referasque superba   115
me spirante domus Paelignae perfidus arma?
haec tibi, cara parens Acca, ad solacia luctus
dona feram, nati ut figas aeterna sepulcro.'
        talia uociferans stricto mucrone ruebat.
ast illi iam tela manu iamque arma fluebant   120
audita patria natisque et coniuge et armis,
ac membra et sensus gelidus stupefecerat horror.
tum uox semanimi miseranda effunditur ore:
'parce, precor, dextrae, non ut mihi uita supersit
(quippe nefas hac uelle frui), sed sanguine nostro   125
ne damnes, o nate, manus. Carthaginis ille
captiuus, patrias nunc primum aduectus in oras,
ille ego sum Satricus, Solymi genus. haud tua, nate,
fraus ulla est. iaceres in me cum feruidus hastam,

---

103 Tyriumque *Damsté* sequentem Γ_S **104** satricus $a\Gamma$: satricos GO : satricis V
105 ceri r1 *corr. in marg.* certi *teste Drakenborchio*   **111** sim a Cm *Ep.* 86 : sum β
112 fatearque ω : fateorque $_S$ **113** solymo L : solimo FGΓ^2 : solino V : sulimo O
114 huic nostras impune manus Cm : hinc nostra impune manu a : hinc uestra impune
manu β : hinc nostra te impune manu Γ^2_S **116** spectante r1m   **117** haec ar1 : nec β
Acca Cm : acta ω : apta Γ^2_S **123** cum O semanimi Ch : semianimi ω **125** hac ar2b1 :
hoc β **127** patria F auectus F : adductus Γ

Silius Italicus *Punica, Book 9*

at his father's bare back. Satricus thought that a Tyrian force had followed him and that a Carthaginian had wounded him. [105] He looked around fearfully for the originator of the unseen blow. Then Solymus the victor ran with youthful strength and came to the spot. He recognized the armor as grim light shone from it. As the moon illuminated it from far off, his brother's shield boss revealed itself before his eyes, and it gleamed close at hand. [110] On fire with sudden anger, the young man cried out:

"As far as I am concerned, Satricus, may I not be your son, born in Sulmo, nor may I be your brother, Mancinus. Let me confess myself to be an unworthy descendant of Solymus of Pergamum if this man is allowed to escape my hands unpunished. Would you carry [115] my brother's noble spoil before my very eyes and treacherously bear away my Paelignian house's glorious armor while I still breathe? Dear mother Acca, I will bring you these gifts as comfort for your mourning, so that you may set them for all time in your son's grave." He called out these words and rushed with his sword drawn. [120] But already the spears and arms had dropped out of Satricus' hands as he heard the names of his homeland and sons and wife and weapons. Cold horror stupefied his senses and his limbs. Then a pitiable voice poured out from his half-dead mouth:

"Spare your hand, I beg you, not so that my life may remain to me [125] (for it would be criminal to want to enjoy it), but so that you don't condemn your own hands, my son, with my blood. I was a captive of Carthage, now returned for the first time to my homeland's shores; I myself am Satricus, of the line of Solymus. My son, there is no crime on your part whatsoever."

48 *Sili Italici Punicorum Liber Nonus*

Poenus eram. uerum castris elapsus acerbis   130
ad uos et carae properabam coniugis ora.
hunc rapui exanimi clipeum. sed iam unice nobis
haec fratris tumulis arma excusata reporta.
curarum tibi prima tamen sit, nate, referre
ductori monitus Paulo: producere bellum   135
nitatur Poenoque neget certamina Martis.
augurio exsultat diuum immensamque propinqua
stragem acie sperat. quaeso, cohibete furentem
Varronem; namque hunc fama est impellere signa.
sat magnum hoc miserae fuerit mihi cardine uitae   140
solamen, cauisse meis. nunc ultima, nate,
inuento simul atque amisso redde parenti
oscula.' sic fatus galeam exuit atque rigentis
inuadit nati tremebundis colla lacertis,
attonitoque timens uerbis sanare pudorem   145
uulneris impressi <et> telum excusare laborat:
'quis testis nostris, quis conscius adfuit actis?
non nox errorem nigranti condidit umbra?
cur trepidas? da, nate, magis, da iungere pectus.
absoluo pater ipse manum, atque in fine laborum   150
hac condas oculos dextra, precor.' at miser imo
pectore suspirans iuuenis non uerba uicesque
alloquio uocemue refert, sed sanguinis atri
sistere festinat cursum laceroque ligare
ocius illacrimans altum uelamine uulnus.   155
tandem inter gemitus miserae erupere querelae:

128 solymi F²L : solimi Fβ **129** cum *om.* GV **130** uerum ut castris *Scaliger*
132 uniceF²GVΓ²O:nunceF:imiteL:uiceΓ **133** armaameexuta*Blass* **136** Marti
Heinsius **138** spirat *Heinsius* cohibete ωCh : prohibete *edd. a* rl **140** sat *a*Γ : sed G :
stat VO **144** tremebundus GΓ²ς **145** attonitoque timens ω : attoniti et nitens *edd.*
a j : attonitumque *Livineius* : attonitumque tenens *uel* uidens *Schrader* : attonito mentis
Summers (1900) 305 **145** et *add. Lefebvre, Schrader* **149** magis] manus *D. Heinsius* :
genas *Schrader, Ernesti* **153** uociue *Schrader* **156** erumpere δ (*corr. in* Γ)

Silius Italicus *Punica, Book 9*   49

"I was a Carthaginian [130] when you eagerly hurled a spear at me. Indeed, I slipped out of that bitter camp and I was hurrying back to you and my dear wife's face. I stole this shield from my dead son. But now you, the only one left to me, bring back these blameless weapons to your brother's grave. Yet let your first concern, son, be to bring [135] the warning to the commander Paulus: he should strive to prolong the war and deny battle to the Carthaginian. Hannibal exults in the gods' augury and hopes for immense slaughter when the battle line draws near. I beg you, hold back raging Varro; for the rumor is that he is the one pushing the battle standards forward. [140] This will have been a great enough consolation at my wretched life's end: to have taken concern for my own people. Now, my son, give your final kisses to the father you found and lost at the same time."

Satricus spoke thus and took off his helmet. His trembling arms aimed for his frozen son's neck. [145] He feared for the stunned young man. He worked hard to find words to soothe his son's shame at the wound he had inflicted and to exculpate his weapon: "Who witnessed our doings, who was present and aware of them? Did not the night bury the error in its dark shadow? Why are you frightened? Son, rather give me your breast to embrace. [150] I myself, your father, forgive your hand, and I pray that you may use that hand to close my eyes at my labor's end." But the wretched young man sighed from the deepest part of his breast. He did not reply in words or in the exchange of conversation or make a sound. Rather, he hurried to stop the flow of dark blood. Swiftly he tore his clothing [155] to tie up the deep wound, crying as he did so. At last, wretched complaints broke out amid his groaning:

50 *Sili Italici Punicorum Liber Nonus*

'sicine te nobis, genitor, Fortuna reducit
in patriam? sic te nato natumque parenti
impia restituit? felix o terque quaterque
frater, cui fatis genitorem agnoscere ademptum.   160
ast ego, Sidoniis imperditus, ecce, parentem
uulnere cognosco. saltem hoc, Fortuna, fuisset
solamen culpae, dubia ut mihi signa dedisses
infausti generis. uerum linquetur iniquis
non ultra superis nostros celare labores.'   165
        haec dum amens queritur, iam deficiente cruore
in uacuas senior uitam disperserat auras.
tum iuuenis maestum attollens ad sidera uultum
'pollutae dextrae et facti Titania testis
infandi, quae nocturno mea lumine tela   170
derigis in patrium corpus, non amplius' inquit
'his oculis et damnato uiolabere uisu.'
haec memorat, simul ense fodit praecordia et atrum
sustentans uulnus mananti sanguine signat
in clipeo mandata patris FVGE PROELIA VARRO,   175
ac summi tegimen suspendit cuspide teli
defletumque super prosternit membra parentem.
        talia uenturae mittebant omina pugnae
Ausoniis superi, sensimque abeuntibus umbris
conscia nox sceleris roseo cedebat Eoo.   180
ductor in arma suos Libys et Romanus in arma
excibant de more suos, Poenisque redibat
qualis nulla dies omni surrexerit aeuo.

161 imperditus *αGVCm Ep.* 86 : impercitus *ΓQ edd. a* p : impeditus O
162 tulisset *Schrader*   165 nostros celare Cm : non hos tolerare b1b2 : nostros
tol(l)erare *ω, Zaia* : nostros scelerare *Summers* : temerare *uel* cumulare *uel*
iterare *Frassinetti*   166 deficiente puella F (ał cruore m.1 marg.) calore
Bothe   171 derigis *α* : dirigis *β*   173 memorans *Heinsius* fodit *αΓ* : fudit *β*
176 ac *αGb*1 : at *Γ* tegimen *α Drakenborch* : tegmen *β*   178 omina LG²*Γ* :
omnia F*β*   179 sensimque *Γ²s* : sensumque *ω*   182 excibat *Γ² edd. vett.*
183 surrexerat p : subluxerit *Heinsius*   184 non *αr*2Ch : nec *β*

Silius Italicus *Punica, Book 9*

"Has fortune thus led you back into your homeland for us, father? Has criminal fortune restored you to your son and your son to his father in this way? You were three and four times lucky, [160] my brother: the Fates took away your opportunity to recognize our father. Look! But I, spared by the Carthaginians, acknowledge my father by wounding him. Fortune, if you had given me doubtful signs of my unfortunate descent, this would have at least been a consolation for my crime. But hiding my sufferings will be left no longer to the hostile [165] gods."

While Solymus, out of his mind, made these complaints, his aged father had lost his blood and loosed his life into the empty air. Then the young man lifted his grieving face to the stars. "Polluted hands," he said, "and Moon, witness of my unspeakable crime, [170] you who lighted the night to guide my weapons into my father's body! No further will these eyes and damned vision violate you." As he spoke thus, at the same moment his sword dug into his chest. He sustained the dark wound and signed his father's orders [175] on the shield with his dripping blood: VARRO, AVOID THE COMBAT! Then he hung the shield from his javelin's tip and collapsed on his lamented parent's limbs.

The gods sent such omens of the coming battle to the Italians. Little by little the shadows withdrew [180] and the night that witnessed this crime yielded to the rosy dawn. The Libyan and the Roman commanders roused their men to arms, each according to his own custom. A day began for the Carthaginians such as never dawned in any age.

52   *Sili Italici Punicorum Liber Nonus*

'non uerborum' inquit 'stimulantum' Poenus 'egetis,
Herculeis iter a metis ad Iapygis agros   185
uincendo emensi. nusquam est animosa Saguntos,
concessere Alpes, pater ipse superbus aquarum
Ausonidum Eridanus captiuo defluit alueo.
strage uirum mersus Trebia est, atque ora sepulcro
Lydia Flaminio premitur, lateque refulgent   190
ossibus ac nullo sulcantur uomere campi.
clarior his titulus plusque allatura cruoris
lux oritur. mihi magna satis, sat magna superque
bellandi merces sit gloria; cetera uobis
uincantur. quicquid diti deuexit Hibero,   195
quicquid in Aetnaeis iactauit Roma triumphis,
quin etiam Libyco si quid de litore raptum
condidit, in uestros ueniet sine sortibus enses.
ferte domos, quod dextra dabit. nil ductor honoris
ex opibus posco. raptor per saecula longa   200
Dardanus edomitum uobis spoliauerit orbem.
qui Tyria ducis Sarranum ab origine nomen,
seu Laurens tibi Sigeo sulcata colono
arridet tellus, seu sunt Byzacia cordi
rura magis centum Cereri fruticantia culmis,   205
electos optare dabo inter praemia campos.
addam etiam, flaua Thybris quas irrigat unda,

185 iter $a\Gamma s$: inter β a metis $aG^2\Gamma$: ametis β Iapygas *Heinsius*   **187** consedere
Schrader   **188** ausonidum Γ^2s : ausonium ω **189** uersus *uel* auersus *uel* immersus
Heinsius pressus *Heinsius, def. Drakenborch* sepulc(h)ro βCh : sepulto $a\Gamma s$ **190** relucent
Schrader   **192** titulus Cm *Ep.* 50, *edd. recc.* : titulis ω, *van Veen* plusque ωCm : plus *edd.*
a rl   **193** sat magna *Watt* (1984) 155 : sat uero ω : uera B *edd.* a l : certa *Heinsius* : clara
Müller (1861) 339 : satis mera satque superque *Blass*   **194** sit Γs : sic ω : est
Liberman   **195** diti Γ^2s : dici ω **196** in] et *Nicander*   **198** ueniet aO : uenient β sorti-
bus Γ^2Os : fortibus ω **199** ferte $a\Gamma^2s$: forte β uictor *edd.* a rl uictor honorus
Barth   **201** uobis aG : nobis Γ **202** sarranum Γ^2s : serranum ω **204** sunt $a$rl : sint
β Byzacia Ch : bizancia FO : bizantia Lβ : buxentia *edd.* a v   **205** Cereris
Liberman   **206** praemia $a$rl Cm *Ep.* 50 : proelia β

Silius Italicus *Punica, Book 9*

"You have no need of words to encourage you," Hannibal said. [185] "You have completed a journey that began at the Pillars of Hercules and you conquered your way to the Iapygian fields. Brave Saguntum is no more. The Alps have yielded to you. The noble Po himself, father of Italian waters, flows in a captive channel. Slaughtered men have overwhelmed the Trebia River, [190] and Flaminius' tomb presses upon the shores of Etruscan Lake Trasimene. Bones gleam far and wide on the battlefields, and no plows dig them up. Yet a day is dawning brighter than these deeds and ready to bring more blood. Let this be great enough glory for me as a reward for my warfare, enough and indeed more than enough. The other rewards for conquest may fall to you. [195] Whatever Rome has carried off from the wealthy Ebro River, whatever glories it has from triumphs in Sicily—even if it has stored away something taken from the Libyan shores—it will fall to your swords, and we will not cast lots to apportion it. Take home whatever your fighting hand brings you. I ask for no rewards [200] from the spoil as your leader. The Roman plunderer despoiled the conquered world through long centuries for your benefit. If you have a Phoenician family name that you can trace back to its origins in Tyre, I will allow you to choose your preferred fields from the rewards: whether Laurentum's territory farmed by Trojan colonists pleases you or Byzacium's fields [205] where grain sprouts a hundredfold are closer to your heart. I will offer in addition the banks which the tawny Tiber River's waves water,

54 *Sili Italici Punicorum Liber Nonus*

captiuis late gregibus depascere ripas.
qui uero externo socius mihi sanguine Byrsae
signa moues, dextram Ausonia si caede cruentam   210
attolles, hinc iam ciuis Carthaginis esto.
neu uos Garganus Daunique fefellerit ora,
ad muros statis Romae. licet auia longe
urbs agat et nostro procul a certamine distet,
hic hodie ruet, atque ultra te ad proelia, miles,   215
nulla uoco: ex acie tende in Capitolia cursum.'
      haec memorat. tum propulso munimine ualli
fossarum rapuere moras, aciemque locorum
consilio curuis accommodat ordine ripis.
barbaricus laeuo stetit ad certamina cornu   220
bellator Nasamon unaque immanior artus
Marmarides, tum Maurus atrox Garamasque Macesque
et Massylae acies et ferro uiuere laetum
uulgus Adyrmachidae, pariter gens accola Nili
corpora ab immodico seruans nigrantia Phoebo.   225
quis positum agminibus caput imperiumque Nealces.
at parte in dextra, sinuat qua flexibus undam
Aufidus et curuo circum errat gurgite campos,
Mago regit. subiere leues, quos horrida misit
Pyrene, populi uarioque auxere tumultu   230
flumineum latus. effulget caetrata iuuentus,

208 *sic* ωCm : gurgitibus late captiuis pascere ripas $\varGamma^2$H *edd. a* rl : gregibus s
209 externo Cm : extremo ω sanguine ωCm : cardine $\varGamma^2 s$ **210** mouens
Ch   **211** attollens δ (*corr. in utroque*) hinc iam $\varGamma^2$ *edd. a* rl : iam hinc ω   **212** heu $\varGamma$
(*corr.*) O   **215** hic Fr1pm Cm : haec F^2Lβ *edd. a* v ruit L   **216** tendo F^2 **218** rupere
van Veen   **219** consilio] consimilem *Heinsius* : ingenio *Liberman*   **221** uasamon GV
arcu rlm   **223** ferro] paruo *Delz (1997)*   **224** Adyrmachidae, pariter *Dausqueius,*
Blomgren (1938) 28–9 : Adyrmachidae pariter, gens *Ernesti, edd. recc.* : patrii *uel* Pharii
Heinsius : et pariter *Drakenborch*   **226** caput *om.* F   **228** aufidus $a\varGamma$: auadus β campos *Liberman* : ripas *codd.*   **230** auxere F^2LG$\varGamma$: anxere O : ausere FV : (et vario)
cinxere *Heinsius* : (et vario) clausere *Summers*

Silius Italicus *Punica, Book 9*   55

where you may pasture captured flocks far and wide. My allies of foreign blood, [210] who carry the Carthaginian Byrsa's battle standards, if you bring back your fighting hand bloodied with Italian slaughter, you may become a citizen of Carthage from that point on. Don't let Mount Garganus or Daunia's shores deceive you: you are standing before Rome's walls. Though the city lies far off in the distance away from our battle, [215] today here is where it falls. I call you to no further battle beyond this, soldiers. Make your way straight from the battle line to the Capitol."

After Hannibal said these things, they threw down the rampart's defenses and rushed over the ditches' barrier. He fit the battle line's order at the landscape's suggestion to the river's curving banks. [220] The barbarian Nasamonian warriors stood on the left wing, ready for battle, together with the Marmaricans, who had enormous limbs. Then came the grim Moors and Garamantians and Macae and the Massylian ranks and the Adyrmachidae, a people happy to live by the sword. Along with them came the people who dwell by the Nile River, [225] whose bodies keep their blackness from the extreme sun. Nealces had been appointed as the head and ruler of these troops. But Mago led on the right side, where the Aufidus River bends and twists its waves and its curving stream wanders around the fields. There came light-armed peoples from the bristling Pyrenees, [230] who enlarged the forces stationed by the river amid a varied uproar. Shield-bearing youths shone forth:

56   *Sili Italici Punicorum Liber Nonus*

Cantaber ante alios nec tectus tempora Vasco
ac torto miscens Baliaris proelia plumbo
Baetigenaeque uiri. celsus media ipse coercet
agmina, quae patrio firmauit milite quaeque   235
Celtarum Eridano perfusis saepe cateruis.
sed qua se fluuius retro labentibus undis
eripit et nullo cuneos munimine uallat,
turritas moles ac propugnacula dorso
belua nigranti gestans ceu mobilis agger   240
nutat et erectos attollit ad aethera muros.
cetera iam Numidis circumuolitare uagosque
ferre datur cursus et toto feruere campo.
   dum Libys incenso dispensat milite uires
hortandoque iterum atque iterum insatiabilis urget   245
factis quemque suis et se cognoscere iactat,
qua dextra ueniant stridentis sibila teli,
promittitque uiris nulli se defore testem,
iam Varro exacta uallo legione mouebat
cladum principia, ac pallenti laetus in unda   250
laxabat sedem uenturis portitor umbris.
stant primi, quos sanguineae pendente uetabant
ire notae clipeo, defixique omine torpent.
iuxta terribilis facies: miseranda iacebant
corpora in amplexu, natusque in pectore patris   255
imposita uulnus dextra letale tegebat.
effusae lacrimae, Mancinique inde reuersus

---

232 uasco *aGΓ²* : uasto *Γ* **233** at L Baliaris *edd. recc.* : Baliares *ω*
234 ipsa O   **239** turritas *Γ²s* : turritae *ω, Heinsius*   **240** molibus v2, *inde omnes praeter* l *usque ad Modium*   **241** erectos *aΓ* : erectus *β* : euectos *Heinsius*
242 nam *Heinsius* uagosque Cm *Ep.* 50 : giros *ω* : citosque *edd. a* j   **243** datur *ωCm* : datum *Γs* **244** incenso FBrl : intenso *Lβ* **245** hortandi *van Veen*
249 legare L   **250** ac *aVOCh* : et G : at *Γs*   **254** iacebat Ch   **255** amplexum *Γs* pectora *Livineius*

Cantabrians before all others, the Vascones who left their heads bare, Balearic islanders who fought their battles by whirling lead slingshot, and the men who dwelled by the Baetis River. Hannibal himself, high on his horse, commanded the middle [235] battle line, which he had strengthened with soldiers from his native land along with Celtic troops drenched often in the Po River. But where the river's flowing waves curved backward and did not guard the formations with any fortification, elephants carried turrets and barricades on their dark backs. [240] They wavered like a mobile rampart and raised high walls up to the sky. It was left to the Numidians to circle swiftly and head down wandering paths and seethe over the whole battlefield.

Hannibal, the Libyan commander, fired up his troops and conferred strength upon them [245] and spurred them on insatiably, urging on each man with memory of his own deeds. He boasted that he recognized from whose hand the rush of a whirring javelin came. He promised his men that he would not miss witnessing any one of them. Meanwhile Varro had taken his legions out of the rampart and set in motion [250] the beginnings of destruction. On his pale waves, Charon the ferryman of the ghosts threw open places for the arriving dead. The front ranks stood fast as Solymus' writing in blood on the hanging shield forbade them to advance. The omen transfixed them, and they were stupefied. Next to them was a terrible sight: the pitiable bodies lay [255] in an embrace, and the son had placed his hand to cover the lethal wound in his father's breast. The soldiers' tears flowed, and grief for Mancinus returned at seeing his

58   *Sili Italici Punicorum Liber Nonus*

fraterna sub morte dolor, tum triste mouebat
augurium et similes defuncto in corpore uultus.
ocius erroris culpam deflendaque facta   260
ductori pandunt atque arma uetantia pugnam.
ille ardens animi 'ferte haec' ait 'omina Paulo.
namque illum, cui femineo stant corde timores,
mouerit ista manus, quae caede imbuta nefanda,
cum Furiae expeterent poenas, fortasse paterno   265
signauit moriens sceleratum sanguine carmen.'
     tum minitans propere describit munera pugnae,
quaque feras saeuus gentes aciemque Nealces
temperat, hac sese Marso cum milite cumque
Samnitum opponit signis et Iapyge alumno.   270
at campi medio (namque hac in parte uidebat
stare ducem Libyae) Seruilius obuia adire
arma et Picentis Vmbrosque inferre iubetur.
cetera Paulus habet dextro certamina cornu.
his super insidias contra Nomadumque uolucrem   275
Scipiadae datur ire manum, quaque arte dolisque
scindent se turmae, praedicit spargere bellum.
     iamque propinquabant acies, agilique uirorum
discursu mixtoque simul calefacta per ora
cornipedum hinnitu et multum crepitantibus armis   280
errabat caecum turbata per agmina murmur.
sic, ubi prima mouent pelago certamina uenti,
inclusam rabiem ac sparsuras astra procellas

---

260 fata *edd. a* rl   **262** omina GΓ^2s : omnia $a\Gamma$, *edd. recc.*   **263** feminei *van Veen*   **266** moriens Γ^2s : mordens ω **267** properae *Heinsius* discribit *Summers*   **268** Afras laeuus *Heinsius*   **269** hac F^{2}GF : ac aVO   **273** umbrosque $a\Gamma$: umbrasque β **274** laeuo *Drakenborch*   **276** quaque *edd. a* p, *Duff, Delz* : quaeque ωCh *edd. recc.*   **279** mistoque L   **280** hinnitu F^{2}G Γ^2O : hynnitu V : innitu LG : inuictu F : hinnitum PCh crepitantibus FGδs, *Delz* : strepitantibus *Modius Ep.* 50, *Bauer* : trepidantibus LO *edd. a* rl   **282** sic tibi O   **283** castra O

Silius Italicus *Punica, Book 9*   59

dead brother. Then the grim omen moved them as well, as did the corpses' similar features. [260] Quickly they revealed the mistake and the pitiable deed to their commander, Varro, and the shield whose message forbade the combat. His spirit on fire, Varro said: "Bring these omens to Paulus. His effeminate breast is full of fear, and this man's hand drenched in an unspeakable killing will move him. [265] Perhaps when the Furies demanded the punishment, he wrote this criminal verse in his father's blood as he died."

Then Varro swiftly assigned the responsibilities for the battle in a threatening tone. Where savage Nealces commanded a line of fierce peoples, he set himself in opposition along with the Marsian soldiers [270] and the Samnites' battle standards and the Iapygians. But in the middle of the battlefield (for he saw Hannibal, the Libyan leader, standing in this part of it), he ordered Servilius to meet his advancing arms and to bring the Picentines and the Umbrians with him. Paulus had charge of the rest of the battle on the right wing. [275] Furthermore, it was Scipio's task to go against sneak attacks by the swift Numidian force. He was ordered to spread the fight wherever the enemy squads divided in cunning trickery for an encirclement.

And now the battle lines drew near one another. Much uncertain noise passed through the troubled ranks as men rushed nimbly forward, horses whinnied [280] from heated mouths, and arms clashed. It was just as when the winds first begin their combats on the seas. The waves on the gulf bring forth pent-up fury and gusts that will drench the stars.

60   *Sili Italici Punicorum Liber Nonus*

parturit unda freti fundoque emota minacis
exspirat per saxa sonos atque acta cauernis   285
torquet anhelantem spumanti uertice pontum.
     nec uero fati tam saeuo in turbine solum
terrarum fuit ille labor. Discordia demens
intrauit caelo superosque ad bella coegit.
hinc Mauors, hinc Gradiuum comitatus Apollo   290
et domitor tumidi pugnat maris, hinc Venus amens,
hinc Vesta et captae stimulatus caede Sagunti
Amphitryoniades, pariter ueneranda Cybele
Indigetesque dei Faunusque satorque Quirinus
alternusque animae mutato Castore Pollux.   295
contra cincta latus ferro Saturnia Iuno
et Pallas, Libycis Tritonidos edita lymphis,
ac patrius flexis per tempora cornibus Hammon,
multaque praeterea diuorum turba minorum.
quorum ubi mole simul uenientum et gressibus alma   300
intremuit tellus, pars impleuere propinquos
diuisi montes, pars sedem nube sub alta
ceperunt: uacuo descensum ad proelia caelo.
     tollitur immensus deserta ad sidera clamor,
Phlegraeis quantas effudit ad aethera uoces   305
terrigena in campis exercitus, aut sator aeui
quanta Cyclopas noua fulmina uoce poposcit
Iuppiter, exstructis uidit cum montibus ire
magnanimos raptum caelestia regna Gigantas.
nec uero prima in tantis concursibus hasta   310

---

284 minacum Ch   **287** in *om. edd. a* r1   **289** intrauit $ar2v$: luctauit β caelo ωCh : caelos r2 *edd. a* v   **290** mauor L   **293** Cybebe *Heinsius, Bentley*   **294** indigetesque $aV^2\Gamma^2O$: indigetosque $G\Gamma$: indigentesque V   **295** alternusque $ar1$: alteriusque β **297** tritonidos ω (tridonidos V titronidos O) Ch : tritonides *edd. a* v   **298** at $\delta\varsigma$ **303** descensum Γ^2r1 : discensum ω (discessum G) Ch   **304** immensos a **305** effudit *Bentley* : effundit r1 *edd. a* v   **306** terrigenum campis *Damsté*   **309** gigantas $ar2$ *Heinsius* : gigantes β

Silius Italicus *Punica, Book 9*   61

They emit menacing sounds over the rocks that they uproot from the sea floor [285] and rip from their caves. They twist the panting ocean into a frothing whirlpool.

Nor indeed in such a vicious whirlwind of fate did this struggle remain only on the earth. Crazy Discord entered heaven and forced the gods to war. [290] Mars and Apollo, his companion, fought on one side, and Neptune, master of the swelling ocean, Venus, out of her mind with grief, Vesta and Hercules, enraged by the slaughter at captured Saguntum. Along with them came honored Cybele and the native gods and Faunus and Quirinus, the ancestor of the Roman people, [295] and Pollux, who shared his soul in alternation with his brother Castor. Against them, Juno, daughter of Saturn, buckled a sword on her side, and Pallas, born from the Libyan Lake Tritonis, and the Carthaginians' native god, Hammon, his horns curving over his temples. There was a great crowd of lesser gods as well. [300] The nourishing earth trembled at their weight and their footsteps as they came on. Some of them parted company and occupied the nearby mountains; others took their place in a deep cloud. The descent to the battle emptied out heaven.

An enormous clamor rose up to the vacated stars. [305] Cries as loud as these once poured forth to the sky from the army of earth-born Giants on the Phlegraean fields. Jupiter, the father of the ages, used a voice as loud as these when he demanded new thunderbolts from the Cyclopes, as he saw the mountains heaped up and the great-spirited Giants attacking his celestial kingdom. Nor indeed was there any spear thrown first

62 *Sili Italici Punicorum Liber Nonus*

ulla fuit. stridens nimbus certante furore
telorum simul effusus, cupidaeque cruoris
hinc atque hinc animae gemina cecidere procella.
ac prius insanus dextra quam ducitur ensis,
bellantum pars magna iacet. super ipsa suorum   315
corpora consistunt auidi calcantque gementes.
nec magis aut Libyco protrudi Dardana nisu
auertiue potest pubes, aut ordine pelli
fixa suo Sarrana manus, quam uellere sede
si coeptet Calpen impacto gurgite pontus.   320
amisere ictus spatium, nec morte peracta
artatis cecidisse licet. galea horrida flictu
aduersae ardescit galeae, clipeusque fatiscit
impulsu clipei, atque ensis contunditur ense.
pes pede, uirque uiro teritur, tellusque uideri   325
sanguine operta nequit, caelumque et sidera pendens
abstulit ingestis nox densa sub aethere telis.
quis adstare loco dederat Fortuna secundo,
contorum longo et procerae cuspidis ictu,
ceu primas agitent acies, certamina miscent.   330
at quos deinde tenet retrorsum inglorius ordo,
missilibus certant pugnas aequare priorum.
ultra clamor agit bellum, milesque cupiti
Martis inops saeuis impellit uocibus hostem.
non ullum defit teli genus. hi sude pugnas,   335
hi pinu flagrante cient, hi pondere pili,

---

311 nimbis *s, edd. vett.*   **312** effusis *s*rlmp cupidaeque *a*r2v : rapidaeque *β* : rabidaeque *Γ²*rlm   **314** ac prius…quam *Burman* : acrius…qua *ω* : acri ast *uel* ast acri *Heinsius* : ac prior…quam *Schrader* : acrius in stragem…qua *Owen* : artius…qua *Damsté* dextra] theca *Liberman*   **317** nisu F*Γ* : uisu L*β*   **318** auertiue *a*δ : auertine GO potest F²*β* (pōt δ) : post *a* pelli *Γ²*rl : belli *ω*   **319** sede *a*G*Γ²* : sedem *Γ*   **320** coeptet *ω*Ch : temptat *Γ²* : temptet (tentet) PQ *edd. a* rl calmen incapto F   **322** flictu F²LG*Γ²*V : flictum *Γ* : fluctu FO   **323** fatiscit G²*Γs* : fatescit *ω*   **327** aethera *van Veen*   **329** et *del. Heinsius*   **334** s(a)euis *aΓs* : seuit *β*   **335** non ullum *a*G²r2 *D. Heinsius* Ch : nec ullum *β* : ullum nec g hi sude G²*Γ*G²*s* : insude *ω*

Silius Italicus *Punica, Book 9*

in such a clash. A roaring cloud of spears poured forth at the same moment, as they competed in rage. On one side and the other, spirits that longed for blood fell in a double whirlwind. A great part of the warriors fell [315] before their crazed hands could draw their swords. Eager men stood atop the very bodies of their comrades and trod on them as they groaned. The Libyan onslaught could not thrust or turn aside the Roman youth, nor could the Carthaginian forces be pushed from their fixed ranks, [320] any more than if the impact of the sea's waves were to begin to tear Gibraltar from its seat.

Blows lacked the space to connect, and the tight-packed men did not have room to fall when they died. Bristling helmets flashed as they struck opposing helmets, shields battered other shields and weakened them, and swords shattered upon swords. [325] Foot trod on foot and man on man. Blood covered the ground so it could not be seen. The javelins thrown in the air made a deep looming night that took away the sky and the stars. Those whom Fortune had allowed to stand in the second rank fought in combat with the lengthy lance's blow and the elongated javelin, [330] just as if they would stir up the front lines. And then the people behind them, in the ranks without glory, competed by hurling their missiles to equal the fighting of those ahead of them. Shouting led the battle onward. Soldiers denied the chance at the combat they so desired harassed the enemy with vicious insults. [335] No kind of weapon was lacking. Some fighters used clubs to stir up the fight, others burning pine branches, some the heavy javelin; still others used rocks and slingshots and swift spears.

64   *Sili Italici Punicorum Liber Nonus*

at saxis fundaque alius iaculoque uolucri.
interdum stridens per nubila fertur harundo,
interdumque ipsis metuenda phalarica muris.
     speramusne, deae, quarum mihi sacra coluntur,   340
mortali totum hunc aperire in saecula uoce
posse diem? tantumne datis confidere linguae,
ut Cannas uno ore sonem? si gloria uobis
nostra placet neque uos magnis auertitis ausis,
huc omnes cantus Phoebumque uocate parentem.   345
uerum utinam posthac animo, Romane, secunda,
quanto nunc aduersa, feras! sitque hactenus, oro,
nec libeat temptare deis, an Troia proles
par bellum tolerare queat. tuque anxia fati
pone, precor, lacrimas et adora uulnera laudes   350
perpetuas paritura tibi. nam tempore, Roma,
nullo maior eris. mox sic labere secundis
ut sola cladum tuearis nomina fama.
     iamque inter uarias Fortuna utrimque uirorum
alternata uices incerto eluserat iras   355
euentu, mediaque diu pendente per ambas
spe gentis paribus Mauors flagrabat in armis,
mitia ceu uirides agitant cum flamina culmos,
necdum maturas impellit uentus aristas,
huc atque huc it summa seges nutansque uicissim   360
alterno lente motu incuruata nitescit.
tandem barbaricis perfractam uiribus acri
dissipat incurrens aciem clamore Nealces.
laxati cunei, perque interualla citatus

337 at *β* (ad O) : ac *α* **338–9** *hoc ordine* Ch   **339** *post*   **342** *Γ, inuerso ordine* rl *edd. a*
m que *om. edd. a* j   **340** speramusne F²*β* : speramusve *α* : speremusne *Blass*
341 aperiri *Heinsius*   **342** tantumne F²GO : tantumue *α*δ considere L   **344** nos
Orl   **347** sitque FOV : sicque L : stetque *Dausqueius* : sisque *Heinsius* : satque *Blass*
(1867) 23, *Bauer*   **361** uirescit *Livineius* : rigescit *uel* resurgit *Schrader*   **362** acris *edd.*
a rl : acer *edd. a* j   **364** lassati L*δ*

Meanwhile shrieking arrows shot through the clouds and the *phalarica*, which the walls themselves feared.

[340] Goddess Muses whose rites I tend, should I hope that my mortal voice could reveal this whole day for successive ages? Are you giving me so much confidence in my tongue that I may sound forth Cannae from my one mouth alone? If my glory pleases you and you do not turn me aside from my great undertaking, call here all your songs and father Apollo. [345] Indeed, Roman, if only you would afterward endure prosperity with courage as great as when you endured adversity! I beg that this may be suffering enough and the gods may not be pleased to test whether Troy's descendants could withstand another war like this. And as you worry about your fate, [350] Rome, put aside your tears, I pray, and honor the wounds that shall always bring you praise. For at no time will you be greater than this, Rome. Soon amid prosperity you will endure such collapse that you will uphold your name solely with the reputation from your defeats.

And already amid her varied changes, Fortune had alternated the men's circumstances [355] and duped their battle fury with uncertain result. Battle blazed in equal force as hope hung for a long time in the middle between the two peoples. It was just like when gentle breezes tug on the green stalks and the wind pushes on ears of grain that have not yet ripened. [360] The whole crop moves here and there and sways back and forth and shines as it curves gently in alternate directions. At last Nealces charged, shouting keenly, and his barbarian forces broke up and shattered the Roman line. The wedge formations were loosened, and the swift enemy rushed in through the openings against the fearful men.

66 *Sili Italici Punicorum Liber Nonus*

irrupit trepidis hostis. tum turbine nigro 365
sanguinis exundat torrens, nullumque sub una
cuspide procumbit corpus. dum uulnera tergo
bellator timet Ausonius, per pectora saeuas
exceptat mortes et leto dedecus arcet.
       stabat cum primis mediae certamine pugnae 370
aspera semper amans et par cuicumque periclo
Scaeuola, nec tanta uitam iam strage uolebat,
sed dignum proauo letum et sub nomine mortem.
is postquam frangi res atque augescere uidit
exitium, 'breuis hoc uitae, quodcumque relictum, 375
extendamus;' ait 'nam uirtus futile nomen,
ni decori sat sint pariendo tempora leti.'
dixit et in medios, qua dextera concita Poeni
limitem agit, uasto conixus turbine fertur.
hic exultantem Caralim atque erepta uolentem 380
induere excelso caesi gestamina trunco
ense subit, capuloque tenus ferrum impulit ira.
uoluitur ille ruens atque arua hostilia morsu
appetit et mortis premit in tellure dolores.
nec Gabaris Sicchaeque uirum tenuere furentem 385
concordi uirtute manus; sed perdidit acer,
dum stat, decisam Gabar inter proelia dextram;
at Siccha auxilium magno turbante dolore
dum temere accelerat, calcato improuidus ense
succidit ac nudae sero uestigia plantae 390

365 trepidus Ch : trepidos *Heinsius* nigri Ch   366 una Br1mp, *Livineius* : ima ω
370 certamine ωCh : certamina Γ, *edd. a* r1   377 decori sat sint *Heinsius* : decoris
adsint ωCh : decori prosint *Withof* : decori assignet *Blass* tempora $a\Gamma$: tempore β
378 dextera r1 : dextra ω 380 calarim Γs : clarim O   383 arua aCm *Ep.* 50 : arma β
384 oppetit *Lefebvre* ut mortis premat *Drakenborch*   385 gabaris BH *Scaliger* : gabari
ω Sicchaeque Ch : sudiaeque F furentem *Delz* : furentes ω 387 decisam] densam
L   390 ac ωCh : et δ sero ωCh : ferro δ

Silius Italicus *Punica, Book 9*

[365] Then a torrent of blood flowed out from battle's dark whirlwind. No corpse fell under a single spear. Even as the Roman warriors feared wounds to the back, they took savage death blows in the chest, and shielded their deaths from disgrace.

[370] Scaevola stood among the first in the middle of the combat. He always loved bitter challenge, and he was equal to any danger. Amid such slaughter he did not want to live; rather, he wanted a death worthy of his ancestor and to die in his name. After he saw that the Romans' circumstances were shattered and destruction was increasing, he said: "Whatever is left of this short life, [375] let us extend its fame. For courage is a useless name unless our deaths should be honorable enough by enduring through time." He spoke thus and gathered himself in a mighty rush and plunged into the middle of the fight, where Nealces was clearing a path with his swift hand.

[380] Here Scaevola attacked Caralis with his sword. Caralis was exulting and wishing to fix the armor he had seized from a slain man on a high tree trunk. In anger Scaevola pierced him with his sword right up to the hilt. He fell forward, collapsing, and bit the hostile earth, stifling death's sufferings on the ground. [385] Nor could Gabar or Siccha hold back raging Scaevola, though they joined hands to cooperate in courageous acts. Even as he stood fast, keen Gabar lost his right hand, as it was cut off in the combat. Great grief overwhelmed Siccha as he hurried in vain to bring help. He trod unawares on Gabar's sword [390] and tripped. Too late, he condemned his bare foot,

68   *Sili Italici Punicorum Liber Nonus*

damnauit dextraque iacet morientis amici.
tandem conuertit fatalia tela Nealcae
fulminei gliscens iuuenis furor. exsilit ardens
nomine tam claro stimulante ad praemia caedis.
tum silicem scopulo auulsum, quem montibus altis   395
detulerat torrens, raptum contorquet in ora
turbidus. incusso crepuerunt pondere malae,
ablatusque uiro uultus. concreta cruento
per nares cerebro sanies fluit, atraque manant
orbibus elisis et trunca lumina fronte.   400
     sternitur unanimo Marius succurrere Capro
conatus metuensque uiro superesse cadenti.
lucis idem auspicium ac patrium et commune duobus
paupertas; sacro iuuenes Praeneste creati
miscuerant studia et iuncta tellure serebant.   405
uelle ac nolle ambobus idem sociataque toto
mens aeuo ac paruis diues concordia rebus.
occubuere simul, uotisque ex omnibus unum
id Fortuna dedit, iunctam inter proelia mortem.
arma fuere decus uictori bina Symaetho.   410
     sed longum tanto laetari munere casus
haud licitum Poenis. aderat terrore minaci
Scipio conuersae miseratus terga cohortis
et cuncti fons Varro mali flauusque comarum
Curio et a primo descendens consule Brutus.   415
atque his fulta uiris acies repararet ademptum
mole noua campum, subito ni turbine Poenus
agmina frenasset iam procurrentia ductor.

391 que *om.* δ (*ins. m.2* Γ)   394 praemia F *marg. m.*1 Lβ : proelia Fδ   396 depulerat *Heinsius*   399 flumina *Liberman*   401 capro rl : caspro ω   403 ac patriae *Heinsius*   404 penestre δ (*corr. in* Γ)   408 uotisque αVΓ² : notisque Gδ   409 uictam V   410 Symaetho ChLF : simaetho OV   411 laetari Γ²s : letali ω   415 discendens F   416 repararat *Heinsius, Bentley*   417 ni F²LV²Γ² : in Fβ

Silius Italicus *Punica, Book 9*   69

and he lay in death thanks to his dying friend's hand. As Scaevola's rage increased, in the end it drew lightning-fast Nealces' fatal weapons. On fire, he leapt forth, and the great fame of his opponent's name prodded him to the reward for killing him. [395] Then he seized a rock torn from a crag which a torrent had brought down from the high mountains. In a frenzy, he hurled it at Scaevola's face. His teeth rattled as the mass struck his cheek and tore off his face. Blood thickened with grisly brains poured through his nostrils. His gory eyes flowed down [400] from his shattered sockets and disfigured forehead.

Marius was laid low as he attempted to help his soul mate Caper. He was afraid to live on if his friend died. The two men had been born on the same day, and poverty was their common inheritance from their fathers. These young men, born in holy Praeneste, [405] had combined their youthful pursuits and farmed adjacent fields. Both wanted and avoided the same things, and their minds were conjoined for life. A rich partnership came from their poor circumstances. They fell together, and from all their vows Fortune granted this one: death together in battle. [410] Their conqueror Symaethus gained honor from their two sets of arms.

But the Carthaginians were not permitted to rejoice for long in such a gift from fate. Scipio was there in menacing terror. He pitied the cohort that was turning its backs in flight. Varro was there too, source of all this evil, and light-haired [415] Curio, and Brutus descended from the first consul. Trusting in these men, the Roman line would have regained the lost battlefield with a new effort—if Hannibal, the leader, had not suddenly rushed in and reined back the hurrying ranks.

70   *Sili Italici Punicorum Liber Nonus*

isque ut Varronem procul inter proelia uidit
et iuxta sagulo circumuolitare rubenti   420
lictorem, 'nosco pompam atque insignia nosco.
Flaminius modo talis' ait. tum feruidus acrem
ingentis clipei tonitru praenuntiat iram.
heu miser! aequari potuisti funere Paulo,
si tibi non ira superum tunc esset ademptum   425
Hannibalis cecidisse manu. quam saepe querere,
Varro, deis, quod Sidonium defugeris ensem!
nam rapido subitam portans in morte salutem
procursu excepta in sese discrimina uertit
Scipio. nec Poenum, quamquam est ereptus opimae   430
caedis honor, mutasse piget maiore sub hoste
proelia et erepti Ticina ad flumina patris
exigere oblato tandem certamine poenas.
stabant educti diuersis orbis in oris,
quantos non alias uidit concurrere tellus,   435
Marte uiri dextraque pares, sed cetera ductor
anteibat Latius, melior pietate fideque.
      desiluere caua turbati ad proelia nube,
Mauors Scipiadae metuens, Tritonia Poeno,
aduentuque deum intrepidis ductoribus ambae   440
contremuere acies. ater, qua pectora flectit
Pallas, Gorgoneo late micat ignis ab ore
sibilaque horrificis torquet serpentibus aegis.

420 circumuolitare   GΓ^2O   :   circum   uolutare αVΓ **421** littorem   L
429 procursu α_ς : pro cursu β excepta in sese *Shackleton Bailey 1959: 174* : incepta sese in
ω : incepta sese δ : incepta ad sese Γ^2r1 : coepta sese in b1 : coepta in sese *Livineius* :
incepta, in sese *Bauer* : *alia, vid. comm.*   **433** poenas $\Gamma^2\varsigma$: poenus ω **434** ab Γ^2 *edd.* a r1
435 quanto *edd.* a r1 alias ω : alios Ch *Bauer* : alio *Heinsius*   **436** macte L
438 desiluere ω *Livineius* : dissiluere δ_ς **441** ater qua ω (acer qua V) : aterque L
442 orbe *Heinsius*

Silius Italicus *Punica, Book 9*

As he saw Varro far off amid the fighting, [420] his lictor rushing around him in a red cloak, he said: "I recognize his entourage and insignia. Flaminius before him was just like this." Then the thundering of his enormous shield announced his keen anger, fired up as he was.

Alas, wretched Varro! Your death would have equalled Paulus', [425] if the gods' anger had not taken from you the chance to fall by Hannibal's hand. How often you will complain to the gods, Varro, that you escaped the Carthaginian's sword! For Scipio rushed forward rapidly and swiftly brought safety in the face of death. He took the danger on himself and turned it away from Varro. [430] Though the honor of the rich spoil had been taken from him, Hannibal was not ashamed to change combat for a greater enemy. Now that a duel was offered to him at last, he wanted to demand recompense for Scipio's father, who had been snatched from him at the Ticinus River. These men, raised on opposite sides of the world, stood against each other. [435] The earth had not seen such men come together at any other time. These men were equal in combat and fighting skill, but the Latin leader Scipio was superior in other respects, and his sense of duty and loyalty were greater.

Mars feared for Scipio, Tritonian Pallas for Hannibal. Troubled at heart, they leapt from their hollow cloud to the battlefield. [440] At the coming of the gods, both battle lines trembled for their fearless leaders. Dark fire flashed widely from the Gorgon's mouth wherever Pallas turned her chest. The horrifying snakes on the aegis emitted hisses.

72 *Sili Italici Punicorum Liber Nonus*

fulgent sanguinei, geminum uibrare cometem
ut credas, oculi, summaque in casside largus 445
undantes uoluit flammas ad sidera uertex.
at Mauors moto proturbans aera telo
et clipeo campum inuoluens Aetnaea Cyclopum
munere fundentem loricam incendia gestat
ac pulsat fulua consurgens aethera crista. 450
       ductores pugnae intenti, quantumque uicissim
auderent, propius mensi, tamen arma ferentes
sensere aduenisse deos et laetus uterque
spectari superis addebant mentibus iras.
iamque ictu ualido libratam a pectore Poeni 455
Pallas in obliquum dextra detorserat hastam,
et Gradiuus opem diuae portare ferocis
exemplo doctus porgebat protinus ensem
Aetnaeum in pugnas iuueni ac maiora iubebat.
tum Virgo ignescens penitus uiolenta repente 460
suffudit flammis ora atque obliqua retorquens
lumina turbato superauit Gorgona uultu.
erexere omnes immania membra chelydri
aegide commota, primique furoris ad ictus
rettulit ipse pedem sensim a certamine Mauors. 465
hic dea conuulsam rapido conamine partem
uicini montis scopulisque horrentia saxa
in Martem furibunda iacit, longeque relatos
expauit sonitus tremefacto litore Sason.
       at non haec superum fallebant proelia regem. 470
demittit propere succinctam nubibus Irim

---

445 e Cd (?)   **447** proturbans αCh : perturbans β celo δ   **448** (a)et(h)n(a)ea FV*Γ²* : ernea LGδ   **449** munera *Heinsius* incendia αV²*Γ²* : incedia β   **452** auderent Bl *Livineius* : audere ω : audere est *Γ²*rl, *Heinsius, Drakenborch* : auderet *edd.* *a* j   **459** ethnaeum L : aetneum F : enaeum O : Aethnaeum V uidebat δ (*corr. in Γ*)   **460** ignescens α*Γ²* : ignoscens β   **465** sensum O   **467** haerentia *Γ²* *edd. vett.*   **469** sason α*Γ*Ch : sanson G*Γ²*s : sasson B *edd.* *a* v   **471** iram δ (*corr. in Γ*)

Eyes shone blood-red so that you might think a double comet was flashing. [445] From the tip of her helmet, a huge whirlwind twisted rolling flames to the stars. But Mars waved his spear and pushed the air forward. He covered the battlefield with his shield. His breastplate, the Cyclopes' gift, poured forth Aetna's fires. [450] The tawny crest rising from his helmet struck the upper air.

The leaders were intent on their duel, each measuring at close quarters how much he would dare to do in turn. Yet they sensed that the gods had come bearing arms. Each man was happy that the gods were observing him and increased the anger in his spirit. [455] And already Pallas' hand had turned aside from Hannibal's chest a spear thrown with a strong cast. The fierce goddess's example taught Mars Gradivus to offer help. Straight away he offered young Scipio a sword forged in Mount Aetna for his combats and ordered him to attempt greater deeds. [460] Then violent virgin Pallas burned deep within, and suddenly her face filled with fire. Her eyes twisted sideways, and her angry face was more frightening than the Gorgon's. She shook the aegis, and all the snakes stretched forth their huge limbs. At her rage's initial blows, [465] Mars himself drew back little by little from the duel. Here the goddess made a swift effort and tore off part of the nearby mountain. In a rage, she hurled the boulder bristling with crags at Mars. Sason Island's shoreline trembled, and it feared the sounds carried over a long distance.

[470] But these battles did not deceive the king of the gods. He quickly sent down cloud-girded Iris

74   *Sili Italici Punicorum Liber Nonus*

quae nimios frenet motus, ac talia fatur:
'i, dea, et Oenotris uelox allabere terris
germanoque truces, dic, Pallas mitiget iras
nec speret fixas Parcarum uertere leges.   475
dic etiam: ni desistis (nam uirus et aestus
flammiferae noui mentis) nec colligis iram,
aegide praecellant quantum horrida fulmina nosces.'
      quae postquam accepit dubitans Tritonia uirgo
nec sat certa diu, patriis an cederet armis,   480
'absistemus' ait 'campo. sed Pallade pulsa
num fata auertet caeloque arcebit ab alto
cernere Gargani feruentia caedibus arua?'
haec effata caua Poenum in certamina nube
sublatum diuersa tulit terrasque reliquit.   485
      at Gradiuus atrox remeantis in aethera diuae
abscessu reuocat mentes fusosque per aequor
ipse manu magna nebulam circumdatus acri
restituit pugnae. conuertunt signa nouamque
instaurant Itali uersa formidine caedem.   490
cum uentis positus custos, cui flamina carcer
imperio compressa tenet caelumque ruentes
Eurique et Boreae parent Corique Notique,
Iunonis precibus promissa haud parua ferentis

---

473 oneotris Q : aenotris Γ^2r2 : (a)enotriis ω elabere δ (*corr. in Γ*)
474 germanoque Ch : germaneque ω : germanique Y^2 476 ni desistis] in dextris F
(*corr. m.2 marg.*)   iam O   477 corrigis *Bentley* : corripis *Blass*
478 aegida *corrector in exemplari ed. Rom., Drakenborch, Bauer* : aegidï *Bentley* (*sic*)
praecellant $a\Gamma^2$: protellant β (procellant δ)   480 sat certa sui *Heinsius*   483 sternere
Blass   487 fusosque $\Xi\Sigma$Ch : fusorque ω : fusoque F^2 : fususque G^2: fusamque Γ^2 *edd.*
a 1   488 nebulam Ch : nebula ω acri $F^2L\beta$: atra $F\Gamma^2$s   489 pugnae FCh : pugnam
$F^2\beta$ 491 tum *edd. vett.* cui Γ^2s : qui ω 493 furique a (*corr. in* F)
494 furentis δ (*corr. in Γ*)

Silius Italicus *Punica, Book 9*

to hold back this excessive violence. Jupiter spoke thus: "Go, goddess, and slip down swiftly to the land of Italy. Tell Pallas to calm her harsh anger at her brother and not to hope to change the Fates' fixed laws. Say also: 'Unless you stop' (for I recognize her fiery mind's disease and swells), 'unless you hold back your rage, you will know how much my bristling thunderbolts outdo your aegis.'"

[479] Tritonian virgin Pallas hesitated after she heard these words. For a long time she was not certain whether she should yield to her father's arms. "Let us leave the battlefield," she said. "But if I, Pallas, am pushed back, will he turn aside Fate and prevent seeing from high heaven the fields of Mount Garganus burning with slaughter?" After she said this, she caught up Hannibal in a hollow cloud and brought him to a different part of the battle. Then she left the earth.

[486] As the goddess departed and returned to the sky, fierce Mars Gradivus called back the Romans' spirits. Concealed in mist, with his own mighty hand he restored them to the bitter fight from where they had scattered over the plain. The Italians turned around their battle standards and reversed their fear, beginning the slaughter anew. Aeolus was the keeper set over the winds, and by his authority a jail holds the storms shut in. Eurus and Boreas and Corus and Notus obey him as they rush through the sky. In response to Juno's entreaty (she offered him no small promises),

76   *Sili Italici Punicorum Liber Nonus*

regnantem Aetolis Vulturnum in proelia campis   495
effrenat. placet hic irae exitiabilis ultor.
qui, se postquam Aetnae mersit candente barathro
concepitque ignes et flammea protulit ora,
euolat horrendo stridore ac Daunia regna
perflat agens caecam glomerato puluere nubem.   500
eripuere oculos aurae uocemque manusque;
uertice harenoso candentes, flebile dictu,
torquet in ora globos Italum et bellare maniplis
iussa laetatur rabie. tum mole ruinae
sternuntur tellure et miles et arma tubaeque,   505
atque omnis retro flatu occursante refertur
lancea et in tergum Rutulis cadit irritus ictus.
atque idem flatus Poenorum tela secundant,
et uelut ammento contorta hastilia turbo
adiuuat ac Tyrias impellit stridulus hastas.   510
tum denso fauces praeclusus puluere miles
ignauam mortem compresso maeret hiatu.
ipse caput flauum caligine conditus atra
Vulturnus multaque comam perfusus harena
nunc uersos agit a tergo stridentibus alis,   515
nunc mediam in frontem ueniens clamante procella
obuius arma quatit patuloque insibilat ore,

495 aetolis Σ^2 *Cluverius* : (a)eoliis $F^2\Gamma^2 s$: (a)eolus ω **497** aetnae Γ^2 : (h)et(h)n(a)e ω
candente Γ, *Bentley* : cadente δ **502** candentes (-is) $a\Gamma^2$: cadentes β **503** in ora Γ :
niora F : mora LG   **504** l(a)etatur LCh : lateatur F : laceratur $F^2\beta$: lacerantur $\Gamma^2 s$ *edd.*
vett. (bacchatur pl lacessuntur g)   **505** tellure et $\Gamma^2 s$: tellure ω iubaeque *Livineius* tellure <equitesque> et miles et arma [tubaeque] *coni. Delz*   **507** in tergum *Barth, edd.* :
interdum ω, *Volpilhac-Lenthéric, Zaia*   **508** secundant ωCh : secundat s
509 hostilia δ (*corr. in* Γ)   **511** perculsus O   **512** m(a)eret $LF^2\Gamma^2 s$: mercet F : marcet β
517 ori *Heinsius*

he let loose into the combat Vulturnus, who rules the Aetolian fields. This avenger pleased her deadly anger. He plunged himself in Aetna's burning abyss and gathered flames and showed forth a fiery face. Then he flew out with a horrifying shriek and blew over the Daunian kingdoms of southern Italy, carrying with him a dark cloud of thick-packed dust. The winds took away sight and voice and hands. Sad to say, Vulturnus shot burning masses from his sandy whirlwind into the Italians' faces and rejoiced as he fought the ranks with the rage that had been commanded.

[504] Then soldiers were laid out on the earth in a mass of ruin, as were their weapons and battle horns. Every lance flew backward as it met the wind and its useless blow fell behind the Romans' backs. These same gusts of wind aided the Carthaginians' weapons. The whirlwind helped along their missiles, just as if they had been hurled from a thong, and the shrieking wind pushed forward the Carthaginians' spears. Next, thick dust clogged the soldiers' throats. They mourned deaths without honor as their windpipes shut. Vulturnus himself buried his tawny head in dark dust and poured much sand in his hair. At one moment, his shrieking wings turned the Romans and pushed them from the back. At another moment, his noisy gale came straight on against their foreheads. He shook his weapons and hissed from a gaping mouth.

78 *Sili Italici Punicorum Liber Nonus*

interdum intentos pugnae et iam iamque ferentes
hostili iugulo ferrum conamine et ictu
auertit dextramque ipso de uulnere uellit. 520
nec satis Ausonias passim foedare cohortes:
in Martem uomit immixtas mugitibus auras
bisque dei summas uibrauit turbine cristas.

  quae dum Romuleis exercet proelia turmis
Aeolius furor et Martem succendit in iras, 525
affatur Virgo, socia Iunone, parentem:
'quantos Gradiuus fluctus in Punica castra,
respice, agit quantisque furens se caedibus implet!
nunc, quaeso, terris descendere non placet Irim?
quamquam ego non Teucros (nostro cum pignore regnet 530
Roma, et Palladio sedes hac urbe locarim)
non Teucros delere aderam, sed lumen alumnae
Hannibalem Libyae pelli florentibus annis
uita atque extingui primordia tanta negabam.'

  excipit hinc Iuno longique laboris ab ira 535
'immo,' ait 'ut noscant gentes, immania quantum
regna Iouis ualeant cunctisque potentia quantum
antistet, coniunx, superis tua, disice telo
flagranti (nil oramus) Carthaginis arces
Sidoniamque aciem uasto telluris hiatu 540
Tartareis immerge uadis aut obrue ponto.'

  contra quae miti respondet Iuppiter ore:
'certatis fatis et spes extenditis aegras.
ille, o nata, libens cui tela inimica ferebas,

---

518 prementes *Heinsius, Håkanson*   **519** et ictu αr2v : dictu β : ducto Γ^2Qr1 : uicto *Blass*   **522** iras Ch   **523** uibrauit αr2v : librauit O : libauit V *Gronovius*   **531** hac LΓ^2s : ac Fβ **533** liby(a)e *uel* libi(a)e V$^2\Gamma^2$: libre β **535** hinc *Delz* : haec ω : hic Γ^2O longisque GV   **538** dissite O : discute *edd.* *a* r1   **539** obstamus *Heinsius* **541** immergere Γ (*corr. in* VΓ)

Silius Italicus *Punica, Book 9*

Sometimes the Romans were intent on combat and already were thrusting their swords toward their enemy's neck. [520] Vulturnus turned aside the effort and the blow and ripped the fighting hand right out of the very wound. Nor was it enough for him to defile the Italian cohorts here and there. He spewed forth winds mixed with roaring at Mars, and twice the whirlwind shook the topmost crest of the god's helmet.

The wind god's fury waged war against the Roman ranks [525] and kindled Mars to anger. Meanwhile virgin Pallas, accompanied by Juno, addressed father Jupiter: "See how great are the waves that Mars Gradivus sends against the Punic camps! See how great the slaughter that fills him as he rages! I ask you, now does it not please you for Iris to come down to earth? [530] I am not here to destroy the Trojans. Let Rome rule with my pledge of security. I have placed a site for the Palladium in this city. Though I would not destroy them, yet I refuse to let Hannibal, the light of Libya that nursed me, be pushed from life in his flourishing youth and for such great beginnings to be snuffed out."

[535] Here Juno took up the argument and spoke in anger from her long struggle: "Let the world know indeed how powerful Jupiter's mighty rule is. Let them know how much power, my husband, you can set against all the gods. Break up the citadel of Carthage with your burning thunderbolt. We beg you for nothing. [540] Make a vast chasm in the earth and plunge the Sidonian ranks into Tartarus's waters or drown them in the sea."

80   *Sili Italici Punicorum Liber Nonus*

contundet iuuenis Tyrios ac nomina gentis   545
induet et Libycam feret in Capitolia laurum.
at cui tu, coniunx, cui das animosque decusque,
(fata cano) auertet populis Laurentibus arma.
nec longe cladis metae. uenit hora diesque,
qua nullas umquam transisse optauerit Alpes.'   550
sic ait atque Irim propere demittit Olympo,
quae reuocet Martem iubeatque abscedere pugna.
nec uetitis luctatus abit Gradiuus in altas
cum fremitu nubes, quamquam lituique tubaeque
uulneraque et sanguis et clamor et arma iuuarent.   555
    ut patuit liber superum certamine tandem
laxatusque deo campus, ruit aequore ab imo
Poenus, quo sensim caelestia fugerat arma,
magna uoce trahens equitemque uirosque feraeque
turrigerae molem tormentorumque labores.   560
atque ubi turbantem leuiores ense cateruas
agnouit iuuenem scintillauitque cruentis
ira genis, 'quaenam Furiae quisue egit in hostem,
en, Minuci, deus, ut rursus te credere nobis
auderes?' inquit 'genitor tibi natus ab armis   565
ille meis ubi nunc Fabius? semel, improbe, nostras
sit satis euasisse manus.' atque inde superbis
hasta comes dictis murali turbine pectus
transforat et uoces uenturas occupat ictu.
    nec ferro saeuire sat est. appellitur atra   570
mole fera, et monstris componitur Itala pubes.

545 iuuenis Tyrios *Bothe* : Tyrius iuuenis ω   548 auertet j : uertet *Γ²β* : uertit α
551 dimittit GO   553 uentis F (*corr. m.2*)   554 litiūque δ (*corr. in Γ*)   563 quae iam
Furiae, quis te egit *Barth*   564 en] an *Barth* : nunc *Schrader* minuci Br2 : minuti
*Calderini in Γ*v : munci F : minici L : numici G : inimici *Γ* ut αVr2v : et Gδ en inimice
deis rursum ut te credere nobis *Odus in Γ*

From his gentle mouth Jupiter spoke in reply: "You are fighting against the Fates and pushing sick hope. O my daughter, you are eagerly bringing hostile arms against the young man [545] who will smash the Carthaginians and gain the name 'Africanus' from these people and bring the Libyan laurel to the Capitol. And the man, my wife, the very man to whom you are giving courage and honor—I am singing Fate—Hannibal will turn his arms from the Italian people. The turning point in this conflict is not far off. The day and hour will come [550] on which Hannibal will wish he had never crossed the Alps."

Thus Jupiter spoke and quickly sent Iris down from Olympus to call back Mars and order him to withdraw from combat. Mars Gradivus did not struggle against the prohibition. He went shouting into the high clouds, even though the battle horns and trumpets [555] and wounds and blood and arms and yells all pleased him.

The battlefield lay open at last, free of the gods' conflicts and relieved of Mars. Hannibal rushed from the furthest point of the field, where he had slowly retreated from the gods' combat. He gave a mighty shout and drew on the cavalry and infantry and the massive elephants [560] with towers on their backs and the straining ballistae. Anger flashed in his bloodstained cheeks when he recognized Minucius, who was harassing the light-armed troops with his sword.

"Look!" Hannibal said. "What Furies or what god has led you against the enemy, Minucius? Do you dare to trust yourself once more against me? [565] Where is Fabius now, the father you got by fighting me? You shameless fool, it should have been enough for you to escape my hands the first time." And then Hannibal's spear accompanied his arrogant words. It pierced Minucius' chest like a shot from the catapult, and its blow stopped the words that he was getting ready in reply.

[570] Nor was raging with swords enough. Hannibal called up the elephants' dark bulk and set these monsters against the Italian youth.

Sili Italici Punicorum Liber Nonus

nam praeuectus equo moderantem cuspide Lucas
Maurum in bella boues stimulis maioribus ire
ac raptare iubet Libycarum armenta ferarum.
immane stridens agitur crebroque coacta   575
uulnere bellatrix properos fert belua gressus.
liuenti dorso turris flammaque uirisque
et iaculis armata sedet. procul aspera grando
saxorum super arma ruit, passimque uolanti
celsus telorum fundit Libys aggere nimbum.   580
stat niueis longum stipata per agmina uallum
dentibus, atque ebori praefixa comminus hasta
fulget ab incuruo derecta cacumine cuspis.
    hic, inter trepidos rerum per membra, per arma
exigit Vfentis sceleratum belua dentem   585
clamantemque ferens calcata per agmina portat.
nec leuius Tadio letum: qua tegmine thorax
multiplicis lini claudit latus, improba sensim
corpore non laeso penetrarunt spicula dentis
et sublime uirum clipeo resonante tulerunt.   590
haud excussa noui uirtus terrore pericli.
utitur ad laudem casu geminumque citato
uicinus fronti lumen transuerberat ense.
exstimulata graui sese fera tollit ad auras
uulnere et erectis excussam cruribus alte   595
pone iacit uoluens reflexo pondere turrim.
arma uirique simul spoliataque belua uisu
sternuntur subita, miserandum, mixta ruina.

---

572 praeuectus *a*GV*Γ²*Ch : prouectus δ*ς* 573 ire] uti *Damsté*
575 immani *Livineius* : immanis *Blass* 577 flaminaque L 578 armata] aptata
Liberman 579 *om.* F (*suppl. m.2 marg.*) uolantem *van Veen*
582 utque *Thilo* 583 derecta *a* (de recta L) GVCh : deiecta δ*ς*
585 exiit Ch 586 furens *Heinsius* 587 nec] hic *Blass* tadio *a*Ch : radio β letum ω :
l(a)euum *Γ²* *edd. a* rl qua β : que *a* 596 pone *a*r2ml : pene β 598 mirandum *Bothe*

Silius Italicus *Punica, Book 9*

He rode his horse before them and ordered the Moors to goad the elephants harder. They guided them into battle with their spears and rushed the herd of Libyan beasts forward. [575] The warlike animals trumpeted deafeningly as they hurried their pace, and steady wounding forced them to move. Towers perched on their dark backs, armed with men and torches and spears. From far above a bitter hailstorm of stones poured down on the Roman soldiers. Here and there, [580] from their mobile rampart on high, the Libyans poured down a cloud of spears. A long palisade of white tusks stood close-packed in ranks. Spears shone close at hand where they had been fastened to the ivory. Their points jutted forth from the curved cones.

Here amid the fearful Romans, an elephant thrust [585] its wicked tusk through Ufens' armor and limbs. It carried him off screaming as it trampled down the ranks. Tadius' death was no lighter. Little by little the tusk's fierce point penetrated where the corslet's multiple layers of linen concealed his side. [590] It bore the man aloft, and his shield resounded. Yet the new danger's terror did not shake the Roman's courage. He used his position close to the elephant's forehead as a chance for glory. He struck the elephant's eyes with his swift sword. The serious wound enraged the beast. It reared toward the sky [595] and shook off its tower, throwing it behind as it raised its legs and turned its bulk. A pitiable sight: the men and weapons and blinded elephant all collapsed at one time in a jumbled heap.

84   *Sili Italici Punicorum Liber Nonus*

spargi flagrantes contra bellantia monstra
Dardanius taedas ductor iubet et facis atrae,   600
quos fera circumfert, compleri sulphure muros.
nec iusso mora. collectis fumantia lucent
terga elephantorum flammis, pastusque sonoro
ignis edax uento per propugnacula fertur.
non aliter, Pindo Rhodopeue incendia pastor   605
cum iacit, et siluis spatiatur feruida pestis,
frondosi ignescunt scopuli, subitoque per alta
collucet iuga dissultans Vulcanius ardor.
it fera candenti torrente bitumine corpus
amens et laxo diducit limite turmas.   610
nec cuiquam uirtus propiora capessere bella:
longinquis audent iaculis et harundinis ictu.
uritur impatiens et magni corporis aestu
huc atque huc iactas accendit belua flammas,
donec uicini tandem se fluminis undis   615
praecipitem dedit et tenui decepta liquore
stagnantis per plana uadi tulit incita longis
exstantem ripis flammam. tum denique sese
gurgitis immersit molem capiente profundo.
     at qua pugna datur necdum Maurusia pestis   620
igne calet, circumfusi Rhoeteia pubes
nunc iaculis, nunc et saxis, nunc alite plumbo
eminus incessunt, ut qui castella per altos

---

599 spargi ωCh : spargere *edd. a* v   **600** ductor *uel* rector *Barth* : uictor ω acre δ (*corr. in Γ*)   **601** conspergi *uel* comburi *van Veen*   **602** coniectis *Calderinus in Γ, Heinsius* : correptis *Schrader*   **603** pastusque Cm *Ep.* 1 : partus ω : raptus $Γ^2$*s edd. vett., Summers* : parcusque O   **609** cadenti δ (*corr. in Γ*)   **610** diducit FGV$Γ^2$: deducit Lδ   **614** *om. edd. vett. excepta* r2, *reduxit Modius Ep.* 1   **619** gurgite summersit *van Veen* immergit F   **621** rh(o)eteia αG²$Γ^2$: rhoetria β   **623** ut $Γ^2$s : ne ω

Varro, the Roman commander, ordered his men to hurl burning firebrands [600] against the warlike beasts and to fill the towers which the elephants carried with sulfur from smoky torches. They did not delay in responding to his order. The elephants' backs shone as the flames heaped up. The noisy wind fed the consuming fire and spread it through their armaments. [605] It was just as when a shepherd on Mount Pindus or Rhodope tosses firebrands and the flames roam eagerly through the woods. The leafy ridges catch fire, and Vulcan's blaze shines forth as it leaps suddenly throughout the high cliffs. The elephants went out of their minds as the glowing pitch scorched their bodies. [610] They forced a ragged path through the ranks. No one had the courage to get close to them and fight. They only dared to strike from far off with spears and arrows. The beasts did not tolerate being burned or the heat scorching their massive bodies. They tossed the fires this way and that and fed them, [615] until at last they threw themselves headlong in the nearby stream's pools. The thin water deceived the elephants. They rushed across the plains beside the still brook, carrying along the banks the fire still blazing forth. Then at last they sank themselves in a deep pool that could receive their bulk.

[620] But where battle was possible, the Roman youth surrounded Moorish elephants that had not yet been set on fire. They attacked them from a distance, now with javelins, other times stones and winged slingshot. They were like men who attack fortified castles on high places

86   *Sili Italici Punicorum Liber Nonus*

oppugnat munita locos atque adsidet arces.
ausus digna uiro, fortuna digna secunda,   625
extulerat dextram atque aduersum comminus ensem
Mincius infelix ausi, sed stridula anhelum
feruorem effundens monstri manus abstulit acri
implicitum nexu diroque ligamine torsit
et superas alte miserum iaculata per auras   630
telluri elisis adflixit, flebile, membris.
       has inter clades uiso Varrone sub armis
increpitans Paulus 'quin imus comminus' inquit
'ductori Tyrio, quem uinctum colla catenis
staturum ante tuos currus promisimus urbi?   635
heu patria, heu plebes scelerata et praua fauoris!
haud umquam expedies tam dura sorte malorum,
quem tibi non nasci fuerit per uota petendum,
Varronem Hannibalemne, magis.' dum talia Paulus,
urget praecipitis Libys atque in terga ruentum   640
ante oculos cunctas ductoris concitat hastas.
pulsatur galea et quatiuntur consulis arma.
acrius hoc Paulus medios ruit asper in hostis.
       tum uero excussus mentem, in certamina Paulo
auia diducto, conuertit Varro manuque   645
cornipedem inflectens 'das,' inquit 'patria, poenas,
quae Fabio incolumi Varronem ad bella uocasti.'

624 assidet (adsidet) *ω* (absidet F) Cm *Ep.* 1 : obsidet P *edd. a* p
626 dextram atque *Γ²s* : dextramque *ω* : dextraque Ch   **627** mincius *ω*Cm : mnicius
r1v : mitius r2 : mutius p *edd. a* l ausi *post* ausus *susp. Delz, qui coni.* infelix, saeui
628 acri] arto *Liberman*   **631** *sic* Cm *Ep.* 1 *ex coniectura Modii* : tellure elisit ac flexit *ω*
(flixit L*Γ²*) : tellure elisis afflixit *Livineius*   **636** plebs *δs* scelerata et *Γ²s* : scelerataque *ω*
639 Hannibalemne F, *Bentley* : Hannibalemue L*β*   **640** praecipitans *edd. a* r1 : prae-
cipitanti Ch   **641** atque oculos Ch cunctas *αΓ²s* : cuncta *β* : iunctas *Heinsius* diducto
*α*GVCh : deducto *δs*

Silius Italicus *Punica, Book 9*   87

and besiege towers. [625] Mincius dared deeds worthy of a man, worthy of favoring Fortune. He raised his fighting hand and went against the elephant at close range, unlucky in his daring. But the monster trumpeted and poured forth a fiery panting breath. Its trunk seized the man in a bitter trap and twisted him in its dire coil. [630] It hurled the wretched man high in the air and, sad to say, it crushed his limbs by smashing them on the ground.

Amid these disasters, Paulus caught sight of Varro in arms and rebuked him: "Why don't we go hand to hand against Hannibal the Carthaginian leader? We promised Rome [635] we would make him stand before your triumphal chariot, his neck bound in chains. Alas for my country, alas for the criminal plebs and their wretched support! In such hard, evil luck they will never tell which man they would more have prayed not to be born: Varro or Hannibal."

As Paulus said these things, [640] Hannibal pressed the Romans as they fled headlong. Before the consul's eyes he hurled all his army's spears into the rushing men's backs. One struck the consul's helmet and shook his armor. This made bitter Paulus fiercer as he rushed into the middle of the enemy.

Then indeed Varro's mind was shaken, as Paulus was separated from him [645] and fought on a remote part of the field. He turned his horse and wheeled about. "My country, you are paying the penalty," he said. "You called me, Varro, to battle while Fabius was still alive."

88 *Sili Italici Punicorum Liber Nonus*

'quaenam autem mentis uel quae discordia fati?
Parcarumne latens fraus est? abrumpere cuncta
iamdudum cum luce libet. sed comprimit ensem 650
nescio qui deus et meme ad grauiora reseruat.
uiuamne et fractos sparsosque cruore meorum
hos referam populo fasces atque ora per urbes
iratas spectanda dabo et, quo saeuius ipse
Hannibal haud poscat, fugiam et te, Roma, uidebo?' 655
plura indignantem telis propioribus hostes
egere et sonipes rapuit laxatus habenas.

648 quaenam autem <tantast> mentis discordia? fati *Liberman* : quidnam autem mentis uult haec discordia? fati *Gärtner*   **649** Parcarumne *Lefebvre, Volpilhac-Lenthéric* : Parcarumque *codd.*   **651** qui ωCh : quis *Γ*² *edd. a* rl nescio qui. deus est? mene *Bothe* : deus. at quae me *Summers* : nece me *Shackleton Bailey* : et nos *coni. Delz* : et mala me *Watt* (1985)   **657** rapuit F²β : rapiat α

Silius Italicus *Punica, Book 9* 89

"What conflict was this in your mind or with fate? Is this a hidden deception by the Parcae? Long before now, I wanted to take my own life and break off all things. But I don't know which god [650] held back my sword and spared me for worse things. Shall I live and bring my shattered fasces, spattered with my men's blood, back to the people? Shall I allow my face to be seen in the angry cities? Hannibal himself could not wish [655] for something more savage than this. Shall I flee and return to see you, Rome?"

As Varro complained still further, the enemy drove him on, their spears jabbing nearer. He loosed the reins, and his horse galloped away.

Commentary

Commentary

1–7. The gods send clear omens of the upcoming defeat, but Varro perversely chooses to interpret them as positive signs. The motif recalls the longer episode before Trasimene, where Flaminius derided the omens despite entreaties from his augur Corvinus; see 5.52–129. Fabius recalls this mistake in addressing his own men: see 15–18n., 32n.

Characters in epic conventionally ignore divine messages when they choose, beginning with Hector's rebuke of Polydamas: Hom. *Il.* 12.243 εἷς οἰωνὸς ἄριστος ἀμύνεσθαι περὶ πάτρης. Unlike Hector, who has already accepted Troy's fall as inevitable, Varro could have chosen to follow Fabius' example and withdrawn his forces. For Varro's contempt for omens, see also 15–16n., 262n. Silius' Sibyl complains about humans' refusal to attend to prophecy: 13.500–1 *sed non sat digna mearum / cura tuis uocum.* See also Stat. *Theb.* 6.935–6 *fata patent homini, piget inseruare, peritque / uenturi praemissa fides.*

The scene recalls Roman epic examples of misinterpretation of omens, both deliberate and mistaken, before a defeat:

(a) Virgil's Turnus misinterprets the metamorphosis of the Trojan ships as a sign that the gods have withdrawn their favor from the Trojans (*Aen.* 9.126–39).

(b) Lucan's *Fortuna* sends clear signs that Pharsalus will be a disaster immediately after Pompey reluctantly chooses to give battle: *BC* 7.151–2 *non tamen abstinuit uenturos prodere casus / per uarias Fortuna notas,* 7.205–6 *o summos hominum, quorum Fortuna per orbem / signa dedit, quorum fatis caelum omne uacauit!*

1. turbato monstris Latio cladisque futurae: referring to the dire omens of the previous book that threatened Roman defeat, introduced at 8.624–5 *nec tanta miseris iamiam impendente ruina / cessarunt superi uicinas prodere clades.* The clausula specifically evokes the closing scene of the previous book, 8.657–8 *clamoribus implet / miles castra feris et anhelat clade futura,* and so accentuates the irony of the Romans' refusal to recognize the impending danger. Marks 2010a: 135 discusses the evocation of Luc. *BC* 1.470 *inrupitque animos populi clademque futuram.* In this scene, Lucan's Romans similarly anticipate Caesar's invasion of Italy, a catastrophe that the narrator compares to Hannibal's assault (*BC* 1.303–5). Lucan's Romans similarly perceive manifest signs of the gods' anger as Rome prepares for Caesar's assault: *BC* 2.1–2 *iamque irae patuere deum manifestaque belli / signa dedit mundus.*

94　　　　　　　　　　*Commentary Lines 2–5*

The book's opening line likely also adapts Verg. *Aen.* 12.246 *turbauit mentes Italas monstroque fefellit*, describing the omen that disrupts the duel between Aeneas and Turnus. Virgil's Latins know their champion will die if the duel proceeds, just as Silius' Paulus knows that his new Roman recruits are not ready to face Hannibal in combat. For similar uses of *turbare* in the context of omens, see Verg. *Aen.* 2.199–200, Ov. *Met.* 11.411 *prodigiis turbatus*, etc. For the clausula, see also Lucr. *DRN* 5.246 *clademque futuram*, Ov. *Met.* 3.191 *cladis…futurae*, Sen. *Phoen.* 280 *cladis futurae*, Luc. *BC* 1.470 (quoted above in this note).

2. signa per Ausoniam prodentibus irrita diuis: *signa…prodentibus* may evoke Luc. *BC* 7.152 (quoted at 1–7n. above). For divine messages "in vain" or their opposite, see Cic. *Leg.* 2.21 *quaeque augur iniusta nefasta uitiosa dira deixerit, inrita infectaque sunto*, Germ. *Arat.* 163 *haec eadem tibi signa dabunt non irrita pisces*, Sen. *NQ* 2.34.2 *non potest hoc auspicium fulmine irritum fieri*, Gell. *NA* 13.14.5 *auesque inritas*. Ausonia referred originally to southern central Italy, but became a metonymy for the whole; see Horsfall's note on Verg. *Aen.* 7.623. Here *Ausoniam* is not simply a synonym of *Latio*. Rather, it emphasizes the contrast between the omens appearing throughout Italy and Rome, where the wrong decisions are being made.

3–4. haud secus ac si fausta forent et prospera pugnae / omina uenturae: the elegant line 3 is composed of three alliterative units. Varro goes beyond Hector's indifference to omens (see 1–7n.) in perversely treating bad omens as good ones. *Fausta et prospera* represent a typical coupling of synonymous adjectives. Spaltenstein is incorrect to claim that the present pairing of adjectives is unique, as there are two prose examples: cf. Cic. *Mur.* 1 *fauste feliciter prospereque*, Fronto *M. Caes.* 5.45 *annum nouum faustum tibi et…prosperum*. *Faustus* is formulaically combined with *felix*; cf. *TLL* 6.1.389.13; for examples in poetry, cf. Lucr. *DRN* 1.100 *exitus ut classi felix faustusque daretur*. For the frequent corruption of *omina* to *omnia* (O$_5$r2), see 262n., 1.342, 4.131, etc. The phrase *uenturae…omina pugnae* recurs at 178n., where Solymus' message is the last of the omens sent in a vain effort to deter the Romans from giving battle at Cannae.

4–5. consul traducere noctem / exsomnis: diligent commanders are conventionally sleepless: cf. 3.172 *turpe duci totam somno consumere noctem*. Varro's excitement before Cannae contrasts with the endurance that Hannibal typically exemplifies (1.245–6 *somnumque negabat / naturae noctemque uigil ducebat in armis*) and that Virtus promises to Scipio (15.110 *insomnes noctes*). In its immature eagerness, Varro's sleeplessness more closely resembles Hannibal's juvenile excitement as he dreamed of his future battles: 1.68–9 *futuras / miscentem pugnas et inania bella gerentem*. Fabius accordingly describes Varro's emotional state in the previous book: 8.338 *tenebras dolet*. Varro should have instead felt the anxious insomnia experienced by Hannibal when Fabius trapped him (7.154–6).

Silius appears to originate the collocation *traducere noctem*, which does not occur again until Auson. *Ephem.* 8.39 *me sinite ignauas placidum traducere noctes.* The compounded form, however, "is little more than an expressive alternative to its simplex counterpart," as Zissos observes on VF *Arg.* 1.251 *ludoque educite noctem.* For other variations, see Verg. *Aen.* 9.166 *noctem custodia ducit / insomnem ludo, Geo.* 3.379 *noctem ludo ducunt,* Stat. *Theb.* 2.74 *insomnem ludo certatim educere noctem* with Gervais's note. *Exsomnis* is a rare alternative to the more common *insomnis* and is found in poetry at Verg. *Aen.* 6.556, Hor. *Carm.* 3.25.9, and Prop. 3.21.6.

5. telumque manu uibrare per umbras: the Carthaginian soldier Maraxes is similarly so eager for battle that he wages war in his sleep: 7.325-7 *ac dirum, in somno ceu bella capesseret, amens / clamorem tum forte dabat dextraque tremente / arma toro et notum quaerebat feruidus ensem.* For the phrasing, see Livy 21.28.1 *uibrantesque dextris tela,* Ov. *Met.* 12.79, Luc. *BC* 7.82 *uibrant tela manus* with Lanzarone's note, etc.

6. ac modo segnitiae Paulum increpitare: Paulus approves of Fabius' defensive strategy. Varro, by contrast, is "hostile to delay" at 24n. *infensusque morae.* Varro here resumes his earlier criticisms of the Fabian strategy as cowardly inactivity; see 8.263 *Fabiumque morae increpitare* and Littlewood 2011: lxiv-lxx. *Segnitiae* in particular recalls Livy 22.44.5 *Varro Paulo speciosum timidis ac segnibus ducibus exemplum Fabium obiceret.*

Lucan attributes to Pompey a comparable reputation for inactivity before Pharsalus and similarly shows him being overruled: Luc. *BC* 7.52-3 *segnis pauidusque uocatur / ac nimium patiens soceri Pompeius,* etc. More generally, Roman epic characteristically defines the fighting commander as an active figure, the opposite of the *segnis.* The narrator characterizes Hannibal accordingly: *Pun.* 1.244-5 *nec cetera segnis / quaecumque ad laudem stimulant.* Murrus prays to Hercules to defend Saguntum through an appeal to his own activity: 1.507 *si tua non segni defenso moenia dextra.* Gestar argues that the Carthaginians possess the active character to defeat the Romans: see 2.347 *indole non adeo segni sumus* with my note. For further examples, see Verg. *Aen.* 9.786-7 *non ... / segnes, miseretque pudetque?,* Stat. *Theb.* 3.17-18 *heu segnes, quorum labor haeret in uno, / si conserta manus,* etc.

Modo ... modo emphasizes Varro's frenzied activity. For *increpitare* construed with accusative and genitive, cf. 8.263 *Fabiumque morae increpitare.* Spaltenstein proposes reading *segnitie;* for this archaic genitive form, see 3.88 *ueneranda fide,* where Drakenborch remarks "malim ... accipere secundum casum, quam sextum." See Verg. *Geo.* 1.208 *die somnique* with Mynors' note, Hor. *Carm.* 3.7.4 *constantis ... fide* (where Nisbet and Rudd reject *fide*), Bömer on Ov. *Met.* 3.341 *fide uocisque,* and Leumann 1977: 285.

6-7. modo acres / exercere tubas nocturnaque classica uelle: Varro's idea of waking the soldiers by sounding the *tuba* at night evokes Valerius' nighttime battle at Cyzicus: VF *Arg.* 3.18 *unde tubae nocturnaque mouit Erinys?* Like Cannae, Cyzicus is a disastrous mistake by an inexperienced commander eager

96   *Commentary Lines 8–12*

for glory. Spaltenstein also suggests a possible adaptation of VF *Arg.* 6.27–8 *acres / sponte sua strepuere tubae,* as the phrase *acres tubae* does not occur previously. Valerius gives the *lituus* a similar sound: *Arg.* 6.107–8 *acres... ad lituos.* Statius may possibly adapt both of his Flavian contemporaries at *Silv.* 5.3.193 *quique tubas acres lituosque audire uolentem.*

The transferred epithet *nocturna* serves the function of a temporal adverb such as *noctu* or an ablative phrase such as *media nocte.* Compare 61n. *crastina signa,* 3.395 *Maenas nocturna,* 7.135–6 *nocturna...furta;* Verg. *Geo.* 1.390 *nocturna...pensa,* VF *Arg.* 7.97 *crastinus ignis,* etc. The phrase *nocturna classica* does not occur next until Drac. *Orest.* 395–6 *nullum nocturna cubantem / classica sollicitent, nullas tuba uerberet aures,* a possible adaptation of Silius' phrase. As an additional verb is not required, Heinsius suggested *bello* or *uallo* in place of *uelle.* Heinsius recognized, however, that the phrase might be modeled on common phrases such as 2.518 *arma uolunt* (found also, with variations, at 11.133, Verg. *Aen.* 7.340, 12.242, Stat. *Theb.* 8.657, etc.) or 15.131 *nullo fera bella uolente.* Drakenborch correctly observed that *uallo* is unlikely, as it occurs two lines below.

Synaloephae blending fifth and sixth feet are rare in epic: *Pun.* 13 times; Verg. *Aen.* 24 times, Ov. *Met.* 18 times, Luc. *BC* 12 times, VF *Arg.* 6 times, Stat. *Theb.* 27 times (figures from http://www.pedecerto.eu/public/). They occur most frequently after prepositions and conjunctions, as here. For the elision of *sine,* see 6.317, 8.18, 10.622, 16.268, 16.623; *ubi,* 6.568, 15.583, 17.264. See Soubiran 1966: 551–2.

8–12. The Carthaginians display a similar eagerness for battle. The Macae head out to feed the army by pillaging the neighboring fields, and thereby provoke the Romans into an initial skirmish. The Romans successfully defeat the Carthaginian raiders (14n.), but their apparent good fortune is "sinister" (9n.) in that it tempts them to continue the attack on the following day and thereby provoke the catastrophic defeat.

8. nec minor in Poeno properi certaminis ardor: the motif adapts Livy 22.41.1 *ceterum temeritati consulis ac praepropero ingenio materiam etiam fortuna dedit.* Hasdrubal's flight across the Alps echoes this line: *Pun.* 15.471 *at non ductori Libyco par ardor in armis.* The intratext contrasts the success at Cannae with the decline in Carthaginian fortunes in the subsequent campaign.

For the initial litotes, see 5.457, Lucr. *DRN* 5.564 *nec nimio solis maior rota nec minor ardor. Properus* and *properare* act as keywords for this opening passage, emphasizing both sides' eagerness to give battle after Fabius' delay: see 18n. *properanti,* 35n. *propere;* Introduction, section 5b. This collocation of *properum certamen* is unique. Silius elsewhere uses the adverb: 15.554 *ni propere alipedes rapis ad certamina turmas. Ardor* for war is a common epic phrase: 1.582 *pugnandi... ardor,* 10.217 *Martius ardor* with Littlewood's note; see further 37n. *pugnae... amore.*

Commentary Lines 9–11   97

9. erumpunt uallo fortuna urgente sinistra: Fortune "presses" the Romans to break forth from their rampart, as the Carthaginians are already devastating the fields. The ablative absolute phrase is an adaptation of Livy 22.43.9 *ad nobilitandas clade Romana Cannas urgente fato profecti sunt*. For Fortune "pressing" on its victims, see also Cic. *Sull.* 91.8 *urget eadem fortuna*, Ov. *Her.* 3.43 *an miseros tristis fortuna tenaciter urget*, QCurt. 5.9.4 *pertinax fortuna Persas urgere non desinit*, etc. Fate is a similar subject: see, e.g., Verg. *Aen.* 2.653 *fatoque urgenti*, Tac. *Germ.* 33.2 *urgentibus imperii fatis*, etc. *Fortuna … sinistra* is an apparently unique collocation, though modeled on similar phrases such as *sinistris / caelicolis* (13.391–2), *diuis … sinistris* (17.584), or *auis sinistra* (Plaut. *Epid.* 182, Cic. *Leg.* 3.9, etc.). Silius' other negative epithets for Fortune include *improba* (5.92–3), *aduersa* (7.10), *impia* (159n.), *titubans* (11.4), *dura* (11.168), and *crudelis* (13.382).

As line 8 is parenthetical, the Carthaginians are not the subject of *erumpunt*. *Erumpere uallo* does not occur elsewhere in poetry; for comparable phrasing, see 2.225–6 *aggere tuto / erupisse* with my note, Livy 6.24.3, 9.37.9 *proruto uallo erupit acies*, etc.

10. consertaeque manus: for "beginning the battle," see Enn. *Ann.* 252 Skutsch *non ex iure manu consertum, sed magis ferro*, quoted at Cic. *Fam.* 7.13.2, Gell. *NA* 20.10.4; cf. Plaut. *Mil.* 3 *conserta manu*, Stat. *Theb.* 3.18 *conserta manus*, VF *Arg.* 3.123 *conseruere manu*, Livy 6.12.8, 7.40.14, 30.31.8, etc. For similar phrasing, see 1.339 *conseruere acies*, 6.316 *consertae campis acie*, etc.

10–11. nam sparsi ad pabula campis / uicinis raptanda Macae: the adjective and ethnonym enclose a triple chiasmus. *Macae* is often a metonym for "North African" (5.184–5, 15.670–1), like several of Silius' other ethnonyms. This people may be the same as the Μακκοῖοι of Polyb. 3.33.15 who contributed troops to Hannibal's army; see *NP* s.v. *Macae*. For its forms, see 89n. Silius elsewhere makes the Macae a nomadic tribe whose Carthaginian rulers force them to inhabit fixed settlements (3.274–7); Livy 22.41.1 describes them as raiders (*praedatoribus*). See *Pun.* 2.60–1 with my note, Pliny *NH* 5.34 *post Nasamonas Asbytae et Macae uiunt*, Bona 1998: 66–7, Talbert et al. 2000: 35 F3, 37 A1. *Sparsi* and *raptanda* accordingly point to the typical mode of life for the Macae as well as their current role as raiders. Contrast the more typical use of *spargere* to denote men and weapons spread over the battlefield: see 94n. *sparsa inter funera*, 1.267 *qua sparsit ferrum, latus rubet aequore limes*, etc.; Enn. *Ann.* 266 Skutsch *spargunt hastas*, Verg. *Aen.* 7.551 *spargam arma per agros*, 11.650, VF *Arg.* 6.427 *sparsique Cytaei*, etc.

The clausula of 10 evokes Caesar's siege of Massilia at Luc. *BC* 3.385 *fontesque et pabula campi*; other poetic occurrences include Ov. *Ibis* 137 *mollia pabula campi*, Coripp. *Ioh.* 6.349. The opening of 11 recalls the Carthaginians' logging raids in order to build rafts to cross the Po: 4.491 *interdum rapta uicinis saltibus alno*.

98 *Commentary Lines 11–14*

11–12. fudere uolucrem / telorum nubem: the image of the sky obscured by weapons recurs frequently in the *Punica*: see 311–12n., 578–80n. For similar phrasing, see 1.311 *telorum ... nube*, 2.37 with my note, 7.595 *telorum nubibus*; for variations, 4.550–1 *hinc Libycae certant subtexere cornus / densa nube polum*, 5.215 *pilorum ... nimbus*, 12.177 *telorum ... nimbum*, 17.66 *condebant iaculis stridentibus aethera nubes*, 17.406–7, Verg. *Aen.* 12.284 *tempestas telorum*, Luc. *BC* 2.261–2 *nec pila lacertis / missa tuis caeca telorum in nube ferentur*. See Gibson on Stat. *Silv.* 5.1.132, Franke 1889: 25–6. Silius applies the epithet *uolucer* to a variety of missiles; see 337n. *iaculoque uolucri*, 2.107 *uolucerque chalybs*, 6.247–8 *hastam ... uolucrem*, 6.274 *uolucres ... sagittae*, 7.646, 14.397.

For "swift clouds," see VF *Arg.* 2.516 *uolucres Rhipaea per ardua nubes*, Ov. *Met.* 1.602 *et noctis faciem nebulas fecisse uolucres*. Though citing these passages, van Veen nevertheless objected to the use of the adjective in hypallage and accordingly proposed *uolucrum*.

12–14. Mancinus' joy in being first to lead the assault complements Varro's poor judgment. His death provokes the subsequent episode of mistaken identity that leads to the deaths of his father and brother; see 89n. This family's tragedy prefigures *in nuce* the greatest catastrophe suffered by the Romans in the Second Punic War. Lines 12–13 feature the maximum number of spondees, followed by 14 with the maximum number of dactyls. Line 12 also features multiple synaloephae, one of which obscures the penthemimeral caesura. The rhythmic progression from slowness to speed conveys the power of Mancinus' assault. Livy 22.15.4 reports the death of a L. Hostilius Mancinus in a cavalry engagement against Numidian raiders near the Vulturnus, which may have suggested Silius' choice of name for this character.

12–13. ante omnes inuadere bella / Mancinus gaudens: for *inuadere bella*, see 8.356 *bella inuasere*, 12.199 *inuadere pugnam*, 17.386, 17.472, Verg. *Aen.* 9.186, 12.712 *inuadunt Martem*. The nominative participle *gaudens* often appears in martial contexts, due in part to the influential model of Verg. *Aen.* 8.702 *scissa gaudens uadit Discordia palla*: *Pun.* 1.325, 7.714, 13.586, Verg. *Aen.* 12.109, Luc. *BC* 1.150, Stat. *Theb.* 7.673, etc.

13–14. hostilique unguere primus / tela cruore cadit: for weapons "anointed" with blood, see Hor. *Carm.* 2.1.4–5 *arma / nondum expiatis uncta cruoribus*. The phrase also applies to smearing poison on weapons: Verg. *Aen.* 9.773 *unguere tela manu ferrumque armare ueneno*. "Enemy blood" recurs at 4.450 *hostili perfusa cruore*, 12.282–3 *cruore / hostili*; cf. 6.625–6 *perfusus sanguine uictor / hostili*. Silius is apparently the only poet to use the phrase; for its use in prose, see V. Max. 3.2.23, 8.1.1, Front. *Strat.* 1.12.4. For the motif of the first fighter to fall, see Verg. *Aen.* 12.460–1 *cadit ipse Tolumnius augur, / primus*, Ov. *Met.* 12.67–8 *Hectorea primus fataliter hasta, / Protesilae, cadis*.

Commentary Lines 14–17   99

The choice between *tingere* and *unguere* resulted from a common palaeographical confusion. Some early editors, such as Dausqueius and Cellarius, retained *tingere*, on the model of 15.757 *tincta cruore*, Ov. *Met.* 9.132 *tincta cruore*, etc. Bentley observed with regard to Hor. *Carm.* 2.1.4–5 that there is a difference between the blood shed during a battle and the blood that has dried afterwards on the weapons.

14. cadit, cadit et numerosa iuuentus: Livy 22.41.2 gives figures for a lopsided Roman victory: *ad mille et septingenti caesi* (on the Carthaginian side), *non plus centum Romanorum sociorumque occisis*. Silius does not mention this initial Roman success, but focuses instead on Satricus' family tragedy and the overwhelming Roman defeat that follows. For similar examples of gemination, see 2.164 *leto letoque* with my note, 3.362 *mouet, mouet*, etc.; Flammini 1983: 100. The change in quantities (*cadīt, cadĭt*) after the main caesura imparts a feeling of speed to the latter half of the verse.

15–18. Varro would have sent the troops into battle in defiance of the omens, had not it been Paulus' day to command them. The motifs of failing to observe the omens and hurrying to one's fate echo Fabius' rebuke of his troops as he reminds them of Flaminius' death at Trasimene: 7.232 *an nondum praeceps uicinaque fata uidetis?* See further 32n.

15. nec pecudum fibras: Livy reports that Paulus consulted the sacred chickens: Livy 22.42.8 *cum ei sua sponte cunctanti pulli quoque auspicio non addixissent*; see Introduction, section 2. Silius includes a consultation of the chickens in the list of omens before Trasimene (5.59–62). By switching the means of consulting the gods to haruspicy, Silius aligns the present omen scene with comparable scenes in Roman epic and tragedy. Seneca provides particularly relevant examples of grim omens presented by the sacrificial animal's *fibrae* that presage impending disaster; see Sen. *Oed.* 357 *magna pars fibris abest*, 377 *infecit atras liuidus fibras cruor*, *Thy.* 757–8 *at ille fibras tractat ac fata inspicit / et adhuc calentes uiscerum uenas notat*. For the phrase *pecudum fibr** and close variants, see Verg. *Aen.* 10.176, Ov. *Her.* 9.39, *Met.* 15.580, Stat. *Theb.* 3.456, *Silv.* 4.8.2.

15–16. Varro et contraria Paulo / auspicia incusante deum compesceret arma: the interlaced word order emphasizes Paulus' reliance on the omens in his determination to resist Varro. There may be an echo of Petr. *Sat.* 122.127 *auspiciis patuere deum*, similarly of ill omens before a destructive battle. For *compesceret*, see, e.g., 8.409–10 *et furialia bella / fulmine compescet*, Sen. *Phoen.* 404 *compesce tela*, *Apoc.* 10.2 *ideo ciuilia bella compescui?*, etc.

17. ni sors alterni iuris, quo castra reguntur: for the alternating command, see Livy 22.45.4–5 *quod summa imperii eo die penes Paulum fuerit. itaque postero die Varro, cui sors eius diei imperii erat.* Cowan 2010: 335 observes the wordplay in lines 17–18: "It is not only the lot but chance (*sors*) which delays the battle, as

100   *Commentary Lines 18–20*

Varro hurtles towards not only disaster but fate (*fata*)." For *ius* of the consul or dictator's *imperium*, see 6.612–13 *cui postquam tradita belli / iura uidet.*

18. arbitrium pugnae properanti in fata negasset: the motif of hurrying into a lost battle evokes Cornelia's lament at Luc. *BC* 8.658 *o saeui, properantem in fata tenetis?* The allusion contributes to the identification of Varro with Lucan's doomed Pompey. See Introduction, section 3a, Marks 2010a: 138, Ariemma 2010: 272. For *arbitrium pugnae,* see the common historiographical phrase *arbitrium belli* (Sall. *BJ* 41.7, Livy 8.2.3, 32.37.5, 44.15.5, Tac. *Ann.* 12.60.16, etc.); see also Vell. 2.85.2 *certaminis arbitrium.* The phrase also evokes the introduction of Varro: 8.251 *et fati foret arbiter unus.* For *properare* as a keyword for this passage, see 8n. The clausula recurs at 6.116 *fata negassent;* cf. 1.107 *fata negarint,* 4.635 *fata negato,* perhaps inspired by Ov. *Met.* 10.634 *fata inportuna negarent,* Luc. *BC* 7.676 *fatisque negatum.*

19–20. quae tamen haud ualuit perituris milibus una / plus donasse die: Paulus desires a longer delay before the battle of Cannae but fails to achieve it. The motif associates him with Lucan's Pompey, who similarly cannot prevent his forces from giving battle at Pharsalus. As Pompey dreams of being in his theater, Lucan's narrator wishes the gods had given him one more day: Luc. *BC* 7.30–1 *donassent utinam superi patriaeque tibique / unum, Magne, diem.* Pompey's wretched troops will not survive the whole day at Pharsalus: see *BC* 7.47–8 *miseri pars maxima uolgi / non totum uisura diem tentoria,* where Lanzarone comments "probabilmente il passo lucaneo è presente" in the present passage of Silius. Lucan's commanders "give" a peaceful day to their country during their preparations for battle at Ilerda: *BC* 4.27–8 *patriaeque et ruptis legibus unum / donauere diem.* See also *BC* 10.432 *donata est nox una duci.*

Wallace 1968: 90 notes Silius' emphasis on temporal markers in narrating the hasty actions of unbalanced commanders such as Flaminius, who springs into action on his *prima dies iuris* (*Pun.* 4.711), and Varro, who *saeuit iam rostris* (8.244) when elected consul. Venus' order to the Cupids *imbellem donare diem* (11.407) is in the opposite context of teaching Hannibal to give the day to drinking in Capua; see *TLL* 5.1.1050.46.

Una dies typically refers to the day of a great battle; here it refers to the one day of delay *before* the massacre. For *una dies* of the day of battle, compare the massacre of the Fabii at the Cremera (2.5 *abstulit una dies* with my note) and its Ovidian versions (Ov. *Fasti* 2.235–6, *Pont.* 1.2.3–4); cf. Enn. *Ann.* 258–60 Skutsch. Lucan's Lentulus similarly looks back on the "one day" of Pharsalus: Luc. *BC* 8.332 *una dies mundi damnauit fata?* with Mayer's note. Valerius' Perses prays for "this one day" to destroy the Argonauts: VF *Arg.* 6.733–4 *dent tamen, oro, / unum illum mihi fata diem.* See *Pun.* 2.5 with my note for the variable gender of *dies.*

For the clausula of 19, see 10.521, 13.80; it apparently originates at Ov. *Met.* 1.325–6, 13.241; cf. Manil. *Astr.* 4.374, Stat. *Theb.* 6.734, 7.128. It creates a typical epic opposition between "one" and "many": see Hardie 1993: 3–10.

Commentary Lines 20–3 101

20–1. rediere in castra, gemente / haud dubie Paulo: Paulus weeps as he foresees the disaster impending when Varro takes command on the following day. The motif of Paulus' grief is introduced at 8.327 *maesto consul sic ore*; see further 65n. Silius is the first extant poet to use the prosaic phrase *haud dubie* (also at 4.421); it is not found again until Ausonius. Zaia *ad loc.* suggests that Silius may have adapted the phrase from Livy, who uses it eighty-eight times.

21–2. qui crastina iura uideret / amenti cessura uiro: for adjectives such as *crastinus* used as temporal adverbs, see 7n.; *TLL* 4.1106.72. For *iura* of transferring consular command, see 6.612–13 *tradita belli / iura*. At the moment, only Paulus sees Varro as *amens*, but after being defeated Varro will accuse himself of *mentis…discordia* (648n.). For the complementarity of the book's opening and concluding sections (1–65, 632–57), see Introduction, section 3a.

22–3. frustraque suorum / seruatas a caede animas: those soldiers saved by Fabius in the previous campaigns. For the phrasing, see 2.361–2 *femina seruet / singultantem animam* with my note, Verg. *Aen.* 10.525, Luc. *BC* 3.697, Stat. *Theb.* 8.638, etc.

23–37. Varro furiously abuses Paulus for delaying the assault. He reminds Paulus that he owes the Roman people for acquitting him at his trial for malfeasance (25–7n.); cf. 8.289–92. He claims hyperbolically that Paulus wants to take the weapons out of his soldiers' hands and give them to the enemy (28–9). He sympathizes with the soldiers for their grief at the delay and promises them they will have to wait no longer (30–2). When the next day gives him command, he will open the gates and send them out (33–6). Indications of Varro's mental instability (23, 36 *turbidus*) and the danger of his insistence on giving battle (37 *pestifero*) bracket his speech.

23. nam turbidus ira: as consul, Varro both shares in and encourages all Latium's mental disturbance: see 1n. *turbato*, 8.349 *turbati mente*. Varro is *turbidus* again at 36; the repetition, common in Silius, emphasizes the commander's unbalanced state. Varro's emotions have accordingly intensified from the previous book, where he was merely "eager": 8.617–18 *auido committere pugnam / Varroni*. While the adjective is common, it may also associate Varro with Virgil's Turnus. The narrator describes Turnus as *turbidus* (Verg. *Aen.* 12.10) at a similar moment, when he insists to Latinus that he will enter the final combat *nulla mora* (*Aen.* 12.11).

Silius applies the epithet *turbidus* to the epic's other reckless commanders, including Hannibal (1.477), Flaminius (5.165, 5.380), Nealces (397n.), Virrius (13.214 *turbidus ausi*), Philip (15.296), and Syphax (17.121). Only Marcellus (12.255) stands out among this group as a thoughtful commander who will later exercise laudable restraint at Syracuse. The clausula *turbidus ira* appears elsewhere at 2.619, where a maddened Saguntine is about to kill his mother, and 12.417, where Hampsagoras commits suicide upon the death of his son. The

102 *Commentary Lines 24–7*

repetition of the clausula associates Varro with these characters' suicidal madness.

Silius appears to have originated the clausula. Statius may allude to it in a contemporary poem on Hercules: *Silv.* 3.1.39 *pacatus mitisque ueni nec turbidus ira.*

24. infensusque morae dilata ob proelia ductor: see 6n. above for Varro's rebuke of what he perceives as Paulus' *segnitia.* Varro's rage at delay aligns him with two Carthaginian warriors:

> (a) Hannibal, who was *impatiensque morae* (8.4) as the result of confinement by Fabius, and who earlier threw aside delay and attacked Saguntum's walls: 2.236 *postposita caede et dilata inuadere pugna*; and

> (b) Maraxes, who wages battle in his sleep (7.325–7) and who must be told by Mago: 7.329–30 *tenebris, fortissime ductor, / iras compesce atque in lucem proelia differ.* See 4–5n.

TLL 7.1.1366.60 interprets *morae* as dative; Spaltenstein correctly observes that it is more likely a genitive of relation like 1.56 *fideique sinister*, 8.316 *indeuia recti*, etc. For *ductor*, see Introduction, section 5b.

25–7. In his consulship of 219, Paulus triumphed over the Illyrians in the Second Illyrian War (Polyb. 3.19). In the following year, however, he and his consular colleague Livius Salinator were tried for malfeasance regarding the distribution of war spoils (Livy 22.35.3, 22.40.3). Salinator was found guilty (Livy 27.34.3, 29.37.13, Front. *Strat.* 4.1.45), but Paulus narrowly escaped conviction. Silius attributes *metus et durae reuerentia plebis* (8.292) to Paulus as a result of this experience; for Salinator, see 15.594–600.

25–6. 'sicine, sic' inquit 'grates pretiumque rependis / Paule, tui capitis?': repeated *sic* is common in the post-Virgilian poets, and slightly favors the choice over *nunc* ω. Wills 1996: 118–19 traces the tradition of this repetition to the soliloquies of Virgil's Anchises (*Aen.* 2.644–5) and Dido (*Aen.* 4.660–2). For instances in Silius, see 4.506–7 *infelix animae, sic, sic uiuasque*, 16.125 *sic, sic, caelicolae*; Heinsius called the present instance "nervose." Duff's translation "repay me" for *rependis* is unnecessarily limiting. In Varro's view, Paulus owes *grates* to the same citizen soldiers who saved him from the death penalty (though *capitis* can also be applied to lesser punishments; see *TLL* 3.0.418.55 "de vita vel de graviore poena rei"). For the repayment motif, see 7.713 *dignum expendamus pretium*; with *rependere*, see Ov. *Am.* 2.8.21, Sen. *Thy.* 530–1, Stat. *Theb.* 7.379, 9.50, etc.

26–7. meruerunt talia, qui te / legibus atque urnae dira eripuere minanti: the *urna* received the votes cast by the jurors pronouncing acquittal, condemnation, or *non liquet*; see Cic. *Att.* 2.5.4, Juv. 13.3–4, etc. For the threat of the laws and urn, see the similar collocation at Hor. *Serm.* 2.1.47 *leges minitatur et urnam.* For the 3+1+1 clausula of 26, see Arribas Hernáez 1990: 234. *Dira* is a

Commentary Lines 28–34   103

neuter adverbial accusative, used nine times in total in the epic; see Fröhlich 2000: 104–5.

28–9. Varro accuses Paulus of ordering the soldiers to return their weapons and hand them over to the enemy. Livy's Varro similarly complains (22.44.6) *se constrictum a collega teneri; ferrum atque arma iratis et pugnare cupientibus adimi militibus*. The treachery motif recalls the comparable moment when Silius' Gestar calls Hanno an *Ausonius miles* sitting in the Carthaginian Senate; see *Pun.* 2.330–2 with my note. Varro's mocking challenge prefigures the actual behavior of the Roman deserter Cinna: 10.476–7 *ad Tyrios namque is sua uerterat arma / credulus aduersis*.

The passage further evokes two comparable moments in Lucan (see Introduction, section 4c):

(a) Caesar's men mutiny in favor of peace rather than continuing to fight for him. Caesar rebukes his men by challenging them to hand their weapons over to Pompey: Luc. *BC* 5.349–51 *quisquis mea signa relinquens / non Pompeianis tradit sua partibus arma, / hic numquam uult esse meus*. As in Lucan, Varro wants his men to continue on a path urged by the leader and condemned as madness by the narrator, which results in devastation for Rome.

(b) Pompey concedes to Cicero's demand to hurry into combat at Pharsalus. Ariemma 2010: 271 observes Silius' appropriation of Luc. *BC* 7.107–9 *placet haec tam prospera rerum / tradere fortunae, gladio permittere mundi / discrimen; pugnare ducem quam uincere malunt*.

Statius may possibly adapt both Silius and Lucan at Stat. *Ach.* 1.791 *tradunt arma patres, rapit irreuocata iuuentus*. Ulixes attempts to trick Achilles into revealing himself and joining a war that will result in Achilles' death and devastation for the Greeks.

28. tradant immo hosti reuocatos ilicet enses: for the use of *immo* "personam opponentis induens," see *Pun.* 2.52 with my note, where Hannibal objects to an actual Roman demand to disarm, and *TLL* 7.1.476.61. *Reuocatos* likely refers to the *enses* that Varro imagines Paulus will call out of his soldiers' hands, rather than functioning as a hypallage for *reuocati* (contra Ruperti).

29. tradant arma iube, aut pugnantum deripe dextris: the anaphora of *tradant* emphasizes Varro's contempt. For *deripere* of snatching weapons, see 10.598–9 *ite ocius, arma / deripite, o pubes, templis*, 10.317–18 *ore / cornipedum derepta fero spumantia frena*. Heinsius' *dextris* is a necessary correction accepted by most modern editors.

30–4. By telling his soldiers to ignore the *signum* for giving battle, Varro speaks against the Roman tradition of *disciplina*. The passage recalls two moments of Lucan's Pharsalus episode (see Introduction, section 4c):

104 *Commentary Line 30*

(a) Cicero's threat to Pompey just before the battle: Luc. *BC* 7.82–3 *uix signa morantia quisquam / expectat: propera, ne te tua classica linquant,* and see also Lanzarone's note on *BC* 7.77–8.

(b) Each of Caesar's men follows *suum munus* and stands *ordine nullo* (Luc. *BC* 7.329–33).

These evocations of Lucan's climactic battle present Varro as both a failed Pompey and a failed Caesar. The thought of restraining the troops does not even cross Varro's mind, and his men's poor order leads to their overwhelming defeat by the Carthaginians.

Livy reports the breach of discipline differently: his soldiers learn that the Carthaginians have apparently abandoned their camp and get ahead of their commander in their desire to plunder: Livy 22.42.7 *et clamore orto a militibus, ni signum detur, sine ducibus ituros, haudquaquam dux defuit; nam extemplo Varro signum dedit proficiscendi.* Livy's Varro errs not in encouraging the soldiers, as Silius has it, but in granting their inappropriate desires. Livy attributes Varro's indifference to *disciplina* to his desire for popularity with his soldiers: Livy 22.42.12 *cum ambitio alterius suam primum apud eos praua indulgentia maiestatem soluisset.*

Livy's subsequent account of the Roman consultant Statorius' effort to train Syphax's Numidian troops emphasizes the point that Roman discipline consists of remaining in *ordines* and following the *signa,* not the disorderly rush that Varro proposes: Livy 24.48.11 *et Statorius ex multa iuuentute regi pedites conscripsit ordinatosque proxime morem Romanum instruendo et decurrendo signa sequi et seruare ordines docuit.*

For passages in which commanders give the troops the *signum* according to *mos,* see *Pun.* 7.383–4 *cui mos tramittere signa / et belli summam primasque iubebat habenas,* Luc. *BC* 10.400 *ut mos, signa dedit castris.*

30. sed uos, quorum oculos atque ora umentia uidi: Varro imagines that the soldiers are weeping as a result of the shame of being forced to "retreat" (31 *uertere…terga*). He exaggerates Paulus' order that simply prevents them from taking the field. Livy similarly reports that the soldiers felt shame, but does not attribute tears to them: Livy 22.45.4 *id uero indignum uisum ab tumultuario auxilio iam etiam castra Romana terreri.* For the pairing of *oculi* and *os,* see 40n., 11.63, 13.394, etc.; *TLL* 9.2.1074.32.

The MSS offer several alternatives to *(h)umentia,* a common attribute of tear-stained faces: Ov. *Met.* 11.464, 14.734 *umentes oculos,* Luc. *BC* 5.737 *umentis…genas,* etc. (At *Pun.* 8.225, Anna Perenna's *umentia…ora* refer to her home in a river, not to tears.) V's *liuentia* indicates a greater degree of grief than is plausible for this situation. Only Statius applies this participle to the face in the context of mourning dead loved ones: Ide in mourning for her sons (Stat. *Theb.* 3.135 *liuentiaque ora*) and Statius himself for his *puer* (*Silv.* 5.5.12

Commentary Lines 31–3 105

liuentesque genas). Heinsius proposed *uuentia*, likely as an effort to account for the reading of V. Forms of *uuescere/uuidus* can indeed sometimes be confused for *umescere/umidus*, e.g., Tibul. 1.9.38. Tears never cause eyes or faces to become *uuidus* in classical Latin, however; as Serv. *ad Ecl.* 10.20 observes, *et 'umidum' est quod extrinsecus habet aliquid umoris, 'uuidum' quod intrinsecus.*

31. uertere cum consul terga et remeare iuberet: *terga uertere* is an extremely common phrase for retreat: see 2.703, 4.329, 7.402, 10.287, 10.380–1, 12.206–7; Verg. *Aen.* 6.491, 8.706, Ov. *Met.* 8.363–4, etc.

32. ne morem et pugnae signum exspectate petendae: a further echo of Fabius' rebuke of the troops (15–18n.) as he reminds them of Flaminius' fate: 7.230–1 *ille ruendi / iam dudum properans signum auspiciumque dedisset.* The maximum number of spondees communicates Varro's sense of being held back. Drakenborch correctly observed that Heinsius' suggestion *Martem* is needless, as *morem et pugnae signum* functions here as a hendiadys. For the phrase *pugnam petere*, see 5.33, 17.340, Livy 1.25.9, etc.

33. dux sibi quisque uiam rapito: the run of three dactyls after the four spondees of the preceding line suggests the soldiers' swiftness in seizing their own path. The men caught in the mud at Trebia are similarly each forced to seize the path for themselves amid disaster: 4.582–3 *dum sibi quisque uiam per inextricabile litus / praeripit.* The text of 13.188–9 *et †superesse / fortunam† sibi quemque ducem* is troubled; see van der Keur *ad loc.* and Watt 1988: 178 for various solutions. The context is clear, however: Fulvius has seen that his men are successful in their assault on Capua and so makes a considered decision to join in the fighting. By contrast, Varro has not yet begun the fight at Cannae and so has no justification for handing over his leadership responsibilities to his men.

Varro's suggestion that each soldier can be his own *dux* tells against an epic tradition of hierarchical command that begins with Hom. *Il.* 2.204–5 οὐκ ἀγαθὸν πολυκοιρανίη· εἷς κοίρανος ἔστω, / εἷς βασιλεύς. Livy's account of Trasimene features a breakdown of Roman order where Flaminius fails to lead and so obliges each man to become his own *dux*: Livy 22.5.6 *apparuitque nullam nisi in dextera ferroque salutis spem esse, tum sibi quisque dux adhortatorque factus ad rem gerendam.* Tacitus evokes the Livian scene in describing the chaos after Otho encourages the soldiers to kill Galba: Tac. *Hist.* 1.38.3 *sibi quisque dux et instigator.* If Silius' phrasing indeed evokes the Livian passage, then it is a further alignment of Varro's incautious leadership at Cannae with Flaminius' at Trasimene. For Cannae as a repetition of Trebia and Trasimene, see 8.38.

The reading *capito* Γ*ς* may have been prompted by phrases such as 12.267 *cursumque furens ad castra capessit*, but it is hardly as well attested as *rapere* for "seizing" a path; see 3.156 *iter liquidum uolucri rapiente carina*, 4.63 *raptum per Celtas iter*, 12.472 *raptum iter est*, Luc. *BC* 4.151–2 *rapuitque... / iter*, etc. In a

106　　　　　　　　　　*Commentary Lines 33–5*

comparable case, modern editors have similarly preferred *rapienda* E over *capienda* A at Sen. *Agam.* 154 *rapienda rebus in malis praeceps uia est*.

33–4. cum spargere primis / incipiet radiis Gargana cacumina Phoebus: for *spargere…radiis*, see Luc. *BC* 3.521–2 *ut matutinos spargens super aequora Phoebus / fregit aquis radios*, Sen. *Med.* 74 *quamprimum radios spargere lucidos* (of Lucifer), etc. *Spargere lumine* is more common: see Lucr. *DRN* 2.144, Verg. *Aen.* 4.584, 9.459, 12.113, VF *Arg.* 3.257, etc. Mount Garganus, modern Gargano, is some 80 km from Cannae and functions here as elsewhere as a metonym for the battle and/or for the region of Apulia: see 212n., 483n., 8.628–9, 13.59–60, 17.600. As often in Silius (see, e.g., my note on 2.60–1), poetic associations are more important than geographic exactitude. For Garganus' poetic associations, see Horsfall's note on Verg. *Aen.* 11.247 *Gargani…Iapygis agris*.

Dausqueius argued for *primus* B, on the example of Verg. *Aen.* 6.255 *ecce autem primi sub limina solis et ortus*, VF *Arg.* 5.331 *rapta toris primi iubar ad placabile Phoebi*. But *radiis* would be bare without an epithet, and *primus* for the sun's rays is well attested: 12.574–5 *primaque rubescit / lampade Neptunus reuocatque Aurora labores*, Verg. *Aen.* 7.148–9 *postera cum prima lustrabat lampade terras / orta dies*, Ov. *Met.* 7.804 *sole fere radiis feriente cacumina primis* (a likely model for the present line), etc.

35. pandam egomet propere portas: Varro proposes to open the gates of the camp himself. He thereby recalls an earlier passage (*Pun.* 8.278–83) comparing him to a charioteer who spurs his horse too fast once the gates are open at the races. His claim that he will do it himself evokes Virgil's Juno, who opens the Gates of War herself (Verg. *Aen.* 7.620–2). This association recalls Varro's role as the instrument of a hostile Juno: see *Pun.* 8.35–8. By volunteering to open the camp's gates, Varro offers Hannibal what the Carthaginian commander could not exact from Fabius or the Saguntines. For *pandere portas*, see 1.300 (Hannibal orders the Saguntines to open their gates), 2.253 (the Saguntines wish they could open the gates for Theron), 12.744 (the Romans rejoice as Hannibal withdraws), 13.302 (the Capuans surrender), 14.118 (Syracuse refuses to open its gates to Marcellus). Virgil is the only other poet to use the phrase: see Verg. *Aen.* 2.27, 6.574, 12.584.

For *properus* as a keyword for the passage, see 8n. Varro acts *propere* again at 267n. *Primus* j was likely the result of dittography from 33 or a correction of *prope* rlmpv.

35. ruite ocius atque hunc: a further association between Varro and Hannibal: 1.458 *ruit ocius amens*. *Ocius* often occurs in the context of commands, but Statius is the only other epic poet to use *ocius* with an imperative: Stat. *Theb.* 10.433 *cuncta ocius effer*, *Ach.* 1.504 *dic ocius*. Silius emphasizes usage that may have connoted the lower genres of poetry; see 2.368–9 with my note for full references and discussion. Seneca, however, may have legitimated the phrase

Commentary Lines 36–7 107

for the high style: see *Thy.* 640 *effare ocius*, and for 35 *propere* with the imperative, see *Agam.* 300 *facesse propere*.

The unusual rhythm contributes to the depiction of Varro's agitated state.
Lines such as Verg. *Aen.* 9.57 *huc turbidus atque huc*, 9.440 *hinc comminus
atque hinc* license the infrequent sixth-foot elision. Silius' half-line may in
fact signal *Aen.* 9.57 specifically; Turnus is *turbidus* like Varro (23n., 36n.)
and is similarly initiating battle (Verg. *Aen.* 9.53 *principium pugnae*). For
clausulae that terminate in conjunction + pronoun, see Arribas Hernáez
1990: 234.

36. ereptum reuocate diem: for Paulus, the extra day was his gift to men otherwise soon to die (19–20n.); in Varro's opposing view, it was a day that was
snatched away from them. The phrase *eripere diem* only appears twice before in
Latin poetry: Verg. *Aen.* 1.88, of the storm that nearly destroys the Aeneadae,
and Manil. *Astr.* 3.19, of the eclipse at Thyestes' banquet; note Sen. *Thy.* 1085
uindica amissum diem of the same event. Silius' uses of the phrase may evoke
both prior loci: Cannae will be a disaster that nearly destroys the Aeneadae and
will be an evil as memorable and world-shaking as Atreus' crime. See *Pun.* 2.5
with my note for the variable gender of *dies*.

36–7. sic turbidus aegra / pestifero pugnae castra incendebat amore: see
23n. for Varro's mental turbidity. The phrasing is a pointed reversal of
Anchises' encouragement of Aeneas in the Underworld: Verg. *Aen.* 6.889
incenditque animum famae uenientis amore. Where Anchises points to a
bright future for Aeneas' descendants, Varro leads his followers to disaster.
Bostar similarly encourages the Carthaginian troops as he returns from the
oracle (*Pun.* 3.714 *impleratque uiros pugnae propioris amore*), while Regulus'
"love of battle" is the comparable error that leads to his capture by Xanthippus
(6.335 *insano pugnae tendebat amore*). There may also be a recollection of
Anna's inflammation of Dido (*Aen.* 4.54 *his dictis impenso animum inflam-
mauit amore*).

The soldiers' eager rush into battle shows that Duff's translation of *incendebat* as conative ("he tried to animate") is incorrect. Varro succeeds in reignit-
ing the troops' sick desire for combat that Fabius had only temporarily
restrained. In spite of Varro's inflammatory rhetoric, Paulus knows that the
inexperienced troops will still be *frigidus* (49n.) when they first see the enemy.
For Hannibal's similarly incendiary effect on his own troops, see 244n. He
pointedly opens his speech before the battle, however, by telling his troops
non uerborum . . . stimulantum . . . egetis (184n.). This claim further emphasizes the contrast between Varro's misplaced confidence and Hannibal's
awareness of his troops' true capacities.

Pestifer amor appears to be a Senecan coinage: Sen. *Phoen.* 38–9 *quid me,
nata, pestifero tenes / amore uinctum?* For poetic compounds in -*fer* and -*ger*, see
Arens 1950. *Amor pugnae* is a common phrase: see 3.714, 6.335 (quoted above in

108 *Commentary Lines 38–43*

this note), Hor. *Carm.* 4.4.12, Ov. *Met.* 3.705, Manil. *Astr.* 4.228; see further 8n. for related phrases. The repetition of *turbidus* and the enclosure of 37 with a rare adjective–noun pairing provide emphatic closure to the passage.

38–43. Two comparisons describe Paulus' reaction to the upcoming battle. As if he were standing on the battlefield after his soldiers have died (39–40), he envisions the future like a mother grieving over a dead child (40–3). The reader's knowledge that Paulus will be killed in the battle increases the scene's pathos. The Roman survivors of Cannae in turn mourn Paulus as their lost father: 10.405–6 *at Pauli pariter ceu dira parentis / fata gemunt.*

The latter comparison draws on two similes in Lucan's *Bellum Civile*:

(a) a comparison of griefstricken Rome as news of the civil war arrives to a mother's frantic attempt to revive her dead child:

> sic funere primo
> attonitae tacuere domus, cum corpora nondum
> conclamata iacent nec mater crine soluto
> exigit ad saeuos famularum bracchia planctus,
> sed cum membra premit fugiente rigentia uita
> uoltusque exanimes oculosque in morte minaces,
> necdum est ille dolor nec iam metus: incubat amens
> miraturque malum.
>
> Luc. *BC* 2.21–8

(b) Cato's comparison of himself to a father burying his child:

> ceu morte parentem
> natorum orbatum longum producere funus
> ad tumulos iubet ipse dolor, iuuat ignibus atris
> inseruisse manus constructoque aggere busti
> ipsum atras tenuisse faces, non ante reuellar
> exanimem quam te conplectar, Roma; tuumque
> nomen, Libertas, et inanem persequar umbram.
>
> Luc. *BC* 2.297–304

Silius' focalization of the simile through the narrator rather than Paulus produces an important contrast with Lucan; see Introduction, section 3a.

38. at Paulus, iam non idem nec mente nec ore: Paulus sees the disaster to come and loses mental composure. Varro will have a similar reaction (644n. *excussus mentem*), but only after seeing the disaster already completed.

Use of the maximum number of spondees, along with monosyllables that disrupt the rhythm, communicate Paulus' astonishment. According to pedecerto.eu (http://www.pedecerto.eu/public/), this line's combination of rhythm and word division is unique, and its pattern of main caesurae and diareses is quite rare (0.45%). For the ablatives of respect used here, compare Glaucus' transformation at Ov. *Met.* 13.958–9 *quae postquam rediit, alium me corpore*

Commentary Lines 39–41

toto / ac fueram nuper, neque eundem mente recepi. The more common phrase in poetry is *eadem mens*: see, e.g., Verg. *Aen.* 5.812 *nunc quoque mens eadem perstat mihi*, VF *Arg.* 6.463 *mens mihi non eadem*, Juv. *Sat.* 5.1 *si te propositi nondum pudet atque eadem est mens*, Claud. *Ruf.* 2.115 *mens eadem cunctis*, etc.

39–40. sed qualis stratis deleto milite campis / post pugnam stetit: an evocation of 7.549–50, where Fabius asks his son: *patiarne ante ora manusque / ciuem deleri nostras?* His successor Paulus now envisions destruction brought upon the entire Roman army. The phrase *stratis… campis* is not rare, but may still be a recollection of Livy 22.59.15 *stratas Cannensibus campis legiones uestras*. For expansions of the motif in this compact phrase, see 505n. *sternuntur tellure et miles et arma tubaeque*, 10.310–11 *saeuis exercitus armis / sternitur, et uictrix toto furit Africa campo*, 12.672–3 *cum sterneret ensis / Aetolos campos*, 16.412–13 *campo / discordes sternuntur equi*, Verg. *Aen.* 11.373 *sternamur campis*, *Il. Lat.* 356 *funditur et totis sternuntur corpora campis*, etc. For *delere* of death in battle, see 532n., 1.514 *dexter ades Phrygiae delenti stirpis alumnos*, 2.185, 16.50 *deleta gentilis pube cateruae*.

40–1. ante oculos atque ora futuro / obuersante malo: the pairing of *oculi* and *ora* occurred shortly before, in Varro's description of the impatient soldiers (30n.). The repetition here emphasizes that Paulus' eyes perceive the true danger that the less experienced soldiers cannot. For imagined visions *ante oculos*, see 11.115–16 *et Capuae pereuntis imago / iam tum erat ante oculos*. For *ante ora* of the imagination, see 10.266–7 *Aetoli tum primum ante ora fuere sorbentes Latium campi*, 12.549–50 *Paulus Gracchusque cruenti / Flaminiusque simul, miseris ante ora uagantur*, 13.394 *uersatur species ante ora oculosque parentum*; *TLL* 9.2.1087.63 "de visu mentis, cordis, animi." *Versari ante oculos* is a common means of invoking the imagination, e.g., nineteen times in Cicero. The compounded form is not as frequent: cf. Cic. *Sest.* 7 *sed mihi ante oculos obuersatur rei publicae dignitas*, *Dom.* 141, Lucr. *DRN* 4.978–9 *per multos itaque illa dies eadem obuersantur / ante oculos*, Livy 2.59.6, 34.36.6, 35.11.3 *Caudinaeque cladis memoria non animis modo sed prope oculis obuersabatur*.

Versare of contemplating evil usually occurs in the context of fear: see Luc. *BC* 6.417 *degeneres trepidant animi peioraque uersant*, Stat. *Theb.* 3.5–6 *tum plurima uersat, / pessimus in dubiis augur, timor*, etc. By contrast, Paulus feels no fear at the impending disaster, only grief.

41. ceu iam spe lucis adempta: for the common metaphor of *lux* as life, see *OLD* s.v. *lux* 6a. For "hope for the light," see Germ. *Arat.* 574 *et spe uenturae solari pectora lucis*, VF *Arg.* 7.413 *fersne aliquam spem lucis?* The participial phrase *adempta spe* is markedly Livian; see 1.53.4, 9.2.12, 23.17.1, 25.6.16. For poetic variations, see Verg. *Aen.* 9.131 *nec spes ulla fugae: rerum pars altera adempta est*, Ov. *Met.* 9.749–50 *spes est, quae capiat, spes est, quae pascit amorem; / hanc tibi res adimit*. Claudian may adapt Silius' phrasing at Claud. *Goth.* 469–70 *prospera sed quantum nostrae spes addita menti, / tantum exempta Getis*.

110   *Commentary Lines 42–65*

42. cum stupet exanimata parens: Lucretius originates the phrase in describing the families stricken by the plague at Athens (Lucr. *DRN* 6.1251–2 *exanimis pueris super exanimata parentum / corpora*), and Virgil describes Dido's bereaved sister Anna as *exanimis* (*Aen.* 4.672). Lucan's Cato similarly applies *exanimis* to the corpse of Rome rather than to himself as stunned parent: see *BC* 2.303, quoted at 38–43n. above. Statius is the first to apply *exanimis* to the stunned mourners, the Theban widows and mothers who discover Tydeus' victims: Stat. *Theb.* 3.115 *at nuptae exanimes puerique aegrique parentes*.

42–3. natique tepentes / nequiquam fouet extremis amplexibus artus: the narrative of Silius' simile evokes both Lucan's simile (*BC* 2.21–8, quoted at 38–43n. above) and Statius' Theban widows and mothers (see 42n.). Anna uses a similar comparison to a grieving mother to describe Dido's mournful embrace of Aeneas' *uestigia*: 8.129 *ceu cinerem orbatae pressant ad pectora matres*. For the recent dead as still warm, see, e.g., Verg. *Aen.* 3.627 with Horsfall's note, *Aen.* 10.555 *truncumque tepentem*, Luc. *BC* 6.621 *tepidique cadaueris*, etc. For the "final embrace" of parents and children, see Sen. *Med.* 552 *liceat ultimum amplexum dare*, *Med.* 848, *Tro.* 761, Luc. *BC* 3.744–5 *ueniam misero concede parenti, / Arge, quod amplexus, extrema quod oscula fugi*, etc. Spaltenstein invokes Homer's comparison of Achilles to a bereft father in his grief for Patroclus: Hom. *Il.* 23.222–3 ὡς δὲ πατὴρ οὗ παιδὸς ὀδύρεται ὀστέα καίων / νυμφίου, ὅς τε θανὼν δειλοὺς ἀκάχησε τοκῆας. However, the Roman passages cited in 38–43n. are much closer in detail.

44–65. Paulus begs Varro not to fight immediately. He appeals to the bad omens, the troops' inexperience, and their fear of Hannibal (44–52). Appeal to the omens recalls the augur Corvinus' similar plea before Trasimene to delay the fight until the omens were better (5.82–100). Paulus next invokes the examples of Fabius' success in preserving his men's lives and Flaminius' defeat (52–5). He returns to the theme of the omens by recalling (or inventing) an ancient prophecy of the Cumaean Sibyl warning about Varro's madness. Paulus claims to be a contemporary prophet who can foresee Roman defeat at Cannae (56–64). Varro rejects these claims as cowardice, as when his men discover the warning left by Solymus. As Ahl, Davis, and Pomeroy 1986: 2534 observe:

> What Varro does not grasp is that his fellow-consul has just done probably the most difficult act of his life: he has humbled himself before a man he believes is unworthy of Rome in an effort to save the city…Paulus has gone as far as he can go, as a good citizen, in opposing Varro.

The Roman survivors of Cannae ruefully recall Paulus' incessant warning at 10.405–9.

At the comparable moment in his narrative, Livy reports only that Paulus acceded unwillingly to Varro's order to fight: Livy 22.45.5 *sequente Paulo quia magis non probare quam non adiuuare consilium poterat*. Silius derives the content of the speech in part from Livy's accounts of Paulus' earlier feuding with

Commentary Lines 44–8 111

Varro. Its occasion and aspects of its argument also recall the comparable moment before Lucan's Pharsalus in which Pompey objects to giving battle (Luc. *BC* 7.87–123). See Introduction, section 4c.

44. 'per totiens' inquit 'concussae moenia Romae': Hannibal has not yet approached the walls of Rome. The *moenia* are used as a metonym for the city, which has been "repeatedly struck" by loss of life in the various Roman defeats preceding Cannae. *Moenia Romae* is one of the most common clausulae in the *Punica* (17 times). Its evocation of a crucial phrase from the *Aeneid*'s proem (*Aen.* 1.7) serves as a leitmotif like *arma uirumque*; see 100n. For the thematic significance of Rome's walls, see von Albrecht 1964: 24–46. *Concussae...Romae* is a unique collocation; it recalls Lucan's comparison of the invasions of Hannibal and Caesar: Luc. *BC* 1.303–5 *non secus ingenti bellorum Roma tumultu / concutitur quam si Poenus transcenderit Alpes / Hannibal.*

45. perque has, nox Stygia quas iam circumuolat umbra, / insontes animas: imminent death threatens Paulus' innocent men; see Cowan 2013 for a comparable narrative involving Minucius. The motif of innocence recalls the words of Livy's Lentulus to Paulus as he offers him a horse to flee from Cannae: Livy 22.49.7 *'L. Aemili' inquit, 'quem unum insontem culpae cladis hodiernae dei respicere debent.'* *Insontes animas* is only found elsewhere of the ghosts of the Underworld. These include Virgil's suicides (Verg. *Aen.* 6.434–6 *qui sibi letum / insontes peperere manu lucemque perosi / proiecere animas*) and Statius' righteous souls admitted by Charon: Stat. *Silv.* 2.1.229 *insontis animas nec portitor arcet.*

The phrasing is modeled on Verg. *Aen.* 2.360 *nox atra caua circumuolat umbra,* used again at Verg. *Aen.* 6.866, Stat. *Theb.* 5.163. For *nox* as death, see 2.574 *nocte obita,* 13.129 *sed iam longo nox uenerat aeuo,* Hor. *Carm.* 1.28.15 *omnes una manet nox,* Verg. *Aen.* 10.746 *aeternam...noctem,* etc. *Stygia umbra* is a common collocation: 5.597, 5.617, 13.784, Luc. *BC* five times, [Sen.] *HO* 1983, etc.

46. cladi parce obuius ire: the phrasing echoes the prophetic soldier's vision from the preceding book: 8.658–9 *miles...anhelat clade futura: / 'parcite, crudeles superi!'* For *parcere* as "avoid" with an infinitive, see 17.27 *parcite...contingere,* Verg. *Ecl.* 3.94 *parcite...procedere* (with Coleman's note on the phrase's colloquial flavor), *Aen.* 3.42 *parce...scelerare,* etc. Lanzarone compares *BC* 7.60 *cladibus inruimus nocituraque poscimus arma.*

For *obuius ire,* see 272–3n., 7.697 *negat obuius ire,* Verg. *Aen.* 10.770 *obuius ire parat,* Ov. *Met.* 7.111 *obuius it,* etc.

47–8. dum transit diuum furor et consumitur ira / Fortunae: Paulus refers to divine anger in wholly generic terms. He does not realize that Cannae represents the high point of Juno's centuries-long persecution of the Trojans/Romans. The phrasing is a chiastic expansion of the far more common phrase

112   *Commentary Lines 48–52*

ira deum: 5.475, 8.332, 14.617, 15.94, Verg. *Aen.* 3.215, 5.706–7, 11.233, Ov. *Met.* 10.399, Livy eleven times, etc. For the phrasing, compare Scylla's rage at Ov. *Met.* 8.106 *consumptis precibus uiolentam transit in iram.*

48–9. nouus Hannibalis, sat, nomina ferre / si discit miles: Livy reports that two-thirds of the Roman army at Cannae consisted of new recruits: Livy 22.41.5 *duas prope partes tironum militum in exercitu esse.* For the soldiers' fear, see Livy 22.12.10 *adsuefaciebant territum pristinis cladibus militem minus iam tandem aut uirtutis aut fortunae paenitere suae.* Polybius' Paulus similarly appeals to the soldiers' inexperience in an effort to exculpate them from their previous defeats and inspire them to victory at Cannae: *Hist.* 3.108.7 οὔτε ταῖς δυνάμεσι κεχρῆσθαι γεγυμνασμέναις, ἀλλὰ νεοσυλλόγοις κἀοράτοις παντὸς δεινοῦ. For the fear caused by Hannibal's name, see 16.15–19 *parta tamen formido manu et tot caedibus olim / quaesitus terror...proque omnibus armis...unum / Hannibalis sat nomen erat.*

49. nec frigidus aspicit hostem: Silius earlier compares the Saguntine soldiers in fear of Hannibal's onslaught to sailors whose hearts turn frigid in a storm: 1.470–1 *frigida nautis / corda tremunt.*

50. nonne uides, cum uicinis auditur in aruis: Duff's "the very sound of his approach" is inaccurate. Fabius has been holding back his men while Hannibal has been ravaging "the nearby fields." For the common phrase *nonne uides,* see 13.844, 15.84; for its Lucretian origins and afterlife, see Schiesaro 1984. For the collocation *uicinis...aruis,* see Verg. *Aen.* 3.500 *uicinaque Thybridis arua.* 52 *arma* likely prompted *armis ω.* A similar error can be observed at 4.293–4, where *arua* and *armis* occur in subsequent lines; cf. 4.293 *arua ωCm : arma edd. a* rl.

51. quam subitus linquat pallentia corpora sanguis: this line and the following create a composite picture of the soldiers' fear. Blood leaves their faces as their weapons "flow" (like blood?) out of their hands, as at 7.701–3 *cecidere et lora repente / et stimuli, ferrumque super ceruice tremiscens / palluit infelix subducto sanguine Maurus.* Valerius apparently introduced the collocation *subitus sanguis,* of sudden flows of blood: VF *Arg.* 2.541 *horrescunt subitoque uident in sanguine puppem* (Hercules kills the sea monster), *Arg.* 6.573 *ingentem subiti cum sanguinis undam* (the death of Zetes). Silius, however, likely employed the collocation applied to fear by adapting elements of passages such as Verg. *Aen.* 3.259–60 *at sociis subita gelidus formidine sanguis / deriguit* (Celaeno's prophecy inspires terror in the Aeneadae) and Ov. *Met.* 7.136 *palluit et subito sine sanguine frigida sedit* (Medea's fear at Jason's danger).

52. quamque fluant arma ante tubas: the soldiers are imagined as dropping their weapons in fear at the sound of Hannibal's war trumpets. For *fluere* of dropping weapons, see 120n. *arma fluebant,* 7.633 *arma fluunt,* 15.378 *fluxerunt*

Commentary Lines 52–4 113

rigidis arma infelicia palmis; Cic. *Phil.* 12.8 *fluent arma de manibus*, Stat. *Theb.* 7.682 *arma fluunt*, *OLD* s.v. *fluo* 12. For soldiers' fear *ante tubas*, see Verg. *Aen.* 11.424 *ante tubam tremor occupat artus.*

52–5. Paulus imagines Varro's objection that he is another *Cunctator* like Fabius Maximus and counters with a suggestive allusion to Flaminius' disaster at Trasimene. His argument recapitulates Fabius' speech to his troops (7.219–52) and Fabius' identification of Varro as an *alter Flaminius* (8.310); see further 422n. and Introduction, section 3a. For Livy's evocation of Fabius and Flaminius in the argument between Paulus and Varro, see Livy 22.44.5 *cum Paulus Sempronique et Flamini temeritatem Varroni, Varro Paulo speciosum timidis ac segnibus ducibus exemplum Fabium obiceret.*

This passage creates a further association between Paulus and Lucan's Pompey. Pompey's forces similarly call him *segnis pauidusque* (Luc. *BC* 7.52) before Pharsalus, the same charges that Varro levels against Paulus and Fabius. In response to Cicero's demand to give battle, he unsuccessfully tries to persuade them *fortissimus ille est / qui, promptus metuenda pati, si comminus instent, / et differre potest* (Luc. *BC* 7.105–7).

52–3. cunctator et aeger, / ut rere, in pugnas Fabius: Paulus reminds Varro that he is out of date; such incomprehension of the goals of Fabius' guerrilla strategy should properly have ended when his troops rescued Minucius. For Fabius as the *Cunctator*, see 7.536 with Littlewood's note, 16.674, Enn. *Ann.* 363 Skutsch, Verg. *Aen.* 6.845–6, etc.; see Littlewood 2011: lxiv–lxx for discussion. For *aeger…in pugnas*, see Ov. *Met.* 12.373–4 *aeger in hostem / erigitur.* For parenthetical *ut rere*, see Verg. *Aen.* 7.437, Stat. *Theb.* 7.196, VF *Arg.* 1.164 *ut reris.*

53. quotcumque sub illis: for the clausula of 54, see Verg. *Aen.* 3.234, Ov. *Fasti* 6.371, Luc. *BC* 4.702, etc. Postgate 1905 proposed *quotcumque* (against *quoscumque ω*) on the basis of the multiple prior references to Fabius' preservation of each of his men's lives, including 6.620–1 *Fabius mirabile quantum / gaudebat reducem patriae annumerare reuersus*, 7.399 *plena tibi castra atque intactus uulnere miles*, 7.730 *senior numerato milite laetus.* Duff's "every soldier whom he led to battle" is inaccurate, since Fabius avoided battle. Zaia retains *quoscumque*, observing *ad loc.* that the adverbial use is rare and mostly prosaic, though found in hexameter at, e.g., Manil. *Astr.* 4.315 *totque dabit uires dominos quotcumque recepit.*

54. culpatis duxit signis, nunc arma capessunt: Paulus does not blame Fabius' standards, though Varro does. In a different context, blameworthy *signa* recall Lucan's civil warriors: *BC* 1.6–7 *infestisque obuia signis / signa*, 3.330 *terribilis aquilas infestaque signa*, 4.217 *damnataque signa.* For the civil war theme of the Cannae episode, see Introduction, section 4b. Baehrens 1872: 631 proposed *non arma* to emphasize the contrast between Fabius' veterans and the "ungeübte Neulinge" under Flaminius.

114   *Commentary Lines 55–65*

55. at quos Flaminius—: Drakenborch *ad loc.* rightly called the aposiopesis "elegantissima." The figure evokes the famous *quos ego* of Virgil's Neptune (*Aen.* 1.135), in the similar context of an effort to save the lives of the Aeneadae against the machinations of a hostile Juno. Silius emphasizes the massive loss of Roman lives in Flaminius' defeat at Trasimene.

This use of the figure appears as the middle of a series of three:

(a) Fabius at 7.248–9 *modo qui—sed parcere dictis / sit melius*, where he similarly avoids direct mention of the disaster that would have occurred had he not chosen to avoid combat;

(b) the present passage; and

(c) Paulus as he nears death and the disaster that he foretold at Cannae comes to fulfillment: 10.289–90 *ille ego—sed uano quid enim te demoror aeger, / Lentule, conquestu?*

Other speakers similarly interrupt themselves as they catalog the Romans' misfortunes, such as Serranus: 6.110 *sed quid ego haec? grauior quanto uis ecce malorum!* For the motif that mentioning a misfortune is likely to provoke it, see 2.54 *effundunt gemitus atque omina tristia uertunt* with my note, and Verg. *Aen.* 2.190–1 *quod di prius omen in ipsum / conuertant.*

55. sed dira auertite, diui!: for the form of the prayer, see Verg. *Aen.* 3.265 *di, prohibete minas; di, talem auertite casum* (where Servius Danielis associates the phrase with augural formulae), 3.620 *di talem terris auertite pestem*, etc. For similar contexts, see 12.329–30 *et ipse / Delius auertet propiora pericula uates*, Cic. *Mur.* 88 *Iuppiter omen auertat*, etc.; *TLL* 2.1323.2–5.

56–65. Paulus appeals to an ancient prophecy by the Cumaean Sibyl that apparently warned the Romans about Varro's madness (56–9). Its fortuitousness and lack of specificity suggest that he made it up on the spot. As a prophecy, however, it is a development on a theme established by three episodes where *uates* figures make warnings that others ignore:

(a) In the debate in the Carthaginian Senate, Hanno presents himself as a Cassandra figure who has already warned the Carthaginians about the dangers of allowing Hannibal to assume command; see 2.285 *haec serus uates Hannon canit* with my note. Hanno sets himself as a figurative *uates* against the Massylian *uates* whose ritual drove Hannibal to insanity (2.298).

(b) Proteus' earlier prophecy to his nymphs, which foretells Cannae but does not blame it on Roman recklessness: see 7.483–4 *damnatoque deum quondam per carmina campo / Aetolae rursus Teucris pugnabitis umbrae* with Littlewood's note.

(c) The Roman soldier who foresees Varro's defeat and flight (8.659–76, esp. 666).

Commentary Lines 56–9 115

Paulus then presents himself as another *uates* whose wisdom has been ignored, along with the Cumaean Sibyl's (60–5). In the complementary scene in the Roman Senate when Scipio proposes invading Africa, he calls Fabius a *uates* who rejected his plan as dangerous (16.653 *atque idem hic uates temeraria coepta canebat*). In contrast to these human *uates* who predict defeat, the prophetic god Apollo indicates that the *uates* warrior Ennius will sing of Roman victories and the glorious leaders who bring them about (12.407–13). Marks 2020 observes the Ovidian narrator's similar claim to be a *uates* at Ov. *Ibis* 243–8.

Both here and elsewhere, Silius epicizes history by presenting the events of the Second Punic War as part of a mythological narrative that stretches from the deep past to the Flavian era; see Introduction, section 4a. Livy's mention of prophecy (25.12.4–9) is likely only peripherally related. He retrospectively indicates that Marcius, a contemporary prophet, had warned the Romans about Cannae in his *carmina*. As is characteristic of prophecy, Marcius does not mention Varro or any specific Roman commander. Val. Max. 1.1.16 shows that there were dozens of retrospectively discovered religious omens pertaining to Cannae.

56. sin nostris animus monitis precibusque repugnat: for the phrasing, see 2.364 *sin fata repugnant*. For the attempt to sway the listener with prayers and warnings, see, e.g., Ov. *Met.* 2.482 *neue preces animos et uerba precantia flectant*, 15.140 *monitis animos aduertite nostris*, etc. For *animus... repugnat*, see, e.g., Cic. *TD* 2.15 *animoque mihi opus est non repugnante*, Sen. *Contr.* 8.6 *repugnantis animi uultus index*.

57. aures pande deo: in spite of Paulus' forceful phrasing, Varro is unlikely to listen to the gods' prophecies, as he has already ignored the omens that open the book; see 1–7 n. For the concept, see *TLL* 2.1510.6 ("in locutionibus, quae animi attentionem significant"). Silius is apparently the first to employ the collocation with *pandere*, which does not appear again until late antiquity: Avien. *Arat.* 292 *pande sacris aurem*, Claud. *Cons. Stil.* 2.47–8 *rumoribus aurem / pandit*, Juvenc. 2.812 *cordis si panditis aures*.

57–8. cecinit Cymaea per orbem / haec olim uates: for *canere* as the typical activity of the *uates*, see 61n., 2.285 (Hanno), 12.409–10 (Ennius), 13.409 (the Sibyl), 13.794 (Scipio longs for the *uates* who will sing of *Romula facta*), 16.653 (Scipio on Fabius); Verg. *Aen.* 5.524, 8.340, etc. For the Sibyl as the *Cymaea uates*, see 8.531 *quondam fatorum conscia Cyme*, 13.400. For song passing throughout the world, see 13.793–4 *ut Romula facta per orbem / hic caneret uates*.

58–9. et te praesaga tuosque / uulgauit terris proauorum aetate furores: the Sibyl as *praesaga uates* sings here of Varro's *furor*, the consul's characteristic mental state (see 23n. and Introduction, section 3a). In a complementary use of

116   *Commentary Lines 60–3*

the motif, the *praesagi uates* encourage Scipio: 16.590 *ad maiora iubent praesagi tendere uates*. *Vulgauit* may be an evocation of the prophecies immediately preceding the outbreak of Lucan's civil war: Luc. *BC* 1.564–5 *diraque per populum Cumanae carmina uatis / uolgantur*. For the motif of consulting the Sibyl in the time of the forefathers, see Ov. *Fasti* 4.157–8 *Roma pudicitia proauorum tempore lapsa est: / Cumaeam, ueteres, consuluistis anum*. The lengthy hyperbaton emphasizes Paulus' accusation of madness; see Introduction, section 5c on figures.

60–1. iamque alter tibi, nec perplexo carmine, coram / fata cano uates: prophecy is conventionally obscure (e.g., Sen. *Oed.* 212 *responsa dubia sorte perplexa iacent*), but Paulus' words are clear. See 56–64n. on the similarity of this scene to those involving Hanno and Fabius.

Perplexo carmine may signal Livy's account of the prophet Marcius' second, more obscure prophecy regarding Cannae, which presents the only other occurrence of the collocated words: Livy 25.12.8 *tum alterum* **carmen** *recitatum, non eo tantum obscurius quia incertiora futura praeteritis sunt sed* **perplexius** *etiam scripturae genere*. For the characteristic obscurity of prophecy, see *Pun.* 7.436 *ambiguus uates* (Proteus), Verg. *Aen.* 6.99 *horrendas canit ambages*, Luc. *BC* 1.638 *multaque tegens ambage canebat*, etc. Marks 2020 notes the correspondence between Paulus' statement and the *Ibis* narrator: Ov. *Ibis* 246–7 'fata canet uates qui tua' dixit 'erit.' / ille ego sum uates.

Fata cano establishes a strong contrast with Jupiter's identical words at 548n. Paulus ironically pretends to be a *uates* in order to speak common sense regarding the likelihood of defeat on the basis of previous battles with the Carthaginians. Jupiter, however, speaks authoritatively about a future that has not yet unfolded. For *canere* as the *uox propria* for prophecy, see, e.g., 3.687 *Marmaricis ales populis responsa canebat*, Verg. *Aen.* 3.444 *fata canit foliisque notas et nomina mandat* with Horsfall's note, VF *Arg.* 5.43 *fata canens*, etc.; *TLL* 6.1.364.81.

61. sistis ni crastina signa: the phrasing is historiographical rather than poetic: see Caes. *BC* 1.79.4 *legionum signa consistere iuberent*, Livy 4.37.11, 9.45.14, 21.32.9 *Hannibal consistere signa iussit*, 28.16.5, etc. For adjectives used as temporal adverbs, see 7n. *nocturna classica*, 21 *crastina iura*.

62–3. firmabis nostro Phoebeae dicta Sibyllae / sanguine: use of the maximum number of spondees in 62 and the enjambement of 63 *sanguine* emphasize Paulus' certainty of the Roman massacre. Further adaptation of Livy's speech of Marcius the *uates* is likely: Livy 25.12.6 *sed neque credes tu mihi, donec compleris sanguine campum*. Paulus' speech continues to evoke Hanno's by evoking his retrospective on the First Punic War: see *Pun.* 2.304 *lauimus Aetnaeas animoso sanguine uallis* with my note. For *firmare*, see *TLL* 6.1.811.80. For the Sibyl as Phoebean, see Ov. *Pont.* 2.2.80; Stat. *Theb.* 4.488 refers to Manto.

Commentary Lines 63–177   117

63. nec Graio posthac Diomede ferentur: Silius employs the traditional narrative in which the Iliadic hero Diomedes emigrated to southern Italy, and accordingly refers to the region in general and Cannae in particular as Diomedes' Aetolian land; see 99n., 495n., 1.125, 3.707, 7.484, 8.241, 8.351, 10.184, 10.266–7, 11.505, 12.673. For the myth, see Horsfall on Verg. *Aen.* 11.225–42.

64. sed te, si perstas, insignes consule campi: for the topos of a battle site made famous by a major victory or defeat, see, e.g., 11.140–1 *ut Trebiae ripas aeterno nomine famae / tradiderit*, Verg. *Aen.* 11.385–6 *passimque tropaeis / insignis agros*; in reference to Cannae, Livy 22.43.9 *ad nobilitandas clade Romana Cannas urgente fato profecti sunt*.

Paulus' prediction that Cannae will become known for Varro's defeat rather than Diomedes' migration responds to three other moments:

(1) Fabius' speech dissuading his troops from combat that will make another place famous for defeat: 7.228–9 *nullum clade noua claraeque fragore ruinae / insignem fecisse locum*.

(2) Hannibal's encouragement of his troops that the association with Diomedes already makes Cannae unlucky for the Romans: 8.241 *infaustum Phrygibus Diomedis nomine campum*.

(3) the narrator's verdict that two Pauluses would have saved the Romans from defeat and deprived Cannae of its fame: 10.29–30 *alter si detur in armis / Paulus Dardaniis, amittant nomina Cannae*.

65. haec Paulus, lacrimaeque oculis ardentibus ortae: Paulus' real tears at the prospect of Roman defeat complement the hypothetical ones that Varro attributed to the soldiers (30n.) on the pretext that they were aggrieved at being held back from combat. Virgil typically attributes burning eyes to men in battle rage (*Aen.* 9.703, 12.101–2, 12.670). Paulus presents the opposite case of a leader who weeps for his men who are about to die in battle. Fabius weeps as his son suggests letting Minucius' men die (7.547); unlike Paulus, however, he can save them from his errant fellow commander. For the motif of Paulus' grief, see 20–1n.

66–177. A grisly episode of parricide and suicide creates a further threatening omen before combat begins. Satricus was taken prisoner in the First Punic War and given as a gift to the king of the Autololes; he serves now as an interpreter as the king campaigns in Italy. As the Carthaginian army nears his home in Sulmo, Satricus escapes from the Carthaginian camp and makes his way at night across the battlefield to the Roman camp. On the way, he strips the armor from his son Mancinus' corpse; for Mancinus' death, see 12–14n. Meanwhile, his other son Solymus goes to look for his brother's corpse and unwittingly wounds his father fatally in the dark on the mistaken assumption that he is a Carthaginian. Before dying, his father absolves him and instructs him to warn

118   *Commentary Line 66*

the Romans not to attack. Solymus nevertheless commits suicide out of grief and *pietas*. As he expires, he writes a message in his own blood warning Varro to flee the combat.

This scene adapts motifs from numerous other epic nighttime episodes and unwitting encounters. Historiographical tradition also presented narratives of family members who killed one another, whether wittingly or unwittingly. As with his other type scenes, Silius creates a unique narrative that both serves the themes of the Cannae episode and establishes a pointed dialogue with epic tradition. His version of the night meeting features a tragedy of unwitting violence between loved ones, inspired by Ovid's fatal encounters between lovers and Valerius' combat between the Argonauts and their hosts at Cyzicus. Satricus' absolution of his son and Solymus' suicide, meanwhile, demonstrate *pietas* taken to a greater extreme than in the night raids of Virgil's *Aeneid* or Statius' *Thebaid*. The command to flee contributes to Varro's typology (175n.) and further associates him with Lucan's Pompey. See Introduction, section 3b for full discussion.

66–9. The narrative introduces Satricus as a soldier of Regulus captured by Xanthippus in the First Punic War and subsequently given as a slave to the king of the Autololes.

66. necnon et noctem sceleratus polluit error: each of the keywords in this line introduces the episode's major narrative movements. The night (*noctem*) is the only witness to the scene: see 169n. *Titania testis*, 180n. *conscia nox sceleris*. The morally ambivalent phrase *sceleratus... error* points to the variable interpretation of Solymus' action. Satricus absolves his son's *error* by claiming it was not *fraus* (128–9n.). Solymus disagrees and commits suicide. Pollution (*polluit*) recurs as Solymus addresses his *pollutae dextrae* (169n.) and claims that his eyes will no longer pollute the moon (172n.). Varro assumes that Solymus' act was parricide, and his *sceleratum... carmen* (266n.) the result of the Fury's punishment. The phrasing likely echoes the question posed by Lucan's narrator to the gods before Pharsalus: Luc. *BC* 7.58–9 *hoc placet, o superi, cum uobis uertere cuncta / propositum, nostris erroribus addere crimen?*

Bruère 1959: 231 observes that the phrase *sceleratus... error* draws a thematic connection to the mistaken murder of Ovid's Actaeon by his dogs: Ov. *Met.* 3.141–2 *fortunae crimen in illo, / non scelus inuenies; quod enim scelus error habebat?* The evocation of the hapless hunter suggests that neither Solymus nor Actaeon should be considered criminally culpable for his errors. For similar efforts at exculpation of *error* through contrast with *scelus*, see Ov. *Trist.* 3.11.34 *quod magis errorem quam scelus esse putes*, 4.10.90 *errorem iussae, non scelus, esse fugae*, Sen. *HF* 1237 *quis nomen usquam sceleris errori addidit?*, [Sen.] *HO* 983 *error a culpa uacat*, etc.

This is the sole example of polluting *error*, but polluting *scelus* is frequent: 13.848–9 *nec par poena tamen sceleri: sacraria Vestae / polluit exuta sibi uirginitate sacerdos,* Cic. *Mil.* 85 *quam ille omni scelere polluerat, Phil.* 11.29 *inexpiabili scelere polluerit,* etc.

67. Xanthippo captus: see 6.301–45 for Marus' account of the Carthaginians' hiring of the mercenary Xanthippus in the First Punic War and his subsequent capture of Regulus. See Polyb. *Hist.* 1.32, Flor. *Epit.* 1.18, Lazenby 1996: 102–6, *NP* s.v. *Xanthippus* 4. Drakenborch correctly rejects Scaliger's suggestion *cretus,* as *captus* points precisely to the events of the first Punic war. For the phrase *Libycis . . . oris* and its alternatives, see 197n.

67–8. Libycis tolerarat in oris / seruitium Satricus: *tolerare . . . seruitium* is a unique collocation, though note Livy 26.4.1 *nec aut famem tolerare seruitia ac plebs poterant.* Satricus' name evokes Satricum, modern Le Ferriere, in the Volscian territory between Antium and Velitrae. Livy 28.11.2 reports a series of omens at Satricum in 206 BC, including lightning strikes and snake infestation. The town had lost its former importance by the Flavian era; cf. Pliny *NH* 3.68 *in prima regione praeterea fuere in Latio clara oppida Satricum, Pometia,* etc.

68–9. mox inter praemia regi / Autololum dono datus: Satricus was taken prisoner and then given as a gift (*dono*) to the king for his good service. Spaltenstein is wrong to interpret *praemia* as *praeda* and to reject Duff's translation "reward." Zaia argues correctly for "ricompensa" through reference to Varro *LL* 5.178 *praeda est ab hostibus capta, quod manu parta . . . praemium a praeda, quod ob recte quid factum concessum* and Serv. *Aen.* 11.78 *nam praeda est quae eripitur, praemium quod offertur.* She also notes the phraseological parallel of Verg. *Aen.* 12.437 *et magna inter praemia ducet.* See also Luc. *BC* 1.341–2 *his saltem longi non cum duce praemia belli / reddantur* with Roche's note. For the common clausula *praemia belli,* see 3.149, Luc. *BC* 5.330, VF *Arg.* 2.114, etc.

The Autololes were a Gaetulian tribe, as the interchangeable use at 79n. suggests; but Silius often uses *Gaetulus* as a metonym for "North African." 3.306–9 attributes remarkable speed to them, a motif that likely recurs at Claud. *Stil.* 1.355–6 *fugaces / Autololes.* See *Pun.* 2.63 with my note, Bona 1998: 70, Talbert et al. 2000: 28 A6.

Dono datus suggests a *figura etymologica,* as at Plaut. *Amph.* 538, *Stich.* 665, Sall. *BJ* 85.38 *datur dono,* Livy 4.51.8 *Hernicis ipsum agerque dono datus,* etc.

69. ob uirtutis honorem: the "honor of courage" should properly have resulted in freedom, as it did, for example, in Claudius' pardoning of the British rebel Caratacus (Tac. *Ann.* 12.37). Here the inappropriate "reward" of exchanging masters subtly reinforces Carthaginian perfidy. For the phrase, see 16.133 *nec a Poenis ulli uirtutis honores.* The phrase first appears as a clausula at VF *Arg.* 1.177, 1.850. That locus is the final line of *Argonautica* 1 and so may have conceivably become memorable through its marked position. The phrase *ob honorem* + genitive can be paralleled, e.g., Gell. *NA* 5.6.5 *'triumphales' coronae sunt*

120   *Commentary Lines 70–2*

aureae, quae imperatoribus ob honorem triumphi mittuntur. For other merits, see, e.g., Cic. *Brut.* 54 *eique ob eam rem honores amplissumos habitos*, Pliny *NH* 7.123 *quod ob meritum honores illi quos Herculi decreuit Graecia*, Pliny *Ep.* 8.6.10, etc.

70–6. Satricus left two children, Mancinus (12–14n.) and Solymus, at home in Sulmo. A brief digression explains the etymology of Solymus' name. The Trojan settler Solymus founded a city named Solymon, which became shortened to Sulmo. Silius expands the briefer version of the etymology at Ov. *Fasti* 4.79–80 *huius erat Solymus Phrygia comes unus ab Ida, / a quo Sulmonis moenia nomen habent*, the sole earlier occurrence of this foundation story. Though the Carthaginians passed through Sulmo earlier in the summer of 216 BC (cf. Livy 22.18.6–7), it is still quite far from Cannae (~275 km).

Bruère 1959: 230 argues that Silius included Sulmo's foundation story here mainly to concentrate the episode's *color Ovidianus*. The fact that Sulmo is roughly 180 km from Satricum further corroborates Bruère's suggestions, as there appears to be no necessary geographic connection between Satricus' residence and the place evoked by his name. See Bona 1998: 185–6. Marks 2020 observes the similarity between Satricus' long exile and Ovid's.

70–1. huic domus et gemini fuerant Sulmone relicti / matris in uberibus nati: Sulmo appeared earlier in the catalog of Roman forces: 8.510 *gelidoque rapit Sulmone cohortes.* Marks 2020 observes that mention of Sulmo and its Paelignian contingent evokes the figure of Ovid the poet, born at Sulmo: *Am.* 2.16.1, 3.15.11, *Fasti* 4.81, *Tr.* 4.10.3, *Pont.* 4.14.49.

The phrasing is modeled in part on Verg. *Aen.* 5.285 *geminique sub ubere nati.* For *domus* "speciatim de patria ut sede natali," see *TLL* 5.1.1974.4. *Uberibus* creates the emotional associations of a loving home (as at, e.g., 3.63 *paruumque sub ubere natum*) rather than a precise chronological indication. Xanthippus' campaign occurred in 255; if the chronology were taken literally, Satricus' children would be close to 40 and their father close to 60 in the summer of 216. Silius creates a similar generational association between the First and Second Punic Wars in the stories of Xanthippus' sons (4.355–400) and Regulus' son Serranus (6.62–589). The point of each of these narratives, as with Silius' invention of a son for Hannibal (3.66–7), is not chronological or genealogical exactitude, but the presentation of the war as *mandata nepotibus arma* (1.18).

71–2. Mancinus et una / nomine Rhoeteo Solymus: for Mancinus, see 12–14n. The epithet *Rhoete(i)us* derives from the town Rhoeteum in the Troad (Hdt. 7.43) and thus means "Trojan," as at, e.g., Verg. *Aen.* 12.456 *ductor Rhoeteius.* Silius is the only poet to use the epithet to mean "Roman"; see 621n. and 2.51 with my note. See Lyne 1987: 11–12 and Bleisch 1999 for Rhoeteum's literary resonances in Virgil's *Aeneid*. The geographers place the *Solymi* south of the Troad in Pisidia or Lycia: Pliny *NH* 5.94 *insident uerticem Pisidae, quondam*

Commentary Lines 72–8 121

appellati Solymi, quorum colonia Caesarea, eadem Antiochia, Strabo 12.573, Steph. Byz. s.v. Σόλυμοι· Σόλυμοι, οἱ νῦν Πισίδαι.

72–3. nam Dardana origo / et Phrygio genus a proauo: these phrases echo and vary 72 *nomine Rhoeteo*. The phrasing is modeled on Verg. *Aen.* 12.225–6 *cui genus a proauis ingens clarumque paternae / nomen erat uirtutis, et ipse acerrimus armis*, also adapted at *Pun.* 2.66 (where, see my note).

73–4. qui sceptra secutus / Aeneae claram muris fundauerat urbem: the use of the maximum number of spondees in line 74 both emphasizes the seriousness of city foundation and recalls that Ovid's brief narrative of Sulmo's foundation also focused on its walls. See Ov. *Fasti* 4.79–80, quoted at 70–6n. above. For walls as the metonym for a city, see 44n. For *fundare urbem*, see Verg. *Aen.* 6.810–11 *urbem / fundabit*, 8.478–9 *fundata... / urbis Agyllinae sedes*.

75–6. ex sese dictam Solymon. celebrata colonis / mox Italis paulatim attrito nomine Sulmo: for the etymology, see Marangoni 2007: 126. For another explicit description of the etymological "disfigurement" of a name, see 3.366 *et quos nunc Grauios uiolato nomine Graium*. Other etymologies, as here, similarly involve the loss of letters or syllables; see *Pun.* 2.58 and 2.67 with my notes. *Celebrata* is a more vivid term for the arrival of settlers than, e.g., 1.288 *aduertere coloni*. For similar rhythm, see 12.358 *inde Ichnusa prius Grais memorata colonis*. For the Romans as *coloni*, see 203n., 4.721 *Maeonios...colonos* (Corythus), 7.160 *numquam tellus mentita colono* (Falernus), 11.546 *Dardanio... colono*, 12.706 *Laurentiue colono*, Verg. *Geo.* 2.385 *Ausonii, Troia gens missa, coloni*, etc. As Horsfall on Verg. *Aen.* 7.85 observes, the first vowel of the adjective *Italus* is typically short, while the first vowel of the noun *Italia* "has been necessarily lengthened."

77–82. The king of the Autololes brought Satricus with him to Italy to serve as his interpreter. As the Carthaginian forces near his home, Satricus escapes from imprisonment and flees unarmed toward the Roman camp.

77–8. at tum barbaricis Satricus cum rege cateruis / aduectus, quo non spretum, si posceret usus: the collocation *barbarica caterua* was apparently a Neronian innovation: Sen. *Ag.* 600 *motam barbaricis equitum cateruis*, Luc. *BC* 7.527 *non bene barbaricis umquam commissa cateruis*. For *caterua* "saepe de barbararum gentium copiis" (*TLL* 3.609.65), see 236n., 3.300, 5.646–7 *cateruis / Boiorum*, 10.452, 17.418, etc.; for application to Romans, see, e.g., 10.495 (Cloelia). For *posceret usus*, see 11.607 *quae belli posceret usus*, Ov. *Met.* 10.37 *pro munere poscimus usum*, etc. Summers proposed genitive *barbaricae...cateruae*, but Delz (app. crit.) argued "abl. qui dicitur militaris fort. ferri potest." Watt 1988: 173 again objected to "the bare ablative," and proposed *tum <in>*. He justified the elision of the monosyllable through reference to 1.257 *cum*, 13.188 *tam*, 14.353 *dum*.

122   *Commentary Lines 79–89*

79. noscere Gaetulis Latias interprete uoces: for the Autololes as Gaetulians, see 69n. Volpilhac-Lenthéric's translation "apprendre la langue latine" is inaccurate. The king has no intention of improving his Latin but expects to receive actionable information in his native language, as at Cic. *Balb.* 28 *in legatione interpretem secum habere*, Caes. *BG* 1.19.3 *cotidianis interpretibus, BG* 5.36.1, QCurt. 10.3.6 *adhibito interprete . . . orationem habuit*, etc.; *TLL* 7.1.2252.61 "respicitur explanatio linguae alienae, translatio". Thilo 1891: 622 observed that the sentence cannot terminate with *uoces* but must continue to 82 *iniquis*.

80–1. postquam posse datum Paeligna reuisere tecta / et patrium sperare larem: alliteration of P- across two lines emphasizes the point that Paelignian Sulmo is home. For *dare* governing an infinitive, see 206n., Lucr. *DRN* 6.1227 *quod ali dederat*, Verg. *Aen.* 1.66 with Austin's note, 5.248 *dat ferre* with Fratantuono and Smith's note, Ov. *Met.* 11.177 *et dat posse moueri*, etc. *Tecta* with a toponym is a common poetic periphrasis because of its convenient metrical shape: see, e.g., 12.607–8 *tecta / Dardana*, 15.308 *Curetica tecta*, Catul. 64.37 *Pharsalia tecta*, Luc. *BC* 5.406 *Minoia tecta*, etc. For *reuisere tecta*, see VF *Arg.* 2.170 *nec tecta uirum thalamosque reuisunt*. For the common collocation *patrium larem*, see 6.439–40 *patrium sine crimine seruat / inuiolata larem*, Hor. *Epod.* 16.19 *lares patrios*, Luc. *BC* 1.278 *patriis laribus*, etc. For *sperare* in the context of home, see Verg. *Aen.* 7.126 *tum sperare domos defessus*. Liberman 2006: 20 proposed *spectare*, as if in parallel to *reuisere*. The paradosis, however:

(a) is *lectio difficilior*, and so unlikely to be the result of corruption from *spectare*;

(b) has the Virgilian precedent quoted immediately above; and

(c) complements action (*reuisere*) with emotion (*sperare*), where *spectare* would simply repeat the action.

81–2. ad conamina noctem / aduocat: the verb develops the personification of a night which is currently complicit in Satricus' plan and will eventually be willing to conceal Solymus' error (148n.). For the phrasing, see 16.515–16 *breuia ad conamina uterque / aduocat*.

82. ac furtim castris euadit iniquis: the collocation *iniqua castra* appears elsewhere only at Hor. *Carm.* 1.10.15 *iniqua Troiae / castra*. *TLL* 7.1.1640.74 classifies these uses as "speciatim i. q. hostilis." 130n. *castris elapsus acerbis* represents a similar idea in an identical *sedes*.

83–9. Satricus fled the Carthaginian camp without arms. He surveys the corpses left on the battlefield from the skirmish in the earlier part of the day. He unwittingly takes the arms belonging to his son Mancinus, who died leading the Roman assault (12–14n.).

Commentary Lines 83–7   123

83. sed fuga nuda uiri: the collocation typically points to a shameful retreat in which combatants have thrown away their arms to run faster, rather than, as here, to aid a prisoner's furtive escape. Examples include Luc. *BC* 4.713–14 *nudataque foeda / terga fuga*, Livy 33.15.11 *postremo fuga ceterorum nudati*, Vell. *Hist.* 2.61.4 *turpi ac nuda fuga*, etc.

83–4. sumpto nam prodere coepta / uitabat clipeo: for *sumere* with a shield, see, e.g., Ov. *Met.* 8.27. Nicander's *quia* for *nam* is a needless change. *Prodere* prepares the contrast between Virgil's hapless Euryalus, betrayed by his greed for the reflecting helmet (see further 106–9n.), and Silius' Satricus, who is initially careful to avoid discovery by the Carthaginians, but ends up being discovered and killed by his son instead. *Vitabat* implies that Satricus had the choice to take a shield from the Carthaginian camp but declined the option, as if he were a prudent participant in an epic night raid. Zaia *ad loc.* observes that this is the sole occurrence of *uitare* + infinitive in the *Punica*; for other examples, see, e.g., Gell. *NA* 10.21.2 *L. Aelius Stilo ut nouo et inprobo uerbo uti uitauerat*.

84. et dextra remeabat inermi: Silius adapts the collocation *dextra inermis*, also at 13.76, from Virgil (*Aen.* 11.672, 12.311, 12.734); the last two loci feature the identical *sedes*.

85–6. exuuias igitur prostrataque corpora campo / lustrat: *exuuias* and *corpora* form a hendiadys for *exuuias corporum*; Zaia compares 6.665 *exuuias Marti donumque Duilius*. For a similar expansion, see 11.374–6 *praeda et captiua leguntur / corpora dereptaeque uiris sub Marte cruento / exuuiae*. For "prostrate corpses," see 17.423 *atque aperit patulas prostrato corpore late / inter tela uias*, [Caes.] *Bell. Afr.* 40.6 *horum corpora... toto campo ac prostrata diuerse iacebant*, Sen. *HF* 1143–4 *unde prostrata ad domum / uideo cruenta corpora?*, *Il. Lat.* 398 *et prostrata necat uesano corpora dente*, etc. *Prostratus* occurs next at 89, followed by 94 *stratum*; on Silius' repetitive style, see Introduction, section 5b. Hannibal "surveys the field" after Cannae (10.450 *lustrabat campos*) and Scipio does the same as he searches for Hannibal at Zama (17.517 *illum igitur lustrans circumfert lumina campo*). See also Luc. *BC* 7.795 *et lustrare oculis campos sub clade latentes*.

86–7. et exutis Mancini cingitur armis / iamque metus leuior: the indication of Satricus' emotional state emphasizes the irony of the situation. The escaped prisoner thinks that he has made himself more secure by arming himself, but he does not know that it will shortly lead to his own death and his son's suicide. Zaia observes the *figura etymologica* that associates 85 *exuuias* with 86 *exutis*. For the clausula of 86, see Verg. *Aen.* 11.536. "Lighter fear" evokes an earlier father–son interaction, where Hannibal addresses his son as *nec Aeneadum leuior metus* (3.70). The Hannibal passage may in turn be in dialogue with Stat. *Theb.* 8.78–9 *faxo haud sit cunctis leuior metus atra mouere /*

124 *Commentary Lines 87–92*

Tartara, where Dis similarly threatens total war. For *leuis* of "affectiones animi," see *TLL* 7.2.1213.56–76.

87–8. uerum, cui dempta ferebat / exsangui spolia et cuius nudauerat artus: *uerum* emphasizes the bizarreness of the image of the father unwittingly despoiling his own son. The narrator describes Satricus through the vocabulary of spoliation, as if he were an enemy stripping the Roman corpses. This identification lends further credibility to Satricus' subsequent claim *Poenus eram* (130n.) as he attempts to justify his son's fatal error. For *ferre* of bearing away spoils, see 8.254, 12.294, Ov. *Met.* 8.87, Sen. *HF* 240, etc.

For the clausula of 88, see 15.697 *carpebat propere et trepidos nudauerat artus*, where Arabus strips Nabis and is killed by Hasdrubal as he does so. The only earlier example of the collocation *nudare artus* occurs at Sen. *Thy.* 763 *denudat artus durus atque ossa amputat,* of Atreus' macabre cookery. Silius has adapted the more frequent *nudare corpus* for the context of spoliation; 10.604 *exsultare leuis nudato corpore Maurus*, Verg. *Geo.* 2.531 (wrestlers stripping), Ov. *Met.* 1.527 (the stripping of Daphne), etc. all occur in different contexts. For the adjective *nudus* of spoliation, see, e.g., Enn. *Ann.* 618 Skutsch *despoliantur eos et corpora nuda relinquunt.*

89. natus erat, paulo ante Mace prostratus ab hoste: for *prostratus*, see 85n. above. *Mace* ω is the ablative singular of nominative singular *Maces* (22n., 5.194); for its other forms, see nominative plural *Macae* (11n., 3.275, 15.670), accusative singular *Macen* (2.60, where, see my note), genitive plural *Macetum* (5 times); Neue and Wagener 1892: 1.34, 1.664.

90–5. While serving as a night watchman, Satricus' other son Solymus searches in the darkness for his brother Mancinus' corpse. Virgil's Nisus is similarly posted as *portae custos* (*Aen.* 9.176) when the idea of the night raid strikes him. Does Solymus leave his post while on duty, as 95n. *furtiua* suggests? Duff's translation "to relieve in his allotted turn the watch" and Volpilhac-Lenthéric's "à son tour devait prendre la garde" suggest that he engages in this search before his watch begins. As Spaltenstein correctly points out, however, he should remain behind the *uallum,* whether or not his watch has begun.

90. ecce sub aduentum noctis primumque soporem: though *aduentus noctis* is not found again until Amm. Marc. 27.2.8, it is a variation of the more common *initium noctis,* found at Val. Max. 8.15.7, Apul. *Met.* three times, Front. *Strat.* 1.8.9, etc. The elevated periphasis *primus sopor* functions as a doublet of the previous phrase. It may perhaps be a Flavian innovation: see VF *Arg.* 8.81 *primi percussus nube soporis,* Stat. *Theb.* 12.7 *et primus post bella sopor.* Spaltenstein compares Verg. *Aen.* 2.268–9 *tempus erat quo prima quies mortalibus aegris / incipit.*

91–2. alter natorum, Solymus, uestigia uallo / Ausonio uigil extulerat: note the alliteration of V- and the chiastic arrangment of the polysyllabic *uestigia*

Commentary Lines 92–7

and *uicissim* around the disyllables *uallo* and *uigil*. For *(ef)ferre uestigia*, see 15.614 *ferens uestigia*, Lucr. *DRN* 6.757–8, Verg. *Aen.* 9.797–8, 11.290, Stat. *Theb.* 9.111–12, etc.; *TLL* 5.2.140.63 "pedem, inde gradus sim." In the present passage, there may be an evocation of Verg. *Aen.* 2.753–4 *qua gressum extuleram, repeto et uestigia retro / obseruata sequor per noctem et lumine lustro*, also in the context of searching for a deceased family member (Aeneas' nighttime search in Troy for Creusa).

92–3. dum sorte uicissim, / alternat portae excubias: for the change of watch, see 7.155–6 *iamque excubias sortitus iniquas / tertius abrupta uigil iret ad arma quiete*. The phrasing recalls the similar moment of Virgil's Nisus and Euryalus scene: Verg. *Aen.* 9.159 *interea uigilum excubiis obsidere portas*, 9.222–3 *uigiles simul excitat, / illi succedunt seruantque uices*.

93–4. fratrisque petebat / Mancini stratum sparsa inter funera corpus: for the repetitiveness of *stratum*, see 89n., 94n., and Introduction, section 5b. For *stratum…corpus,* see Lucr. *DRN* 6.1265, Ov. *Met.* 14.800–1 *strata est tellus Romana Sabinis / corporibus strata estque suis*, Livy 25.26.10, Luc. *BC* 7.671, etc. For *sparsa…funera,* see Luc. *BC* 6.103 *spargere funus*; see also VF *Arg.* 6.427–8 *sparsique Cytaei / funera miscebant*. Zaia observes that anastrophe of *inter* assists the alliteration *stratum–sparsa*.

95. furtiua cupiens miserum componere terra: *furtiua* is a transferred epithet, in place of the adverb *furtim* (82n.); for other examples, see Ov. *Her.* 14.126 *corpora furtiuis insuper adde rogis*, *TLL* 6.1.1644.2. For *cupiens* with the infinitive, see *TLL* 4.1432.11. For *componere* of burial, see Hor. *Serm.* 1.9.28, Ov. *Fasti* 5.426, *TLL* 3.2116.22.

96–9. Solymus catches sight of a man whom he believes to be an enemy and hides in a nearby tomb. Bruère 1959: 231 compares Thisbe's concealment when startled by the lion (Ov. *Met.* 4.99–100); see 81–2n. and 108–9n. Statius' Amphion sees Hopleus and Dymas: Stat. *Theb.* 10.391–2 *nescio quid uisu dubium incertumque moueri / corporaque ire uidet*.

96. nec longum celerarat iter: for *celerare* with travel, see 12.479 *celerare ad moenia*, 15.208 *praegreditur celeratque uias*, Verg. *Aen.* 8.90 *iter inceptum celerant*, etc.; *TLL* 3.758.10.

96–7. cum tendere in armis / aggere Sidonio uenientem conspicit hostem: a classic example of "deviant focalisation" in the terms of Fowler 1990. The narrator knows that the approaching man is the refugee Satricus, who has no intention of attacking the Romans. Solymus, by contrast, sees him as a *hostis…in armis* because of the direction that he is coming from and his armor. Contrast 104 *credens*, where Satricus mistakenly believes that he has been attacked by a Carthaginian.

126   *Commentary Lines 98–100*

98. quodque dabat fors in subitis necopina: for *dabat fors*, see 10.143–4 *namque hoc de strage iacentum / fors dabat*, Verg. *Aen.* 7.554 *quae fors prima dedit*, Ov. *Met.* 1.452–3 *quem non / fors ignara dedit*, VF *Arg.* 4.620 *fors etiam optatam dabitur contingere pellem*, etc. This substantive use of *in subitis*, as at 7.527 *in subitum*, appears to be prosaic. It is perhaps also a contemporary fashion, as it is found elsewhere only at Pliny *NH* 7.143 *ut necesse erat in subito*, Pliny *Ep.* 2.3.2 *multa lectio in subitis*, Tac. *Agr.* 18.5 *ut in subitis consiliis*. The substantive adjective *necopina* complements the sense of unexpectedness indicated by *fors in subitis*. The phrase is likely a variation on Verg. *Aen.* 8.476 *fors inopina*; the collocation occurs elsewhere only at Cic. *Acad.* 1.29 *non numquam quidem eandem fortunam, quod efficiat multa improvisa et necopinata nobis.*

98–9. sepulcro / Aetoli condit membra occultata Thoantis: for ancient tombs located throughout the epic landscape, see Hom. *Il.* 2.793 τύμβῳ ἐπ᾽ ἀκροτάτῳ Αἰσυήταο γέροντος, 11.166 παρ᾽ Ἴλου σῆμα παλαιοῦ Δαρδανίδαο, 23.331 σῆμα βροτοῖο πάλαι κατατεθνηῶτος, Verg. *Aen.* 11.850–1 *regis Dercenni terreno ex aggere bustum / antiqui Laurentis*, Ov. *Met.* 15.296 *est prope Pittheam tumulus Troezena*, etc. For Silius' dialogue with Ovid's Pyramus and Thisbe episode, see 96–9n. and Introduction, section 3b. The phrasing evokes Enn. *Ann.* 126 Skutsch *heu quam crudeli condebat membra sepulcro*, Verg. *Aen.* 10.558 *condet humi patrioque onerabit membra sepulcro*, and was widely adapted thereafter. Silius uses the common phrase *condere sepulcro* (*TLL* 4.0.151.80) ironically; like Ovid's Thisbe, Solymus is not yet dead but soon will be. For the proleptic use of *occultata*, see, e.g., Verg. *Aen.* 3.237 *scuta latentia condunt*. For the "near golden" arrangement of line 99, see Introduction, section 5c.

Thoas is the king of the Aetolians at Hom. *Il.* 2.638, 4.527 Θόας Αἰτωλὸς, and he led the Aetolians to colonize Bruttium, according to Strabo 6.1.5. See Bona 1998: 16, Nicol 1936: 142–3. Spaltenstein and Fucecchi 1999: 308 observe that reference to him here should evoke associations with Diomedes, the other Aetolian hero who migrated to southern Italy. For southern Italy as "Aetolian," see 63n. There is likely also an association with Thoas king of Lemnos, a father saved from murder by his daughter Hypsipyle (A.R. *Arg.* 1.609–26, VF *Arg.* 2.410–13, Stat. *Theb.* 5.239–51, etc.). Evocation of him here emphasizes the irony of Solymus' murder of his father. *Pun.* 4.769, 14.260 *Thoanteae* clearly refer to the king of Tauris who presided over human sacrifice. For other heroes named Thoas, see Zaia *ad loc.*

100. inde, ubi nulla sequi propius pone arma uirumque: Spaltenstein claims that *propius* is "une précision superflue" with *sequi* and proposes to take it with 101 *uidet* in opposition to the translations of Duff and Volpilhac-Lenthéric. The collocation of *sequi + prope/ius* is well attested, however: Plaut. *Bacch.* 723, Livy 6.32.10 *cum Romanus exercitus prope uestigiis sequeretur*, etc. Zaia further observes that *propius–pone* forms part of a sequence of alliterations, continued in 101 *uidet-uestigia*, 103–4 *sequentum / Satricus*, etc. Word order further supports the

Commentary Lines 101–9   127

construction. For *arma* as a typical metonymy for *armati*, see 2.36, 2.303, 2.394, etc. with my notes; Verg. *Aen.* 10.150 with Harrison, Stat. *Theb.* 4.394 with Parkes, *TLL* 2.600.44. Landrey 2014 argues that many of Silius' collocations of *arma* and *uir* are explicit evocations of the opening of the *Aeneid*; see further 597n.

101. incomitata uidet uestigia ferre per umbras: *incomitata* functions as a hypallage for *incomitati*; *TLL* 7.1.984.26 s.v. *incomitatus* shows that it is typically applied to individuals. The collocation *uidere uestigia* is common (15.603, 16.691–2, Ov. *Am.* 1.8.97) and overlaps once more with Ovid's Pyramus episode: Ov. *Met.* 4.105 *serius egressus uestigia uidit in alto*. See Introduction, section 3b.

102–3. prosiliens tumulo contorquet nuda parentis / in terga haud frustra iaculum: Solymus' leaping forth from the tomb to hurl his unerring javelin increases the shock of the scene. *Nuda...terga* recalls that Satricus has only armed himself with Mancinus' shield and so has no armor on his back. For the collocation, see 10.470, Luc. *BC* 4.713–14 (quoted at 83n. above), *Il. Lat.* 543, etc. Silius is the only epic poet to use the litotes *haud frustra*, again at 5.417 and 7.22; it appears elsewhere in poetry only at Plaut. *Pseud.* 683 and Cic. *Arat.* 114.

103–4. Tyriamque sequentum / Satricus esse manum et Sidonia uulnera credens: Satricus' mistaken assumptions regarding his attacker continue to contribute to the scene's irony. The doubling of the adjectives *Tyrius* and *Sidonius* is licensed by passages such as Verg. *Aen.* 4.544–5 *an Tyriis omnique manu stipata meorum / inferar et, quos Sidonia uix urbe reuelli*, Sen. *Oed.* 712–14 *Castalium nemus / umbram Sidonio praebuit hospiti / lauitque Dirce Tyrios colonos*, Stat. *Silv.* 1.5.39 *quaeque Tyri niveas secat et Sidonia rupes*. Damsté proposed *Tyrium* (i.e., *Tyriorum*), which Delz (app. crit.) commends as "fort. recte." *Sidonia* functions as the equivalent of a genitive, such as the one found at 14.434 *uoluitur in fluctus Lycchaei uulnere Cydnus*. For the clausula, see 10.130 *uulnera credit*.

105. auctorem caeci trepidus circumspicit ictus: for *auctor* of a wound, see Verg. *Aen.* 9.748, Ov. *Met.* 5.133, 8.418 *uulneris auctor*, Stat. *Theb.* 9.558 with Dewar's note. The Roman *editio princeps* (r1) printed the meaningless *ceri*, which Drakenborch found corrected by hand to *certi* in an exemplar. But this is clearly a banalization, and *caecus ictus* is well attested: Lucr. *DRN* 2.136, Ov. *Fasti* 1.623, Livy 34.14.11, etc. For the variation *caecum uulnus*, see Verg. *Aen.* 10.733, Ov. *Her.* 4.20, *Met.* 7.342, etc.

106–9. Moonlight reflected from Mancinus' shield leads Solymus to the mistaken assumption that a Carthaginian has stolen his brother's arms. Silius' careful phrasing recombines two Virgilian scenes with an Ovidian one (see Introduction, section 3b):

(a) The helmet stolen by Euryalus reflects the moonlight and betrays him to the Latins: Verg. *Aen.* 9.371–4 *iamque propinquabant castris murosque subibant / cum* **procul** *hos laeuo flectentis limite cernunt, / et galea*

128 *Commentary Lines 106–9*

Euryalum sublustri noctis in umbra / **prodidit** *immemorem* **radiisque** *aduersa* **refulsit**. See 107n. *fulsit*, 108n. *procul, luna prodente*, 109n. *radiauit*. In both passages, stolen armor betrays its wearer and leads to fatal consequences. See further 83–4n.

(b) Aeneas' recognition of Pallas' *balteus*, taken by Turnus: Verg. *Aen.* 12.942–3 *et* **notis** *fulserunt cingula bullis* / *Pallantis pueri.* See 107n. *et notis fulsit.* Adaptation of this moment extends to the description of Solymus' anger (110n.) and his words as he hurls his spear (114n.). The evocation of the *Aeneid*'s conclusion emphasizes the contrast of *pietas*: the sight of a dead loved one's *spolia* leads Aeneas to righteous revenge, but Solymus to a terrible mistake.

(c) Bruère 1959: 231 compares the moment when Ovid's Thisbe catches sight of the lion by the light of the moon: Ov. *Met.* 4.99 *quam procul ad lunae radios Babylonia Thisbe* / *uidit.* This is the closest verbal link between this episode of the *Punica* and the Pyramus and Thisbe episode. See further 98–9n.

106–7. uerum ubi uictorem iuuenili robore cursus / attulit: the language evokes the typical battlefield pursuit, e.g., Catul. 64.340 *persaepe uago uictor certamine cursus* (of Achilles), Verg. *Aen.* 9.559–60 *quem Turnus pariter cursu teloque secutus* / *increpat his uictor* (see further 113–14n.). The collocation *iuuenile robur* originates at Colum. *RR* 4.3.4. Either this line or Calp. Sic. 4.85 *perpetuamque regit iuuenili robore pacem* (if this poet was indeed active in the Neronian period) first adapts the phrase for poetry; it is found elsewhere only at *CLE* 387.10 and 1278.7. For *ferre cursus*, see 8.89 *rettulit in thalamos cursum,* [Verg.] *Aetna* 127, Prop. 2.34.33, etc.

107. et notis fulsit lux tristis ab armis: *tristis* prefigures the tragic recognition scene to follow. The phrase may have been adapted from Sen. *Med.* 793 *sic face tristem pallida lucem* / *funde per auras,* Medea's prayer to Hecate immediately before committing filicide. The foreshadowing of Roman defeat may potentially evoke the other use of the phrase, Livy 9.6.3 *tamen ipsa lux ita deforme intuentibus agmen omni morte tristior fuit,* of the Roman army sent under the yoke by the Samnites.

108–9. fraternusque procul luna prodente retexit / ante oculos sese et radiauit comminus umbo: the moon "betrays" Mancinus' shield to his brother Solymus but does not yet disclose its bearer's identity. Every other extant pairing of *procul* and *comminus* occurs as part of an opposition between "far" and "near"; *PHI* eight times, *TLL* 10.2.1557.50. To take *procul* as part of an opposition would require limiting it to *luna*, contrasting the distant moon with the nearby shield boss. Spaltenstein instead explains *procul* as "à côté," as at 7.294 *stat procul hasta uiri terrae defixa propinquae,* if one accepts Delz's conjecture *stat* for *haud* ω. Attestation of this meaning of *procul* comes from Verg. *Ecl.* 6.16 *serta procul tantum capiti delapsa iacebant* with Servius' comment SERTA PROCVL *modo 'prope', id est iuxta.* If this view is correct, *comminus* helps to clarify the meaning of *procul*.

Commentary Lines 110–13 129

The ending of 109 recalls Hannibal's terrifying arms that overwhelm the Saguntines; see 2.211 *ac simul aerati radiauit luminis umbo* with my note. Statius may have adapted the phrasing of 109 at *Ach.* 1.852 *radiantem ut comminus orbem*, which is the only other collocation of *radiare* with *comminus*.

Kyle Gervais (*per litteras*) suggests replacing *procul* with *orbis*, which has the advantage of motivating the *–que* and *et* and does not require attributing an unusual meaning to *procul*. Arguments in favor of *procul*, however, are (a) that it creates a double chiasmus enclosing this couplet, formed by the adjective-noun pairing *fraternus–umbo* and the adverbs *procul* and *comminus*; and (b) the echo of Verg. *Aen.* 9.372, quoted at 106–9n. above.

110. exclamat iuuenis subita flammatus ab ira: a further recollection of the *Aeneid*'s conclusion (see further 107n. and 114n.), here of Aeneas' reaction to seeing Pallas' *balteus*: Verg. *Aen.* 12.946–7 *furiis accensus et ira / terribilis*. The collocation *subita ira* is common (Ov. *Met.* 9.574, 10.683, Manil. *Astr.* 4.187, etc.), as is *ira subit* (Verg. *Aen.* 2.575, Ov. *AA* 3.373, Luc. *BC* 3.142, etc.). Statius uses a similar clausula at *Theb.* 12.714 *ingemit et iustas belli flammatur in iras. Flammatus* is *simplex pro composito,* as the following examples suggest: Cic. *ND* 1.42 *ira inflammatos*, Phil. 12.26 *hic ira dementiaque inflammatus*, Livy 2.6.7 *inflammatus ira.*

111–18. Solymus claims he would be no worthy son or brother if he allowed his brother's killer to escape unpunished. For oaths with a similar "I am not" or "I would not be" structure, see Hom. *Il.* 2.257–64, Ov. *Met.* 3.271–2 *nec sum Saturnia, si non / ab Ioue mersa suo Stygias penetrabit in undas*, Petr. *Sat.* 81.6 *nam aut uir ego liberque non sum, aut noxio sanguine parentabo iniuriae meae*, etc. Solymus fully identifies himself through his relatives and his birthplace. The oversupply of information in the soliloquy creates a darkly comic effect by emphasizing his ignorance of his listener's identity.

111. non sim equidem Sulmone satus tua, Satrice, proles: emphatic alliteration of S- marks the line. Statius uses *satus* and *proles* in a comparable collocation: Stat. *Theb.* 5.436 *prolem Calydone satam*. See also *Il. Lat.* 248–9 *simul et Iouis inclita proles / Sarpedon claraque satus tellure Coroebus*, where the two words for "descendant" refer to different individuals. Müller 1861: 284 commended *sum β* against *sim α* Cm *Ep.* 86, but his metrical argument does not aid in the choice of mood. Soubiran 1966: 412 gives examples of *sim* in synaloepha at Prop. 2.13.8 *tunc ego sim Inachio notior arte Lino*, Ov. *Trist.* 5.8.2 *te quoque sim, inferius quo nihil esse potest.*

112–13. nec frater, Mancine, tuus fatearque nepotem / Pergameo indignum Solymo: the repeated vocatives and possessive adjectives (111 *tua, Satrice*, 112 *Mancine, tuus*) increase the pathos. *Esse* is commonly omitted after *fateor*; see *TLL* 6.1.339.60. This is the first occurrence of *nepos indignus*, found next at Stat. *Ach.* 1.955 *ne qua det indignos Thetidi captiua nepotes*. Ovid apparently

130   *Commentary Lines 113–16*

originates the collocation *nepos dignus: Met.* 14.810 *dignoque nepoti, Pont.* 2.8.33 *perque tuos uel auo dignos uel patre nepotes.* For Solymus' Trojan descent, see 72n.

113–14. si euadere detur / huic nostras impune manus: Solymus' words echo those of Turnus as he rampages in the Trojan camp (see 106–7n.): Verg. *Aen.* 9.560–1 *nostrasne euadere, demens, / sperasti te posse manus?* The echo of the Rutulian hero's rage creates a further irony that emphasizes Solymus' tragic error. Turnus furiously kills numerous enemies and receives multiple comparisons to animal predators (*Aen.* 9.551–5, 563–6), while Solymus is about to kill one enemy in the mistaken belief that he is avenging his brother. Silius uses the expression *si detur* again at 4.196–7, 7.133–4, 12.150 *si quando euadere detur.* It is found frequently in comedy (Plaut. *Cist.* 308, *Mil.* 1157, Ter. *Eun.* 647, etc.), but used in epic only at Ov. *Met.* 1.175, 6.545. For *euadere manus*, see 567n., 7.628–9.

114–19. Solymus thinks an unknown Carthaginian has killed his brother Mancinus and taken his armor. He promises his mother to bring home Mancinus' arms to preserve her son's memory. There is a further recollection of the *Aeneid*'s conclusion (see 107n. and 110n.), here of Aeneas' words as he kills Turnus: Verg. *Aen.* 12.947–8 *tune hinc spoliis indute meorum / eripiare mihi?* Solymus' challenge as he throws his spear may also evoke through reversal the complaint of Virgil's Priam to Pyrrhus, though the connection is less direct: Verg. *Aen.* 2.538–9 *qui nati coram me cernere letum / fecisti et patrios foedasti funere uultus.* Priam throws his spear uselessly, while Solymus does so successfully; Priam attempts to avenge his son's death, while Solymus unwittingly causes his father's death. *Ante oculos* is a further potential link to the scene between Priam and Pyrrhus: *Aen.* 2.531 *ut tandem ante oculos euasit et ora parentum.* See further 40–1n.

114–15. tu nobile gestes / germani spolium ante oculos: Seneca apparently originates the collocation *nobile spolium* at *HF* 544 *detraxit spolium nobile corpori.* Silius is the only other poet to employ it, here and at 5.37 *nobile Gergeni spolium.* For the collocation *gestare spolia*, see Manil. *Astr.* 1.783 *et spolia et nomen, qui gestat in alite Phoebum*, Sen. *Ben.* 7.27.2 *hic spolia cruenta manu gestat*, [Sen.] *HO* 411 *spolia gestantem*, QCurt. 6.6.5, etc.

115–16. referasque superba / me spirante domus Paelignae perfidus arma?: Solymus' reference to the arms as belonging to his *domus* rather than specifically to his deceased brother illustrates how he thinks of his family as an indissoluble unit rather than as separate individuals—even as he unwittingly destroys that family. The phrase *superba...arma* is a doublet of 114–15 *nobile...spolium.* The collocation is apparently unique, though modeled on phrases such as *superbum decus* (3.232, 10.398–9), 10.563 *insigne superbum*, etc. In similar phrases, *superbus* applies to the arms' location; see VF *Arg.* 2.544–5

Commentary Lines 117–19 131

aptatque superbis / arma umeris (where Hercules' shoulders are clearly more superb than his armor), Stat. *Theb.* 2.733–4 *figamque superbis / arma tholis* (where Tydeus promises votive offerings that will make the shrine superb).

The phrase *me spirante* appears earlier only at Livy 40.8.17. It is a resonant alternative to phrases such as *me uiuente* (Ov. *Met.* 12.228) or *ego uiuus* (Caes. *BC* 3.64.3, Cic. *Planc.* 101). The alternative *spectante* r1m is both banalizing and needless after *ante oculos* of the preceding line. For *Paelignae*, see 80n. *Perfidus* is a standard epithet for the Carthaginians in the *Punica*, a motif introduced in the epic's proem: 1.5–6 *sacri cum perfida pacti / gens Cadmea.* Solymus' use of the epithet further ironizes him, as he is the one committing a treacherous action.

117–18. haec tibi, cara parens Acca, ad solacia luctus / dona feram: see 113–14 for Solymus' address to the men of his family. In addressing his mother, he varies the structure with pronoun instead of possessive adjective. Only two other individuals, both mythological, appear to have had the name *Acca*: Romulus' nurse (Ov. *Fasti* 5.453, Gell. *NA* 7.7, etc.) and Camilla's companion (Verg. *Aen.* 11.823; see Horsfall's note). Silius' attribution of the name to a third-century Roman mother is part of his project of mythologizing his historical material. *Pun.* 4.462–5 may present the acrostic ACCA, at the moment in which Scipio takes the battlefield at the Ticinus in order to rescue his father. After observing that due caution must be taken before identifying and interpreting acrostics, Zaia comments that "è significativo che esso compaia in correlazione del passo in cui Silio descrive Scipione in quanto *exemplum* di pietà filiale verso il padre." On acrostics in Latin poetry, see Damschen 2004.

For *cara parens,* see 13.624 with van der Keur's note. The clausula is modeled on Verg. *Aen.* 11.62, in the similar context of a parent's funeral honors for a child. As Pallas' honors were small consolation for his father Evander's tremendous grief, so the implication is that Mancinus' arms will be small (but nevertheless indispensable) consolation for Acca. For other uses of the clausula, see 13.392 (Scipio resists consolation for his father and uncle's death), Stat. *Theb.* 9.569; in other *sedes,* see 10.619; see also Stat. *Silv.* 3.3.31 *dabimus solacia dignis / luctibus.*

Drakenborch commended *nec β* with a question mark at the sentence's end, in order to make 117–18 an indignant rhetorical question like 114–16. But Solymus' error appears more tragic if he emphatically promises consolation for his mother before realizing he has killed his father.

118. nati ut figas aeterna sepulcro: *aeterna* is a transferred epithet for adverbial *aeterne* or *in aeternum* (3.136, 13.873); see *TLL* 1.1148.23. For dedicating arms, see 13.65 *armaque Laurenti figebat Troia luco* with van der Keur's note, 14.650 *armaque fixa deis,* Verg. *Aen.* 1.248–9 *armaque fixit / Troia,* Stat. *Theb.* 2.733–4 *figamque superbis / arma tholis* with Gervais's note, etc.

119. talia uociferans stricto mucrone ruebat: the line is an adaptation of Verg. *Aen.* 10.651–2 *talia uociferans sequitur strictumque coruscat / mucronem,* where

132   *Commentary Lines 120–3*

Turnus pursues the false image of Aeneas created by Juno. The evocation of Turnus' failure to perceive reality is a further reminder of Solymus' delusion. The line opening is also found at *Pun.* 7.116, Verg. *Aen.* 2.679, Stat. *Theb.* 6.177, 10.219.

120–2. Satricus drops his arms and freezes in horror as he hears Solymus mention his homeland, wife, children, and the owner of the arms that he has stripped. *Armis* is the unexpected element in the list of conventional emotional attachments. Its inclusion emphasizes the bizarreness of the scene.

120. ast illi iam tela manu iamque arma fluebant: for repeated *iam*, see Verg. *Aen.* 2.530 with Horsfall's note; *TLL* 7.1.118.11. Wills 1996: 107 observes that "separated gemination is infrequent"; 518n., 6.263, 14.581, 15.723, 16.134, 16.375 *iam iamque* is more common. For *iamque* followed by *iam,* see, e.g., 4.682–3. For *fluere* of dropping weapons, see 52n. Marcellus similarly drops his weapons in shock as his son is wounded in an ambush: 15.377–8 *tum patriae tremuere manus, laxataque luctu / fluxerunt rigidis arma infelicia palmis.*

121. audita patria natisque et coniuge et armis: for comparable lists of conventional emotional attachments, see Ov. *Her.* 12.161–2 *deseror amissis regno patriaque domoque / coniuge,* Sen. *Tro.* 1170 *natam an nepotem, coniugem an patriam fleam?, Phoen.* 663 *patriam penates coniugem flammis dare?,* etc.

122. ac membra et sensus gelidus stupefecerat horror: "cold fear" descends from Hom. *Il.* 9.2 φόβου κρυόεντος, rendered in the Latin poets as *gelidus* and/ or *frigidus.* See 5.390–1 *gelidusque sub ossa / peruasit . . . horror,* 6.169–70 *tacitus penetrauit in artus / horror et occulto riguerunt frigore membra,* Lucr. *DRN* 6.1011 *frigidus horror,* Verg. *Aen.* 3.29–30 *mihi frigidus horror / membra quatit gelidusque coit formidine sanguis,* Ov. *Her.* 16.67 *gelidusque comas erexerat horror, Met.* 9.290–1 *frigidus artus . . . / horror habet,* Sen. *Tro.* 457 *gelidus horror,* etc.; *TLL* 6.2.1729.7.

For fear's stupefaction, see Verg. *Aen.* 5.643 *stupefactaque corda,* Livy 5.39.5 *stupefecit publicus pauor.* The Fury who attacks the Saguntines similarly leaves one of her victims *stupefactus membra* (*Pun.* 2.624; see my note). This Saguntine comes to his senses and throws away his ax before he kills his wife. In the present passage, the family violence occurs without the Fury's intervention and serves instead as a warning to the Romans to avoid battle at Cannae. *Sensus* and *stupefacere* do not appear together before Silius. Prudentius may accordingly adapt this line at *Psych.* 585 *mentis Auaritia stupefactis sensibus haesit.*

123–32. Satricus absolves his son and explains why he was running from the Carthaginian camp.

123. tum uox semanimi miseranda effunditur ore: McClellan 2021 notes the paradox of Satricus' ability to deliver a speech from "a half-dead mouth." The phrase *effundere uocem/s* originates at Enn. *Ann.* 553 Skutsch; see 3.696, 13.448

Commentary Line 124–6 133

with van der Keur's note, Verg. *Aen.* 5.482, etc.; *TLL* 5.2.223.77. The phrase *semanimi…ore* is an original collocation (García Amutxastegi *ad loc.*) modeled on phrases such as Enn. *Ann.* 484 Skutsch *semianimes…oculi*, Luc. *BC* 8.669–70 *uoltus / semianimis Magni*, etc. For a similar choice between the syncopated form *semanimi* Ch and *semianimi* ω, see 5.515 *semiusta* OV : *semusta alii*. For syncopated -i-, see also 2.681 *semambusta* with my note, 3.16 *semusta*. For unsyncopated choices, see Horsfall's note on Verg. *Aen.* 3.578 *semustum*.

124. parce, precor, dextrae, non ut mihi uita supersit: the pseudo-Senecan Hyllus uses similar language to forgive Deianira for her unwitting mistake of killing his father Hercules. She refuses to believe him, as Solymus refuses to believe in his father's forgiveness. She orders him instead to kill her as punishment and claims his hands will be blameless: [Sen.] *HO* 1001–2 *scelus remitto, dexterae parcent tuae / Eumenides ipsae*. The line opening *parce precor* is common: Tib. *Eleg.* 1.8.51, Ov. *Met.* 2.361, *Fasti* 2.451, etc.; it is found in other *sedes* at 17.286, Hor. *Carm.* 4.1.2, Sen. *HF* 1015, Luc. *BC* 6.773, etc. Lanzarone compares Luc. *BC* 7.729 *parcendum ferro manibusque* "per la costruzione di *parco*, nel senso di 'non adoperare', con sostantivi indicanti mezzi di offesa." The clausula is modeled on Verg. *Geo.* 3.10 *modo uita supersit* and used again at 15.607 *si uita supersit*.

125. quippe nefas hac uelle frui: Satricus does not explain why it would be *nefas* for him to want to live on. Possible reasons include, in descending order of plausibility:

(a) He does not wish to live on after the death of his son, like Mopsus, who kills himself after losing two sons at Saguntum; see 2.138–47 with my note.

(b) He regards himself as justly slain because he was "an enemy" (130 *Poenus eram*) at the time.

(c) He may think that he would have to fight his son if Solymus were not convinced of his identity.

Imilce uses similar phrasing in speaking of the proposed sacrifice of her child: 4.797 *aut si uelle nefas superos fixumque sedetque*.

125–6. sed sanguine nostro / ne damnes, o nate, manus: Satricus resumes his absolution of his son's hands at 150n. *absoluo pater ipse manum*. Despite Satricus' effort to absolve his hands, Solymus believes that his hands are already polluted with his father's blood and so death is the only option; see 169n. There is likely another evocation of the pseudo-Senecan Deianira (see 124n.). The Nurse asks her mistress: [Sen.] *HO* 909 *cur tuas damnas manus?* Like Silius' Solymus, Deianira is resolved on suicide; she replies: *HO* 910–11 *damnat meas deuictus Alcides manus: / placet scelus punire*. Seneca's Amphitryon similarly forgives his son Hercules' murderous hands: Sen. *HF* 1319 *hanc manum amplector libens*.

134   *Commentary Lines 126–131*

126–7. Carthaginis ille / captiuus, patrias nunc primum aduectus in oras:
Spaltenstein correctly observes that *ille* is not simply emphatic here but also
establishes a contrast with a prior state of being, as at 566n., 6.476–8 *fuit ille nec
umquam, / dum fuit, a duro cessauit munere Martis / Regulus*, 12.15–16 *sed non
ille uigor qui ruptis Alpibus arma / intulerat*, etc. Line 127 is adapted from Verg.
Aen. 3.108 *Teucrus Rhoeteas primum est aduectus in oras*. For variations on the
clausula, see 5.10 *aduexerat oras*, 17.158 *deuexerat oras*.

128. ille ego sum Satricus, Solymi genus: for the identification by name and
genus, see Verg. *Aen.* 1.378–80 *sum pius Aeneas…/ Italiam quaero patriam, et
genus ab Ioue summo*. Like Aeneas, Satricus exemplifies *pietas* in his forgiveness
of his son and was also in search of his home. For the line opening, see 15.59 *illa
ego sum*; for a similar introduction through ethnic affiliation, see 11.177 *ille ego
sanguis / Dardanius* (Decius Magius). The phrasing originates in the elegists:
Prop. 4.9.38, Tib. 1.6.31, Ov. *Met.* 4.226, *Fasti* 3.505, etc. Marks 2020 argues that:

> one might recognize the formula as Ovidian; for in pre-Silian Latin there are twenty-
> eight instances of the collocation *ille ego*…twenty-two of which are in Ovid, and of the
> twelve instances in which it is followed by the verb *sum*…nine appear in Ovid.

One such Ovidian example is particularly pertinent because of its reference to
Sulmo: Ov. *Trist.* 4.10.1–3 *ille ego, qui fuerim…/ Sulmo mihi patria est*. For
Solymi, see 70–6n.

128–9. haud tua, nate / fraus ulla est: for *fraus* as "crime" without the sense of
deception, see *TLL* 6.1.1269.22 ("laxiore sensu i. q. actio improba, scelesta, ini-
uria"). The Pseudo-Senecan Hyllus (see 124n.) similarly forgives Deianira with
the observation: [Sen.] *HO* 983 *error a culpa uacat*. This clausula is one of 63 in
the *Punica* of type 1+2+2, the so-called *si bona norint* pattern. They occur
roughly half as frequently (0.51%) as in Virgil (1.2%). See 151, 306, 335, 529, 600,
2.332 *non latet hostis* with my note, etc.; Arribas Hernáez 1990: 243.

129–30. iaceres in me cum feruidus hastam, / Poenus eram: Satricus excul-
pates his son by asserting that someone emerging from the direction of the
Carthaginian camp would likely be an enemy. Satricus' claim to be a pseudo-
Carthaginian recalls Fabius' earlier characterization of Varro as a consul for the
Carthaginians: 8.332–3 *consul datus alter, opinor, / Ausoniae est, alter Poenis*.
Silius employs the clausula again at 1.386 and 5.320; see also *Il. Lat.* 777, Coripp.
Ioh. 8.397. For variations, see 7.327 *feruidus ensem*.

130. uerum castris elapsus acerbis: a similar idea to 82n. *castris euadit iniquis*,
in an identical *sedes*. For similar phrasing, but a different context, see Stat. *Theb.*
8.173 *dilapsaque numina castris*.

131. ad uos et carae properabam coniugis ora: for Satricus' *coniunx* Acca, see
117–18n. For the conventional epithet *cara* or *carissima* applied to *coniunx*, see

Commentary Lines 132–6 135

TLL 4.343.71. For the clausula, see 17.334 *coniugis ora*, Ov. *Met.* 4.595; for other periphrases with *os*, see, 2.491, 4.139, Verg. *Aen.* 7.575; *TLL* 9.2.1088.12 ("de tota forma, figura").

132. hunc rapui exanimi clipeum: the uncommon adjective may recall 42n. *exanimata parens.* Satricus' words as he loses both his children and his own life evoke Paulus' grief for the loss of the Roman soldiers (his symbolic children) along with his own life.

132–6. Satricus gives his son his final instructions: bury his arms with his brother's corpse and warn Varro not to give battle.

132. sed iam unice nobis: the motif of "the one son left to me" recalls two earlier moments: when Imilce begs an absent Hannibal to save their *unica proles* from sacrifice (4.785–6); and when Marus returns Serranus to his mother Marcia and she observes: 6.580 *hunc certe mihi reddis.*

133. haec fratris tumulis arma excusata reporta: irony contributes to the scene's pathos: Solymus will not live to construct a tumulus for his brother. For *tumuli* used as a poetic plural for singular, see 13.462, Prop. 4.7.54, Mart. 9.30.5. For placing arms in a tumulus, see 2.675–6 *arma.../ imponit tumulo*, Verg. *Aen.* 11.6 *constituit tumulo fulgentiaque induit arma*, *Aen.* 11.592–3 *et arma / inspoliata feram tumulo patriaeque reponam*, etc. Spaltenstein is incorrect to cite 12.253 *reportans* as a parallel for a phrase where the destination does not yet exist. Pedianus successfully carries off Cinyps' helmet and has no specific destination in mind.

    Blass' conjecture *arma a me exuta* produces an inelegant series of synaloephae. As Van Veen observed, there is no need to emend *excusata*, nor was Bauer correct to associate *excusata* with 146 *telum excusare laborat.* In the present line, Satricus excuses himself for any injury to Mancinus' memory caused by dressing in his armor, while at 146 he forgives Solymus for throwing his spear in error.

134. curarum tibi prima tamen sit, nate: *curarum prima* is found only in poetry at 3.62 *curarum prima exercet subducere bello.* For *cura* + dative + infinitive, see *TLL* 4.1456.19.

134–5. referre / ductori monitus Paulo: *referre monitus* is a variation on the more common *referre dicta*: 11.600 *dicta referre*, Verg. *Aen.* 3.169–70 *longaeuo dicta parenti / haud dubitanda refer*, *Aen.* 10.491 *memores mea dicta referte*, Ov. *Met.* 9.581 *dicta refert*, etc. For *ductori*, see 24n.

135–6. producere bellum / nitatur: the phrase recalls Fabius' strategic skill: 1.681 *et melior clauso bellum producere ferro.* Here it would also be wiser for Varro to defer combat. Marks 2020 reads the initial N of *nitatur* as inaugurating the acrostic NASVS, formed from the initial letters of 136–40, and thus evoking the presence of Ovid (albeit very distantly).

136   *Commentary Lines 136–9*

136. Poenoque neget certamina Martis: Silius employs the clausula at 15.440, 15.823, 16.203; see also [Tib.] 3.7.98, Ov. *Met.* 8.20; it occurs in other *sedes* at *Pun.* 12.274, Verg. *Aen.* 12.73, 12.790. The phrase is a variation on the slightly more common *certamin* pugnae,* which occurs as a clausula at 370n. 12.297, 13.876, 17.546; Lucr. *DRN* 4.843, Verg. *Aen.* 11.780, Ov. *Met.* 12.180, *Il. Lat.* 562. Silius does not use *certamin* belli,* found at Lucr. *DRN* 1.475, 5.1296, Verg. *Aen.* 10.146, Stat. *Theb.* 5.690, etc.

Heinsius' suggestion *Marti* can be paralleled by 8.579 *exhaustae mox Poeno Marte Cerillae,* Luc. *BC* 3.350 *obsessum Poeno gessit quae Marte Saguntum.* But 12.274–5 *Martis certamine sisti / posse ducem Libyae* shows that Hannibal himself can be identified as separate from "Punic Mars," his troops. Leaving the text as is accordingly enables focus on the three commanders: Paulus (135), Hannibal (136 *Poeno*), and Varro (139).

137–41. Satricus explains that Varro should not give battle because divine augury supports Hannibal's eagerness for combat. It will be consolation enough for him to have warned his fellow Romans. Solymus preempts part of his father's consolation by proceeding to commit suicide, though he does write his warning for Varro in blood (173–7n.). In a further irony, Varro preempts consolation for both father and son, both by ignoring the warning and by refusing to believe in Solymus' guiltlessness (262–6n.).

137. augurio exsultat diuum: a recollection of Anna Perenna's inspiring prophecy to Hannibal, which he immediately conveyed to his troops (8.226–41). Hannibal's acquisition of valid, actionable information from the gods (who elsewhere typically deceive him) contrasts with Varro's contempt for the clear message sent by the negative omens; see 1–7n. For Anna's role at Cannae, see Marks 2013.

137–8. immensamque propinqua / stragem acie sperat: *propinqua…acie* recalls 50n. *uicinis aruis:* Hannibal and his forces are a menacing presence long before the battle commences. 278n. *propinquabant acies* is in a different sense: the armies draw closer in order to engage in combat.

138–9. quaeso, cohibete furentem / Varronem: for Varro's *furores,* see 59n. and Ariemma 2010: 247–8. For holding back madness or madmen, see 11.98 *impatiens ultra gemitu cohibere furorem,* Cic. *Phil.* 3.5 *nisi unus adulescens illius furentis impetus crudelissimosque conatus cohibuisset, rem publicam funditus interituram fuisse.*

139. namque hunc fama est impellere signa: it might seem implausible that Satricus, an escaped prisoner of war who has not yet returned to the Roman lines, should have such good information about the politics of the Roman camp. Livy reports, however that Hannibal knew everything about the discord between the Roman consuls: Livy 22.41.5 *et omnia ei hostium haud secus quam*

Commentary Lines 140–3   137

sua nota erant: dissimiles discordesque imperitare. The phrase *fama est* introduces indirect discourse at 12.126, 12.365, 13.86, 14.21, Verg. *Aen.* 3.578, etc. The collocation *impellere signa* is unique. Possible inspiration may have come from phrases such as Verg. *Aen.* 8.3 *impulit arma,* Luc. *BC* 5.41 *tollite signa, duces, fatorum impellite cursum, BC* 5.757 *impulerint acies,* etc.

140–1. sat magnum hoc miserae fuerit mihi cardine uitae / solamen: *magnum . . . solamen* ironizes the typical consolation for epic death, falling to a great warrior in battle (on which, see 426n.); the present situation is entirely the opposite.

The phrasing evokes Pompey's argument that dying in far-off lands will at least bring the consolation that his son-in-law Caesar will not touch his corpse, for good or ill: Luc. *BC* 8.314–16 *sat magna feram solacia mortis / orbe iacens alio, nihil haec in membra cruente, / nil socerum fecisse pie.* The recollection of Pompey's self-consolation emphasizes the differences of Satricus' fate: he is close to home, and he has been killed by a loving son rather than a hostile son-in-law. The phrase *sat magnus/a* is rare in poetry (Prop. 2.7.16, 2.13.25, Luc. *BC* 5.660, 8.314, VF *Arg.* 6.548); *satis* is more common. Silius uses the phrase six times in total (193n., 5.118, 6.122, 6.343, 10.366). The use of the rare form implies that Pompey is being alluded to here and that Silius elsewhere adapts a phrase that Lucan had taken from elegy and licensed for historical epic.

Cardine uitae is a unique phrase, perhaps modeled on phrases such as Luc. *BC* 7.381 *turpes extremi cardinis annos.* See Lanzarone's note for the astrological background of the image.

141. cauisse meis: Satricus speaks as if the Roman forces were family. As Paulus dies at Cannae, he similarly instructs Lentulus not to rescue him but to send a warning, in this case to close Rome's gates against Hannibal (10.281).

141–3. Satricus desires to embrace his son before dying and thereby allow Solymus to perform the child's duty of catching the parent's last breath; see Austin's note on Verg. *Aen.* 4.684–5. Enjambement at the end of a long speech provides emphasis to the concluding word *oscula,* which adds emotional force to the father's forgiveness of his son.

141–3. nunc ultima, nate, / inuento simul atque amisso redde parenti / oscula: Bruère 1959: 231 compares Thisbe's use of the "found and lost once more" motif upon discovering Pyramus' suicide: Ov. *Met.* 4.156–7 *quos certus amor, quos hora nouissima iunxit, / conponi tumulo non inuideatis eodem.* Spaltenstein adds Daedalus' loss of Icarus: Ov. *Met.* 8.231 *at pater infelix, nec iam pater.* Seneca appears to have originated the collocation *ultima oscula* at *Marc.* 3.2 *non licuerat matri ultima filii oscula gratumque extremi sermonem oris haurire,* a variation on phrases such as *ultimus amplexus,* which he uses in his tragedies (*Tro.* 761, *Med.* 552, 848). The phrase then appears in each of the Flavian poets: VF *Arg.* 4.373 *ultima tum patriae cedens dedit oscula ripae, Arg.* 8.6 *ultima*

138 *Commentary Lines 143–6*

uirgineis tunc flens dedit oscula uittis, Stat. *Theb.* 12.417–18 *ignem miserae post ultima quaerunt / oscula.*

The extreme hyperbaton and enjambement heavily emphasize *oscula,* as the reader is kept wondering what final gift the father wishes from his son; see Introduction, section 5c. The infrequent phrase *reddere oscula* may recall Seneca's Andromache instructing her doomed son Astyanax: *Tro.* 808–9 *sume quae reddas tuo / oscula parenti.* The collocation occurs elsewhere only at Ov. *Met.* 10.256 *oscula dat reddique putat,* Pliny *Pan.* 24.2 *nec osculum manu reddis,* Drac. *Orest.* 246; *TLL* 11.2.491.69.

143–6. Satricus removes his helmet and attempts to embrace his astonished son. He sees that he must speak further in order to convince Solymus of his guiltlessness.

143–4. sic fatus galeam exuit atque rigentis / inuadit nati tremebundis colla lacertis: Solymus is frozen (*rigentis*) with fear, as his father was at 122n. *Inuadere colla* appears earlier only at Cic. *Phil.* 2.77 *in collum inuasit* (see Ramsey's note), quoted at Gell. *NA* 6.11.6; see also Petr. *Sat.* 20.8 *ceruicem eius inuasit.* The phrase's mixture of violence and tenderness is characteristic of this episode. Trembling is a typical attribute of aged characters in Latin epic; see *Pun.* 2.648 with my note, 11.330, etc., and Ripoll 2003. Lyne's note on [Verg.] *Ciris* 256 observes that Silius' eight uses of *tremebundus* are far more frequent than other poets', e.g., Verg. once, Ov. once, VF twice, Stat. three times. For Silius' use of adjectives in –*bundus,* see Pianezzola 1965.

145. attonitoque timens uerbis sanare pudorem: *attonito* recalls *rigentis* two lines earlier. For *sanare* through language, see [Caes.] *BG* 8.38.2 *animos consolatione sanat,* Sen. *Contr.* 2.3.14 *demens uideor qui uno uerbo sanari possum?,* Sen. *Ira* 1.16.2 *tu longius iam processisti quam ut possis uerbis sanari.*

This line has attracted numerous efforts at emendation, as *timens* appeared to some editors to suggest that the father is afraid to relieve his son's *pudor* but then works hard to do so in the next line. Along with earlier editors, for example, Summers 1900: 305 thought that "the words *timens . . . sanare pudorem . . .* suit so ill" *telum excusare laborat.* He suggested *mentis* for *timens* on palaeographical grounds, as *mētis* could easily be read as *mens.* Blomgren 1938: 25 provided the most straightforward explication of the paradosis without recourse to emendation. He observed that *laborat* governs both the infinitives *sanare* and *excusare,* while *timens* governs the dative *attonito.* The principal caesura further helps to demarcate *attonitoque timens* as a syntactic unit. Duff's translation illustrates this interpretation, which I have followed. Examples of verbs of fearing with the dative include 2.31 *portisque focisque timebis,* 7.721 *sibimet metuens,* 9.439 *Mauors Scipiadae metuens, Tritonia Poeno,* etc.

146. uulneris impressi <et> telum excusare laborat: Satricus excuses his son's weapon and then follows up in 150 by absolving the hand that threw it. For

Commentary Lines 147–9 139

uulneris impressi, see 1.550 *impressum coniecta cuspide uulnus*, [Sen.] *HO* 1626 *multo uulnere impresso*, Pliny *Pan.* 6.1; for application to the weapon, see Sen. *Thy.* 1057 *ferro uulnera impresso dedi*. Lefebvre supplied the necessary *et*. Though providing the correct interpretation of the preceding line, Blomgren 1938: 26–8 argues that asyndeton is preferable here and provides several examples of asyndeton in Silius.

147–8. Satricus attempts to reassure Solymus that no one saw his error. Solymus will counter that the moon was his witness (169n.).

147. quis testis nostris, quis conscius adfuit actis?: the pair of questions recalls the procedure of the Roman law court. For the kinds of question that an advocate might ask about witnesses, see Quint. *Inst.* 7.2.54 *adulterium obicis: 'quis testis? quis index?'. <proditionem>: 'quod pretium? quis conscius?'* The phrasing adapts Stat. *Theb.* 3.175–6 *qui conscius actis / noctis*, similarly of a grisly series of murders. For an earlier adaptation of the witness motif to epic, see the Ovidian Ajax's dismissal of Ulixes' night raid in the *iudicium armorum*: Ov. *Met.* 13.15 *quae sine teste gerit, quorum nox conscia sola est*. The distribution of *nostris . . . actis* as the conclusion to each question creates an elegant symmetry. The question *quis testis* typically appears in the context of witnessing crime: Cic. *Rab.* 10 *num quis testis Postumum appellauit?*, Sen. *Contr.* 7.1.23, Sen. *Phaed.* 724 *secreta cum sit culpa, quis testis sciet?*, etc.

148. non nox errorem nigranti condidit umbra?: Satricus earlier called on the night to aid his escape from the Carthaginian camp (81–2n.); here he appeals to it to persuade his son of his guiltlessness. For night burying objects in shadow, see 12.613 *et terras caeco nox condit amictu*, 13.254 *et ni caeca sinu terras nox conderet atro*, Luc. *BC* 4.472–3 *nam condidit umbra / nox lucem dubiam*, etc. For Solymus' action as an *error* rather than a crime, see 66n. For *nigrans umbra*, see 12.122, 12.647. The participle *nigrans* typically replaces other adjectives for "dark" in epic (e.g., 7.690, 12.620, *OLD* s.v.); see Horsfall's note on Verg. *Aen.* 6.243. Silius uses it far more frequently (nineteen times) than the other epic poets (Verg. five times, Ov. one time, Luc. zero times, VF two times, Stat. eight times).

149–51. Satricus urges his son to abandon his fear and shame, embrace him, and perform a final act of *pietas* by closing his eyes in death. His words to his son replay Aeneas' words to his father Anchises in the Underworld: Verg. *Aen.* 6.697–8 *da iungere dextram, / da, genitor, teque amplexu ne subtrahe nostro*. See Wills 1996: 93 on the significance of repeated *da*. The evocation of this famous demonstration of filial *pietas* emphasizes Satricus' forgiveness of his son's error. The roles of son and father continue to be switched at 157–60n., where Solymus' despairing plea to his father evokes Anchises' speech to Aeneas.

149. cur trepidas? da, nate, magis, da iungere pectus: Silius uses repeated *da* elsewhere in prayer contexts: 7.217 *da famae, da, Musa, uirum*, 12.643–4 *da*,

140   *Commentary Lines 150–2*

summe deorum, / da, pater. For *magis* with imperatives, see Stat. *Theb.* 4. 543–4 *Argolicas magis huc appelle precando / Thebanasque animas.* For *magis* in the sense of "rather, instead," see *OLD* s.v. 6.

In place of *magis,* Schrader proposed *genas,* modeled on the similar context of VF *Arg.* 3.309–10 *fas tamen est conferre genas, fas iungere tecum / pectora et exsangues miscere amplexibus artus.* Jason embraces the corpse of his former host Cyzicus, whose people the Argonauts unwittingly destroyed in the night-time battle. Repetition of *fas* further recalls the Virgilian encounter between Aeneas and Anchises. D. Heinsius corrected to *manus* in order to create a closer parallelism with *pectus,* but N. Heinsius observed that *manum* appears in the subsequent line. The example of Verg. *Aen.* 6.697–8 (quoted at 149–51n. above) supports *manus / manum.*

150–1. Satricus forgives Solymus' guiltless hand and begs his son to use it to close his eyes. Two first-person verb forms (*absoluo, precor*) and two references to his son's hand (*manum, dextra*) enclose the father's prayer in chiasmus.

150. absoluo pater ipse manum: a recapitulation of 126n. *ne damnes, o nate, manus,* where, see further on the motif of the bloodstained hand.

150. atque in fine laborum: for human life as *labor,* see 13.519–20 *quando uitae tibi causa labores / humanos iuuisse fuit* (Scipio to the Sibyl), Hor. *Serm.*1.9.59–60 *nil sine magno / uita labore dedit mortalibus,* Verg. *Aen.* 5.688–9 *si quid pietas antiqua labores / respicit humanos,* etc. For the tradition of death as the end of labors, see Cic. *Tusc.* 1.115 (= *frg. poet.* 37, Eur. frg. 449) *quí labores mórte finissét grauis,* etc. In the tragic manner, Silius often refers to life as suffering to be ended. See, for example, 1.85 *curis mortalibus* (Dido's suicide), 11.186–8 (Decius on the advantages of suicide), 13.263 *pulsis uiuendi e pectore curis* (Virrius' preparation for suicide), etc.

151. hac condas oculos dextra, precor: for closing a dead loved one's eyes, see Sen. *Contr.* 9.4.5 *oculos meos fili manus operiant,* Ov. *Trist.* 4.3.43–4 *supremoque die notum spectantia caelum / texissent digiti lumina nostra tui,* Luc. *BC* 3.739–40 *tacito tantum petit oscula uoltu / inuitatque patris claudenda ad lumina dextram,* Pliny *NH* 11.150, etc. *Hac* emphasizes Satricus' forgiveness of his son: he wants the same hand that killed him to close his eyes. 10.58 *hanc … animam* and 15.362–3 *his, / his umeris* offer similar example of emphasis "de secunda persona"; see *TLL* 6.3.2704.35.

151–5. Solymus ignores his father's fatalism and frantically tries to bandage the mortal wound that he inflicted. He delays speaking in order to concentrate on his work before breaking out in lamentation. See 166–7n.

151–2. at miser imo / pectore suspirans iuuenis: see 128n. for the 1+2+2 clausula of 151. The phrasing is modeled on Verg. *Aen.* 1.371 *suspirans imoque trahens a pectore uocem,* also of a son interacting with a parent of whose identity

Commentary Lines 152–6   141

he was initially ignorant, and Ov. *Met.* 2.655–6 *suspirat ab imis / pectoribus*, etc. Silius employs similar phrasing at *Pun.* 4.777 *et inclusum suspirat pectore Bacchum*. For recapitulation of Verg. *Aen.* 11.377 *dat gemitum rumpitque has imo pectore uoces*, see 156n.

152–3. non uerba uicesque / alloquio uocemue refert: alliteration of V-emphasizes the repetition of words referring to conversation. For Silius' repetitive style, see Introduction, section 5b. For *uices* of conversation, see Verg. *Aen.* 6.535 *hac uice sermonum*, Ov. *Her.* 21.18 *colloquii… uices*, VF *Arg.* 2.664–5 *hasque inter uariis nox plurima dictis / rapta uices*, etc.; see also 15.283 *haec atque his paria alterno sermone serebant*. Spaltenstein is incorrect to state "nous n'avons pas de parallèle en prose": cf. Livy 9.3.4 *his in uicem sermonibus*, Apul. *Met.* 3.19.1 *ad haec dicta sermonis uicem refero*.

153–4. sed sanguinis atri / sistere festinat cursum: *ater* is a conventional epithet for blood; see Introduction, section 5b for contrast with *niger*. For application to *sanguis*, see 173–4n., 399–400n., 8.644, 13.566, 15.364–5, Enn. *Trag.* 297, Verg. *Aen.* 3.28 with Horsfall's note, 3.622, Livy 38.21.9, Ov. *Met.* 12.256, VF *Arg.* 6.708, Stat. *Theb.* 6.211–12, etc. For application to *cruor*, see 10.510, Verg. *Aen.* 4.687, 9.33, 11.646, Hor. *Epod.* 17.31–2, Stat. *Theb.* 8.711. Stat. *Silv.* 3.4.24–5 *festinantia sistens / fata salutifero mitis deus incubat angui* also uses the oxymoronic collocation *sistere festinare* in the context of healing. No other classical poet uses *cursus* as the technical term for blood flow; see Sen. *Ira* 3.9.4, Cels. *Med.* 2.1.19, 4.2.2 *sanguinis ex naribus cursus*, 5.26.22, [Quint.] *DM* 8.16.

154–5. laceroque ligare / ocius illacrimans altum uelamine uulnus: note the run of L- sounds. Bruère 1959: 231–2 compares Ovid's Cephalus and Procris story, which features a similar attempt by the killer to bandage the fatal spear wound that he inflicted on his loved one: Ov. *Met.* 7.848–9 *scissaque a pectore ueste / uulnera saeua ligo conorque inhibere cruorem*. Virgil's Anna similarly attempts to staunch her dying sister's blood: Verg. *Aen.* 4.687 *atros siccabat ueste cruores*. Memory of the failure of these earlier efforts adds to the pathos of Solymus' present endeavor.

156. tandem inter gemitus miserae erupere querelae: Statius' Creon displays similar reactions as he buries his son Menoeceus: Stat. *Theb.* 12.71 *et gemitus tandem erupere paterni*. For the additional emphasis of *tandem*, see VF *Arg.* 3.509 *ingemuit Iuno tandemque silentia rumpit*. All three Flavian passages are likely adaptations of Virgil's Sinon episode (Verg. *Aen.* 2.128–9 *uix tandem… / composito rumpit uocem*). as *tandem rumpere* does not otherwise occur in poetry in the context of breaking into speech. For *rumpere* of breaking into speech or tears, see 4.728 *ac rumpit ducis haud spernenda uoce quietem*, 8.299 *inuitus uocem hanc e pectore rumpam*, Verg. *Aen.* 3.246 *rumpitque hanc pectore uocem*, 11.377 (on which, see 151–2n.), etc. *Miserae… querelae* are Ovidian: Ov. *Met.* 2.342, *Fasti* 4.481.

142   *Commentary Lines 157–60*

157–60. Solymus' speech evokes Anchises' welcome of Aeneas in the Underworld: Verg. *Aen.* 6.687–8 *uenisti tandem, tuaque exspectata parenti / uicit iter durum pietas?* See 149n. for the allusion to the Underworld scene and the inversion of the roles of father and son. Solymus' words also echo Catullus' lament for his brother (Catul. 68.92–3 *ei misero frater adempte mihi, / ei misero fratri iucundum lumen ademptum*), especially in the noun shift of 158.

157–8. sicine te nobis, genitor, Fortuna reducit / in patriam?: the clausula may be a topical evocation of Domitian's temple of *Fortuna Redux*, built soon after the emperor's return from the Sarmatian campaign in 93. See Mart. 8.65 with Schöffel 2002 and Claud. *VI Cos. Hon.* 1 with Dewar's note. For returning to the *patria*, see 6.621 *gaudebat reducem patriae adnumerare reuersus* (Fabius rejoices that he has brought his men back alive), Livy 22.60.13 *reduces in patriam ad parentes, ad coniuges ac liberos facit* (Torquatus' rebuke of the soldiers for not rescuing themselves at Cannae).

158–9. sic te nato natumque parenti / impia restituit?: Wills 1996: 278 lists the repetition *nato natumque* as an example of a noun shift with variation comparable to Catul. 68.92–3 (quoted at 157–60n. above), Luc. *BC* 5.14 *non Magni partes sed Magnum in partibus esse*, etc.; see Introduction, section 5c. Silius is the only author to call Fortune *impia*, though note Val. Max. 9.11.*ext.* 1 *impietas fortunae*. For Silius' other negative epithets for Fortune, see 9n. 157 *reducit ...* 159 *restituit* is characteristic of Silius' repetitive style.

159–60. felix o terque quaterque / frater: Solymus' words adapt the laments of two Virgilian fathers:

  (a) Aeneas' lament during the storm: *Aen.* 1.94–6 *o terque quaterque beati, / quis ante ora patrum Troiae sub moenibus altis / contigit oppetere!* Aeneas claims that Trojans who died in view of their fathers were thrice and four times luckier than a man like him who will die unknown at sea. Like the Trojans whom Aeneas envies, Solymus will die in his father's presence.

  (b) Evander's lament for his son Pallas: *Aen.* 11.158–9 *tuque, o sanctissima coniunx, / felix morte tua neque in hunc seruata dolorem!* Evander's wife was lucky to die before her son and so be spared from his present grief. Like Evander, Solymus praises his brother Mancinus' fortunate ignorance. He did not know either how his father died or about his brother's guilt.

160. cui fatis genitorem agnoscere ademptum: *agnoscere* and 162 *cognosco* create a paradoxical turn on Roman parents' choice to recognize children as their own. For use in this context, see Sen. *Contr.* 2.4.2, Val. Max. 9.15.3, Suet. *Claud.* 15.2, etc.; Shaw 2001. Silius offers a tragic inversion of the typical situation of father recognizing son. One son was deprived of the opportunity to recognize his returned father, and the other regrets that he has done so while murdering

Commentary Lines 161–5   143

him. Similar language appears in Tacitus' account of the murder of Julius Mansuetus: *Hist*. 3.25 *agnitus agnoscensque et exsanguem amplexus*; see Introduction, section 3b. See also Stat. *Theb*. 7.354 *Iphitus asper agit, genitor cui nuper ademptus*. *Adimere* with an infinitive is an infrequent construction; see 425–6n., Hor. *Epist*. 1.19.9 *adimam cantare*, Ov. *Pont*. 1.7.47, *TLL* 1.685.29.

161–2. ast ego, Sidoniis imperditus, ecce, parentem / uulnere cognosco: recognizing a long-absent warrior through his wound may distantly evoke Eurycleia's recognition of Odysseus (Hom. *Od*. 19.361–475), though the context is necessarily quite different. Both *Sidoniis imperditus* and 10.416 *imperdita corpora Poenis* are modeled on Verg. *Aen*. 10.430 *o Grais imperdita corpora*; see also Statius' adaptation at *Theb*. 3.84–5 *imperdita Tydeo / pectora*. The Virgilian allusion certifies *imperditus* and makes *impercitus* ΓQ *edd. a* p highly unlikely. This variant would also represent the only occurrence of *impercitus* since Plautus (*Cas*. 833, *Amph*. 500). For *cognoscere* + ablative, see *TLL* 3.1512.41.

162–3. saltem hoc, Fortuna, fuisset / solamen culpae: *saltem…fuisset* may evoke Verg. *Aen*. 4.327–8 *saltem si qua mihi de te suscepta fuisset / ante fugam suboles*, where Dido similarly looks for a consolation for her loss of Aeneas. Like Dido, Solymus does not receive the consolation he desires and so proceeds to commit suicide.

163–4. dubia ut mihi signa dedisses / infausti generis: Solymus would rather be an illegitimate child and have a reason to live than be his father's legitimate son and thus condemn himself to die. For the theme of the extinction of a household line, see Introduction, section 3b. Reference to the *signa generis* may evoke an inversion of Aegeus' recognition of Theseus: Ov. *Met*. 7.422–3 *cum pater in capulo gladii cognouit eburno / signa sui generis facinusque excussit ab ore*. Recognition *by* his father saves Theseus' life; by contrast, recognition *of* his father condemns Solymus to suicide. There may be a further evocation of Seneca's *Thyestes*, in which Atreus initially doubts his sons' legitimacy (*Thy*. 240 *dubius sanguis*) and then satisfies himself of it through his crime (*Thy*. 1098–9 *liberos nasci mihi / nunc credo*). Solymus cannot avoid either recognition of his legitimacy as his victim's son or his responsibility for killing his father. The phrasing may also recall Statius' Polynices and Eteocles; Adrastus regards their short tempers that lead to their brawl on his doorstep as the *signa* of their distinguished ancestry: Stat. *Theb*. 1.445–6 *haud humiles tanta ira docet, generisque superbi / magna per effusum clarescunt signa cruorem*. For the conditional use of *ut* meaning "provided that," see L&S s.v. *ut* II.C.4.e.

164–5. uerum linquetur iniquis / non ultra superis nostros celare labores: Solymus indirectly announces his plans to convert his misfortune into a warning for Varro; see 253n. For impersonal passive *linquere* governing an infinitive, see 4.626 *et uix cernere linquitur undas*; with *ut*, Lucr. *DRN* 2.914, 5.795; *TLL* 7.2.1462.48. *Iniquis…superis* recapitulates 157–9 *Fortuna…impia*. For the

144 *Commentary Line 166*

gods' proverbial unfairness, see, e.g., Verg. *Aen.* 2.257 *fatisque deum defensus iniquis,* Prop. 2.18.13, Ov. *Met.* 10.611, *Fasti* 5.299, *Trist.* 3.2.27 *di, quos experior nimium constanter iniquos.* Solymus' reference to *labores* echoes Satricus' reference to his own death as the end of labors; see 150n. Now the suffering that they have undergone will become known to all.

Celare Cm has attracted efforts at emendation. This reading supports the theme of concealment that has run throughout the episode (81–2n., 95n., 98–9n., 105n., 148n.). Solymus proposes to turn from the night's concealment to converting their deaths into a public spectacle in the (unachieved) hope of deterring Varro from combat. Summers proposed *scelerare,* which could have become corrupted to *celare.* This would lay the blame for the current situation more fully on malevolent gods, but reference to their conscious intervention has, in fact, been conspicuously absent throughout the episode; *iniquis... superis* refers to life's general unfairness. Accordingly, Delz pointed to 147 and 163 as evidence that the gods were not conscious witnesses of the bloodshed.

Frassinetti 1989: 149 offered a series of suggestions: *temerare, cumulare, iterare.* None of these is particularly convincing. *Temerare* is similar to Summers' *scelerare.* With regard to the last two, Solymus has not suggested that he is a man of constant sorrow, rather that the one misfortune of losing his father has been more than enough. Kyle Gervais (*per litteras*) notes that of these suggestions, *cumulare* is most attractive, as it could have become corrupted to *celare.*

Zaia *ad loc.* supports *tol(l)erare* b1b2, as the gods' frustration with human criminality is a common topic. *Tolerare labores* is a frequent collocation, and it occurs as a clausula at Ov. *Met.* 9.289, 15.121, Luc. *BC* 9.588, 9.881; see also *tolerate labores* at Cic. *Carm.* 23.1 Blänsdorf, and Ov. *AA* 2.669. Delz's response to Summers also applies here: the gods have been unfair, but they have not witnessed or intervened. *Tol(l)erare* may also have been influenced by 168 *attollens.*

166–7. Satricus dies amid his son's laments. Bruère 1959: 232 compares the expiration of Ovid's Procris: *Met.* 7. 859–61 *paruae fugiunt cum sanguine uires / dumque aliquid spectare potest, me spectat et in me / infelicem animam nostroque exhalat in ore.* See 153–5n. Silius employs similar phrasing at 10.455–6 *seminecem extremo uitam exhalabat in auras / murmure deficiens iam Cloelius.* Both passages of Silius adapt Verg. *Aen.* 11.617 *uitam dispergit in auras,* modeled in turn on Lucr. *DRN* 3.544 *(anima) dispersa per auras.*

166. haec dum amens queritur, iam deficiente cruore: for death from blood loss, see Ov. *Met.* 5.96 *sanguine defectos cecidit conlapsus in artus;* for *deficere* of death more generally, see also 10.455–6 (quoted at 166–7n. above), Lucr. *DRN* 5.887 *membraque deficiunt fugienti languida uita,* VF *Arg.* 3.179–80 *iam candor et anni / deficiunt uitaque fugit decus omne soluta,* etc. A declamatory passage that also involves the context of parricide, [Quint.] *DM* 1.11.5 *nec cruor ante deficit?,* may be a reminiscence of this scene.

Commentary Lines 167–70 145

167. in uacuas senior uitam disperserat auras: the phrasing is modeled on Verg. *Aen.* 11.617 *uitam dispergit in auras.* For variations on the common motif of the dying soul dispersing into the air, see 5.642–3 *moriens fugiente per auras / hac anima,* 6.39–40 *supremus fessi tenuis tum cessit in auras / halitus,* 10.577 *aetherias anima exultans euasit in auras,* etc. *Vacuus* is a typical epithet for air: Verg. *Geo.* 3.109 *aera per uacuum, Aen.* 12.592 *uacuas it fumus ad auras,* Ov. *Met.* 6.398, 12.469, 15.220, etc. See Introduction, section 5b for the contrast of *senior* with *senex.* See Ripoll 2003 on elderly figures in Flavian epic. For the clausula, see, e.g., 5.456 *dispersit in auras,* Lucr. *DRN* 3.544 *dispersa per auras,* Verg. *Aen.* 11.795 *dispersit in auras,* etc.

168–72. Solymus resolves to die in order to expiate his guilt and remove his pollution from the gods' sight. His address to the moon is a further inversion of Virgil's Nisus and Euryalus scene. Virgil's Nisus prays to the moon as a *dea praesens* to guide his spear and help him avenge Euryalus (*Aen.* 9.404–9); Solymus blames the moon for guiding the spear which killed his father.

168. tum iuuenis maestum attollens ad sidera uultum: the introduction to Solymus' speech evokes an earlier moment when Serranus, another dutiful son who has lost his father, addresses the gods: 6.101 *hic iuuenis maestos tollens ad sidera uultus;* see also 6.466 *tum palmas simul attollens ac lumina caelo.* The repetition points to the meaningful opposition between the two moments: Serranus celebrates his father's *exemplum* and is restored to his mother, while Solymus kills his father and then himself. The second half of the line is common: Ov. *Met.* 1.731, *Fasti* 2.75, Stat. *Theb.* 9.453, varied at *Pun.* 12.319 *tollebat ad aethera uultus.*

169. pollutae dextrae: Solymus' view of his hands and his deed recalls the narrator's introduction to the episode (66n. *sceleratus polluit error*) and looks forward to Varro's verdict (264n. *manus... caede imbuta nefanda*). In formal terms, the killer's address to his own hands recalls Seneca's Hercules at the similar moment when he realizes he has murdered his family: Sen. *HF* 1236 *o nouercales manus,* 1281 *agedum, dextra.* For the Senecan theme of self-apostrophe, see Star 2006. Silius likely plays on the contrast of the two murderers' situations: Amphitryon can slowly talk Hercules down from suicide through the fifth act of *Hercules Furens,* but Satricus dies before he is able to persuade Solymus.

169–70. et facti Titania testis / infandi: Solymus' indication of the moon as the witness of his crime provides a response to his father's question *quis testis?* (147n.). For *Titania* in reference to the moon or Diana, see 10.538, Ov. *Met.* 3.173, Stat. *Theb.* 1.337 *Titanis,* etc. For the gods as *testes* of deeds, see 15.112 *testes factorum stare arbitrabere diuos.* The narrator shortly after refers to the *conscia nox* (180n.) that observed Solymus' parricide.

146 *Commentary Lines 170–4*

170–1. quae nocturno mea lumine tela / derigis in patrium corpus: Solymus blames the moon for providing the light that enabled him to strike his father; see 108n. *luna prodente.* Dominik 2018 suggests an evocation of Thyestes' consumption of his children (Sen. *Thy.* 795 *nocturna…lumina*), but the collocation is quite frequent. *Tela derigis* may be a conscious echo of the prayer of Virgil's Nisus *rege tela* (*Aen.* 9.409). *Derigis* is present for perfect in order to indicate a continuing state, as at 2.142 *concidis*, 13.365 *dat*, 14.172 *das*, 16.464 *dat*, 17.37 *creas*, 17.295 *portas*; see Spaltenstein's note on 2.142 and Roosjen 1996 on 14.171–2. The same choice between the manuscript alternatives *derig-* and *dirig-* occurs at 2.92.

171–2. 'non amplius' inquit / 'his oculis et damnato uiolabere uisu': Solymus draws on the commonplace that eyes that have witnessed crimes become culpable and polluting, even if they do not belong to consciously guilty parties. Lucan's Sextus says to his brother Gnaeus after their father Pompey's murder at Luc. *BC* 9.127–8, *oculos, germane, nocentis / spectato genitore fero.* Seneca's Messenger reports Oedipus as saying as he blinds himself at Sen. *Oed.* 976–7, *iam iusta feci, debitas poenas tuli; / inuenta thalamis digna nox tandem meis.*

173–7. Solymus stabs himself and uses his own blood to inscribe the warning to Varro to avoid combat, as his father had requested. For the motif, see the story of Othryades, the Spartan general who reputedly used his own blood to sign a trophy Διὶ τροπαιούχῳ: Sen. *Suas.* 2.16, Val. Max. 3.2.*ext.* 4, Plut. *Mor.* 306b, Ampelius 14.4. By making his Solymus write a warning, however, Silius reverses the goal of Othryades' exploit. Marks 2010c: 132 associates both this completed suicide and Varro's suicide wish (649–51n.) with the civil war themes of books 4–10, "all signs of a city collapsing in on itself."

173. haec memorat, simul ense fodit praecordia: Silius employs the speech formula again at 217n. Heinsius suggested *memorans* to match the Virgilian formula (*Aen.* 5.641, 5.743, 10.680), but the three verbs in two lines suggest the rapidity of Solymus' action. *Praecordia* is a unique variation on the expected *uiscera* or *ilia*. See, e.g., 5.255–6 *subsidensque ilia nisu / conantis suspensa fodit* (Lentulus kills Syrticus), 6.544 *fodiunt ad uiscera corpus* (the death of Regulus), Ov. *Ibis* 625, Luc. *BC* 4.511 *cum calido fodiemus uiscera ferro* (the Opitergian suicide), *BC* 7.309 (Caesar's suicide threat), etc.

173–4. et atrum / sustentans uulnus mananti sanguine signat: the wound is "dark," as blood is conventionally *ater* (153n.). *Sustentans* adds a gruesome physical detail: Solymus is obliged to hold up his intestines as he writes his message. Haymitch in *The Hunger Games: Catching Fire* does the same in order to survive a duel to the death; Collins 2009: 201. Albanus cannot do the same at 4.383–4 and so his guts spill out and fill up his shield. The motif can also be found in Plutarch's account of Cato the Younger's suicide (*Cato Minor* 70.6).

Spaltenstein correctly observes that Ruperti's references to Ov. *Her.* 1.114 and VF *Arg.* 6.276 are not relevant to the present context, as both are figurative rather than concrete uses of *sustentare*. *Signare* recalls Aeneas' inscription on the shield he took from Abas: *Aen.* 3.287 *rem carmine signo*. Instead of commemorating a defeat that has already occurred, Solymus uses his inscription in an attempt to prevent the upcoming defeat. "Signing in blood" derives from Ovid's various descriptions of metamorphosed birds: *AA* 2.384 *signatum sanguine pectus*, *Met.* 6.670 *signataque sanguine pluma*, *Met.* 12.125 *signatum sanguine Cycnum*.

175. in clipeo mandata patris FVGE PROELIA VARRO: Solymus follows one of his father's instructions (to warn Varro) but not the other (to stay alive). The phrase *mandata patris* recalls Verg. *Aen.* 9.312 *multa patri mandata dabat portanda*, Ascanius' attempt to bear a message to his father through Nisus and Euryalus. There may also be an evocation of Sen. *Phoen.* 36 *perage mandatum patris*, where Oedipus, another parricide, similarly seeks death. Numerous allusions throughout this scene have reinforced its tragic theme of inadvertent violence against family members prompted by divine hostility.

Varro responds to Solymus' warning in a different sense: he flees from the battle once it has been lost, and his cowardly flight becomes a rhetorical focal point for Rome's enemies. Like Solymus, he also contemplates suicide as he flees from the battlefield; see 649–50n. See also 426–7n.

The order to flee the battle evokes Lucan's Pharsalus episode. Dominik 2006: 125 compares Solymus' inscription to the narrator's admonition to Pompey at Luc. *BC* 7.689 *fuge proelia dira*, as well as Palaemon's warning to Adrastus at Stat. *Theb.* 8.138 *uerte gradum, fuge rector*. Tipping 2010: 366 compares the narrator's self-exhortation (which, like the narrators of Lucan and Statius, he subsequently ignores) to forgo narration of the battle: Luc. *BC* 7.552 *hanc fuge, mens, partem belli tenebrisque relinque*.

176. ac summi tegimen suspendit cuspide teli: *tegimen* is a common metonymy for pieces of armor such as helmets and shields: see Verg. *Aen.* 7.632 with Horsfall's note. Silius uses the syncopated forms of *teg(i)men* twenty-six times versus unsyncopated *tegimen* eight times, occupying the fifth foot in all but three instances. For items of armor hanging from spears, see 7.295 *et dira e summa pendebat cuspide cassis*. The pleonasm created by *summi...teli* and *cuspide* is characteristic: see 5.488 *summi fastigia montis*, 12.625, 6.644 *summi qua uertice montis*, 7.295, Verg. *Aen.* 2.458 *summi fastigia culminis*, Stat. *Theb.* 8.496 *summa...in cuspide*, etc.

177. defletumque super prosternit membra parentem: *defletum* reflects Solymus' grief for his deceased father and also anticipates the perspective of Varro's men as they discover father and son lying together in death; see 260n. *deflendaque facta*. Silius reverses elements of the Saguntum episode in order to

148   *Commentary Lines 178–80*

emphasize Roman *pietas*. Various Saguntine parents kill themselves to lie on the bodies of their children, such as Mopsus (2.145–6 *delapsus pondere prono / membra super nati moribundos explicat artus*) and the mother of the identical twins (2.649 *ambiguos cecidit super inscia natos*). Here the Roman son demonstrates *pietas erga patrem* by committing suicide in order to lie across his father's body. In contrast to the Saguntines' despair, he hopes that his warning to Varro will bring a positive outcome for his fellow soldiers. The adjective–noun enclosure concludes the narrative unit; see Introduction, section 5.

178–83. Dawn rises on the day of Cannae. It is August 2, 216 BC, but the epic does not specify historical time. It is more significantly the morning after a night of tragic events. Silius varies the conventional epic description of dawn in order to align this scene with the dawn of Lucan's Pharsalus. These elements are:

- (a) the slowness of the night's yielding to the sun (179n. *sensim*) ~ Lucan's sun which is reluctant to rise: Luc. *BC* 7.1–2 *segnior, Oceano quam lex aeterna uocabat, / luctificus Titan*;
- (b) the night's awareness of Solymus' parricide (180n. *conscia*) ~ the crime of Erictho's necromancy that precedes Pharsalus;
- (c) Cannae's uniqueness in history for the Carthaginians (182–3n.) ~ Pharsalus' uniqueness in Roman history, as it reverses all the preceding years of Rome's fate: Luc. *BC* 7.426–7 *sed retro tua fata tulit par omnibus annis / Emathiae funesta dies.*

178–9. talia uenturae mittebant omina pugnae / Ausoniis superi: the echo of 3–4n. *pugnae / omina uenturae* resumes the theme of Varro's destructive stupidity in ignoring the gods' clear messages. At 3–4n. he ignores the omens sent to all of Italy; here he ignores an omen specifically addressed to him (cf. 262–6n.). Line 178 is the only "golden" line of book 9; see Introduction, section 5c.

179. sensimque abeuntibus umbris: *sensim* is both a naturalistic description of the slow arrival of dawn and a recollection of Lucan's Pharsalus episode (see 178–83n.). *Sensum* ω was likely provoked by 180 *conscia*. Silius uses *sensim* eighteen times, a word that elevated poetry generally avoids: Ov. *Met.* twice, Luc. *BC* once.

180. conscia nox sceleris roseo cedebat Eoo: the first half of the line marks the end of the Solymus episode by echoing the wording of its opening line; see 66n. *noctem sceleratus polluit error.* The adjective *conscia* recapitulates Satricus' question regarding witnesses (147n. *quis conscius affuit actis?*) and Solymus' reply (169n. *Titania testis*).

The phrase *conscia nox* originates in Ovid; see *Met.* 6.588 *nox conscia sacris* (a Bacchic festival), *Met.* 13.15 (quoted at 147n.), VF *Arg.* 3.211 *lentis haeret nox*

Commentary Lines 181–3 149

conscia bigis (simile of Vesuvius' eruption), Stat. *Ach.* 1.926 *et intrepidos nox conscia iungit amantes* (Achilles and Deidamia). It is likely a development of Virgil's *conscia sidera*: see Verg. *Aen.* 9.249, Stat. *Theb.* 12.393. Though it is quite common in prose, *conscia sceleris* appears in earlier poetry only at Ov. *Met.* 10.366–7 *pietatis nomine dicto / demisit uultus sceleris sibi conscia uirgo.* Ovid's Myrrha tricks her father into sleeping with her and soon after prays for punishment. Silius may suggest an association here with another story of mistaken identity between parents and children that ends in the guilty child's death.

"Rosy dawn" adapts the Homeric formula ῥοδοδάκτυλος Ἠώς, *Il.* 1.475, 6.175, 9.705, etc. The elegant arrangement of line 180 opposes the night of crime with the day of bloodshed to follow. The motif is frequent in Latin poetry: Propertius is the first to adapt the phrase into this form (Prop. 3.24.7 *roseo collatus Eoo*); other examples include Verg. *Aen.* 6.535 *roseis Aurora quadrigis*, 7.26 *Aurora in roseis fulgebat lutea bigis*, VF *Arg.* 2.261, etc. Silius varies the phrasing slightly at 4.481–2 *ab aequore Eoo / surgebant roseae media inter caerula flammae.*

181–2. ductor in arma suos Libys et Romanus in arma / excibant de more suos: the parallelism of the line and a half conveys both commanders' eagerness for combat. The repetition of *arma* further suggests their excited shouting. Other instances of repetition of *arma* occur in similarly agitated contexts, such as 4.98 *arma, uiri, capite arma, uiri*, 11.133 *arma, arma Hannibalemque uolunt*, and 12.168–9 *arma, cruentus / hostis adest, capite arma, uiri.* Wills 1996: 62–3 observes that through these examples, Silius "shows his own eagerness for constant variation" of the models presented by Hor. *Carm.* 1.35.15 *ad arma cessantes, ad arma*, Verg. *Aen.* 2.668 *arma, uiri, ferte arma*, etc.

For *ductor*, see 24n. For "rousing to arms," see 5.191–2 *ceu ductor ad arma / exciret Tyrius*, 14.193 *exciti populi atque urbes socia arma ferebant*, Luc. *BC* 1.239–40 *stratisque excita iuuentus / deripuit sacris adfixa penatibus arma*, Stat. *Theb.* 4.146–7 *suus excit in arma / antiquam Tiryntha deus*, 9.316 *ipse excitus in arma.*

182–3. Poenisque redibat / qualis nulla dies omni surrexerit aeuo: for the "no greater day" motif in Lucan's Pharsalus episode, see 178–83n. Statius adapts the "no such day" motif in his prayer that no age remember the day of the brothers' duel: Stat. *Theb.* 11.577–9 *omnibus in terris scelus hoc omnique sub aeuo / uiderit una dies, monstrumque infame futuris / excidat, et soli memorent haec proelia reges.* Like both these earlier combats, Cannae will be both unspeakable and unforgettable. Silius uses the "no greater for all time" motif again in describing a mighty Carthaginian ship: *Pun.* 14.385–6 *qua nulla per omne / egressa est Libycis maior naualibus aeuum.* The verb *surgere* is an epic *vox propria* with the dawn, and so Heinsius' *subluxerit* is needless. The phrase is the equivalent of the Homeric ἠώς ... ὄρνυθ' (*Il.* 11.1–2, 19.1–2); see *Pun.* 11.454, Verg. *Aen.* 3.588, *Aen.* 11.1 with Horsfall's note, Luc. *BC* 4.155, etc.

150 *Commentary Lines 184–6*

184–216. Hannibal addresses his troops. For differences between Silius' version and Polybius 3.111, the only extant full-length version, see Introduction, section 3c. Silius also adapts elements from Livy's version of Hannibal's exhortation at the Ticinus (185–6n., 209–11n.).

184–91. Hannibal reminds his troops of their accomplishments to date. They have destroyed Saguntum, conquered the Italian peninsula's two great northern natural boundaries (the Alps and the Po), and won victory at Trasimene. Hannibal frequently references these conquests of natural boundaries in exhortations to his troops: see 6.706–8, 7.147–50, 12.79–82, etc.; Bona 1998: 124–5.

184. 'non uerborum' inquit 'stimulantum' Poenus 'egetis': Polybius' Hannibal similarly claims his men have no need for inspiring words (*Hist.* 3.111.5). For stimulating words, see Ov. *Met.* 14.495 *instimulat uerbis*, Apul. *Met.* 4.30 *uerbis quoque insuper stimulat.* For the motif that words are unnecessary, see Ov. *Fasti* 2.734 *non opus est uerbis, credite rebus*, Sen. *Ep.* 16.2 *itaque non opus est tibi apud me pluribus uerbis aut adfirmatione tam longa*, etc. For phrasing with *egere*, see *Rhet. Her.* 4.68 *res non egent longae orationis*, Cic. *Brut.* 263 *uerborum non egens*, etc. The near synonyms *stimuli* and *uerbera* frequently occur together; see, e.g., Luc. *BC* 1.208 *se saeuae stimulauit uerbere caudae*, 4.759 *uerberibus stimulisque coacti*, Stat. *Theb.* 6.460 *nec iam sufficiunt stimuli, non uerbera*, etc. There may accordingly be a possible *figura etymologica* associating *uerba* and *uerbera*.

185–6. Herculeis iter a metis ad Iapygis agros / uincendo emensi: Hannibal also appeals to his troops' journey from Spain to Italy before the battle of Ticinus (4.59–66), and the Carthaginians do so as Mago returns to report the victory at Cannae (11.134–46). Livy's Hannibal similarly recalls the Carthaginian journey before Ticinus: Livy 21.43.13 *ab Herculis columnis, ab Oceano terminisque ultimis terrarum per tot ferocissimos Hispaniae et Galliae populos uincentes huc peruenistis.* Hannibal plans to march on Rome directly after his victory, and so the journey that began for him at the edge of the world will ideally culminate at its center.

For the *metae Herculeae* as the edge of the world, see 1.141–2 *atque hominum finem Gadis Calpenque secutus*, /...*Herculeis...columnis*, 16.149 *tu, quando Herculeis finisti proelia metis*, Luc. *BC* 3.278 *et Herculeis aufertur gloria metis*, *TLL* 8.0.865.83 ("de mundi finibus extremis"), Bona 1998: 41. For *iter*...*emensi*, see 13.1, Verg. *Aen.* 7.160, 11.244, Luc. *BC* 9.735, etc. Heinsius' *Iapygas* is unnecessary; see Verg. *Aen.* 11.247 *Iapygis agris*, Ov. *Met.* 15.52 *Iapygis arua*, etc.

186. nusquam est animosa Saguntos: Saguntum's resistance against overwhelming odds, culminating in the mass suicide of its citizens, is the subject of *Punica* 1–2. Hannibal mentions his troops' sack of the city in his exhortation before Ticinus: 4.62 *Rutulam fumasse Saguntum.* The city's grim fate is

Commentary Lines 187–8   151

remembered throughout the epic: 292–3n., 3.2 *non aequo superum genitore euersa Sagunti*, 3.564 *casus metuit iam Roma Sagunti*, 5.160 *passamque infanda Saguntum*, 7.280 *arta fames poenas miserae exactura Sagunti*, 12.431–2 *Petilia…/ infelix fidei miseraeque secunda Sagunto*, 17.493–4 *claro deletum…Marte Saguntum*. For reference to the obliteration of epic cities, see Verg. *Aen.* 2.325 *fuimus Troes, fuit Ilium*, Prop. 2.8.10 *et Thebae steterunt altaque Troia fuit*.

For *nusquam est*, see *OLD* s.v. 2. For application of *animosus* to cities, see 6.303 *animosa Therapne*, 11.16 *animosa Tarento*; *TLL* 2.88.38. The gender of Saguntum varies: feminine here, as at 292n. *captae…Sagunti*, 2.105 with my note, 2.284, 2.541, 2.662 *totam…Saguntum*, 4.62, 5.160, 6.701, 11.143, 15.409, Livy 21.19.1 *Sagunto excisa*, Stat. *Silv.* 4.6.83 *immeritae…Sagunti*; neuter at 17.328 *deletum…Saguntum*, Luc. *BC* 3.350 *obsessum…Saguntum*, Livy 21.21.1 *Sagunto capto*. See Zwiener 1909: 139.

187. concessere Alpes: for the crossing of the Alps, see 3.477–646. Virgil's Jupiter foretells this moment in the *concilium deorum*: Verg. *Aen.* 10.11–13 *adueniet iustum pugnae (ne arcessite) tempus, / cum fera Karthago Romanis arcibus olim / exitium magnum atque Alpis immittet apertas*. For mountains "yielding," see, e.g., 3.495 *Ossaque cum Pelio cumque Haemo cesserit Othrys* (mountains that yield to the Alps' immense height); *TLL* 4.8.55. Schrader's *consedere* may have been prompted by phrases such as 2.313 *subsident Alpes*, 8.648 *non Alpes sedere loco*.

187–8. pater ipse superbus aquarum / Ausonidum Eridanus captiuo defluit alueo: the Araxes, enslaved by its Roman bridge, is the model for the captive river in Latin poetry; see Verg. *Aen.* 8.728 *pontem indignatus Araxes*, Stat. *Silv.* 1.4.79 *patiens Latii iam pontis Araxes*, etc.; Babnis 2019. Silius reverses this motif of Roman triumphalism by putting it in Hannibal's mouth. For Hannibal's crossing of the Po after Ticinus, see 4.485–92; in prophecy, see 1.131–2 *fluit ecce cruentus / Eridanus*. For the Po as *pater*, see 4.690–1, 12.217; as the greatest of the Italian rivers and the source of others, see Verg. *Geo.* 1.482 *fluuiorum rex Eridanus* with Mynors's note. The Tiber is more characteristically the "father" river for the Romans, beginning with Enn. *Ann.* 26 Skutsch *pater Tiberine*; see Verg. *Geo.* 4.369, Livy 2.10.11, [Ov.] *Epic. Drus.* 221, etc.; Jones 2005. *Pater aquarum* is an original collocation, but modeled on Virgil's application of *rex*, and perhaps on Colum. *RR* 10.200 *nunc pater aequoreus, nunc et regnator aquarum*.

As *lectio difficilior*, the reading *Ausonidum Γ²s* is preferable to *Ausonium ω*; for the Grecizing form, see 7.80, 8.300, 13.348, Verg. *Aen.* 10.564 (where, see Servius' note on its formation), Ov. *Fasti* 2.94, etc. Silius is the first to bring *defluere alueo* into poetry: see Livy 5.37.7, QCurt. 9.8.30, Mela 3.41. For the disyllabic scansion of *alueo*, see 3.450 *ac propere in pontem lato ruit incitus alueo*, 4.602, 14.428, Verg. *Aen.* 7.33 *adsuetae ripis uolucres et fluminis alueo*, 6.412, 7.303, 9.32, Ov. *Met.* 1.423, Tib. 2.1.49, etc.

152 Commentary Lines 189–200

189. strage uirum mersus Trebia est: a moment foretold in the Massylian priestess' prophecy (1.45–9) and fulfilled in the actual battle (4.663–5). The motif of a river "drowned" by slaughter originates in the Homeric river battle (*Il.* 21.218–20); see also Luc. *BC* 2.209–20, of the Tiber choked by the Sullan massacres. For the line opening *strage uirum*, see 17.602, Luc. *BC* 3.627, Stat. *Theb.* 7.591, VF *Arg.* 3.276. *Mergere* reprises the Massylian priestess's prophecy and looks forward to Cannae; see 1.50–1 *dum Cannas tumulum Hesperiae campumque cruore / Ausonio mersum sublimis Iapyga cernam*, TLL 8.0.834.9.

Mersus is a deliberately paradoxical word choice, as it is usually rivers that cause drowning. Heinsius suggested *uersus* or *auersus*, implying that the corpses had deflected the course of the river, as well as *immersus*, on which he commented "malim." He also conjectured *pressus*, but then retracted it. Drakenborch took up the suggestion, citing 4.621 *et clausit magna uada pressa ruina* (of an elephant's corpse stopping the flow of the Trebia) and Claud. *IV Cos. Hon.* 630 *corporibus premitur Peuce.*

189–90. atque ora sepulcro / Lydia Flaminio premitur: for Flaminius' exemplary fate at Trasimene, see 55n. The phrase is a reversal of the typical funerary wish *sit terra tibi leuis*, for which, see *TLL* 7.2.1202.73. *Sepulc(h)ro* βCh with *premitur* is preferable to *sepulto* aΓs, as it is more plausible to visualize a monumental tomb pressing down on the Etruscan shores. Zaia compares *CLE* 1135, 1272, etc., and Stat. *Silv.* 2.7.93 *angusto Babylon premit sepulcro* with Newlands' note. For Trebia's location in the *ora...Lydia*, see 4.719 *Lydorum in populos*.

190–1. lateque refulgent / ossibus: Silius' phrasing is a unique amplification of Verg. *Aen.* 12.36 *campique ingentes ossibus albent* (on which, see Tarrant's note), which in turn prompted phrases such as Ov. *Fasti* 1.558, Sen. *Oed.* 94 *et albens ossibus sparsis solum* (the Sphinx's depredations), Tac. *Ann.* 1.61 *medio campi albentia ossa* (Varus' slaughtered forces at the Teutoburger Wald), etc. It is unobjectionable that bones shine "brightly" here rather than are "white," as in the tradition. The hyperbole evidently appeared unacceptable to Schrader, however, who suggested the equally unique phrase *relucent*.

191. ac nullo sulcantur uomere campi: then, as now, wartime forces farmers to stop their activities. Personified Tellus complains at 15.532–3 *nulla mihi floret bucis felicibus arbor: / immatura seges rapido succiditur ense.* For Tellus' role in the *Punica*, see Augoustakis 2010c: 144–55. Virgil and Lucan make similar observations on the civil war: Verg. *Geo.* 1.506–7 *non ullus aratro / dignus honos, squalent abductis arua colonis*; Luc. *BC* 1.28–9 *horrida quod dumis multosque inarata per annos / Hesperia est desuntque manus poscentibus aruis.* For *sulcare uomere*, see Luc. *BC* 1.168–9 with Roche's note.

192–200. Hannibal promises his troops the plunder from the battle and reiterates that he needs no material reward. He offered similar encouragement to the troops when crossing the Alps: 3.512 *commotum promissis ditibus agmen.* For

Commentary Lines 192–3   153

the comparable moment in Livy's Cannae narrative, see Livy 21.43.6 *quicquid Romani tot triumphis partum congestumque possident, id omne uestrum cum ipsis dominis futurum est*; 21.43.9 *tempus est iam opulenta uos ac ditia stipendia facere.* For the repetition *quicquid...quicquid...quin...si quid,* see 2.539–40 with my note, and 13.527–9 with van der Keur's note.

192–3. clarior his titulus plusque allatura cruoris / lux oritur: Cannae will bring a greater title and more Roman bloodshed than any previous battle that the Carthaginians have fought. Hannibal will be able to return to this feat as consolation for his expulsion from Italy: 17.608 *non ullo Cannas abolebis, Iuppiter, aeuo.* For the *clarus titulus,* see 4.496–7 *multusque in imagine claris / praefulgebat auus titulis.* For *tituli* gained in battle, see Ov. *Fasti* 2.16 *per titulos ingredimurque tuos* with Robinson's note. For *plus* with the genitive, see 12.228 *nituit plus fronte decoris,* L-H-S 112–13, 165–6. For the metrically convenient phrase *lux oritur,* see Hor. *Serm.* 1.5.39, Ov. *Fasti* 1.71.

The *titulus* to be gained by the victory at Cannae is distinct from the *lux* that will bring more bloodshed. For an unambiguous distinction between the two, see Ov. *Fasti* 4.675–6 *ut titulum imperii cum primum luce sequenti / Augusto iuueni prospera bella darent.* Van Veen objected, however, that reading *titulus* means "pendet τὸ *his*" and thus preferred *titulis* ω. The "hanging" *his* is unobjectionable, however: see, e.g., 13.571 *tristior his Acheron,* 17.432 *saeuior his Latius.*

193–5. Hannibal wants only the glory of victory, not its material rewards. He needs no *merces* (194) like the mercenary Xanthippus and so will leave the booty for his troops to plunder; see further 199–200. His goal is *gloria* alone, as when, for example, he complains about being deceived at Zama: 17.550 *tantumne obstat mea gloria diuis?* For the tradition, see Verg. *Aen.* 9.194–5 *nam mihi facti / fama sat est,* 10.468–9 *sed famam extendere factis, / hoc uirtutis opus,* etc. See Ripoll 1998: 244–7.

Hannibal thereby transcends the Roman stereotype of the "greedy, commercial" Carthaginian, for which, see Starks 1999 and Ciocarlie 2008. For the motif that the *sapiens* needs only honor, see Cic. *De Orat.* 3.102 = *Trag. Rom. inc. frg.* 30 *sapiens uirtuti honorem praemium, haud praedam petit, Phil.* 5.35 *neque enim ullam mercedem tanta uirtus praeter hanc laudis gloriaeque desiderat,* etc. For greed among Roman epic leaders, see Coffee 2009.

Hannibal will achieve glory from Cannae, but not the additional glory of conquering Rome. Jupiter's admonition in a dream deterring him from Rome recalls this scene by echoing the phrasing of 193: 10.366 *sat magna, o iuuenis, prensa est tibi gloria Cannis.*

193. mihi magna satis, sat magna superque: *sat magna* Watt 1984: 155 : *sat uero* ω. The trochaic scansion of *uĕrŏ* ω has prompted suspicion. There are two parallels in Flavian poetry: VF *Arg.* 5.321 *sin uero preces* and Stat. *Theb.* 2.187 *nos uero*

154 *Commentary Lines 194–8*

uolentes. None occurs from earlier periods, however, and none will occur again until the Christian poets of late antiquity, e.g., Paul. Nol. *Carm.* 21.643, 29.5, Paul. Petric. *Mart.* 4.434, 4.632. Furthermore, Wijsman rejects the *uero* found in the manuscripts at VF *Arg.* 5.321 *sin uero preces*, as final –o is long in all other instances of *uero* in Valerius. This leaves Stat. *Theb.* 2.187 *nos uero uolentes* (with Gervais's note) as the only currently unchallenged contemporary parallel. Liberman 2006: 21 adds Sen. *Phaed.* 1082 as a further example of trochaic *uĕrŏ*.

The manuscript alternative *uera* B *edd. a* l and Heinsius' suggestion *certa* do little to help the problem, as it is not the veracity or certitude of Hannibal's glory that is at issue but its scope. Müller 1861: 339 argued that correption of final –o does not occur with particles at this period and so proposed *clara.* Blass's *satis mera satque superque* is too extensive an intervention. I have followed Watt 1984: 155, who proposes repeated *magna* on the example of the repetition of *optima* at 10.222–3 *Seruilius, optima belli, / post Paulum belli pars optima*. Watt suggests that *uero* may have been inserted as a stopgap after *magna* dropped out. 10.366 *sat magna* (quoted at 193–5n. above) offers further support.

194. bellandi merces sit gloria: for looking beyond material benefit (*merces*) in war, see Verg. *Aen.* 10.532–3 *belli commercia Turnus / sustulit ista prior iam tum Pallante perempto*; see Coffee 2009 for discussion. Glory can substitute for "mercenary" rewards in peaceful contexts as well. Ovid's Mamurius, for example, asks Numa for glory as his *merces* for constructing the *ancilia: Fasti* 3.389–90 *merces mihi gloria detur, / nominaque extremo carmine nostra sonent.* Liberman 2006: 21 proposes *est*, since "glory is enough for Hannibal," but Hannibal has not actually won the battle yet.

194–5. cetera uobis / uincantur: *uobis* is dative of advantage, "for your benefit." Hannibal certainly intends to make his own contribution to the effort of conquering.

195. quicquid diti deuexit Hibero: for the richness of the Iberian mines, see 1.228 *hic omne metallum, TLL* 5.1.1591.6; for a different characterization of the Ebro, see 8.323 *crudo quae uenit Hibero*. For *deuehere* of rivers, see Verg. *Geo.* 4.293 *usque coloratis amnis deuexus ab Indis.*

196. quicquid in Aetnaeis iactauit Roma triumphis: for the Carthaginian defeat in the Sicilian campaign of the First Punic War, see 2.304–10 with my note; for Aetna as a metonym for Sicily, see 2.304 *lauimus Aetnaeas animoso sanguine uallis.*

197–8. quin etiam Libyco si quid de litore raptum / condidit: Hannibal promises his soldiers that they may even retain Carthaginian property previously captured as war prizes by the Romans in the First Punic War. For *Libyco . . . litore*, see 6.673; the phrase derives from Verg. *Aen.* 11.265 *Libycone habitantis litore*

Commentary Lines 198–201   155

Locros? and is found also at VF *Arg.* 6.411–12. The phrase is a variant on the
more common *Libycis... oris*; see 67n., 11.377, 13.481, 14.289, 17.402, Verg. *Aen.*
1.377, Ov. *Rem.* 797, etc.

198. in uestros ueniet sine sortibus enses: for this meaning of *uenio*, see OLD
s.v. 13 "to come (to) as a possession," as at, e.g., Livy 3.6.9 *ad eos summa rerum
ac maiestas consularis imperii uenerat*. For *sortibus*, see Verg. *Aen.* 9.271 *excipi-
am sorti*. Reference to the *sortes* also contrasts Hannibal and his Carthaginians
with Homer's Agamemnon and the Achaeans. The Achaeans apportion their
spoil by lot, and their commander Agamemnon demands the choicest portion.
The complaints of Homer's Achilles and Thersites evince frustration with this
system of division; see Hom. *Il.* 1.148–71, 2.225–42.

199. ferte domos, quod dextra dabit: a challenge by Virgil's Turnus features
similar brevity and may be a potential model for this line: Verg. *Aen.* 10.650 *hac
dabitur dextra tellus quaesita per undas*. It may also stand behind Hannibal's
vaunt at Saguntum: 1.398–400 *'narrabis... hanc' inquit 'dextram, quae iam post
funera uulgi / Hannibalem uobis comitem dabit.'* For *ferre domos*, see Stat. *Theb.*
4.649, *TLL* 5.1.1976–7.

199–200. nil ductor honoris / ex opibus posco: Hannibal reasserts his lack of
need for spoils; see 193–4n. For *ductor* as opposed to *dux*, see 24n. Barth
inquired "quid opibus cum honore?" and accordingly suggested *nil uictor honorus*. Heinsius responded "sed *honor* etiam pro munere nonnumquam ponitur," as at Ov. *Met.* 11.216–17 *nec... Telamon sine honore recessit / Hesioneque
data potitur*, 13.41 *nos inhonorati et donis patruelibus orbi*, etc. For the frequent
manuscript confusion of *ductor* with *uictor*, see 600n., Luc. *BC* 3.71 *uictor* V :
ductor Ω, etc.

200–11 Hannibal promises rewards of land allotments to Carthaginian citizens and grants of Carthaginian citizenship to allied troops. Livy's Hannibal
makes these offers before Ticinus: see Livy 21.45.5–6 *agrum sese daturum esse
in Italia, Africa, Hispania, ubi quisque uelit... qui sociorum ciues Carthaginienses
fieri uellent, potestatem facturum*. See Introduction, section 3c.

**200–1. raptor per saecula longa / Dardanus edomitum uobis spoliauerit
orbem:** Hannibal speaks similarly of Roman rapacity when exhorting his
troops at Saguntum: see 2.51–3 *Rhoeteius immo / aeternum imperitet populis
saeclisque propaget / regna ferox* with my note. The narrator's complaint about
the rapacity of provincial governors (14.684–8) features similar phrasing:
14.688 *nudassent auidae terrasque fretumque rapinae*. For *saecula longa*, see Ov.
Met. 4.67, 15.446, Luc. *BC* 2.116, etc. The "conquered world" derives from Ov.
Fasti 4.255–6 *ut Roma potens opibus iam saecula quinque / uidit et edomito
sustulit orbe caput*; see also *AA* 1.177 *ecce parat Caesar, domito quod defuit orbi*,
Fasti 4.861 *quotiens steteris domito sublimis in orbe*, Verg. *Geo.* 2.114 *extremis*

156   *Commentary Lines 202–5*

domitum cultoribus orbem. As often, Hannibal's complaints about Roman domination evoke Augustan eulogies of Rome.

202. qui Tyria ducis Sarranum ab origine nomen: for *ducere nomen*, see 11.178–9 *cui nomina liquit / ab Ioue ducta Capys magno cognatus Iulo*, 16.428 *qui pecudum ducunt ab origine nomen*, 17.33 *prisca ducens Clausorum ab origine nomen*, Verg. *Aen.* 10.145 *hinc nomen Campanae ducitur urbi*. For *ducere* as "derivare," see *TLL* 5.1.2153.55, which cites Hor. *Carm.* 3.27.75 *tua sectus orbis / nomina ducet*.

The narrative of Hamilcar's ancestry introduces the Sarranian motif: 1.72–3 *Sarrana prisci Barcae de gente uetustos / a Belo numerabat auos*. The adjective *Sarranus*, as a synonym for "Tyrian," derives from Phoenician Ṣr, meaning "rock"; see *NP* s.v *Tyrus*. *Sarranus* enters Latin poetry at Verg. *Geo.* 2.506 *Sarrano…ostro*, where Servius' note (inaccurately) observes *quae enim nunc Tyros dicitur, olim Sarra uocabatur a pisce quodam, qui illic abundat, quem lingua sua 'sar' appellant*. For the juxtaposition of the synonyms *Tyrius* and *Sarranus*, see 3.256–8 *Sabratha tum Tyrium uulgus Sarranaque Leptis / mittebat*.

203–4. seu Laurens tibi Sigeo sulcata colono / arridet tellus: for the Romans' land as Laurentine, see 1.605, 1.659, 8.28, 12.706 *Laurentiue colono*, etc. For *Sigeo* as "Roman," see 1.665 *Sigeis duxistis auis*. According to Spaltenstein, only Silius uses *Sigeus* to mean "Roman." For the Romans as *coloni*, see 75n.

204–5. seu sunt Byzacia cordi / rura magis centum Cereri fruticantia culmis: the fertility of Byzacium, near the Syrtis Minor, was widely attested in antiquity. For the attribution of hundredfold returns, see Varro *RR* 1.44.2 *in Africa ad Byzacium…ex modio nasci centum*, Pliny *NH* 5.24 *fertilitatis eximiae, cum centesima fruge agricolis faenus reddente terra*. See also Polyb. *Hist.* 3.23.2, Pliny *NH* 17.41, 18.94, *NP* s.v. *Byzacium*. These attestations permit the rejection of the uncomprehending alternatives *Bizantia* Lβ or *Buxentia* edd. *a* v. Statius is apparently the first Latin poet to bring the phrase *magis cordi* into poetry: see Stat. *Theb.* 1.652–4 *an illud / lene magis cordi quod desolata domorum / tecta uides*.

The verb *fruticare* first appears in poetry at Calp. Sic. *Ecl.* 6.37 (if this poet was indeed active in the Neronian period, rather than subsequent to Silius) and then next at Juv. 9.15. *Ceres* is a metonym for *fruges*, explicated at Cic. *De Orat.* 3.167 *Cererem pro frugibus* and glossed at Ov. *Met.* 5.655–6 *dona fero Cereris, / latos quae sparsa per agros / frugiferas messes alimentaque mitia reddant*; see Michalopoulos 2001: 83. The juxtaposition *Cereri fruticantia* may accordingly be an alternative *figura etymologica*. For Ceres' *culmi*, see Hor. *Serm.* 2.2.124 *ac uenerata Ceres, ita culmo surgeret alto*, Manil. *Astr.* 3.629 *tum Cererem fragili properant destringere culmo*, etc.

Liberman 2006: 21 proposes *Cereris* with *culmis*, which is entirely plausible. But the phrase may conceivably be modeled on "pleasing to Ceres," as at 1.237

nec Cereri terra indocilis nec inhospita Baccho, 14.130 *Cereri placitos*. Alliteration of C- unifies the line and a half.

206. electos optare dabo inter praemia campos: the phrase *electos optare* combines near synonymous words (cf. Serv. *Aen.* 3.509 *alii 'optatae' electae uel expetitae accipiunt*) and so constitutes another example of Silius' typical repetition with variation; see Introduction, section 5b. For *dare* governing the infinitive, see 80n.; Verg. *Aen.* 5.247–8 *muneraque in nauis ternos optare iuuencos / uinaque et argenti magnum dat ferre talentum* may suggest the phrasing of the present line. For the frequent manuscript confusion of *praemia* with *proelia*, see 16.523.

207. addam etiam, flaua Thybris quas irrigat unda: as Spaltenstein observes, *addam* continues the sense of "permit" from 206 *dabo*. For the Tiber's tawny waves, see 1.607 *in pontum flauo descendit gurgite Thybris*, Enn. *Ann.* 453 Skutsch, Verg. *Aen.* 9.816–17 *ille suo cum gurgite flauo / accepit uenientem, Epic. Drusi* 221 *ipse pater flauis Tiberinus adhorruit undis*, etc. For the clausula, see Ov. *Met.* 14.633, *Pan. Mess.* 60, Calp. Sic. *Ecl.* 7.68.

208. captiuis late gregibus depascere ripas: the captured flocks on the Tiber's banks recall the Po's enslaved channel at 187–8n. *Late* conveys the Carthaginians' intended mastery over Italy. *Captiuus grex* is found only at Sen. *Phoen.* 575 *adulta uirgo, mixta captiuo gregi*. For the typical notion, see Livy 26.34.5 *pecua captiua*, Ov. *Her.* 1.52 *incola captiuo quae boue uictor arat*, etc. The construction with *depascere* has been varied, as the cattle are typically in the accusative and the places where they pasture are typically in the ablative; see, e.g., Verg. *Geo.* 3.143 *saltibus in uacuis pascunt*, Ov. *Fasti* 5.640 *pascebat sparsas utraque ripa boues*. Claudian reverses Hannibal's promise in Eridanus' rebuke of Alaric in retreat: Claud. *VI Cos. Hon.* 182–3 *nec iam cornipedem Thybrino gramine pascis, / ut rebare, tuum?*; see Dewar 1994.

209–10. qui uero externo socius mihi sanguine Byrsae / signa moues: the Byrsa is the acropolis of Carthage, used metonymically for the city itself: see 2.363 *quis procul a Tyria dominos depellere Byrsa* with my note. Virgil's Venus relates the legend of its purchase by Dido: *Aen.* 1.367 *mercatique solum, facti de nomine Byrsam*. Ruperti conjoined *socius* with *Byrsae*; I have followed Spaltenstein in my translation, who conjoins it with *mihi* and makes *Byrsae* dependent on *signa*.

210–11. dextram Ausonia si caede cruentam / attolles, hinc iam ciuis Carthaginis esto: the striking image of troops raising bloody hands to attest to their eligibility for rewards previews the slaughter to follow shortly. Silius adapts Enn. *Ann.* 234–5 Skutsch *hostem qui feriet †erit (inquit) mi† Carthaginiensis, / quisquis erit. cuiatis siet*. Skutsch observes that Cic. *Balb.* 51, the source for the Ennius passage, apparently reveals Cicero's thought that

158   *Commentary Lines 212–14*

Ennius was the first to assign to Hannibal an offer that theoretically could have been made by any Carthaginian commander.

Though this motif is embedded in historiographical tradition, it also responds to Lucan's narrative of inclusion and exclusion from citizenship. At the outbreak of the war, Laelius proudly tells Caesar at Luc. *BC* 1.373–4, *nec ciuis meus est, in quem tua classica, Caesar, / audiero*; see Roche's note. At Pharsalus, Caesar implicitly contradicts Laelius by insisting that his men not strike Pompeian fugitives in the back. He instead orders them to regard them as fellow citizens; see Luc. *BC* 7.318–19 *uos tamen hoc oro, iuuenes, ne caedere quisquam / hostis terga uelit: ciuis qui fugerit esto* with Lanzarone's note. Hannibal's offer of citizenship earned through bloodshed thereby creates an additional point of contact with Caesar, each at his moment of greatest triumph in his respective poem.

"Bloody with slaughter" is a common collocation: see Verg. *Aen.* 1.471 *Tydides multa uastabat caede cruentus*, Ov. *Her.* 6.162 *erret inops, exspes, caede cruenta sua*, Sen. *HF* 919 *manus cruenta caede et hostili expia*, etc. Silius has added *variatio* by placing the common phrase in chiasmus.

212–16. Hannibal forecasts a quick end to the war; his troops will proceed directly from victory at Cannae to besieging the Capitol (216n.). His words recall those of Livy's Maharbal after Cannae: 22.51.2 *'immo ut quid hac pugna sit actum scias, die quinto' inquit, 'uictor in Capitolio epulaberis'*. Silius briefly introduces Maharbal at Trebia (4.562), but does not show him again after this moment. Hannibal does not put this plan of marching on Rome in action, however; he moves instead into winter quarters at Capua. Hannibal's own hesitation, not Rome's distance from Cannae (214n.), causes his strategic error. Livy's Maharbal accordingly accuses him of ignorance of how to use the victories he wins: Livy 22.51.4 *uincere scis, Hannibal; uictoria uti nescis*.

212. neu uos Garganus Daunique fefellerit ora: for Garganus as a metonym for Apulia, see 33–4n. For its pairing with the similarly metonymic "shores of Daunus," see 499n., 13.59–60 *non Garganus nec Daunia tellus / debentur nobis*. Daunus was the father of Turnus in Virgil, and his kingdom became a metonym for Apulia and southern Italy; see Verg. *Aen.* 10.616 with Harrison's note.

213. ad muros statis Romae: for the motif of Rome's walls, see 44n. Earlier, both Saguntum and the Alps were seen as proxies for Rome itself: 1.270 *extremis pulsat Capitolia terris*, 1.384–5 *fallax Poene, iaces; certe Capitolia primus / scandebas uictor*; 3.509–10 *nunc, o nunc, socii, dominantis moenia Romae / credite uos summumque Iouis conscendere culmen*. Cannae has become Rome's proxy now that Hannibal's forces have won a series of victories in Italy. See Dominik 2003 and 2006.

213–14. licet auia longe / urbs agat: for the phrasing of *auia longe*, Delz (app. crit.) compares Luc. *BC* 5.375 *auius Hydrus* and Amm. Marc. 27.5.6 *longius*

Commentary Lines 214–18 159

agentes Greuthungos bellicosam gentem aggressus est. For *agat* as *sita est*, see Sall. *BJ* 89.7 *Africa, quae procul a mari incultius agebat,* Tac. *Germ.* 42 *iuxta Hermunduros Naristi agunt, TLL* 1.1402.56 ("de populis, saepe i. q. situm esse, habitare, colere").

214. et nostro procul a certamine distet: the phrase is unique to Silius and appears next in reference to Hannibal's pursuit of the phantom at Zama: 17.546 *diuersa spatio procul a certamine pugnae.*

215. hic hodie ruet: the double emphasis of *hic hodie* extends the representation of Cannae as a crucial day in history: see, e.g., 19–20n. *una…die,* 183n. *nulla dies.* For *ruere* of a city, see, e.g., Verg. *Aen.* 2.363 *urbs antiqua ruit.*

215-16. atque ultra te ad proelia, miles, / nulla uoco: in his enthusiasm, Hannibal assumes there will be no fighting between Cannae and the Capitol, because no Roman soldiers will be left alive to defend it after the upcoming slaughter. Mago makes the same claim immediately after the battle: 10.385–6 *accipe muros / Iliacos portasque tibi sine Marte patentis.* Hannibal refuses, however, and so earns the criticism of not knowing how to use a victory; see Livy 22.51.

216. ex acie tende in Capitolia cursum: for the common collocation *tendere cursum,* see 10.73, 17.589, Lucr. *DRN* 5.631, Verg. *Aen.* 2.321, etc.

217-43. Hannibal disposes his troops. For the contrast between Silius' account of the disposition and the historiographical accounts, see Introduction, section 3c.

217. haec memorat: for the speech formula, see 173n.

217-18. tum propulso munimine ualli / fossarum rapuere moras: for throwing down the *uallum,* see 7.101–2 *ruite ad portas, propellite uallum / pectoribus.* Hannibal's actions at Cannae once more (see 210–11n.) reflect those of Lucan's Caesar at Pharsalus, where he gives a similar order to his men. See Luc. *BC* 7.326 *sternite iam uallum fossasque implete ruina* with Lanzarone's note.

Livy uses similar phrasing to describe a Roman attack on a Samnite fortification: Livy 9.14.9 *cum pars fossas explerent, pars uellerent uallum atque in fossas proruerent.* For *munimine ualli,* see 238n., 7.528–9 *uallique tenet munimine turmas / Ausonius,* 16.41 *coepti munimina ualli, TLL* 8.1655.33. Lucan first introduces the pleonastic phrase in poetry: Luc. *BC* 6.290 *transierat primi Caesar munimina ualli.* For pleonasm, see 176n. Statius' Thebans hardly dare progress outside the rampart after the Argives withdraw: Stat. *Theb.* 12.9–10 *et munimina ualli / soluere.*

For *mora* of defenses, see 13.108 *morantia claustra,* Verg. *Aen.* 9.143 *fossarum morae,* Stat. *Theb.* 10.196–7 *morasque / frangite portarum,* 11.244 *portarumque moras.* The periphrasis may be an example of "deviant focalization" (cf. Fowler

160 *Commentary Lines 218–21*

1990), reflecting both commanders' perspective that any obstacle to giving battle is an unacceptable *mora*.

Van Veen argued for *rupere*, as *rapere moras/am* is unattested and the phrase *rumpere moras/am* is very well attested: 8.215, Verg. *Aen.* 4.569, Ov. *Met.* 15.583, Luc. *BC* 2.525, etc. Spaltenstein notes 3.156 *iter... rapiente* can serve as a model for construing as *rapuere iter per fossarum moras*.

218–19. aciemque locorum / consilio curuis accommodat ordine ripis: the words are carefully arranged, with the noun–adjective pair *curuis... ripis* interlaced with the two ablative nouns. In contrast to Varro's recklessness, Hannibal thinks carefully about his occasion and manner of giving battle. As Silius is the only source to make the Aufidus curve, it is likely a conventional use of the epithet, as at 15.621–2, Ov. *Met.* 9.450, Luc. *BC* 1.397, 1.420, etc. See 227n.

TLL 4.456.45 offers no parallel for this usage of *consilio*, but Spaltenstein accurately interprets the phrase as *consilio pro locis sumpto*. (*Capto* might be more idiomatic; cf. *OLD* s.v. 1.) Heinsius' proposal *consimilem* is banalizing. Liberman 2006: 21 proposes *ingenio* on the example of 14.283 *ingenio portus* and inquires, "Is it a confusion of words which have the same metrical value and are near in point of sense?"

220–6. A catalog of the North African ethnic groups under Nealces' command on the left wing. In contrast to Silius, Livy puts the Gallic and Iberian troops on the left wing under Hasdrubal and the Numidians on the right under Maharbal: Livy 22.46.2 *Gallos Hispanosque equites prope ripam laeuo in cornu aduersus Romanum equitatum*; 22.46.7 *duces cornibus praeerant sinistro Hasdrubal, dextro Maharbal*.

Nealces' forces include Nasamones, Marmaricans, Moors, Garamantians, Macae, and Massylae. Many of these ethnonyms are often used throughout the epic as unspecific synonyms for "North African," as their frequent pairings suggest. Examples include 2.62–4 (with my notes), *Garamas* and *Marmaricus* (7.628–9, 11.181–2, etc.), *Garamas* and *Nasamon* (16.630). The Adyrmachidae and Massylians also appear consecutively in the catalog of 3.278–83.

220. barbaricus laeuo stetit ad certamina cornu: the keyword *barbaricus* introduces the multiethnic catalog to follow. Silius employs the clausula once more at 274n.

221. bellator Nasamon: the ethnographic tradition knows the Nasamones as plunderers who profit from shipwrecks in the dangerous Syrtis: see 1.408 *Nasamon...populator*, 3.320–1 *Nasamon, inuadere fluctu / audax naufragia*. Decius, the Capuan loyalist, will soon refer to them as *semihomines* (11.180). See Luc. *BC* 9.439–41 with Wick's note, QCurt. 4.7.19, Talbert et al. 2000: 37 D2, 38 B3, Bona 1998: 73. Like the Garamantes (222n.), the Nasamones may conceivably have been of topical interest. Domitian "forbade the Nasamones to exist" (Dio 67.4.6 Ναsαμῶνας ἐκώλυσα εἶναι) after their rebellion in 85–6.

Enjambed *bellator* completes the lengthy hyperbaton; see Introduction, section 5c. Application to North African warriors evokes the poem's introductory description of Libya: 1.218–19 *altrix bellorum bellatorumque uirorum / tellus*. For the phrase *barbaricus… bellator*, see 5.415 *delerat leto bellator barbarus annos*, applied to a Massylian warrior at Trasimene. Horsfall on Verg. *Aen.* 11.553 suggests that the noun *bellator* may be of Ennian origin. Silius uses *bellator* twenty-one times, far more frequently than the other epic poets: Verg. *Aen.* seven times, Ov. *Met.* one time, Luc. *BC* zero times, VF *Arg.* three times, Stat. *Theb.* six times. For Silius' use of substantives in –*tor*, see 24n.

221–2. unaque immanior artus / Marmarides: ancient Marmarica was located between Egypt and Cyrenaica; its inhabitants were conquered by Roman forces likely in AD 2 (*NP* s.v. *Marmarica*). Silius typically uses *Marmaricus* as a metonym for "North African" (7.84, 8.215, 11.182, etc.) and often pairs it with reference to the Garamantes (222n.). The Marmaricans are described as healers of snakebites at 3.300–2, as at Luc. *BC* 9.891–3; see Wick's note and Bona 1998: 69. Individual Marmarican characters include Cothon (164n.) and the giant Othrys (5.437). See *TLL* 7.1.441.34 for *immanis* with the accusative of relation. *Immanior* highlights the Marmaricans' great size, as attested by Othrys, and so the alternative *arcu* r1m should be rejected.

222. tum Maurus atrox Garamasque Macesque: *atrox* (*ater*) may be a calque on the false etymology associating the Moors with (ἀ)μαυρός, "dark". See 2.439 *nigri…Mauri* with my note, 8.267 *adustus corpora Maurus* with Ariemma's note, 17.632 *incocti corpora Mauri*, Luc. *BC* 4.678–9 *concolor Indo / Maurus* with Asso's note, etc. The Garamantes were a Berber people of Libya, whom Silius also describes as *atrox* at 12.749; see *NP* s.v. *Garamantes*, Bona 1998: 70–2. Tac. *Hist.* 4.50.4 describes them as a *gentem indomitam et inter accolas latrociniis fecundam*. For the Macae, see 11n.

These North African peoples may conceivably have been of contemporary interest to Silius' audience. C. Velius Rufus received honors for suppressing the tribes of Mauretania sometime between AD 85 and 87: *NP* s.v. *C. Velius Rufus, AE* 1903.368 *duci exercitus Africi et Mauretanici ad nationes quae sunt in Mauretania comprimendas*. Tac. *Hist.* 4.50.4 also records the defeat of a Garamantian force during a raid on Lepcis Magna by Roman auxiliaries in the war of AD 68–9.

223. et Massylae acies: Pliny *NH* 5.30 localizes the Massylians between the Ampsaga River and Carthage. In the catalog of Carthaginian forces, Silius employs Virgil's mythical geography to place them in the garden of the Hesperides: *Pun.* 3.282–3 *quin et Massyli fulgentia signa tulere, / Hesperidum ueniens lucis domus ultima terrae*; cf. Verg. *Aen.* 4.484 *Hesperidum templi custos*. Silius' Anna recalls Virgil's Massylian priestess (8.98–101), and another priestess presides at Hannibal's oath (1.101, 2.297–8). Syphax is their ruler at 16.170–1. See Bona 1998: 68.

162 *Commentary Lines 225–6*

223–4. et ferro uiuere laetum / uulgus Adyrmachidae, pariter gens accola Nili: the Adyrmachidae appeared in an earlier catalog of Hannibal's forces (3.278–81), where they were distinguished by their sickle-shaped swords. Pliny *NH* 5.39 places them in Libya Mareotis along with the Marmarides. Delz 1997: 168 observes that the phrase *uiuere laetum* forms a deliberate contrast to their *tristes epulae* (3.280–1). See 231n. for the assignment of their *caetra* to other Iberian troops. Spaltenstein suggests the possibility of a *figura etymologica* connecting *ferro uiuere laetum* to *Adyrmachidae*, evoking Greek μάχη or μάχαιρα. For *laetus* governing an infinitive, see 3.575 *laeta domare labores*, 8.615 *laetos cingere ferrum*, etc.; *TLL* 7.2.885.83, L-H-S 350–1.

Gens accola Nili is a contraction of Verg. *Geo.* 4.287–8 *nam qua Pellaei gens fortunata Canopi / accolit effuso stagnantem flumine Nilum*. For *accola* of river dwellers, see 11.25 *Eridani tumidissimus accola*, Verg. *Aen.* 7.728–9 *amnisque uadosi / accola Volturni, pariterque Saticulus asper*, etc. According to Hdt. 4.168, the Adyrmachidae dwelled east of Plynus, a North African port between Cyrenaica and the Nile Delta; cf. Pliny *NH* 5.39, Ptol. *Geog.* 4.5.22, Bona 1998: 67–8, *NP* s.v. *Plynus*. Though the homeland of the Adyrmachidae was some distance from the Nile, Silius' geography is often as inaccurate as that of the other Latin poets; see, e.g., my note on 2.60–1n. Thus, it is certainly possible to interpret the phrase *gens accola Nili* as being in apposition with *Adyrmachidae*. 3.265 *Aethiopes, gens haud incognita Nilo*, similarly places the Ethiopians on the Nile.

Drakenborch argued correctly, however, that the comma should be placed before *pariter* to distinguish the Nilotic troops from the Adyrmachidae; see Blomgren 1938: 28–9. 293n. *Amphitryoniades, pariter ueneranda Cybele* is a relevant parallel, as *pariter* is similarly found with the second element. Verg. *Aen.* 7.728–9, quoted above in this note, shows the structure that Silius is adapting. Heinsius endeavored to correct *pariter* to *patrii* or *Pharii*, while Drakenborch supplied *et*, but neither expedient is required. Both here and at 293 *pariter* can be used without a connective, and the pause at the principal caesura helps to clarify the apposition. For further examples, see, e.g., Sen. *Ag.* 754–5 *uos, umbrae, precor, / iurata superis unda, te pariter precor*.

225. corpora ab immodico seruans nigrantia Phoebo: for the racist misconception that black skin results from burning by the sun, see 222n. and 3.268–9 *his simul immitem testantes corpore solem / exusti uenere Nubae; LSJ* s.v. Αἰθίοψ, Ov. *Met.* 1.774, 2.235–6 *sanguine tum credunt in corpora summa uocato / Aethiopum populos nigrum traxisse colorem* with Bömer's notes and Michalopoulos 2001: 21, Manil. *Astr.* 4.758–9 *ardent Aethiopes Cancro, cui plurimus ignis: / hoc color ipse docet*, Luc. *BC* 10.131 *pars sanguinis usti* with Berti's note. For the immoderate African sun, see, e.g., 2.60 *iniquo... sole*, 3.268 *immitem... solem*, 7.866 *solis iniqui*, etc.

226. quis positum agminibus caput imperiumque Nealces: no Nealces is historically attested at Cannae, but the name appears in Roman epic: see 15.448,

Commentary Lines 227–8 163

Verg. *Aen.* 10.753, VF *Arg.* 3.191. Livy 22.46.7 attributes command of the African troops to Maharbal, Polybius 3.114.7 to Hanno. The pairing of *caput* and *imperium* is infrequent and may be inspired by historiographical examples such as Livy 22.32.5 *ac pro capite atque arce Italiae urbe Romana atque imperio geratur*, Vell. 2.101.2 *cum duo inter se eminentissima imperiorum et hominum coirent capita*.

227–34. A catalog of the Iberian peoples under Mago's command on the right wing: Pyreneans, Cantabrians, Balearic islanders, and inhabitants of the Baetis region. By contrast, Livy places Mago in the center with his brother Hannibal, and Maharbal's Numidians on the right wing: 22.46.3 *dextrum cornu Numidis equitibus datum*, 22.46.7 *duces cornibus praeerant sinistro Hasdrubal, dextro Maharbal; mediam aciem Hannibal ipse cum fratre Magone tenuit*. See 220–6n. and Introduction, section 3c.

227–8. at parte in dextra, sinuat qua flexibus undam / Aufidus: see 219n. on the curving Aufidus, the modern Ofanto River in southern Italy, and Bona 1998: 126. Silius alternately describes the Aufidus as *stagnans* (617n., 10.89 *stagnantis consul molitur proelia ripas*) and *rapidus* (11.507–8 *umentis rapido circumdat gurgite campos / Aufidus*). As in the latter passage, Horace makes it a fast-flowing river: *Carm.* 3.30.10 *uiolens*, 4.9.2, *Serm.* 1.1.58 *acer*. Spaltenstein suggests that Horace may have been thinking of a different section of the river, but limnological verisimilitude is not likely to be the issue in either poet. Silius' rivers are part of a poetic landscape where literary associations override other considerations. The epic's representations of the Cinyps and the Hebrus are parallel examples; see 2.60 *Cinyphiumque Macen* and 2.74–5 *saxosis nemora alta iugis cursuque fatigant / Hebrum* with my notes. By the end of the battle, the river will be flowing in blood: see 10.319–20.

The phrasing may be adapted from Manil. *Astr.* 1.692 *sinuat flexus*, 5.14 *sinuantia flexus* (of constellations); see also Ov. *Met.* 11.553 *unda, uelut uictrix, sinuataque despicit undas* (the waves that drown Ceyx). Note also Silius' phrases for curving battlefield formations: 4.318 *aut illi laeuos sinuant in cornua gyros*, 6.226 *cetera sinuatis glomerat sub pectore gyris*.

228. et curuo circum errat gurgite campos: *curuo…gurgite* redoubles the preceding line's *sinuat…flexibus undam*. See 4.650 *curuato gurgite*, adapted from Verg. *Aen.* 3.564 *curuato gurgite*. Silius can also pair the preceding line's *sinuare* with *gurges*: 13.27 *sinuati gurgitis*, 15.173–4 *sinuatos gurgite…/ anfractus pelagi*. See Ov. *Met.* 14.51 *paruus erat gurges, curuos sinuatus in arcus* for a comparable reduplication; see also *TLL* 6.2.2364.6. For *errare* applied to a river, see *TLL* 5.2.808.72.

I have accepted Liberman's convincing correction *campos* for *ripas* of the MSS (2006: 21). The reading *ripas* may appear to be supported by the example of the Metaurus at 15.621–3 *qua curuatas sinuosis flexibus amnis / obliquat ripas*

164   *Commentary Lines 229–31*

refluoque per aspera lapsu / in sese redit. Liberman argues, however, that 228's close similarity to 219 *consilio curuis accommodat ordine ripis* prompted the intrusion of *ripas*. The example of 11.507–8 *umentis rapido circumdat gurgite campos / Aufidus* confirms the likelihood of *campos*. In both passages, the Aufidus River wanders around the surrounding fields rather than its own banks.

229. Mago regit: see 227–34n. for Mago's role at Cannae.

229–30. subiere leues, quos horrida misit / Pyrene, populi: for Hannibal's recruitment of the Pyrenean forces, see 3.415–41 and Augoustakis 2003. Here, however, *Pyrene* is more likely used as a metonym for Iberia as a whole, as 230 *uario* suggests; see 1.190 *mox et Pyrenes populi et bellator Hiberus,* 13.699 *Pyrenes populos,* 14.35 *Pyrene misit populos,* 15.451 *Pyrenes... tellus,* 16.278, etc. For light-armed Iberian troops, see 4.549 *instat Hiber leuis et leuior discurrere Maurus,* Luc. *BC* 4.9 *Vettonesque leues,* Livy 22.46.6 *Hispani linteis praetextis purpura tunicis, candore miro fulgentibus, constiterant,* etc. *Horrida* refers to both the steepness of the Pyrenees and the proverbial ferocity of the Iberian troops; see 17.641 *fera Pyrene nec mitis Hiberus,* Sen. *Phaed.* 69 *siue ferocis iuga Pyrenes,* etc. For the adjective's use *de barbaris,* see *TLL* 6.3.2993.22.

230–1. uarioque auxere tumultu / flumineum latus: the variety of the forces suggests that 230 *Pyrene* is a metonym for all Iberia. For Hannibal's multiethnic army, see 3.221 *castra quatit clamor permixtis dissona linguis* and Dewar 2003. For the varied Pyrenean forces, see, e.g., 16.277–8 *uariosque subacta / Pyrene misit populos.* The phrase *uario tumultu* does not appear in poetry until the Flavian era: Stat. *Theb.* 1.516, 5.348, Claud. *Cos. Stil.* 1.162.

    (H)ausere FV and *anxere* O, neither of which makes sense in context, arose as easy palaeographical confusions. Interpreting *auxere* as *impleuere,* however, has given difficulty. Heinsius suggested *cinxere,* which can indeed be used in reference to a group of people, e.g., Ov. *Pont.* 4.9.17 *dumque latus sancti cingit tibi turba senatus.* Summers 1900: 305 suggested *clausere,* "closed the way to the river side" on the example of Livy 22.47.2 *nullo circa ad euagandum relicto spatio hinc amnis hinc peditum acies claudebant.*

    Håkanson 1976; 21 preserves the MS reading by identifying the *flumineum latus* not as the riverbank itself (as do, e.g., Ernesti and Ruperti), but as Hannibal's flank stationed on it, on the example of Livy 22.46.2 *Gallos Hispanosque equites prope ripam laeuo in cornu aduersus Romanum equitatum.* Volpilhac-Lenthéric follows this interpretation in her translation ("à l'aile adossée au fleuve"), as I have in mine, in contrast to Duff's "filling the river-banks." For *latus* as a riverbank, see Ov. *Fasti* 1.501 *fluminis... latus, TLL* 7.2.1028.65.

231. effulget caetrata iuuentus: for *fulgere* of armed warriors, see 2.79 *fulgentem tegmine laeuam* with my note, 12.232–3 *egregium cristis et casside nota / fulgentem,* etc. The Adyrmachidae (see 223–4n.) were introduced as carrying

Commentary Lines 232–4   165

the *caetra* at 3.278–9 *uersicolor contra caetra et falcatus ab arte / ensis Adyrmachidis ac laeuo tegmina crure.* The passage evokes the arms carried by Virgil's Oscans: Verg. *Aen.* 7.732 *laeuas caetra tegit, falcati comminus enses.* As Servius *ad loc.* knew, however, the *caetra* was more appropriately carried by Hannibal's forces than by Italians: LAEVAS CAETRA TEGIT *caetra est scutum loreum, quo utuntur Afri et Hispani.* Silius' assignment of the *caetra* to the other Iberian troops follows, e.g., Caes. *BC* 1.39.1 *caetratae ulterioris Hispaniae cohortes,* Livy 21.21.12 *tredecim milia octingentos quinquaginta pedites caetratos misit in Africam* (i.e., from Iberia), Luc. *BC* 7.232 *illic pugnaces commouit Hiberia caetras,* etc. For *caetratus* applied to the peltasts in the Macedonian forces, see Livy 33.4.4 *ad hoc duo milia caetratorum, quos peltastas appellant,* 33.8.7 *Philippus cum caetratis et cornu dextro peditum,* etc.

232. Cantaber ante alios nec tectus tempora Vasco: for a comparable pairing, see 5.197 *Cantaber et galeae contempto tegmine Vasco.* Both of these Iberian peoples were introduced as mercenaries at 5.195–7. *Ante alios* recalls the similar priority accorded to the Cantabrians in the earlier catalog: see 3.326–7 *Cantaber ante omnis, hiemisque aestusque famisque / inuictus palmamque ex omni ferre labore.* The Vascones' lack of helmets (cf. 3.358 *aut Vasco insuetus galeae,* 5.197) is a mark of their primitive society, as at Tac. *Germ.* 6.1 *paucis loricae, uix uni alterive cassis aut galea.* For *tectus* with an accusative of relation, see, e.g., 8.375 *aere caput tecti,* Ov. *Met.* 12.291 *prima tectus lanugine malas,* Luc. *BC* 6.625 *maestum tecta caput,* etc. For the Vascones' localization between the Ebro and the Pyrenees, see Pliny *NH* 3.22, 4.110; Bona 1998: 78–9.

233. ac torto miscens Baliaris proelia plumbo: for the Balearic islanders' deadly expertise with the slingshot, see 1.314 *hic crebram fundit Baliari uerbere glandem,* 3.365 *funda bella ferens Baliaris et alite plumbo,* 5.193 *torta Baliaris saeuus habena,* Verg. *Geo.* 1.308–9, Luc. *BC* 3.709–11, Strabo *Geog.* 3.5.1 ὅμως σφενδονῆται ἄριστοι λέγονται, etc. For *torto…plumbo,* see, e.g., Ov. *Met.* 4.709–10 *tantum aberat scopulis, quantum Balearica torto / funda potest plumbo medii transmittere caeli.* The chiastic arrangement of adjective–noun and participle–object surrounding *Baliaris* provides a visual image of the slingshot circling around the warrior's head. For chiastic arrangement, see Flammini 1983 and Introduction, section 5c. *Miscere proelia* is a common phrase in the *Punica* and elsewhere: see 1.266, 2.152 with my note, 4.355–6, 10.427, 14.155, 14.521, 15.667, 15.673, 16.48, 17.383; for *miscere* with other words for combat, see 330n. *certamina miscent,* 1.69 *miscentem pugnas,* 2.528 *miscentem bella,* etc.

234. Baetigenaeque uiri: the Baetis is the modern Guadalquivir River in southern Spain. Hasdrubal harasses Baetica (1.146) before Hannibal assumes command, the peoples of the region form part of the catalog at 3.391–405, and the Romans send troops there as part of the Spanish campaign: 12.687–8 *summissaque Baetis ad oras / auxilia.* Silius is the only classical Latin author to use the

166   *Commentary Lines 234–8*

compounds *Baetigena* and *Baeticola,* which he appears to have coined on the model of Verg. *Aen.* 11.700 *Appenninicola* and Ov. *Met.* 15.432 *Appenninigena.* See Bona 1998: 41.

234–5. celsus media ipse coercet / agmina: as the commander, Hannibal rides high on his horse, as at 1.249–50 *celsus et in magno praecedens agmine ductor / imperium perferre suum,* etc.; see also 1.161 *sublimis.* The phrasing recombines descriptions of Hannibal's two major models from earlier epic, Virgil's Turnus (Verg. *Aen.* 9.27–8 *Messapus primas acies, postrema <u>coercent</u> / Tyrrhidae iuuenes, <u>medio</u> dux <u>agmine</u> Turnus*) and Lucan's Caesar (Luc. *BC* 1.245 *et* **celsus medio** *conspectus in* **agmine** *Caesar*). For *coercere* as *regere,* see *TLL* 3.1436.14, Ov. *Pont.* 3.3.61 *sic regat imperium terrasque coerceat omnis,* Luc. *BC* 2.9 *qua cuncta coercet,* etc.

235–6. quae patrio firmauit milite: *patrio…milite* is in contradistinction to Livy 22.46.3, where Hannibal places the African troops at the wings and the Gauls and Iberians in the center. Silius employs the phrase again at 12.343 *Sardoas patrio quatiebat milite terras;* these are apparently the only uses in classical poetry.

235–6. quaeque / Celtarum Eridano perfusis saepe cateruis: *perfusis saepe* refers to dwelling by the Po and thus washing frequently in it, as at 8.450–1 *et lauat ingentem perfundens flumine sacro / Clitumnus taurum.* Compare "drinking" the river at 8.367 *sceptriferi qui potant Thybridis undam.* Prior models include Verg. *Geo.* 2.146–7 *hinc albi, Clitumne, greges et maxima taurus / uictima, saepe tuo perfusi flumine sacro* and Luc. *BC* 3.203–4 *Mysiaque et gelido tellus perfusa Caico / Idalis.* For the Celts as inhabitants of the Po valley, see 11.25 *Eridani tumidissimus accola, Celtae.* For *cateruis,* see 77n.

237–43. Hannibal stations the elephant troops where the river provides no natural defense. 8.670 *ac uictrix insultat belua campis* announced the presence of the elephants, and they go into battle at 570n. The historiographical sources indicate that the elephants perished of cold before Cannae, nor is it fully accepted that Carthaginian elephants carried turrets into battle; see Introduction, section 3 for full discussion. Silius includes the elephants here in order to provide *variatio* to the combat narrative and to emphasize the extraordinary nature of the battle. He describes the elephants in paradoxical terms, as moving walls or fortifications. The turrets or howdahs that they carry are variously described as "towers," "fortifications," and "walls": 239 *turritas moles ac propugnacula,* 241 *muros.* The comparison to city defenses suggests the pairing of immense size with mobility.

237–8. sed qua se fluuius retro labentibus undis / eripit: for the construction with *qua,* compare 1.211 *sed qua se campis squalentibus Africa tendit.* Virgil's tide simile may have inspired the phrasing of the latter part of the line: Verg.

Aen. 11.627–8 *nunc rapidus* <u>retro</u> *atque aestu reuoluta resorbens / saxa fugit* <u>litusque</u> *uado labente relinquit.* The clausula adapts Ov. *Met.* 11.138 *labentibus obuius undis, Met.* 14.633.

238. et nullo cuneos munimine uallat: Hannibal's troops threw down "the rampart's defenses" at 217n.; here the turn in the river affords no natural defense. For the imagined geography of the Aufidus, see 219n. and 227n. *Cunei* can be generic "squads," rather than specifically "wedges;" see *TLL* 4.1404.39. For the contrast between their typical density and uncharacteristic looseness, see 364n. *Cuneos...uallat* may have been inspired by Luc. *BC* 6.184 *tunc densos inter cuneos compressus et omni / uallatus bello uincit, quem respicit, hostem.*

239–40. turritas moles ac propugnacula dorso / belua nigranti gestans: the elephants carry *turres* at 596n., 4.599 *uis elephantorum turrito concita dorso,* 17.621 *et posuit gestatas belua turris*; see, e.g., Lucr. *DRN* 5.1302 *inde boues Lucas turrito corpore,* Pliny *NH* 8.27 *turres armatorum in dorsis ferunt,* Juv. 12.109–10 *dorso ferre cohortis, / partem aliquam belli, et euntem in proelia turrem,* Florus 1.18.28 *cum turribus suis beluas.* There has been considerable scholarly debate over the particular species of elephant employed by the Carthaginians and whether they carried turrets into combat. Rance 2009: 106 concludes: "The positive evidence for specifically Carthaginian use of elephant turrets is undeniably slight, but even those studies which argue a negative case concede the possibility of the exceptional use of turrets in a variety of contexts— ceremonial, propagandistic or poliorcetic." Heinsius read *turritae ω,* in apposition with the elephants themselves rather than their turrets, as at 559–60 *feraeque / turrigerae molem.* Difficulties result, however, from the parallelism of *moles* and *propugnacula.*

For the elephant as a *moles,* see 571n., 3.463–4 *atras...moles,* Colum. *RR* 3.8.3 *India perhibetur molibus ferarum mirabilis,* Flor. *Epit.* 1.22 *Hasdrubal...cum exercitu nouo, nouis uiribus, noua belli mole ueniebat.* See Stat. *Theb.* 4.47 *ingenti turritae mole Cleonae* with Parkes's note. The Roman troops attack the *propugnacula* with fire at 604n. Virgil licenses the word for epic (*Aen.* 4.87, 9.170, 9.664), but Silius is the only other epic poet to use *propugnacula* until Claudian; see also Hor. *Epod.* 1.2, Stat. *Silv.* 3.3.101. Silius characteristically refers to the elephants as *beluae* (five times in this book, fourteen times in total). For the elephants' dark backs, see 577n. *liuenti dorso,* 4.618 *stat multa in tergo et nigranti lancea dorso.*

240–1. ceu mobilis agger / nutat: a studied oxymoron, as *agger* typically refers to stationary fortifications. Compare 579–80 *uolanti...aggere.* The contrast between the "nodding" elephants and the "straight walls" (turrets) that they "lift to the sky" emphasizes the paradoxical nature of the sight. The elephants' bodies are like moving ramparts. *Molibus* v2 is difficult and the repetition after 239 *moles* is unlikely.

168   *Commentary Lines 241–51*

241. et erectos attollit ad aethera muros: for *erectus* as "elatus, altus," see *TLL* 5.2.785.20, Sen. *Marc.* 18.5 *erectos…montes*; for *ad aethera*, compare 4.145–6 *erectus in auras / it sonipes.* Heinsius' suggestion *euectos* obscures the contrast between nodding elephants and straight turrets. Varro orders his troops to attack the turrets, again described as *muros* (601n.), with fire at 599–601. *TLL* 8.1687.55 cites this line along with Claud. *Eutr.* 2.284 (referring to Cybele's mural crown) as examples of figurative poetic uses of *murus*.

    Attollit ad aethera recalls another terrifying monster, the serpent of the Bagrada River: 6.223–5 *adsultans aethera lambit /…/ immensum attollit corpus.* The phrase *attollere muros* typically refers to the walls that a city raises to protect iself, as at 3.384 *Sarmaticos attollens Vxama muros,* 15.508–9 *'quos Roma,' inquit 'quos altius, oro, / attollit muros',* Verg. *Aen.* 11.130 *fatalis murorum attollere moles,* etc. The association between the elephants and city walls continues the image of vastness looming over the frightened foot soldiers.

242–3. cetera iam Numidis circumuolitare uagosque / ferre datur cursus: alliteration of C- and the interlaced alliteration of F- continue across both lines. Silius draws on Virgil's characterization of the *Numidae infreni* (see *Aen.* 4.41 with Pease's note) at 1.215 *Numidae, gens inscia freni.* This passage and 1.215 are Silius' sole uses of forms of *Numidae* (following Delz's readings); he elsewhere refers to them as *Nomades* (sixteen times; see 275n.). Virgil varies *Numidae* (once) and *Nomades* (three times); Ovid, Manilius, and Lucan refer exclusively to *Numidae*; Statius varies the names in the *Silvae*, but his sole epic reference is *Theb.* 10.415 *Numidae.* Silius is accordingly the only successor to follow Virgil's practice in epic.

    Circumuolitare and *uagos…cursus* are etymological glosses of Νομάδες; see Luc. *BC* 4.677 *Numidaeque uagi,* etc. For the Numidian horsemen's characteristic battle tactics, see Polyb. *Hist.* 3.72.10 διὰ τὸ τοὺς Νομάδας ἀποχωρεῖν μὲν εὐχερῶς καὶ σποράδην, ἐπικεῖσθαι δὲ πάλιν ἐκ μεταβολῆς τολμηρῶς καὶ θρασέως· τὸ γὰρ τῆς Νομαδικῆς μάχης ἴδιόν ἐστι τοῦτο. The emphasis on confusion of the enemy rather than speed allows rejection of *citos* (*edd. a* j). Earlier poets applied *uagos…cursus* to the wandering stars: Sen. *Phaed.* 962, Luc. *BC* 10.203. Silius assigns the phrase to movement on the battlefield, as here and at 5.630. See further 275n. *Nomadumque uolucrem.*

    Heinsius' tentative suggestion *nam* obscures the emphasis on the Numidian troops' ceaseless motion.

243. et toto feruere campo: for the battlefield seething with soldiers, see Lucr. *DRN* 2.40–1 *per loca campi / feruere cum uideas belli,* VF *Arg.* 6.588 *toto iamdudum feruere campo,* Stat. *Theb.* 3.314 *late deferuere campo,* etc. Slaughter rather than fast-moving cavalry makes the battlefield seethe at 483n. *feruentia caedibus arua.*

244–51. Hannibal exhorts his forces and promises to recognize each of his soldiers' accomplishments. Meanwhile, Varro moves the Roman troops outside

Commentary Lines 244–6 169

the fortification. Flaminius similarly recognizes the accomplishments of individual soldiers before Trasimene at 5.165–85. Both that scene and the present recall Caesar's promise before Pharsalus to recognize his men's deeds individually: Luc. *BC* 7.287–9 *cuius non militis ensem / agnoscam? caelumque tremens cum lancea transit / dicere non fallar quo sit uibrata lacerto.* For Lucan's Caesar as a model for Hannibal, see Stocks 2014: 61–70. As Spaltenstein observes, Varro neglects to deliver the "encouragements de rigueur," an inspiring speech before combat. The absence of a speech can accordingly be read as a further sign of Varro's haste and inattention to the necessities of battle.

244. dum Libys incenso dispensat milite uires: *dum Libys* followed by 249 *iam Varro* reflects the similar movement of the earlier episode introducing Varro to the narrative: 8.242–4 *dum…Poeni…/ iam… Varro.* Both commanders have an incendiary effect on their troops; for Hannibal, see 1.345 *accensae exultant mentes,* 2.36 *incensi dictis animi* with my note, 17.293–4 *ignifero mentes furiabat in iram / hortatu,* etc.; for Varro, see 37n. *incendebat.* The phrase *dispensare uires* appears in poetry only here and in the boxing match of Stat. *Theb.* 6.766 *cunctatus uires dispensat.* The phrase's appearance for the first time in both Flavian poets suggests that this may be a possible instance of bidirectional influence (see Introduction, section 5a). Hannibal fights with cunning against the maddened Varro, just as Alcidamas husbands his strength against the stronger Capaneus.

245. hortandoque iterum atque iterum insatiabilis urget: the series of elisions conveys the sense of speed. For the repetition of *iterum,* see 7.393 *hunc iterum atque iterum uinctum,* 10.364 *iterumque iterumque tremendum,* Verg. *Aen.* 8.527 *iterum atque iterum fragor increpat ingens;* Wills 1996: 116–17. *Insatiabilis urget* suggests an overtrumping of Varro's exhortation of the Roman troops (267n. *minitans*). Silius applies the adjective *insatiabilis* only to Hannibal (here) and his opposite Scipio (13.218, 13.755). The adjective is rare in poetry, occurring previously only at Lucr. *DRN* twice, Ov. *Ibis* 172, and Stat. *Theb.* 11.87–8 *miserum insatiabilis edit / me tradente caput; TLL* 7.1.1837.8. Statius' application of the adjective to Tydeus may accordingly be an instance of bidirectional influence; see Introduction, section 5a. The collocation of *hortari* and *urg(u)ere* is not common; it appears first at Livy 10.5.3 *urgent itaque alii alios hortanturque signiferos ut ocius eant* and next at VF *Arg.* 3.550 *simul Alcides hortatibus urget.*

Van Veen objected to *hortando* with 246 *factis* and so proposed *hortandi* depending on *insatiabilis.*

246. factis quemque suis et se cognoscere iactat: for *facta* as the achievements of war, see 1.55 *facta ad Mauortia* (the young Hannibal's ambition), 3.607 *at tu transcendes, Germanice, facta tuorum* (Jupiter's prophecy for Domitian), 4.361–2 *Marte probare genus factisque Lacona parentem / ardebant* (the sons of Xanthippus), etc. Hannibal's pride (*iactat*) in observing his men is matched by

170   *Commentary Lines 247–50*

his disappointment after Cannae when they fail to conquer Naples: 12.50 *talia iactabat famaeque pudore futurae.*

247–8. qua dextra ueniant stridentis sibila teli / promittitque uiris nulli se defore testem: the sound of the missiles will permit Hannibal to determine which soldiers launched them and fulfill his promise to be their witness. The motif recalls the similar claim of Livy's Hannibal before the battle at the Ticinus to have been a witness of his troops' deeds: Livy 21.43.17 *nemo est uestrum . . . cui non idem ego uirtutis spectator ac testis notata temporibus locisque referre sua possim decora.* As the battle begins at Cannae, however, so many spears are hurled at once that no one can tell who was the first to cast his (see 310–11n.). The motif recalls a similar promise made by Lucan's Caesar at Pharsalus to recognize his men's individual spear casts. See Luc. *BC* 7.288–9 *caelumque tremens cum lancea transit, / dicere non fallar, quo sit uibrata lacerto* with Lanzarone's note. The theomachy episode offers a *Steigerung* of the motif of observation by a superior, as Mars and Pallas watch their respective champions; see 453–4n.

    Missiles are conventionally strident and resonant. For *stridentis*, see 311–12n. *stridens nimbus certante furore / telorum*, 338n. *stridens . . . harundo*, 17.66 *iaculis stridentibus*, Verg. *Aen.* 5.502 *neruo stridente*, *Aen.* 11.863 *extemplo teli stridorem aurasque sonantis*, Stat. *Theb.* 10.536 *stridentia tela*, etc. For *sibila*, see 2.99 *sibila . . . arcus*, VF *Arg.* 6.201–2 *dum sibila respicit Iron / Cuspidis Argiuae, Pyliam latere accipit hastam*, etc.

249–51. Charon rejoices as Varro moves his troops from the rampart to begin combat and opens his domain to receive the massive influx of dead souls. These reactions are typical of the Underworld powers at the prospect of impending war. It is also a topos of civil war poetry; see Introduction, section 4b. See Luc. *BC* 3.16–17 *praeparat innumeras puppes Acherontis adusti / portitor; in multas laxantur Tartara poenas* (Julia), *BC* 6.799–800 *regni possessor inertis / pallentis aperit sedes* (as seen by the ghost raised by Erictho); Petr. *Sat.* 121.117–19 *uix nauita Porthmeus / sufficiet simulacra uirum traducere cumba; / classe opus est.*

249. iam Varro exacta uallo legione: Skutsch on Enn. *Ann.* 292 observes that Ennius applied the term *legiones* to Hannibal's army; see also Skutsch's note on *Ann.* 326. Lucan generally avoids the *terminus technicus*, using it only at *BC* 7.219. The mythological poets use it comparatively frequently (Verg. *Aen.* seven times, Stat. *Theb.* twice, VF *Arg.* four times) "in its original sense of 'muster' or 'levy'"; see Harrison's note on Verg. *Aen.* 10.120. Silius' usage (six times) follows the mythological poets.

249–50. mouebat / cladum principia: *mouere principia* and *cladum principia* are both apparently unique collocations. *Mouere principia* is a variation on Stat. *Theb.* 4.212 *scelerumque ingentia semina mouit* (see 244–51n. for context), itself adapted from Ov. *Am.* 3.1.59. *Cladum principia* is similarly adapted from Sen.

Phoen. 279–80 *iacta iam sunt semina / cladis futurae.* Phrasing and context may vary Eriphyle's treachery in Statius: see Stat. *Theb.* 4.211–13 *sic Eriphylaeos aurum fatale penates / inrupit scelerumque ingentia* **semina mouit**, / *et graue Tisiphone risit gauisa futuris.* Like Varro, Eriphyle too "moves the beginnings" of disaster in the foolish hope of short-term gain, and the Fury rejoices. For *mouere* with an abstract object, compare 12.437 *miranda mouens*, 13.97 *extrema mouebat*, Stat. *Theb.* 10.178 *rerum extrema mouens*, etc.

250–1. ac pallenti laetus in unda / laxabat sedem uenturis portitor umbris: Silius' Sibyl observes that Charon always has adequate space for the newly dead: 13.759–61 *nullo non tempore abundans / umbrarum huc agitur torrens, uectatque capaci / agmina mole Charon, et sufficit improba puppis.* For *laxabat*, see 244–51n. The reference to Charon's happiness (*laetus*) is a *figura etymologica* on his name: see Serv. *ad Aen.* 6.299 CHARON κατὰ ἀντίφρασιν *quasi* ἀχαίρων, VF *Arg.* 6.158–9 *gaudet iam nocte quieta / portitor.* It is also a deliberate reversal of the Virgilian Charon: Verg. *Aen.* 6.315 *nauita… tristis.* Charon's joy further recalls Death's gaping rictus during the sack of Saguntum; see *Pun.* 2.548 *Mors graditur uasto caua pandens guttura rictu* with my note.

Pallenti… unda is found earlier only at [Tib.] 3.5.21 *pallentes undas*, but the Underworld is typically *pallens*: 3.483 *Tartareus regni pallentis hiatus*, 13.408 *regna… pallentia*, [Verg.] *Aetna* 78 *Ditis pallentia regna*, Luc. *BC* 6.800 (quoted at 249–50n.above), etc. *Portitor* is the characteristic poetic title for Charon: see Verg. *Geo.* 4.502 *portitor Orci*, *Aen.* 6.298 with Horsfall's note, 6.326 *portitor ille Charon*, Ov. *Met.* 10.73, Luc. *BC* 3.17 (quoted at 249–51n. above), VF *Arg.* 6.159, etc. A careful pattern of alliteration unites the pair of lines: *pallenti–portitor, laetus–laxabat, unda–umbris.*

252–61. The Roman troops discover the bodies of Solymus and his father Satricus. The grim omen (*triste… augurium*) unnerves them. They display the scene and its message to avoid combat (*uetantia*) to their commander Varro. Solymus achieves his desire to convert his family's misfortune into a warning for the Roman forces (see 164–5n.), but Varro derisively dismisses it (see 262–6n.).

252–3. stant primi: initial position is typical for *stare*; see 370n., 434n., 581n. For *stant primi*, see 370n. *stabat cum primis*, 2.321 *stant prima inter signa senes*, Stat. *Theb.* 2.225 *stant ordine primi*, etc. As Charon was the subject of the preceding lines, there may have been a recollection of another Charon passage, Verg. *Aen.* 6.313 *stabant orantes primi transmittere cursum.*

252–3. quos sanguineae pendente uetabant / ire notae clipeo: Silius appears to have originated the phrase *sanguineae… notae*, adapted by Claud. *Ruf.* 2 *praef.* 10 *sanguineas belli rettulit unda notas.* The verb *uetare* with the infinitive is not uncommon; for *uetare + ire*, see Ov. *Her.* 10.88, Luc. *BC* 7.578, 10.203, Stat. *Theb.* 2.3, etc.; Zaia observes the similarity of the augural context of Hor. *Carm.* 3.27.15 *teque nec laeuus uetet ire picus.*

172   *Commentary Lines 253–9*

253. defixique omine torpent: the pause at the principal caesura suggests the astonished soldiers coming to a halt. *Omine* repeats 178n. *omina* and anticipates 258–9n. *triste... augurium.* It is likely that Silius has "corrected" Stat. *Theb.* 1.490–1 *stupet omine tanto / defixus senior* in order to recall more directly Hor. *Epist.* 1.6.14 *defixis oculis animoque et corpore torpet.* The verb *stupere* is the more frequent reaction to an omen: see, e.g., Verg. *Aen.* 10.249–50, VF *Arg.* 5.95–6 *omina Mopsus dum stupet,* Livy 3.47.6, 22.53.6 *cum stupore ac miraculo torpidos defixisset,* etc.; see *TLL* 5.1.341.62.

254. iuxta terribilis facies: the phrase is common; a relevant prior application can be found in Lucan's description of Erictho: *BC* 6.517 *terribilis Stygio facies pallore grauatur.*

254–5. miseranda iacebant / corpora in amplexu: *iacere in amplexu* typically refers to the erotic embrace: Ov. *Am.* 3.8.12 *huius in amplexu, uita, iacere potes,* Stat. *Silv.* 1.2.52–3 *alma Venus... iacebat / amplexu duro Getici resoluta mariti,* etc. Silius adapts it here and at 17.470–1 *Heriumque iacentem / amplexus* for the embrace of death.

255–6. natusque in pectore patris / imposita uulnus dextra letale tegebat: Solymus' spear struck his father in the back, but presumably (*pace* Spaltenstein) with enough force to penetrate to the front of his body, in particular as Satricus was not wearing armor; see 102–3n. *nuda parentis / in terga.* Solymus' hand now modestly covers the wound he inflicted. Satricus had asked *da iungere pectus* (149n.) and now receives his wish. The clausula of 255 is rare, recurring only at 13.618, Ov. *Fasti* 5.71, and Luc. *BC* 9.133 *uidi ego magnanimi lacerantes pectora patris,* again of a father's death in the sight of his son. For *imponere* with hands, see 8.110 *meque sua ratibus dextra imposuisset,* Stat. *Theb.* 11.586 *uirgo autem impositae sustentat pondera laeuae.* For *uulnus... letale,* which occurs six times in Silius, see Verg. *Aen.* 9.580, 11.749, Stat. *Theb.* 11.535–6, etc.

257–8. effusae lacrimae, Mancinique inde reuersus / fraterna sub morte dolor: the troops mourn Mancinus both as their fallen hero and as the unwitting cause of his family's suffering and their own. *Effundere lacrimas* is a common phrase, like *effundere fletus*; a relevant prior application can be found in the reunion of Virgil's Aeneas and Anchises (Verg. *Aen.* 6.686 *effusaeque genis lacrimae*). For the death of Mancinus, see 12–14n. The adjective *fraterna* similarly replaces genitive *fratris* at Catul. 68.19 *fraterna... mors,* Verg. *Geo.* 3.518 *fraterna morte,* *Aen.* 9.736, etc. For *sub morte,* see Spaltenstein's note on 3.217, which compares 373n. *sub nomine,* 431n. *sub hoste,* 3.217 *sub omine,* 11.244 *sub ira,* etc. as examples in which *sub* "marque très généralement la circonstance, ce qui implique de cas en cas la cause, l'instrument, etc." See *OLD* s.v. *sub* 11.

258–9. tum triste mouebat / augurium: *triste... augurium* recapitulates 253n. *omine.* The phrase evokes its only earlier appearance, Verg. *Aen.* 5.7 *triste per* *augurium Teucrorum pectora ducunt,* of Dido's death, which, like Solymus, Aeneas caused unintentionally. Claud. *DRP* 3.125–6 adapts the phrase in an unrelated context.

259. et similes defuncto in corpore uultus: for Roman culture's emphasis on the similar appearance of father and son, see Guastella 1985. The phrasing likely evokes Stat. *Theb.* 5.227 *heu similes perituro in corpore uultus,* in the similar context of family murder among the Lemnian women. The line also evokes Luc. *BC* 6.631 *et uocem defuncto in corpore quaerit,* in the similar context of an ill omen occurring before a climactic battle, in this case Sextus' necromantic consultation before Pharsalus.

260. ocius erroris culpam deflendaque facta: for Solymus' *error,* see 66n. For *culpa erroris,* see, e.g., Cic. *Marcell.* 13 *etsi aliqua culpa tenemur erroris humani, scelere certe liberati sumus,* [Sen.] *HO* 983 *error a culpa uacat,* Gell. *NA* 11.16.9 'sed huius' inquam 'tui erroris culpam esse intellego in mea scilicet infacundia,' etc. The narrator's reference to the events as *deflenda...facta* recapitulates 177n. *defletum...parentem.*

261. ductori pandunt atque arma uetantia pugnam: for *ductori,* see 24n. For reporting to the commander with *pandere,* see 6.206 *et ductori singula pando. Arma uetantia* recapitulates the message that Solymus wrote on his shield: 175n. *fuge proelia Varro.*

262–6. Varro shows contempt for the grisly scene and claims that these omens would only persuade his timid colleague Paulus. He disdains Solymus as a parricide, and his suicide and warning in blood as justified punishment by the Fury. For Varro's contempt for omens, see 1–7n., 15–16n.

262. ille ardens animi: a variation on the more common *ardens animus* (Livy 1.46.2, Man. *Astr.* 4.220, 4.570, Juv. 15.52, etc) or the Virgilian phrase *ardent animi* (Verg. *Aen.* 2.316). As Spaltenstein observes, *TLL* 2.486.44 classifies this use of *animi* as either locative or genitive of relation. The genitives in the other examples given by the *TLL,* Stat. *Theb.* 11.152 *ardet inops animi, Theb.* 1.662 *ardentem tenuit reuerentia caedis,* do not depend on *ardere.*

262. 'ferte haec' ait 'omina Paulo': for the frequent corruption of *omina* to *omnia* (aγ), see 3–4n.

263. namque illum, cui femineo stant corde timores: during the debate in the Carthaginian Senate, Gestar similarly accuses the more prudent Hanno of effeminacy: see 2.360–1 with my note. Spaltenstein's note suggests that *stare* simply functions as a synonym of *esse,* as at, e.g., 8.43 *quamquam inter Latios Annae stet numen honores,* 16.683–4 *et opima pace quieta / stat tellus.* Poetic tradition, however, appears to determine the use of *stare* when referring to the heart's emotions, as at, e.g., Luc. *BC* 7.339–40 *stat corde gelato / attonitus,* VF

174   *Commentary Lines 264–7*

Arg. 5.288–9 *stat pectore fixum / Aeetae sociare manus*, Stat. *Silv.* 2.1.12–13 *stat pectore demens / luctus et admoto latrant praecordia tactu*, Prud. *Perist.* 10.713 *stat in piorum corde pietas fortior*, etc. Van Veen suggested *feminei*, on the example of 13.17 *femineam Tyriae labem*, Sen. *Med.* 42 *pelle femineos metus*. The clausula is modeled on Catul. 64.99, and found also at *Pun.*12.324, Stat. *Ach.* 1.42.

264. mouerit ista manus, quae caede imbuta nefanda: Varro's view conforms with Solymus' view of his own hands (169–70n.) but disregards Satricus' absolution of his son. The phrase *caede imbuta* evokes its only previous occurrence in poetry, the murder of Lucan's Pompey: Luc. *BC* 10.334 *mens inbuta semel sacra iam caede*. For *imbuere* as *polluere*, see *TLL* 7.1.429.33. For *nefanda caedes*, see 10.585, Ov. *Met.* 15.174, Luc. *BC* 4.259, etc. The clausula is adapted from Catul. 64.397 *sed postquam tellus scelere est imbuta nefando*, also of family violence.

265. cum Furiae expeterent poenas: reference to the Furies' punishment of criminal sons recalls the frequent jibes leveled at Hannibal: 1.443–4 *quaenam te, Poene, paternae / huc adigunt furiae?* (Daunus at Saguntum), my note on 2.296 *exagitant manes iuuenem furiaeque paternae* (Hanno in the Carthaginian Senate), etc. For *expetere poenas,* see 13.543–4 with van der Keur's note, Sen. *Med.* 256, etc.; *TLL* 5.2.1694.72.

265–6. fortasse paterno / signauit moriens sceleratum sanguine carmen: Varro cruelly suggests that Solymus augmented his crime by writing in his father's blood rather than his own. Alliteration of S- emphasizes Varro's contempt, as at Eur. *Med.* 476–7; see Clayman 1987. Varro's reference to Solymus' inscription as a *carmen* evokes Paulus' earlier claim to be a *uates* when he similarly urged against giving battle (56–65n.). Both have warned Varro against battle with prophetic force. For *signare carmen*, see 174n., Verg. *Aen.* 3.287 *rem carmine signo*, similarly of writing on a shield, Ov. *Met.* 2.326 *signant quoque carmine saxum. Sceleratum…carmen* points back to the introduction to the scene: see 66n. *sceleratus…error.* For signing in blood, see 174n.

    The line as a whole adapts Ov. *Met.* 5.293 *tundit humum moriens scelerato sanguine tinctum*, describing the death of Pyreneus who fell off a tower while chasing the Muses. See Marks 2020 for further discussion of possible engagement with Ovid's poem and career.

267–77. Varro disposes the Roman troops, putting the forces under his own command in opposition to Nealces'. The listing of his forces further suggests his obliviousness. He leads some of Rome's traditional enemies, such as the Marsians and Samnites, and both the Samnites and Iapygians will defect to Hannibal after Cannae (Livy 22.61.11–13). Livy puts Varro on the left wing and Paulus on the right: Livy 22.45.8 *consules cornua tenuerunt, Terentius laeuum, Aemilius dextrum.* Silius earlier placed Nealces on the left wing (220–6n.),

Commentary Lines 267–70 175

which more likely means "the Romans' left" than a departure from Livy. See Introduction, section 3c.

267. tum minitans propere describit munera pugnae: *minitans* is a lesser parallel to Hannibal's encouragement of his troops, *insatiabilis urget* (245n.). Haste is one of Varro's characteristic attributes; he earlier promised to open the gates *propere* (35n.) to send his men to battle. The evocation of this earlier passage makes Heinsius' *properae* less likely. His argument for the genitive is certainly correct, however, at 15.604 *properi signum accursus* against *propere ω. Munera pugnae* is a variation on the more common *munera belli*: see Ov. *Met.* 13.296 *me duri fugientem munera belli*, Varro *Menipp.* 223 *fera militia / munera belli ut praestarem*, Livy 24.35.7 *inter se munera belli partiti sunt*, etc. *TLL* 5.1.662.78 rejects editorial efforts to correct *describere* to *discribere* when the verb means *definire, determinare* (cf. *OLD* s.v. 5), and accordingly Summers' *discribit* should be rejected. For *describere munus,* see Q. Cic. *Pet.* 20, 57.

268–9. quaque feras saeuus gentes aciemque Nealces / temperat: Nealces' "feral" troops will be described as "barbarian forces" (362n. *barbaricis...uiribus*) when they break the Roman line. Enjambement emphasizes the carefully chosen verb *temperat*. The verb contrasts Nealces' ability to effectively deploy his putatively wild men with Varro's erosion of the Roman troops' discipline. For the correlatives *qua...hac*, see 14.241–2, 15.147, 15.239–40, 15.621–3, etc.

Heinsius suggested *Afras laeuus gentes*, recalling that Nealces leads the left wing. Drakenborch added 16.180 *Africa bella* (Cm *Ep.* 74) : *fera bella* (*edd. a* l) as a partial parallel, but concluded that such extensive changes did not appear to be necessary.

269. hac sese Marso cum milite: the *Marsica pubes* were introduced in the catalog of 8.495–509; see Bona 1998: 181. Livy 22.9.5 reports on Hannibal's devastation of Marsian territory, and Marsian troops later volunteer to serve in the Roman fleet (Livy 28.45.19). The Marsi and Samnites fall together as Cannae becomes a massacre: 10.314–15 *passim signa iacent, quae Samnis belliger, et quae / Sarrastes populi Marsaeque tulere cohortes.*

269–70. cumque / Samnitum opponit signis: the Samnites, Rome's fiercest Italian opponents, fought three wars against the Romans, which ended in 304 BC, less than a century before Cannae. Lucan recalls their apparently undiminished hostility: *BC* 2.137–8 *Romanaque Samnis / ultra Caudinas sperauit uolnera Furcas!* Here the Samnites are temporarily allied with the Romans against the Carthaginian invaders. The catalog preceding Cannae recalls their recent hostility: 8.562–3 *adfuit et Samnis, nondum uergente fauore / ad Poenos, sed nec ueteri purgatus ab ira.* After Cannae, however, the Samnites defect to Hannibal, along with other peoples of southern Italy: 11.7–8 *saeuior ante alios iras seruasse repostas / atque odium renouare ferox in tempore Samnis*; Livy 22.61.11 *defecere autem ad Poenos hi populi...Samnites praeter Pentros.*

176   *Commentary Lines 270–7*

270. et Iapyge alumno: for the *Iapygis agros,* see 185n. The Iapygian peoples are fighting on their home territory and will also defect to Hannibal after Cannae: 11.10 *ambiguis fallax mox Apulus armis.* For *alumnus* as inhabitant of a territory, see 8.424 *Picenae...telluris alumnos,* 11.182 *Marmarico...alumno,* 14.52 *Ephyraeis...alumnis,* Stat. *Theb.* 4.638 *Lernaeos...alumnos,* etc.; *TLL* 1.1796.52.

271–2. at campi medio (namque hac in parte uidebat / stare ducem Libyae) Seruilius: Servilius leads the middle formation in Livy as well. As predicted at 8.664–6, he dies in the latter phases of the battle: 10.222–3 *Seruilius, optima belli, / post Paulum belli pars optima.* For Servilius' command, see Livy 22.40.6 *consulum anni prioris M. Atilium, aetatem excusantem, Romam miserunt, Geminum Seruilium in minoribus castris legioni Romanae et socium peditum equitumque duobus milibus praeficiunt;* 22.45.8 *consules cornua tenuerunt, Terentius laeuum, Aemilius dextrum: Gemino Seruilio media pugna tuenda data.*

272–3. obuia adire / arma: for *obuia (ad)ire,* see 46n. For *obuia arma,* see 5.240–1 *namque obuia ferre / arma quis auderet,* 13.217–18 *ruit obuia in arma / Scipio* with van der Keur's note, Verg. *Aen.* 9.56–7 *non obuia ferre / arma uiros,* Stat. *Theb.* 9.110 *nec in obuia concitus arma.* The phrase *obuia tela* appears in similar contexts: 7.147, Stat. *Theb.* 6.772, etc.

273. et Picentis Vmbrosque inferre iubetur: the Picentines and Umbrians were introduced together in the catalog preceding Cannae (8.424–67). Like the Marsi and Samnites (see 269–70n.), they also fall together: 10.312–13 *hic Picentum acies, hic Vmber Martius.../ procumbit.* The Picentines earlier fought heroically at Trasimene (5.208–19). The phrase with *inferre arma* is a variation on the more common *inferre signa* or the Virgilian *inferre acies.* See Verg. *Aen.* 10.364 *Arcadas, insuetos acies inferre pedestris,* Luc. *BC* 3.498 *ultro acies inferre parant,* Sil. *Pun.* 15.725–7 *turmis abeuntibus infert / cornipedem; TLL* 7.1.1380.23–31.

274. cetera Paulus habet dextro certamina cornu: alliteration of C- unifies the line; see 220n. for an earlier use of the clausula. Drakenborch's *laeuo* would conform with Livy and would necessitate a similar emendation at 227. Cosack 1844: 34 pointed out that *dextro* could be interpreted as "the enemy's right wing," which would place Paulus on the left, as in Livy. Yet, as he observes, it makes little sense to emend Silius in order to match Livy.

275–7. Varro instructs Scipio to prepare his troops against a Numidian ambush. The consul has learned something from the Carthaginian ambushes that doomed Flaminius at Trasimene and almost destroyed Minucius. Yet neither Varro nor his inexperienced troops can match Hannibal's tactical skill and seasoned forces. Scipio's command was introduced earlier at 8.546–61. Livy 22.53.1–3 mentions Scipio's presence at Cannae as a military tribune in command

Commentary Lines 275–81 177

of the second legion; cf. App. *Hann.* 26. Silius innovates by specifying Scipio's role and his subsequent exploits.

275. his super insidias contra Nomadumque uolucrem: for the anastrophe *his super*, see 1.60 *his super* with Feeney's note, 2.271 *bello super* with my note, etc. See Parkes' note on Stat. *Theb.* 4.201–2 for anastrophe of prepositions in Statius. The Numidians are traditionally swift horsemen: see Luc. *BC* 4.746 *Numidaeque fugaces* with Asso's note. *Nomadum* is Silius' more typical means of referring to the Numidians (sixteen times); see 242–3n. on *Numidae*.

276. Scipiadae datur ire manum: *Scīpĭō* is inadmissible in hexameter verse, and so the patronymic periphrasis (again in this book at 439n.) provided a convenient alternative. The poets associate the name with the thunderbolt, following the tradition associated with the *gens*. Thus, 7.106–7 *atque ubi nunc sunt fulmina gentis / Scipiadae?* is modeled on Lucr. *DRN* 3.1034 *Scipiadas, belli fulmen, Carthaginis horror*, Verg. *Aen.* 6.842–3 *geminos, duo fulmina belli, / Scipiadas, cladem Libyae*. See Marks 2005: 192–206 for full discussion.

276–7. quaque arte dolisque / scindent se turmae: the hendiadys *arte dolisque* recapitulates 275 *insidias*. The phrase is modeled on Verg. *Aen.* 2.152 *ille dolis instructus et arte Pelasga*; see also Stat. *Theb.* 12.183 *tunc mouet arte dolum*, Claud. *Ruf.* 1.97 *meque etiam tradente dolos artesque nocendi, TLL* 5.1.1863.77–9. The elements of the phrase recur later in the battle as the Carthaginians employ a stratagem that results in Galba's death and the capture of a standard: *Pun.* 10.188–90 *Tyrius quos fallere doctus / hanc ipsam pugnae rector formarat ad artem; succinctique dolis*. A *turma* was originally a small detachment of Roman cavalry (*OLD* s.v. a); it refers here to the Numidian cavalry detachments. The poets can apply the term to larger units, however (as at 6.241, Luc. *BC* 1.474, etc.), non-Roman forces (as here, 1.656, Stat. *Theb.* 4.125), as well as to noncombatants (Ov. *Am.* 2.13.18, Stat. *Theb.* 2.131).

Duff and Delz read *quaque*, likely a humanist conjecture, which appears first in the Parma edition (p). Other editors (Bauer, Summers, Budé) have favored the manuscript reading *quaeque*. For the indicative *scindent*, compare 10.525 *rubebit* and see Lindblom 1906: 65–6.

277. praedicit spargere bellum: likely modeled on Luc. *BC* 2.682 *spargatque per aequora bellum, BC* 3.64; perhaps adapted at Tac. *Ann.* 3.21 *spargit bellum*, *Agr.* 38.3 *spargi bellum nequibat*. See *TLL* 2.1839.81–5. For variations, see *spargere arma*: see Verg. *Aen.* 7.551 *spargam arma per agros, Aen.* 11.191 *sparguntur et arma*, Luc. *BC* 6.269–70 *armaque late / spargit*, etc. For *praedicere* in a military context, see *TLL* 10.2.566.64.

278–81. The armies shout and clash their weapons as they approach each other before joining in combat. This motif is a characteristic part of battle narrative; see 5.393, 12.181–3, 17.386–7. For earlier examples, see, e.g., Hom. *Il.* 11.500 βοή

178 *Commentary Lines 278–81*

δ' ἄσβεστος, 20.374 ὦρτο δ' ἀϋτή, Enn. *Ann.* 428 Skutsch *tollitur in caelum clamor exortus utrimque*, Luc. *BC* 7.475–84. See 282–6n. for discussion of Silius' adaptation of the simile at Hom. *Il.* 14.394–5.

278. iamque propinquabant acies: the line opening is common, occurring elsewhere at 6.169, 12.691, 17.605, Verg. *Aen.* 2.730, 5.159, 9.371, etc.

278–9. agilique uirorum / discursu: *agili ... discursu* is unparalleled, but clearly modeled on phrases such as Ov. *Met.* 2.720–1 *sic super Actaeas agilis Cyllenius arces / inclinat cursus*, Stat. *Silv.* 4.3.32 *nec cursus agiles*. The phrase *uirorum discursu* appears in historiographers such as Liv. *Per.* 117 and Flor. *Epit.* 1.22.

279–80. mixtoque simul calefacta per ora / cornipedum hinnitu: a variation on Verg. *Aen.* 12.66 *calefacta per ora cucurrit*. Earlier epic uses *cornipes* sparingly, but this elevated synonym for "horse" occurs frequently in Silius and Statius. See 2.72 with my note, Verg. *Aen.* 6.591, Stat. *Theb.* 7.589 with Smolenaars' note, etc. An alliterative sequence in C- begins here and runs through line 281; note also Silius' frequent use of chiastic word order.

280. et multum crepitantibus armis: *crepitantibus armis* FGδ⁵ is a common phrase: 16.30 *agens crepitantibus agmina caetris*, Ov. *Met.* 1.143 *crepitantia concutit arma*, *Met.* 15.783 *arma ... crepitantia*, Mart. 9.20.7 *Curetes texere Iovem crepitantibus armis*, etc. The closer poetic parallels for the phrase and its participation in the alliterative sequence in C- make it on balance slightly more likely than the alternatives. *Strepitantibus armis* derives from Modius *Ep.* 50; for parallels for this phrase, see Tib. 2.5.73 *atque tubas atque arma ferunt strepitantia*; see also Verg. *Aen.* 9.808–9 *strepit adsiduo caua tempora circum / tinnitu galea et saxis solida aera fatiscunt*, 10.567–8 *Iouis cum fulmina contra / tot paribus streperet clipeis, tot stringeret ensis*. The phrases *crepitus armorum* (Livy 25.6.21, 38.17.5, Pliny *NH* 2.148, etc.) and *strepitus armorum* (Sall. *BJ* 60.2, QCurt. 3.5.11, Petr. *BC* 134, etc.) are both more common.

Trepidantibus LO does not seem to fit the context; both armies entered the battle with great eagerness (181–2n., 244–5n., etc.), and there is as yet no reason for them to be frightened.

281. errabat caecum turbata per agmina murmur: a sophisticated recombination of three Virgilian passages:

- (a) The shouting through the disturbed ranks evokes Verg. *Aen.* 11.296–7 *uariusque per ora cucurrit / Ausonidum turbata fremor*.
- (b) *caecum ... murmur* adapts Virgil's comparison of the divine council to an oncoming storm: Verg. *Aen.* 10.98–9 *cum deprensa fremunt siluis et caeca uolutant / murmura uenturos nautis prodentia uentos*. This is a "window" allusion (Thomas 1986), in which Silius looks through the Virgilian simile to the battlefield context of its Homeric original. See

Commentary Lines 282–6 179

Hom. *Il.* 14.398–401 οὔτ’ ἄνεμος τόσσόν γε περὶ δρυσὶν ὑψικόμοισι / ἠπύει, ὅς τε μάλιστα μέγα βρέμεται χαλεπαίνων, / ὅσση ἄρα Τρώων καὶ Ἀχαιῶν ἔπλετο φωνὴ /δεινὸν ἀϋσάντων, ὅτ’ ἐπ’ ἀλλήλοισιν ὄρουσαν. For *caecus* referring to sound, see 14.60 *caecos...fragores*, Verg. *Aen.* 12.591 *murmure caeco*, Stat. *Theb.* 4.499 *caeca...murmura*, etc.; *TLL* 3.46.4.

(c) *errabat* recalls a Virgilian simile comparing the planting of trees to armies about to join battle: Verg. *Geo.* 2.282–3 *necdum horrida miscent / proelia, sed dubius mediis Mars errat in armis.*

For "near golden" lines, see Introduction, section 5c.

282–6. An extended simile compares the armies' approach to the battle of the winds. The simile elevates the conflict above the ordinary human level. It thereby prepares for the subsequent narratives of the gods' descent to the battlefield (287–303n.) and the incapacitating assault by the Vulturnus wind (491–523n.).

Silius' simile is a composite of motifs drawn from earlier poetry. The motif of the winds' *certamen* is as ubiquitous in epic as the sea storm, to which it is conceptually related. An extended Iliadic simile compares the clash of Achaean and Trojan ranks to the battle of Eurus and Notus in the mountains: Hom. *Il.* 16.765–71 ὡς δ’ Εὖρός τε Νότος τ’ ἐριδαίνετον ἀλλήλοιιν / οὔρεος ἐν βήσσῃς βαθέην πελεμιζέμεν ὕλην / φηγόν τε μελίην τε τανύφλοιόν τε κράνειαν, / αἵ τε πρὸς ἀλλήλας ἔβαλον τανυήκεας ὄζους / ἠχῇ θεσπεσίῃ, πάταγος δέ τε ἀγνυμενάων, / ὣς Τρῶες καὶ Ἀχαιοὶ ἐπ’ ἀλλήλοισι θορόντες / δῄουν, οὐδ’ ἕτεροι μνώοντ’ ὀλοοῖο φόβοιο.

Barchfeld 1880: 27 suggested that the present simile also adapts the first part of an Iliadic triple simile describing the armies' battle cries: Hom. *Il.* 14.394–5 οὔτε θαλάσσης κῦμα τόσον βοάᾳ ποτὶ χέρσον / ποντόθεν ὀρνύμενον πνοιῇ Βορέω ἀλεγεινῇ. For an army's advance compared to a high wind raising the waves, see Hom. *Il.* 4.422–8, Verg. *Aen.* 7.528–30.

The battle of the winds is a frequent subject for similes in the *Punica*; see, e.g., 3.658–61, 4.321–3, 7.569–74, while actual battles of the winds occur at 12.617–22 and 17.236–58. For discussion of Silius and the meteorological sublime, see Schrijvers 2006.

282. sic, ubi prima mouent pelago certamina uenti: allusion to the "contest of the winds" occurred earlier at 7.569–70 *non grauiore mouent uenti certamina mole.* Virgil refers to the winds' *proelia* (Verg. *Geo.* 1.318 *omnia uentorum concurrere proelia uidi*), Ovid to their *bella* (Ov. *Met.* 11.490–1 *omnique e parte feroces / bella gerunt uenti fretaque indignantia miscent*). The Flavian poets begin referring to it as a *certamen*: VF *Arg.* 4.270 *uentis certantibus*, Stat. *Theb.* 6.299–300 *aut litore in uno / Aeolus insanis statuat certamina uentis.*

283. inclusam rabiem ac sparsuras astra procellas: for the winds' *rabies*, see Hor. *Carm.* 1.3.14 *rabiem Noti*, [Verg.] *Aetna* 171 *uenti rabies*, Ov. *Trist.* 2.1.149–50

180   *Commentary Lines 284–8*

ac ueluti uentis agitantibus aequora non est / aequalis rabies continuusque furor,
etc. For *inclusam,* see *OLD* s.v. *includo* 2c. For the association of the winds'
madness with the sea, see 2.290 *uenturam pelagi rabiem Caurique futura* with
my note. The motif of winds that drench the stars appears elsewhere at 3.652
perfundens sidera Syrtis, 17.450 *undantem torquet perfundens nubila tabem,*
Verg. *Aen.* 1.567 *et rorantia uidimus astra, Aen.* 3.423 *sidera uerberat unda,* etc.

284–6. Each of these lines commences with a third-person verb form, produc-
ing a repetitive effect that suggests the beat of waves against the shore. See also
498–500.

284. parturit unda freti: the birth metaphor suggested by *parturit* appears in earlier epic, but with different verbs: Luc. *BC* 5.567 *flatusque incerta futuri / turbida
testantur conceptos aequora uentos,* VF *Arg.* 5.521–2 *ceu tumet atque imo sub gurgite
concipit austros / unda silens.* The verb *parturire* is used nowhere else with *unda*
until two imitations of Silius in late antiquity: Ennod. 2.93.1 *parturit unda sitim,
quam splendens conca ministrat,* Coripp. *Ioh.* 6.24 *aestuat unda tumens et sacros
parturit ignes.* For the "wave of the gulf," see 2.591 *spumantisque freti praeceps
immergitur undis,* Ov. *Fasti* 3.568 *insula, quam Libyci uerberat unda freti,* etc.

**284–5. fundoque emota minaces / exspirat per saxa sonos atque acta cau-
ernis:** *fundoque emota* varies other references to raising waters from the deep:
Pun. 4.322–3 *molemque profundi /... gestant,* 17.283 *emoti... ponti,* etc.; see also
the description of Charybdis: 14.255 *e fundo iaculantem ad sidera puppes.*
"Menacing sounds" elsewhere refer to the Porta Scelerata (7.48–9 *minaci... sonitu*) and Vulcan's roaring at the Campi Phlegraei (12.140 *sonitu... minaci*). *TLL* 5.2.1904.7 lists line 285 as the sole example of *exspirare* with sound.

286. torquet anhelantem spumanti uertice pontum: this line recombines
prior models from Virgil (Verg. *Geo.* 4.529 *spumantem undam sub uertice torsit*) and Lucan: Luc. *BC* 1.371 *Arctoo spumantem uertice Rhenum,* 3.631 *uicinum
inuoluens contorto uertice pontum;* see Marks 2010: 136. For battle compared to
the foaming waves, see the Homeric simile describing the Trojan advance at
Hom. *Il.* 13.797–9 ἐν δέ τε πολλὰ / κύματα παφλάζοντα πολυφλοίσβοιο θαλάσσης, /
κυρτὰ φαληριόωντα. See also Verg. *Aen.* 7.528–30. For *torquere* as the characteristic motion of the sea or rivers, see 1.592–3 *uerticibus torquet rapidis mare,
fractaque anhelant / aequora,* 3.475 *spumanti uertice torquens* (the Druentia).
Spaltenstein observes that Silius is the sole poet to apply *anhelare* to the sea,
here, at 1.592–3, as well as at 8.629–30 *anhelans / Aufidus* to a river. See Feeney's
note on 1.592–3 and *TLL* 2.66.73. "de terris, campis, mari, sim."

287–95. As at Virgil's Actium, numerous gods descend from Olympus to the
battlefield.

287–8. nec uero fati tam saeuo in turbine solum / terrarum fuit ille labor:
turbo characteristically refers to the world's upheaval: 1.40–1 *atque in regna*

Latini / turbine mox saevo uenientum haud inscia cladum, 11.521–2 *uidi cum turbine saeuo / Ausonia et sonitu bellantis fusa per agros*, Cic. *Pis. 20 in maximis turbinibus ac fluctibus rei publicae*, etc. The phrase *fati... turbine* evokes Flaminius' folly at Trasimene in particular: 5.54 *excussus consul fatorum turbine mentem*, where the phrase *excussus... mentem* prefigures Varro (644n.). The gods hid their faces from the sight of the last major Roman defeat at Trasimene (5.201–7). Now they have become active participants in the combat. *Labor... terrae* typically refers to war or travel, as at 4.53 *pelagi terraeque laborem*, 6.503 *terrarum pelagique pati caelique labores*, VF *Arg.* 5.575 *terraeque marisque labores*, etc.

288–9. Discordia demens / intrauit caelo superosque ad bella coegit: the catalog of deities commences with *Discordia*, the personification of civil war. By giving her pride of place, Silius draws a strong thematic association between Cannae and Roman civil conflict. See Introduction, section 3d for discussion of the *Discordia* tradition in Roman epic. Varro attributes his unexpected survival of the battle to *discordia fati*; see 648n.

For the dative *caelo*, cf. 6.498 *puppi properantem intrare*, Verg. *Aen.* 5.451 *it clamor caelo*, etc.; TLL 7.2.58.58–63. Van der Keur comments on *Pun.* 13.814 *intrauitque casae*: "The construction of *intrare* with a dative is common in Silius (though not as frequent as with an accusative), but not elsewhere." The erroneous reading *lustrauit* in place of *intrauit* similarly occurs at *Pun.* 13.814.

290. hinc Mauors, hinc Gradiuum comitatus Apollo: Mars will stay on earth to participate in a brief theomachy with Pallas; see 438–85n. Apollo's support of the Romans determines his decision to accompany Mars. He earlier reacted with grief to the defeat at Trasimene: 5.204–5 *et Delum peruectus Apollo / tristem maerenti solatur pectine luctum*. He will later intervene directly in combat to rescue the poet Ennius (12.405–19). Silius marks the difference between his version of Cannae and Virgil's Actium by assigning Apollo no significant role. The first syllable of *Grādīuum* is scanned long except at a line end: 15.15, 15.337, Ov. *Met.* 6.427, VF *Arg.* 4.602, 5.650. Here it completes a stately run of three spondees.

291. et domitor tumidi pugnat maris, hinc Venus amens: for the periphrasis referring to Neptune, see Verg. *Aen.* 5.799 *Saturnius... domitor maris*, Sen. *Phaed.* 1159 *profundi... dominator freti*, *Med.* 4 *profundi... dominator maris*. Note also the extension to Neptune's children: Verg. *Aen.* 7.691, 9.523, 12.128 *Messapus, equum domitor, Neptunia proles*. Venus' reaction parallels her grief at Trasimene: 5.203–4 *disiectaque crinem / inlacrimat Venus*.

292–3. hinc Vesta et captae stimulatus caede Sagunti / Amphitryoniades: the Vesta which Aeneas brought from Troy now serves Rome as the symbolic link to its Trojan origins. As Hannibal crosses the Alps, Venus asks Jupiter where she may safely move Vesta: 3.565–6 *quo Troiae extremos cineres sacramque*

182   *Commentary Lines 293–5*

ruinam / Assaracique larem et Vestae secreta feramus? TLL 3.0.50.18 lists this
line as the sole example of *caedes* "de urbe deleta." For the variable gender of
Saguntum, see 186n. Hercules, founder of Saguntum (1.273–95), attempted in
vain to protect his city in *Punica* 2 but was forced to yield to Juno's hostility; see
2.475–512 with my discussion.

293. Amphitryoniades, pariter ueneranda Cybele: a single Greek name occupies the first hemiepes in order to create a resonant four-word hexameter; 6.183
and 12.119 feature similar uses of the name *Amphitryoniades*. Cybele's cult
arrives at Rome toward the end of war, as shown in Silius' narrative of Claudia
Quinta (17.1–47). Here the goddess expresses early support for the Romans. For
the comma before *pariter*, see 224n. Heinsius suggested *Cybebe* on the grounds
of quantity (Cybēbe, Κυβήβη vs. Cybĕle, Κυβέλη), as he did in a similar context
at Claud. *DRP* 1.212. A similar choice occurs at 8.363, Luc. *BC* 1.600, Colum. *RR*
10.220, etc., where editors have supported both alternatives; see *TLL Onom.* s.v.

294. Indigetesque dei Faunusque satorque Quirinus: the *Indigetes dei* were a
variable group of Italian deities whose identity and etymology remain debated;
see *NP* s.v. *Indiges* for the alternatives. Aeneas as *Iupiter Indiges* appeared earlier
at 8.39 *tum diua Indigetis castis contermina lucis*; Scipio swears by the *Indigetes*
at 10.436. There may be a recollection of Lucan's reference to these gods in
mourning for Rome as Caesar invades Italy: Luc. *BC* 1.556 *Indigetes fleuisse
deos*. A similar disaster for Rome is about to unfold at Cannae.

The presence of *–que* indicates that Faunus and Quirinus are distinct from
the *Indigetes*, as do the prior poetic models for this line: Verg. *Geo.* 1.498 *di
patrii Indigetes et Romule Vestaque mater*, and Ov. *Met.* 15.862 *dique Indigetes
genitorque Quirine*. Duff's placement of the *Indigetes* in apposition with Faunus
and Quirinus is, therefore, incorrect.

Faunus is the father of Virgil's Latinus (*Aen.* 7.47). His other progeny play a
role in the *Punica*: the *Apenninicolae...Fauni* (5.626) scatter during the earthquake at Trasimene, and the Rutulians are described as *Faunigenae* (8.356).

This is the sole application of *sator* to Romulus Quirinus; see further 306n. It
functions as an elevated alternative for his more common epithet *pater*; cf.
8.646 *patris...Quirini*, Verg. *Aen.* 6.859 *patri...Quirino*, etc. Zaia observes
that *sator* likely references Romulus' role as founder of the city, as at 3.364
Tlepolemus sator, 11.262 *muris sator*.

295. alternusque animae mutato Castore Pollux: the presence of the Dioscuri
at Cannae recalls their aid to the Romans at the battle of Lake Regillus, a battle
that similarly threatened the survival of Rome; see Livy 2.19–20, D.H. *Ant.
Rom.* 6.10–13. For the evocation of Lake Regillus in Augustan culture, see
Rebeggiani 2013.

Alternus indicates that the Dioscuri were imagined as sharing a single soul
on alternate days; see 13.805 *alternam lucem peragebat in aethere Pollux* with

Commentary Lines 296–8 183

van der Keur's note, Hom. *Od.* 11.303–4 ἄλλοτε μὲν ζώουσ᾽ ἐτερήμεροι, ἄλλοτε δ᾽ αὖτε / τεθνᾶσιν, Verg. *Aen.* 6.121 *fratrem Pollux alterna morte redemit*, Ov. *Fasti* 5.719 *alterna fratrem statione redemit*, etc. For the occurrence of *alternus* with a genitive of relation, see *TLL* 1.1756.71; in collocation with *mutare*, see Stat. *Theb.* 5.722, 11.336–7.

The clausula is modeled on Hor. *Epist.* 2.1.5 *Romulus et Liber pater et cum Castore Pollux*, a similar list of native Roman deities. VF *Arg.* 3.330, 3.723 in turn adapt the Horatian clausula.

296–9. Juno, Pallas, and Hammon lead the Carthaginian gods against the Roman gods. Juno and Pallas' opposition to the Romans derives from their persecution of the Trojans in Virgil's *Aeneid*. The Budé editors' suggestion that their inclusion evokes the oath of Hannibal to certify his treaty with Philip (Polyb. 7.9.2) is accordingly irrelevant. Juno will intervene again at Cannae in disguise as Metellus in an effort to dissuade Paulus from seeking a heroic death (10.45–91).

296. contra cincta latus ferro Saturnia Iuno: for Juno in combat, see also Venus' expression of concern at 11.392 *ualet illa manu, ualet illa lacertis. Cincta* recalls Juno's role in leading the Greek troops during the sack of Troy: Verg. *Aen.* 2.612–14 *hic Iuno… agmen / ferro accincta uocat.* There may also be an evocation of Sen. *HF* 695 *et cincta ferro Bella*, where "Wars" are part of a list of personifications that Theseus and Hercules saw in the Underworld. For *cingor* with the accusative of relation *latus,* see, e.g., Ov. *Am.* 3.8.14 *ense latus cinctum, Fasti* 2.784 *ense latus cinxit,* Stat. *Theb.* 4.41 *ferro cingi latus,* etc.; *TLL* 7.2.1026.71. For the clausula, see Verg. *Aen.* 3.380 (seven times in total), Ov. *Met.* 4.448, Germ. *Arat.* 545, etc.

297. et Pallas, Libycis Tritonidos edita lymphis: reference to Pallas' North African birth suggests an additional reason for her support for the Carthaginians. She was born near Lake Tritonis: 3.322–3 *huc, qui stagna colunt Tritonidos alta paludis, / qua uirgo, ut fama est, bellatrix edita lympha,* 4.533, Luc. *BC* 9.350–4, Stat. *Theb.* 2.722–3 *seu Libyco Tritone tu repexas / lota comas* with Gervais's note. Homer knows Pallas as τριτογένεια (*Il.* 4.515, 8.39, 22.183), which gave rise to numerous interpretations, including birth from Lake Triton: see, e.g., Eur. *Ion* 871–2 θεὰν / λίμνης τ᾽ ἐνύδρου Τριτωνιάδος, and (influentially for Roman poets) A.R. *Arg.* 4.1309–11. See further 479n. *Tritonia uirgo.*

298. ac patrius flexis per tempora cornibus Hammon: chiastic word order reinforces a visual image of the horns on either side of Hammon's head, a distinctive part of the god's representation. Ov. *Met.* 5.328 and Luc. *BC* 9.514 each employ the same clausula as here; for *corniger Hammon,* see, e.g., *Pun.* 3.10, 14.572, VF *Arg.* 2.482, etc. For chiastic arrangement in the *Punica,* see Flammini 1983. The description of curving horns on Hiarbas' headgear features similar phrasing: 1.416 *insignis flexo galeam per tempora cornu.* See also 14.438–9,

184   *Commentary Lines 299–303*

describing Hammon's image on a ship. For Hammon's role and his various off-
spring in the *Punica*, see 2.59 with my note, 5.357, 13.768, etc. For *patrius* applied
to a god, see Stat. *Theb.* 4.111, *Silv.* 4.8.19; *TLL* 10.1.761.47–51.

299. multaque praeterea diuorum turba minorum: the shift between enumeration by name and reference to a collective recalls the Actium narrative on
Virgil's Shield of Aeneas: Verg. *Aen.* 8.698 *omnigenumque deum monstra et
latrator Anubis.* The opening phrase *multaque praeterea* is a favorite of Lucretius,
who uses it eight times, Virgil four times, Ovid three times, and then not again
until Silius, who uses it only here. Virgil adapts the phrase slightly to conclude
a catalog of competitors at the funeral games: Verg. *Aen.* 5.302 *multi praeterea,
quos fama obscura recondit.*

300–3. Earth trembles as Olympus empties and the gods take their seats on
clouds and mountains to observe the combat. Ripoll 2006: 244 compares the
similar motif of the emptied sky in Petronius' civil war poem: Petr. *Sat.*
124.264–6 *sentit terra deos mutataque sidera pondus / quaesivere suum; namque
omnis regia caeli / in partes diducta ruit.*

**300–1. quorum ubi mole simul uenientum et gressibus alma / intremuit tel-
lus:** Mago's report of the battle to the Carthaginian Senate includes the motif of
Earth trembling: 11.518 *intremit et tellus et pulsus mugit Olympus.* Though the
result of a different cause, trembling also recalls the earthquake at Trasimene:
5.387 *intremuere simul tellus et pontus et aether.* The armies shake as two gods,
Mars and Pallas, approach closer; see 440–1n.

For the gods' massive size and weight, see, e.g., 6.426 *humana maior species
erat*, 15.21 *haud paulum mortali maior imago*, Hom. *Il.* 21.407 ἑπτὰ δ' ἐπέσχε
πέλεθρα πεσών (Ares), Verg. *Aen.* 2.591–2 *qualisque uideri / caelicolis et quanta
solet* (Venus). See 447–50n. for reference to Mars' tremendous size.

The phrase *alma Tellus* originates at Ov. *Met.* 2.272 *alma...Tellus.* It may
have been perceived to be a *figura etymologica*, as Servius observes on *Aen.*
10.252 ALMA PARENS IDAEA DEVM *alma proprie est tellus ab eo quod nos alat,
abusiue tamen etiam aliis numinibus hoc epitheton datur.* Servius overstates the
case for abuse, however, as indicated by examples such as *alma Fides* (Enn.
Trag. 350), *alma Venus* (Lucr. *DRN* 1.2), *alma Ceres* (Verg. *Geo.* 1.7), etc.

**301–3. pars impleuere propinquos, / diuisi montes, pars sedem nube sub alta /
ceperunt:** this moment recombines Homeric and Virgilian models of divine
spectatorship. Homer's Zeus sits on Ida to observe the combat (Hom. *Il.* 8.47–
52), whilst Virgil's Juno watches from a cloud (Verg. *Aen.* 12.792 *fulua pugnas de
nube tuentem*; cf. *Aen.* 9.639–40). Elsewhere, Silius' gods watch from similar
vantage points. For mountains, see 1.548 (Juno), 4.667 (Venus and Vulcan),
5.206–7 (Juno), 6.598 (Jupiter), 6.697 (Dione); for clouds, see 2.534, 17.342
(Juno), 12.405 (Apollo). In specifying these different locations, Silius emphasizes the particularity of the gods' observation; they are engaged more intently

Commentary Lines 303–4 185

on the action than when they watch from Olympus, their typical vantage point. See Lovatt 2013 for full discussion.

For *implere* as *occupare*, see 14.277–8 *Syracusae...muros / milite collecto uariisque impleuerat armis*, 17.63–4 *campos pariter uallesque refusas / litoraque implerat*, 17.378 *et terras implere uolet redeuntibus armis*; *TLL* 7.1.631.22–39. Spaltenstein interprets *sub nube* as a contamination of the "naturel" *in nube* with phrases such as *sub caelo* or *sub aethere* (327n.), and compares Verg. *Aen.* 7.768 *caeli...sub auras*. For *sedem capere*, see *Pun.* 6.131–2 *sedem / ceperat alma Fides*.

303. uacuo descensum ad proelia caelo: Silius emphasizes that the gods have left Olympus empty through their departure and so puts the Virgilian phrase *uacuo...caelo* to a new purpose. The phrase refers to a clear sky at Verg. *Aen.* 5.515 and Stat. *Theb.* 3.459; at Man. *Astr.* 1.472, it refers to a sky where the full moon's light has allowed the constellations to appear more clearly without being obscured by lesser stars. Stat. *Theb.* 10.78 *uacuis...in astris* indicates Juno's anger at Jupiter's absence from the sky for the purposes of adultery. 304 *deserta...sidera* recapitulates the motif.

304–9. The battlefield noise recalls the Giants' shouting as they stormed Olympus and Jupiter's shouting as he demanded thunderbolts in order to stop them. Great battles in Roman epic conventionally replay aspects of the Gigantomachy. Hannibal's invasion threatens chaos; Scipio, the son of Jupiter, will eventually restore human and divine order, as his father did at the battle of Phlegra. This simile creates a further correspondence with the comparison of Scipio in triumph to Hercules after he helps the gods to conquer the Giants: *Pun.* 17.649–50 *aut cum Phlegraeis confecta mole Gigantum / incessit campis tangens Tirynthius astra*. Gigantomachy serves as the point of comparison linking the Romans' worst moment at Cannae to their recovery after Zama. See Introduction, section 3d. Silius elsewhere uses two briefer comparisons to Giants to describe the vast size of the Gallic warriors: 4.275–6 *quantus Phlegraeis Telluris alumnus in aruis / mouit signa Mimas caelumque exterruit armis*; 5.110–13. Hannibal's visit to the Campi Phlegraei also features a brief Gigantomachy narrative (12.143–51).

304. tollitur immensus deserta ad sidera clamor: a chiastic "near golden" arrangement elevates the narrative register for both the commencement and conclusion (309n.) of the Gigantomachic comparison. Shouting that reaches the sky is a traditional epic motif: 7.733 *clamorem tollens ad sidera*, 16.319 *tollitur in caelum furiali turbine clamor*, Hom. *Il.* 2.153, 12.338 ἀϋτὴ δ᾽ οὐρανὸν ἷκεν, 17.424–5, Verg. *Aen.* 2.338 *sublatus ad aethera clamor*, *Aen.* 2.488 *ferit aurea sidera clamor*, etc.; *TLL* 3.1259.35–7. The phrasing here evokes Enn. *Ann.* 428 Skutsch *tollitur in caelum clamor*, adapted at Verg. *Aen.* 11.745 and 12.462. *Immensus* derives from Verg. *Aen.* 11.832–3 *immensus surgens ferit aurea clamor /*

186 *Commentary Lines 306–9*

sidera. The gods' departure from Olympus (303n.) has left the stars deserted; for a parallel, see [Sen.] *HO* 468 *descendat astris Luna desertis licet.* See *Il. Lat.* 1055 and Coripp. *Ioh.* 5.33 for other adaptations of these lines.

305–6. Phlegraeis quantas effudit ad aethera uoces / terrigena in campis exercitus: for the Phlegraean fields as the traditional site of the Gigantomachy, see 12.143–51. For the Giants as earth-born monsters, see 4.275 (quoted at 304–9n. above), Ov. *Met.* 5.325 *terrigenam... Typhoea*, Luc. *BC* 3.316 *aut si ter- rigenae temptarent astra Gigantes*, etc. The latter half of line 305 is adapted from Verg. *Aen.* 8.70 *talis effundit ad aethera uoces*. For the suffix *-gena*, see 234n. Damsté's conjecture (1911: 115) *terrigenum campis* is banalizing.

306. aut sator aeui: *sator* + genitive is a typical epic means of referring to Jupiter: 4.430 *rerum sator*, Verg. *Aen.* 1.254 *hominum sator atque deorum*, Stat. *Theb.* 7.155 *diuum sator optime*, etc. Silius originates the phrase *sator aeui* and uses it once more in senatorial debate as Scipio justifies his plan to invade Africa: 16.664–5 *hoc sator aeui / Iuppiter aeterni monet*. The repetition of the unique phrase associates Jupiter, the opponent of the Giants in the Cannae episode, with his son Scipio, who will similarly destroy his enemies and re-establish order in his country. The phrase may potentially have been inspired by Prop. 4.2.55–6 *sed facias, diuum sator, ut Romana per aeuum / transeat...turba*. For the 1+2+2 clausula, see 128n.

307–8. quanta Cyclopas noua fulmina uoce poposcit / Iuppiter, exstructis uidit cum montibus ire: Jupiter asks for new thunderbolts in order to dislodge the mountains that the Giants heaped up, as at Verg. *Geo.* 1.283 *ter pater exstruc- tos disiecit fulmine montis*. For the Cyclopes as makers of the thunderbolts, see 5.71–2 *concutiens tonitru Cyclopum rapta caminis / fulmina*. The quantity of the first syllable of *Cycl-* is variable, as it is formed by a mute and a liquid; see Enn. *Ann.* 319 with Skutsch's note; for example, it is short at 448n. The only other occurrence of the clausula of 307 is Stat. *Theb.* 9.621, which may be an example of bidirectional influence; see Introduction, section 5a. For the Giants' heaping Pelion on Ossa in order to storm Olympus, see 3.495 *Ossaque cum Pelio*, Hom. *Od.* 11.313–16, Verg. *Geo.* 1.281 *ter sunt conati imponere Pelio Ossam*, etc.

Silius adapts the *figura etymologica* that associates *Phlegraeis*/φλέγειν (305n.) and *fulmina*, found at Ov. *Met.* 10.151 *sparsaque Phlegraeis uictricia fulmina campis*; see Michalopoulos 2001: 145 and Introduction, section 5c. These *noua fulmina* point to Silius' role as a successor to Ovid, and also to the "new" thunderbolts that Jupiter will hurl at Hannibal, the latter-day theomach, as he approaches Rome.

309. magnanimos raptum caelestia regna Gigantas: for the chiastic "near golden" arrangement, see 304n. and Introduction, section 5c. *Magnanimos* is a calque on the Homeric μεγάθυμος, which Silius elsewhere applies exclusively to human beings. The line is adapted from Ov. *Pont.* 4.8.59 *sic affectantes caelestia regna Gigantas*.

Commentary Lines 310–16 187

310–16. The first exchange of missiles causes many casualties, even before the soldiers draw their swords. In their eagerness to clash, they trample the bodies of their own comrades. Roman military assaults typically began with the *hastati* throwing *pila* at the enemy, as in Silius' account of Trasimene: 5.214–15 *funditur unanimo nisu et concordibus ausis / pilorum in Poenos nimbus*. See Daly 2002: 183 for a reconstruction of this tactic at Cannae.

310–11. nec uero prima in tantis concursibus hasta / ulla fuit: so many spears are hurled at once that no one can tell who was the first to cast his, just as at 366–7n. no soldier falls from a single spear. The scale of the combat negates Hannibal's promise to recognize his soldiers' individual accomplishments (247–8n.). The epic emphasis on the first spear cast reflects its connection to fetial ritual. Thus, at Ticinus, the prophet Bogus is first to cast his spear: 4.134–5 *contorquet primus in hostis / ceu suadente deo et fatorum conscius hastam.* Virgil's Turnus performs a similar role: Verg. *Aen.* 9.51–3 'ecquis erit mecum, *iuuenes, qui primus in hostem*—? / *en,' ait et iaculum attorquens emittit in auras, / principium pugnae.* See also Luc. *BC* 9.470–5.

311–12. stridens nimbus certante furore / telorum simul effusus: for the image of the sky obscured by weapons, see 11–12n. and Skutsch's note on Enn. *Ann.* 266 *fit ferreus imber*, which he suggests is a description of Cannae. For *stridens*, see 247n. *Effusus* recalls the typical phrase (*ef*)*fundere tela*; cf. *TLL* 5.2.218.50–62.

312–13. cupidaeque cruoris / hinc atque hinc animae gemina cecidere procella: epic poets typically use the motif of the "killer killed" for individuals, as at 10.194–201 (Galba and Amorgus), 15.691 *praedam animamque simul uictori uictor ademit*, Verg. *Aen.* 9.573 *Ortygium Caeneus, uictorem Caenea Turnus.* Here Silius scales up the motif to apply it to the front lines of both armies. For the clausula of 312, see 13.174, Ov. *Trist.* 1.6.9. The phrases flanking the central word *animae* emphasize that the clouds of missiles coming from both sides struck the soldiers. Contrast the arrangement of similar words at 15.516–17 *nunc geminum Hannibalem, nunc iactant bina coire / hinc atque hinc castra,* Verg. *Aen.* 1.162–3 *hinc atque hinc uastae rupes geminique minantur / in caelum scopuli.* For the metaphor of missiles as a storm, see 11–12n.

314. ac prius insanus dextra quam ducitur ensis: either Silius or Calp. Sic. 1.59 (if this poet was indeed active in the Neronian period) is first to apply *insanus* to *ensis*. For the insanity of epic warfare, see 4.100 *ad pugnas Martemque insania concors*, 6.6 *insani Mauortis opus*, Verg. *Aen.* 7.461 *scelerata insania belli* with Horsfall's note, etc.; Hershkowitz 1998. Spaltenstein compares Luc. *BC* 7.490–1 *odiis solus ciuilibus ensis / sufficit, et dextras Romana in uiscera ducit.* For the clausula, see 8.340, Manil. *Astr.* 1.391.

The reading *acrius...qua* ω, retained in the Budé, has attracted numerous attempts at emendation. *Ac prius...quam* is Gronovius' solution, varied by

188   *Commentary Lines 315–20*

Schrader's *ac prior;* the missile volley caused great destruction before the hand-to-hand combat began. Owen 1909: 255–6 argues that *prius* represents an unacceptable departure from Livy 22.47, which focuses on the hand-to-hand fighting, and proposes *acrius in stragem... qua.* Exaggerated departure from Livy's narrative has been the whole point of this passage, however. Damsté 1911: 115 proposed *artius... qua,* looking forward to 321 *artatis;* but repetition of the idea here would be intrusive.

Liberman 2006: 22 observes that *dextra* is "a mere verse-filler," which he correctly observes "are not rare in this poet." His proposal of the uncommon word *theca* is an unlikely solution, however. It will not serve as a substitute for *uagina,* on the model of 8.340 *dum uagina ducitur ensis.*

315. bellantum pars magna iacet: the indication that a significant percentage of combatants are dead in the first moments of the battle suggests the scale of the bloodshed to come. Silius elsewhere applies *pars magna* to an individual's death, that of Appius at Trasimene (5.328–30 *iacet... / Italae pars magna ruinae / Appius*), on the model of Verg. *Aen.* 2.6 *quorum pars magna fui.* For the epitaphic use of *iacet* in epic, see Dinter 2005. For examples in the *Punica,* see 5.373–4 *iacet Appius hasta / ad manis pulsus nostra,* 11.566 *et iacet in campis Latium,* 15.340 *iacet campis Carthaginis horror,* etc.

315–16. super ipsa suorum / corpora consistunt auidi calcantque gementes: Verg. *Aen.* 12.271 *corpora constiterant contra, quos fida crearat,* similarly of a man dying from a spear cast, is both the source of the line opening and the likely inspiration for the multiple alliteration of C-. Zaia *ad loc.* compares Caes. *BG* 2.27.3–4 for the motif of men treading on their own dead due to the crowded combat.

317–20. The infantry ranks stand fast against the first assault. For the Romans' endurance, see Livy 22.47.4 *sub equestris finem certaminis coorta est peditum pugna, primo et uiribus et animis par dum constabant ordines Gallis Hispanisque.* A simile compares the combatants to Calpe, the Rock of Gibraltar, which remains unmoved even as the waves strike it. Silius earlier used the comparison to describe the battle cries at Trasimene: 5.395–6 *ceu pater Oceanus cum saeua Tethye Calpen / Herculeam ferit.*

The simile of the rock in the ocean is a traditional component of battle narrative: Hom. *Il.* 15.618–19 ἠΰτε πέτρη / ἠλίβατος μεγάλη πολιῆς ἁλὸς ἐγγὺς ἐοῦσα (the Greeks stand fast against Hector), Verg. *Aen.* 10.693–4 *uelut rupes uastum quae prodit in aequor, / obuia uentorum furiis expostaque ponto* (Mezentius takes the battlefield), Stat. *Theb.* 9.91 *ceu fluctibus obuia rupes* (Hippomedon stands against the Thebans), etc.

There may also be a recollection of Valerius' narrative of Hercules' combat with the sea monster: VF *Arg.* 2.522–4 *non illa magis quam sede mouetur / magnus Eryx, deferre uelint quem uallibus imbres. / iam breuis et telo uolucri non*

Commentary Lines 317–25 189

utilis aer. Both passages offer the same succession of motifs: the simile of the immobile mountain followed by an indication that the space between the combatants is too short for the proper use of weapons (321–2n.). Silius may implicitly "correct" his older Flavian contemporary by restoring the simile from a fantasy scene of monster combat to its original battlefield context. See Marks 2010b for Silius' dialogue with Flavian mythological epic.

For use of the simile to describe events off the battlefield, see Verg. *Aen.* 7.586 *ille uelut pelago rupes immota resistit* (Latinus resists the calls for war), Ov. *Met.* 9.40–1 *haud secus ac moles, magno quam murmure fluctus / oppugnant* (Hercules cannot move Achelous in their wrestling match).

317–18. nec magis aut Libyco protrudi Dardana nisu / auertiue potest pubes: for the Romans as Dardanians, see 70–6n. The poets frequently use the phrase *pubes* + ethnonym to describe a military detachment. Though not employed as a clausula here, its metrical shape can be convenient for that purpose. See 571n. *Itala pubes,* 621n. *Rhoeteia pubes,* 1.291 *Daunia pubes,* 8.495 *Marsica pubes,* etc.; Verg. *Aen.* 5.450 *Trinacria pubes,* Ov. *Met.* 7.56 *pubis Achiuae,* etc.; *TLL* 10.2.2433.67.

318–19. aut ordine pelli / fixa suo Sarrana manus: for *Sarrana,* see 202n. Like *pubes* in the preceding line, *manus* + ethnonym similarly describes a military detachment and can form a convenient clausula. See, e.g., 3.544 *Alpina... manus,* 7.629 *Marmaridumque manus,* 8.602 *Troiana manus,* etc.; Verg. *Aen.* 2.29 *Dolopum manus, Aen.* 7.43 *Tyrrhenamque manum,* Luc. *BC* 2.532 *Romana manus,* etc.

319–20. quam uellere sede / si coeptet Calpen impacto gurgite pontus: for the phrase *uellere sede,* see Cic. *Verr.* 2.5.186. The clausula of 320 originates in Cicero's *Aratea* (*Div.* 1.14) and occurs frequently thereafter; in the *Punica* at 1.197, 12.117, 12.440. Virgil adapted it for a comparison of the advancing and retreating battle lines to the tide: Verg. *Aen.* 11.624 *qualis ubi alterno procurrens gurgite pontus.*

321–5. The opposed ranks press tightly together in hand-to-hand combat. Wills 1996: 201 calls this passage "the culmination of battle polyptoton in Latin poetry," comparable to Stat. *Theb.* 8.398–9 *iam clipeus clipeis, umbone repellitur umbo, / ense minax ensis, pede pes et cuspide cuspis.* Briefer polyptota appear at Ticinus and Trasimene: Sil. *Pun.* 4.352–3 *teritur iunctis umbonibus umbo, / pesque pedem premit,* 5.219 *pressoque impellunt pectore pectus.* The figure originates at Hom. *Il.* 13.130–1 φράξαντες δόρυ δουρί, σάκος σάκεϊ προθελύμνῳ· / ἀσπὶς ἄρ' ἀσπίδ' ἔρειδε, κόρυς κόρυν, ἀνέρα δ' ἀνήρ, adapted at Enn. *Ann.* 584 Skutsch *premitur pede pes atque armis arma teruntur,* Verg. *Aen.* 10.361 *haeret pede pes densusque uiro uir,* Ov. *Met.* 9.43–5 *eratque / cum pede pes iunctus, totoque ego pectore pronus / et digitos digitis et frontem fronte premebam,* etc.

190　　　　　　　　　*Commentary Lines 321–5*

Silius signals a specific allusion to Homer by including clashing helmets (*galea…galeae* ~ κόρυς κόρυν), a motif which Latin poets had hitherto left unadapted. The inclusion of this motif emphasizes that Cannae is as desperate for the Romans as the battle for the ships was for the Achaeans. The polyptoton also signals the fulfillment of Virgil's similarly polyptotic curse pronounced by Dido: Verg. *Aen.* 4.628–9 *litora litoribus contraria, fluctibus undas / imprecor, arma armis: pugnent ipsique nepotesque.* Dido's revenge on Aeneas' descendants has come to pass in the disaster of Cannae.

321–2. amisere ictus spatium, nec morte peracta / artatis cecidisse licet: the infantry are packed so close together that there is no room for the men to fall when they die. Livy, by contrast, attributed lack of maneuverability only to the cavalry at this stage of the battle: Livy 22.47.2 *frontibus enim aduersis concurrendum erat, quia nullo circa ad euagandum relicto spatio hinc amnis, hinc peditum acies claudebant.*

Silius used the motif earlier at Trebia: 4.553 *nec artatis locus est in morte cadendi.* Language and context point most closely to Sulla's massacres in Lucan: Luc. *BC* 2.201–4 *densi uix agmina uolgi / inter et exangues inmissa morte cateruas / uictores mouere manus; uix caede peracta / procumbunt, dubiaque labant ceruice.* For the use of the motif more generally, see Verg. *Aen.* 10.432–3 *extremi addensent acies nec turba moueri / tela manusque sinit,* Luc. *BC* 4.781–2 *non arma mouendi / iam locus est pressis, stipataque membra teruntur, BC* 7.494–5 *uixque habitura locum dextras ac tela mouendi / constiterat gladiosque suos conpressa timebat.*

Spaltenstein claims that *morte peracta* "étonne." It is no more, however, than an adaptation of Luc. *BC* 2.203 *caede peracta,* and the same phrase can be found at Stat. *Theb.* 3.94 *et toruum in morte peracta.*

322–3. galea horrida flictu / aduersae ardescit galeae: Verg. *Aen.* 9.667 *dant sonitum flictu galeae* is the source of the otherwise rare word *flictus.* It is found elsewhere only at Pacuv. *Trag.* 335 *flictus nauium,* which Silius adapts for his sea battle at *Pun.* 14.558 *remorumque fragor flictuque sonantia rostra.* For *ardescere* here as "fervescere, aestuare," see *TLL* 2.488.64; contrast its use in the context of drinking at 11.302. Zaia notes the imitation by Claud. *Carm. Min.* 53.77–9 *splendentior igni / aureus ardescit clipeus, galeaeumque nitentes / arrexere iubae.*

323–4. clipeusque fatiscit / impulsu clipei, atque ensis contunditur ense: Lucan similarly employs the motif of swords breaking on other swords at Pharsalus: Luc. *BC* 7.573 *confractique ensibus enses.* See also *Il. Lat.* 955–6 *ensem terit horridus ensis, / collatusque haeret pede pes et dextera dextrae.* For *fatiscit,* see Verg. *Aen.* 9.809 *et saxis solida aera fatiscunt, TLL* 5.2.609.71. *Impulsu clipei* recapitulates *flictu… galeae* of the preceding lines.

325. pes pede, uirque uiro teritur: the wording closely follows Verg. *Aen.* 10.361, while *teritur* recalls Enn. *Ann.* 584 Skutsch *teruntur* (quoted at 321–5n. above).

Commentary Lines 325–9

325–7. Shed blood conceals the ground and thrown spears conceal the sky. The latter motif evokes the Persians' threat at Thermopylae (Hdt. 7.226), on which, see also Cic. *Tusc.* 1.101 *solem prae iaculorum multitudine et sagittarum non uidebitis.* It is an amplification of the common epic motif of clouds or deluges of missiles, on which see 11–12n. The hyperbolic description of battle's effect on the natural world is characteristic of Silius' approach to the sublime; see Schrijvers 2006. For the motif at Lucan's Pharsalus, see Luc. *BC* 7.519–20 *ferro subtexitur aether / noxque super campos telis conserta pependit* with Lanzarone's note. Statius adapts the motif at *Theb.* 8.411–12 *exclusere diem telis, stant ferrea caelo / nubila, nec iaculis artatus sufficit aer;* see Augoustakis' note.

325–6. tellusque uideri / sanguine operta nequit: the earth is similarly covered in blood at 4.162–3 *arua natant, altusque uirum cruor, altus equorum / lubrica belligerae sorbet uestigia turmae,* 17.412 *gentilemque bibit tellus inuita cruorem.*

326–7. caelumque et sidera pendens / abstulit ingestis nox densa sub aethere telis: so many missiles have been thrown that the air has become dense. Luc. *BC* 7.520 (quoted at 325–7n. above) may have inspired the transferred use of *pendens.* The word more typically refers to the clouds themselves, as at 17.358 *pendenti nube,* Verg. *Geo.* 1.214 *nubila pendent,* Ov. *Met.* 1.268 *pendentia nubila,* etc. *Abstulit* appears in descriptions of nightfall (12.647 *abstulerat terras nigrantibus Hesperus umbris*) or of the onset of storms, as at Verg. *Aen.* 3.198–9 *inuoluere diem nimbi et nox umida caelum / abstulit; TLL* 2.1335.12. Van Veen 1893 proposed *sub aethera,* as *pendens...nox* would be better construed "cum verbo ingerendi". The clausula of 327 is adapted from Verg. *Aen.* 12.578 *et obumbrant aethera telis.*

328–32. Silius describes the second rank of men behind the hand-to-hand fighters, who wield the *conti.* Behind them, an *inglorius ordo* fires missiles at the Carthaginians. The description conforms to epic tradition; it was not a priority to reflect the likely disposition of Roman forces at Cannae.

Parallelism unites the component phrases of the sentence: 328 *quis...* 331 *at quos,* 328 *loco...secundo...* 330 *primas...acies,* 331 *retrorsum...* 332 *priorum.* The disposition of forces conforms to epic's conventional contrast between the hand-to-hand fighter and the missile fighter's putative "treachery." This contrast begins with the scene in which Homer's Athene convinces Pandarus to shoot at Menelaus and break the truce; *Il.* 4.104 τῷ δὲ φρένας ἄφρονι πεῖθεν. Virgil's Arruns similarly asks no glory for shooting Camilla from a distance: Verg. *Aen.* 11.790–2.

328–9. quis adstare loco dederat Fortuna secundo, / contorum longo et procerae cuspidis ictu: the *contus,* a long lance, is not meant to be thrown, and so *longo* is used as a hypallage for *longorum.* Note the different use of 612n. *longinquis...iaculis,* where thrown spears strike "from far off." Virgil introduced the *contus* to Latin poetry to mean a ship's pole; see Verg. *Aen.* 5.208 with

192   *Commentary Lines 330–35*

Fratantuono and Smith's note and *Aen.* 9.510 with Hardie's note. Silius' Nero carries Hasdrubal's head on a *procera… cuspide* (15.813); see also 6.277 *pondere conti.*

Silius elsewhere attributes the *contus* to the Sarmatians (15.684–5 *conti / Sarmatici*), following VF *Arg.* 6.162 *ingentis frenator Sarmata conti.* Valerius was "the first to designate… the *contus* as a cavalry lance and as something specifically Sarmatian" (Syme 1929: 130). For a similar reference in Statius, see Stat. *Ach.* 2.132–4 *quo turbine contum / Sauromates…/ tenderet.* Stover 2012: 9–11 persuasively rejects Syme's conclusion regarding the overall dating of the *Argonautica.* The topicality of Domitian's Danubian wars need not have been the reason for the mention of the *contus*, and the incursion of the Roxolani in AD 69 suffices. The clausula is common: 4.612, 13.197, Verg. *Aen.* 7.756, etc.

330. ceu primas agitent acies, certamina miscent: Spaltenstein characterizes the line's initial phrase as a combination of *agitare proelium* and *in prima acie uersari. Miscere* is commonly used with combat words (see 233n.); 12.394 *miscebat primas acies* recalls this line. Silius is the only poet, however, to use *miscere* with *certamen.* See also 5.302, Livy 2.19.5, 41.19.4.

331. at quos deinde tenet retrorsum inglorius ordo: as missile fighters, the *inglorius ordo* would correspond to the *uelites.* There may be a recollection of Virgil's Arruns here, who concludes his prayer to guide his shot with a reminder that it brings no glory: Verg. *Aen.* 11.793 *patrias remeabo inglorius urbes.*

332. missilibus certant pugnas aequare priorum: this line fills out the *tibicen* at Verg. *Aen.* 9.520 *missilibus certant.* In doing so, it functions as a metapoetic signal: Silius' Cannae narrative has "matched" the prior poet's fight. For *certare* + infinitive, see 2.348 *certant…anteire*, 3.695 *concurrere certant*, 4.24 *certant… accersere*, etc. For the clausula, see 8.147 *aequare priores.*

333–4. ultra clamor agit bellum, milesque cupiti / Martis inops saeuis impellit uocibus hostem: Lanzarone compares the soldiers' shouting at Pharsalus: Luc. *BC* 7.367–8 *plures tantum clamore cateruae / bella gerent.* Duff compares QCurt. 6.1.10 *et qui extra teli iactum erant, clamore inuicem suos accendebant,* but (as Spaltenstein correctly objects) the situations are not directly comparable. The Spartan and Macedonian forces in the Curtius passage cannot all occupy the narrow battleground and so inspire the combatants by shouting. Silius' soldiers, by contrast, harass the enemy with shouting. For *inops* with the genitive, see 5.631 *mentis inops*, 12.66 *inops animi*, etc. Claudian adapts the final phrase at *P&O* 73 *postquam fulmineis impellens uiribus hostem.*

335. non ullum defit teli genus: an evocation of Verg. *Aen.* 2.467–8 *nec saxa nec ullum / telorum interea cessat genus* and perhaps more distantly *Aen.* 9.509–10 *telorum effundere contra / omne genus Teucri.*

Commentary Lines 335–40 193

335–6. hi sude pugnas, / hi pinu flagrante cient, hi pondere pili: triple gemination reflects the confusion of battle, continued at 338–9 *interdum... interdum.* See also 622n. *nunc... nunc... nunc.* Statius' description of the Arcadians' varied arms features similar gemination of *hic*: Stat. *Theb.* 4.302–3 *his arcus, his tela sudes, his cassida crines / integit.* For the gemination of *hic*, see Wills 1996: 78, though he does not comment on this particular instance; see Introduction, section 5c. See 128n. for the 1+2+2 clausula of 335. For *pinus* as a metonym of *taeda*, see Verg. *Aen.* 7.397 *flagrantem... pinum, Aen.* 9.72 *pinu flagranti.* A phrase formed by *ponder-* with a weapon in the genitive creates a common clausula: 1.336 *pondere teli*, 1.523 *pondere plumbi*, 2.246 *pondera clauae*, etc.

337. at saxis fundaque alius iaculoque uolucri: *TLL* 6.1.1549.10–23 lists only this line and 10.151 *funda procul per inane uoluta* as the sole occurrences of *funda* in the sense of "missile, quod funda mittitur" in poetry. But this seems overly precise. The *funda* is part of a conventional list of weapons, as at VF *Arg.* 3.96 *saxa facesque atras et tortae pondera fundae*; Stat. *Theb.* 10.856–7 *ingentia saxa / roboraque et ualidas fundae Balearis habenas.* For the epithet *uolucer* applied to missiles, see 11–12n. For the clausula, see Luc. *BC* 9.720 *iaculique uolucres* (referring to snakes).

338. interdum stridens per nubila fertur harundo: for the anaphora of *interdum*, see 335–6n. For *stridens*, see 247n., 311n.

339. interdumque ipsis metuenda phalarica muris: the *phalarica* is similarly described as a danger to city walls at 1.354 *uix muris toleranda lues.* Soldiers wrapped incendiary material around the top end of the weapon's shaft and lit it shortly before casting. Livy 21.8.10–12 describes its construction and operation in detail. For its earlier appearances in the poets, see Enn. *Ann.* 557 with Skutsch's note, Verg. *Aen.* 9.705, Luc. *BC* 6.198, etc.

340–5. Narrators in epic traditionally invoke the Muse before a great battle commences: Hom. *Il.* 2.484–93, Verg. *Aen.* 12.500–4, Stat. *Theb.* 8.373–4, etc. Here Silius combines the invocation with variations on the topoi of incapacity (341 *mortali... uoce*) and "many mouths" (343 *uno ore*). Both topoi occur in the Trebia narrative (4.525–8), but the narrator does not invoke the Muses. The Trasimene narrative (5.420–4) and the encomium of Ennius (12.387–92) both feature an invocation and a claim of incapacity, but not the "many mouths" topos, on which, see Gowers 2005.

340. speramusne, deae, quarum mihi sacra coluntur: the narrator similarly makes hope part of the incapacity topos in his encomium of Ennius: 12.387–8 *non equidem... sperarim.* The poet is traditionally the worshiper of the Muses: see Hor. *Carm.* 3.1.3 *Musarum sacerdos*, Verg. *Geo.* 2.475–7 *me uero primum dulces ante omnia **Musae**, / **quarum** sacra fero ingenti percussus amore, / accipiant,* etc. Silius' Homer is dressed as the Muses' worshiper: 13.779–82 *caste cui uitta*

194 *Commentary Lines 341–53*

ligabat / purpurea effusos per colla nitentia crines...frons sacra uiro. Silius'
Domitian inverts the relationship of dependency, as the Muses bring him their
sacra: 3.619–20 *huic sua Musae / sacra ferent.*

341–2. mortali totum hunc aperire in saecula uoce / posse diem: for the contrast between the poet's mortal voice and the Muses' divine voices, see 340–5n.
The *saecula* are "future ages, posterity" (*OLD* s.v. 8). For the topos, see 2.511 *in
saecula mittam* with my note, 8.371 *nascens in saecula uirtus*, 12.312 *factoque in
saecula ituro*; Luc. *BC* 8.608 *in saecula mittet*, VF *Arg.* 1.99 *in saecula tollat* with
Zissos' note. For the repeated motif of Cannae as a crucial day, see 19–20n.
una...die, 183n. *nulla dies*, 215n. *hic hodie*.

Blass supported Heinsius' *aperiri*, but *sperare* in Silius is typically followed by
personal rather than impersonal constructions. Examples include 10.20 *et
sperat iam tangere dextra*, 12.388 *sperarim tanto digne pro nomine rerum /
pandere.*

342–3. tantumne datis confidere linguae, / ut Cannas uno ore sonem: for the
"many mouths" topos, see 340–5n. Examples include Hom. *Il.* 2.488–92, Enn.
Ann. 469 Skutsch, Verg. *Aen.* 6.625–7.

343–4. si gloria uobis / nostra placet: the poet's prayer to please the Muses
evokes the Virgilian narrator's prayer: Verg. *Geo.* 2.475–7 *me uero...Musae.../
accipiant.*

344. neque uos magnis auertitis ausis: for the poet's pride in his great undertaking, see 7.163 *quamquam magna incepta uocent*. For the topos of epic as a
tremendous work of daring, see Verg. *Geo.* 1.40 *audacibus...coeptis, Aen.* 7.45
maius opus moueo, Luc. *BC* 1.68 *immensum...opus*. The verb *auertere* can be
used with or without the accompanying preposition *ab*; see 520n., 548n., 12.202
coeptoque auertit suprema in fata ruentem, etc.

345. huc omnes cantus Phoebumque uocate parentem: *parens* is an honorific
title for Apollo Musagetes, as the Muses are daughters of Zeus and Mnemosyne. See
13.538–9 *nec dedignanda parenti / carmina fuderunt Phoebo* with van der Keur's
note, and Stat. *Theb.* 1.696. For Phoebus as *pater*, see 4.526, Stat. *Silv.* 1.6.1, etc.

346–53. The narrator instructs the Romans of his own day to perceive the historic
defeat as a measure of their ability to bear adversity. Subsequent ages brought
prosperity, with its concomitant corruption. Silius' Jupiter employs a similar
argument in his prophecy to Venus as Hannibal crosses the Alps (3.570–629). He
describes the Second Punic War as a salutary test of Roman morals before a subsequent period of moral decline (3.580–1 *blandoque ueneno / desidiae uirtus
paulatim euicta senescit*). This passage also prefigures the complementary apostrophe to Carthage, similarly on the theme of Roman morals, at the conclusion of
the Cannae episode: see 10.657–8 *haec tum Roma fuit: post te cui uertere mores /
si stabat fatis, potius, Carthago, maneres* with Littlewood's note.

Commentary Lines 346–9

The topos is familiar from Roman historiography and rhetoric, e.g., Sall. *BCat.* 10, *BJ* 41.2 *metus hostilis in bonis artibus ciuitatem retinebat*; see Jacobs 2010. Lucan adapts the topos at *BC* 1.161 *et rebus mores cessere secundis*.

The address to a generic Roman (346 *Romane*) evokes the *Romane, memento* exhortation delivered by Virgil's Anchises in the Underworld (Verg. *Aen.* 6.851–3). Lucan similarly apostrophizes the Romans before and after the battle of Pharsalus (Luc. *BC* 7.205–13); see Fucecchi 1999. Each passage points to a new epoch; the Golden Age for Virgil's Augustan subjects, subjugation under the Caesars for Lucan's Romans. Silius similarly marks defeat at Cannae as the commencement of a new period of moral decline. For apostrophe in Lucan, see D'Alessandro Behr 2007.

The exhortation to Rome (349–52) not to weep for the defeat at Cannae evokes two earlier scenes:

(a) Jupiter's prophecy as Hannibal crosses the Alps. He consoles Venus with the thought of Rome's future greatness, which culminates in the reign of Domitian. Rome will be the greater for its losses: 3.571 *pelle metus,* 3.584–5 *iamque tibi ueniet tempus quo maxima rerum / nobilior sit Roma malis.* For Venus and the *parce metu* motif, see Hershkowitz 1997.

(b) Marus tells Serranus to stop weeping for his father Regulus and admire his endurance instead: 6.537–8 *tu quoque, care puer, dignum te sanguine tanto / fingere ne cessa atque orientis comprime fletus.*

346–7. uerum utinam posthac animo, Romane, secunda, / quanto nunc aduersa, feras: for the contrast of *secundum* and *aduersum*, see Verg. *Aen.* 9.282 *tantum fortuna secunda / aut aduersa cadat*, Claud. *Stil.* 1.285 *peruigil euentusque sibi latura secundos / maior in aduersis micuit.*

347–8. sitque hactenus, oro, / nec libeat temptare deis: L offers the alternative *sic*, and numerous conjectures have been proposed, including Blass' *sat*, which Duff adopts. The example of 4.795–6 *hactenus, oro, / sit*, however, suggests that correction is not necessary.

348. an Troia proles: a unique collocation, likely modeled on Virgilian phrases such as *Cyllenia proles* (*Aen.* 4.258), *Neptunia proles* (*Aen.* 7.691, 9.523, 10.353, 12.128), etc. The periphrasis replaces a genitive and offers a convenient metrical shape, as at *Pun.* 2.3 *Tirynthia proles* (where, see my note), 13.630 *Cyllenia proles*, 14.356 *Arethusia proles*; see Harrison on Verg. *Aen.* 10.353. *Troius* in the sense of "Roman" is relatively rare (12.331 *Troianos...labores*, 16.655 *gens Troiana*, 16.678–9 *Troia...moenia*); *Dardanus* is more common.

349. par bellum tolerare queat: Fabius promises the Carthaginians a *priori / par...bellum* (2.388–9 with my note). The motif of testing the Romans' limits of endurance echoes Jupiter's prophecy: 3.373–4 *hac ego Martis / mole uiros spectare paro atque expendere bello.*

196 *Commentary Lines 349–57*

349. tuque anxia fati: for *anxius* with the genitive, see 12.492 *anxius euentus, TLL* 2.202.68. For the clausula, see [Verg.] *Culex* 353 *copia nunc miseris circumdatur anxia fatis*. Ussani 1950: 123 suggested possible imitation, but this is unlikely, as there is little connection between the contexts. *Anxia* in the fifth foot creates a common and convenient clausula, as at 2.285 *anxia rupi*, 10.108 *anxia nido*, Ov. *Met.* 1.623 *anxia furti, Met.* 9.275 *anxia curis*, etc.

350. pone, precor, lacrimas: *pone* is *simplex pro composito* for *deponere*; see *TLL* 10.1.2656.8. This phrase is modeled on Ov. *Met.* 14.762 *pone, precor, fastus, Fasti* 1.480 *siste, precor, lacrimas*.

350–1. et adora uulnera laudes / perpetuas paritura tibi: McClellan 2021 notes the physicality of the metaphor, which envisions Rome as a body that may weep (350 *lacrimas*) and suffer wounding. The lines further echo Jupiter's prophecy: 3.588–90 *hi* [i.e., Paulus, Fabius, and Marcellus] *tantum parient Latio per uulnera regnum / quod luxu et multum mutata mente nepotes / non tamen euertisse queant*.

351–3. nam tempore, Roma, / nullo maior eris. mox sic labere secundis / ut sola cladum tuearis nomina fama: *fama* varies 350 *laudes*. For the clausula of 353, see 3.263, 11.140 *ut Trebiae ripas aeterno nomine famae*. It is common in Lucan: *BC* 5.468, 6.257, 6.604, 10.544.

354–7. The course of the battle wavers. As is typical of Silius' repetitive style, variation of the same idea creates emphasis: *uarias... uices, alternata, incerto... euentu, mediaque diu pendente*. The motif of an uncertain struggle reprises the epic's proem: 1.7–8 *quaesitumque diu, qua tandem poneret arce / terrarum Fortuna caput*. Cannae represents a moment at which Fortune could have given Carthage rule of the world. Lucan's Pharsalus narrative similarly uses the topos of Fortune's variability in battle: Luc. *BC* 7.487–8 *rapit omnia casus / atque incerta facit quos uult Fortuna nocentes*.

354–5. iamque inter uarias Fortuna utrimque uirorum / alternata uices: *iamque* resumes the narration of events after the lengthy apostrophe. For the phrase *uarias... uices*, see Tib. 1.9.64, [Sen.] *Epig.* 18.64, 31.2, etc. For the clausula of 354, see *Il. Lat.* 530. For the opening of 355, see Ov. *Met.* 15.409, [Verg.] *Mor.* 29, etc.

355–6. incerto eluserat iras / euentu: for the phrasing, see Stat. *Theb.* 11.648 *et iam laeta ducum spes elusisse duorum* [i.e., Fortuna]. Both lines are variations on the more common motif of *Fortuna ludens*, for which, see Verg. *Aen.* 11.427 *lusit... Fortuna* with Horsfall's note, and Hor. *Carm.* 2.1.3 *ludumque Fortunae* with Nisbet and Hubbard's note. For "uncertain outcome," see 8.208 *incertos rerum euentus*.

356–7. mediaque diu pendente per ambas / spe gentis paribus Mauors flagrabat in armis: for hope hanging in the balance, see Ov. *Fasti* 3.680 *pendet ab* *officio spes mihi magna tuo*, Sen. *Epig.* 18.7 *spes nescit uinci, spes pendet tota futuris*, etc. Until the reader arrives at 357 *spe*, however, *pendente* also suggests the related topos of *Fortuna pendens*, for which, see Ov. *Met.* 8.12 *et pendebat adhuc belli fortuna*, Luc. *BC* 2.41 *dum pendet fortuna ducum*, Livy 28.17.7 *quibus ex fortuna pendet fides*, etc. Spaltenstein correctly observes that *flagrabat* is closer to "faisait rage" (e.g., 1.435 *flagrantia bella*) than the classification "ardere, nitere" at *TLL* 6.1.847.22; cf. Verg. *Aen.* 12.167 *flagrans clipeo*. For the common collocation *paribus... armis*, see 2.132 with my note, 4.381, 14.526; six times in Verg. *Aen.*

358–61. A simile compares the wavering battle lines to crops swaying in the wind. The simile is modeled in part on the Homeric comparison describing the Achaeans' departure for the ships: Hom. *Il.* 2.147–9 ὡς δ' ὅτε κινήσῃ Ζέφυρος βαθὺ λήϊον ἐλθὼν / λάβρος ἐπαιγίζων, ἐπί τ' ἠμύει ἀσταχύεσσιν, / ὣς τῶν πᾶσ' ἀγορὴ κινήθη. Silius' wind is gentler (358 *mitia*, 361 *lente*) and thus creates a sharper contrast between the peaceful cropland and the violent battlefield. Sen. *HF* 699 *nec adulta leni fluctuat Zephyro seges* draws the scene in miniature. Ov. *Am.* 1.7.54–5 reproduces the topos in an erotic context.

358–9. mitia ceu uirides agitant cum flamina culmos, / necdum maturas impellit uentus aristas: repetition (*uirides, necdum maturas*) emphasizes that the crops are new, and accordingly more flexible than mature ones and more likely to bend in the wind. The gentle wind earlier appeared at 6.527–8 *moderato flamine lenes / uexerunt Zephyri*. For the phrase "mature crops," see Verg. *Geo.* 1.348, Ov. *Fasti* 5.357 (both in the same *sedes*), Manil. *Astr.* 4.558, etc.

360–1. huc atque huc it summa seges nutansque uicissim / alterno lente motu incuruata nitescit: for the "shining" of new crops, see Lucr. *DRN* 1.252 *at nitidae surgunt fruges ramique uirescunt / arboribus*. *Vicissim* and *alterno* recapitulate the alternation motif introduced in 354–7n.

362–6. Nealces' troops break the Roman line and slaughter ensues. In Livy 22.47 and Polybius 3.115, the Romans initially break through Hannibal's line but then are encircled and slaughtered. Silius foreshortens the narrative to emphasize the slaughter of the Romans rather than Hannibal's deception. For Nealces, see 226n.

362–3. tandem barbaricis perfractam uiribus acri / dissipat incurrens aciem clamore Nealces: *perfractam... aciem* is a unique collocation in poetry; see 11.398 *profliganda acies, quam non perfregerit ensis*. The collocation appears in prose at Tac. *Hist.* 4.20.3 *sic tenuem nostrorum aciem perfringunt*. The reference to Nealces' troops as *barbaricis... uiribus* reprises 268n. *feras... gentes*.

Acri... clamore is also a unique collocation in poetry, though note Verg. *Aen.* 9.791 *acrius hoc Teucri clamore incumbere magno*. For similar phrases, see, e.g., 3.230 *acrius infremuit*, 15.711 *acrius... urget*, Ov. *Met.* 3.704 *fremit acer equus*.

198   *Commentary Lines 364–9*

The collocation appears in prose at [Cic.] *Rhet. Her.* 3.21, Livy 2.55.6 *indignantium pro se acerrimus erat clamor*, Petr. *Sat.* 136.13, etc.

364. laxati cunei: the Carthaginian breakthrough loosens the Roman wedges. Livy 22.47.5 reports the opposite movement, where a closely formed Roman battle line breaks through the Carthaginian *cunei*. The *cuneus* is ideally a close formation, conventionally *densus*: see Verg. *Aen.* 12.457–8 *densi cuneis se quisque coactis / adglomerant*, Luc. *BC* 6.184 *tunc densos inter cuneos conpressus*, Apul. *Met.* 4.26 *denso conglobatoque cuneo*, etc. *Laxati* varies 363 *dissipat*. "Loosening" the *cunei* appears to be Silius' innovation, an extension of phrases such as *laxare acies* (5.381–2, Livy 27.18.17), *laxare manipulos* (Caes. *BG* 2.25.2, Front. *Strat.* 2.6.2); see *OLD* s.v. *laxo* 1b. Ammianus adapts the phrase at Amm. Marc. 24.1.3 *laxatis cuneis*. The image is inverted at the Metaurus, where a Roman wedge breaks the Celtic line: *Pun.* 15.716–17 *hos impulsu cuneoque feroci / laxat uis subita*. For *cunei* elsewhere as "squads" rather than "wedges," see 238n.

364–5. perque interualla citatus / irrupit trepidis hostis: the prosaic *interuallum* is common in didactic poets (Lucr. *DRN* thirteen times, Germ. *Arat.* twice, Man. *Astr.* four times), but otherwise rare in poetry: *Pun.* 12.382, Verg. *Aen.* 5.320, Hor. *Epist.* 2.2.70, Prop. *Eleg.* 3.21.31, then not again until late antiquity. For the comparative rarity of *irrumpere* with the dative, see *Pun.* 2.378 *ceu templo irrumperet hostis* with my note, 10.583 *nondum portis irruperit hostis*, Verg. *Aen.* 6.528 *irrumpunt thalamo*, and *TLL* 7.2.444.74–5.

365–6. tum turbine nigro / sanguinis exundat torrens: the phrasing evokes the fire that consumes the Saguntines: see 2.630–1 *densum qua turbine nigro / exundat fumans piceus caligine uertex* with my note. Cannae represents similar devastation for the Romans on a larger scale. Dark blood appears before Cannae as an omen: 8.644–5 *atro sanguine flumen / manauit Iouis in templis*. The "torrent of dark blood" recurs in Silius' Underworld, retroactively creating an association between Cannae and Hell: see 13.566 *torrens Cocytos sanguinis atri* with van der Keur's note. For the clausula of 365, see also 12.148, 15.631, Verg. *Geo.* 1.320. The river of blood is an epic motif; see 5.431–2 *fluit impia riuis / sanguineis uallis*, Verg. *Aen.* 9.456, Luc. *BC* 4.785 with Esposito's note, *BC* 7.292, *BC* 7.637 with Lanzarone's note, etc.

366–7. nullumque sub una / cuspide procumbit corpus: no soldier fell from a single spear, just as at 310–11n. there was no first spear to be thrown. The hyperbolic claims emphasize the vast sizes of the opposed forces. For estimates of the force sizes, see Introduction, section 2.

367–9. At the beginning of the battle, the proud Romans fear the dishonor of wounds to the back and so seek to take wounds in the chest. Later in the battle, after the reversal, Paulus must exhort them to remain similarly steadfast: see

Commentary Lines 367–73   199

10.7–8 *pectoribus ferrum accipite ac sine uulnere terga / ad manes deferte, uiri* with Littlewood's note. For taking mortal wounds in the chest, see 4.194 *exceptum pectore letum*. For the dishonor and cowardice of wounds to the back, see 10.62–3 *non hostica tela / excipias tergo, superos precor* (Paulus to Juno in disguise as Metellus), 15.717–21 (the Celts at the Metaurus experience *patrius genti pauor*), Ov. *Fasti* 2.211–12 *diffugiunt hostes inhonestaque uulnera tergo / accipiunt* (the Fabii initially slaughter the Etruscans at the Cremera), VF *Arg.* 6.520–1 *sed trepidae redeunt et uerso uulnera tergo / accipiunt* (Absyrtus' shield terrifies his enemies), etc.

367–8. dum uulnera tergo / bellator timet Ausonius: for *bellator*, see 221n.; for pairing of the noun with an ethnonym, see 1.190 *bellator Hiberus*, 3.403 *bellator Arauricus*, etc.

368–9. per pectora saeuas / exceptat mortes et leto dedecus arcet: for *mortes* in the specific meaning of "tela," see Luc. *BC* 7.517 *inde cadunt mortes* with Lanzarone's note, Stat. *Theb.* 6.793 *mille cauet lapsas circum caua tempora mortes*, *TLL* 8.1505.2. The more likely meaning, however, is "causa mortis," as at *TLL* 8.1504.71.

Spaltenstein correctly interprets *leto* as *a leto*, "from death," as at 1.84 *caelique arcebant lumine*, or possibly dative on the model of 5.490–1 *defendere nescia morti / dedecus*. Ruperti opted for instrumental ablative, "by dying," followed by Duff, "by death [they] avoided dishonour;" similarly Volpilhac-Lenthéric: "la mort, du déshonneur, le sauve." The narrator's focus, however, is on the heroic manner of the Romans' death. They fear the wounds to the back that would compromise their *decus*. Skutsch's note on Enn. *Ann.* 389 observes Silius' avoidance of an ambiguous ablative in a different passage: "in Sil. 13.380 *liceat pugnanti occumbere letum* the accusative seems to be chosen to avoid the ambiguity which would arise from *leto*."

370–9. Scaevola stands fast in the face of overwhelming force, like his legendary ancestor Mucius Scaevola, who fearlessly faced Lars Porsenna (Livy 2.12). Scaevola was introduced in the catalog preceding Cannae through his connection to his ancestors: 8.383 *ducit auis pollens nec dextra indignus auorum*. He carries an image of the legendary Mucius on his shield (8.384–9), and the Romans grieve his noble death after the battle: 10.404 *grauis illic Scaeuola bello*. As McGuire 1995: 112 observes, the historical Q. Mucius Scaevola did not die at Cannae, as he was praetor for 215 bc (Livy 23.24.4). See 415n. for a similar connection between another Roman at Cannae (Brutus) and his legendary ancestor. For the significance of Silius' names of Roman characters at Cannae, see Introduction, section 4b.

370–3. An elegantly composed sentence that commences with the strong spondee *stabat* and emphatically enjambs its subject *Scaevola* at the sentence's midpoint. Scaevola displays the epic hero's typical contempt for life and eagerness

200 *Commentary Lines 370–6*

to risk death in search of a great name. 371 *aspera…periclo* and 377 *decori* evoke the Senate's response to the news of Hannibal's crossing of the Alps: 4.35–7 *tamen crudam contra aspera mentem / et magnos tollunt animos. iuuat ire periclis / ad decus et dextra memorandum condere nomen.* Lucan's Scaeva has a similar contempt for death (*BC* 6.246 *mortis amor*), but not the same patriotic interest in defending his country from foreign invaders or in achieving a memorable name. Lucan's narrator condemns him for only aiding Caesar's eventual tyranny (*BC* 6.257–72). Silius may have created his *decus*-seeking Scaevola in part as a response to this figure.

370. stabat cum primis mediae certamine pugnae: initial position is typical for *stare*; see the similar 252n. *stant primi*. Initial *stabat* occurs six times in Silius, four times in Verg. *Aen.*, six times in Ov. *Met.*, seven times in Stat. *Theb. Cum primis* recalls the organization of the ranks, for which, see 328–32n. *Mediae* accordingly means "in the middle" of battle, as Nealces was earlier identified as leading the left wing (226n.). For the clausula, see 136n.

371–2. aspera semper amans et par cuicumque periclo / Scaeuola, nec tanta uitam iam strage uolebat: that the wise man holds steady through life's *aspera* is a typical Stoic idea, which epic applies in a nontechnical sense to its heroes. Examples include Sen. *Prov.* 5.9 *contra fortunam illi tenendus est cursus; multa accident dura, aspera, sed quae molliat et conplanet ipse, Ep. Mor.* 31.7 *animi est ipsa tolerantia quae se ad dura et aspera hortatur ac dicit, 'quid cessas? non est uiri timere sudorem.'* For the topos of death as one answer to *aspera*, see *Pun.* 2.576 *quis telum ingens contra aspera mors est* with my note. For possession of a spirit equal to the danger, see Livy 1.26.12 *ipsius parem in omni periculo animum*, QCurt. 8.14.14.3 *par animo meo periculum uideo*, etc.

373. sed dignum proauo letum et sub nomine mortem: Scaevola's *proauus*, the legendary Mucius, did not die in his confrontation with Lars Porsenna, but demonstrated steadfastness in the face of death. For the use of *sub*, see 258n., and contrast Curio's inglorious death by drowning: 10.214 *sine nomine mortis.* The only other examples of the inclusion of *letum* and *mors* in the same line are in lists of Underworld personifications: Sen. *Oed.* 652 *Letum Luesque, Mors Labor Tabes Dolor*, Petr. *BC* 257 *Letumque Insidiaeque et lurida Mortis imago.* These nouns occur more frequently in neighboring lines. For Silius' characteristic repetition with varied diction, see Introduction, section 5b.

374–5. is postquam frangi res atque augescere uidit / exitium: for *frangi res*, compare 1.560, Verg. *Geo.* 4.240 *res miserabere fractas*, Sen. *NQ* 3.pr.6 (of Hannibal's defeat), *TLL* 6.1.1247.19, etc. *Aug(esc)ere exitium* is a unique collocation, likely modeled on *augere periculum* (Caes. *BC* 3.64.2, Pliny *Ep.* 6.20.15, etc.).

375–6. breuis hoc uitae, quodcumque relictum, / extendamus: Scaevola does not seek to prolong his life but the persistence of his fame after death. The topos

Commentary Lines 376–89   201

evokes Fides' promise to the Saguntines: see 2.511 *extendam leti decus, atque in saecula mittam* with my note. Both passages are ultimately modeled directly on the Virgilian Jupiter's words to Hercules: Verg. *Aen.* 10.467–9 *stat sua cuique dies, breue et inreparabile tempus / omnibus est uitae; sed famam extendere factis, / hoc uirtutis opus.* See also Stat. *Theb.* 4.33 *uitasque extendere* with Parkes's note. The ending of 375 is modeled on Ov. *Met.* 11.543, *Fasti* 2.579 *quodcumque relictum est*, each in a different context.

376. ait 'nam uirtus futile nomen': for the potential for *uirtus* to become a empty name, see 6.548–9 *dum uirtutis uenerabile nomen / uiuet* (of Regulus' enduring example), Hor. *Epist.* 1.17.41–2 *aut uirtus nomen inane est, / aut decus et pretium recte petit experiens uir*. For the related topos that *uirtus* can become the fine name that conceals crime, see Luc. *BC* 1.667–8 *scelerique nefando / nomen erit uirtus*.

377. ni decori sat sint pariendo tempora leti: for the clausula, see 10.35 *iunxit fera tempora leti*.

378–84. Scaevola plunges into the middle of the fray and kills Caralis. Aspects of the combat recombine several different combats of Virgil's Aeneas:

(a) 379 *limitem agit* is modeled on Verg. *Aen.* 10.514 *ardens limitem agit ferro*, of Aeneas' pursuit of Turnus immediately after his killing of Pallas.

(b) Caralis' desire to affix spoils to a tree (380–1) evokes Aeneas' trophy displaying Mezentius' spoils: Verg. *Aen.* 11.5–6 *ingentem quercum decisis undique ramis / constituit tumulo fulgentiaque induit arma*.

Three possible further allusions in this passage to Aeneas' combats include:

(a) 379 *turbine fertur* evokes Verg. *Aen.* 12.855, of the Dira's descent to incapacitate Turnus. As the clausula only occurs otherwise at *Pun.* 12.538, Lucr. *DRN* 5.632, and *Il. Lat.* 893, its comparative infrequency suggests the possibility of allusion here.

(b) 382 *capuloque tenus* evokes one of Aeneas' murders during his rampage (Verg. *Aen.* 10.536), but this is a more common collocation.

(c) Caralis "bites the dust" as he dies, like Virgil's Pallas, but so do many other epic victims; see 383–4n.

The combined effect is to associate Scaevola strongly with Aeneas and thus contrast him further with Lucan's Scaeva. This brief vignette of a minor hero's exploits dramatizes the moral benefits and hazards of *uirtus*.

Delz 1987: L refers to lines 378–9 in constructing his two stemmata for the transmission of the *Punica*: "uno carmen usque ad versum 9, 378, ubi codex *Γ* exemplar mutavit, altero a 9, 379 ad finem complectente."

378–9. dixit et in medios, qua dextera concita Poeni / limitem agit, uasto conixus turbine fertur: *Poenus* refers to Nealces, who was the last Carthaginian

202 *Commentary Lines 380–4*

to be mentioned (363), and who turns to attack Scaevola at 392. Duff is, therefore, incorrect to identify Hannibal as the *Poenus*, though that is a typical metonym for him.

380. hic exultantem Caralim: *Caralis* is the ancient name for Cagliari in Sardinia, which was assigned to the Carthaginian Empire after the First Punic War (Polyb. 3.22.8–9) and did not become a Roman possession until 238 BC. The island revolted numerous times, most pertinently the revolt led by Hampsicora in 215 BC with Carthaginian support (Livy 23.40–1); Silius presents a narrative of the rebellion at 12.342–419. The name is accordingly appropriate for a Sardinian warrior allied with Carthage. For toponyms as personal names, see 410n. *Symaetho*, 1.380 *Aradum* with Spaltenstein's note, 2.104 *Meroe*, 2.160 *Thapsum*, etc.

380–1. atque erepta uolentem / induere excelso caesi gestamina trunco: carefully interlaced word order suggests the spoils in the tree's branches. For the topos of erecting a trophy to display spoils taken in combat, see *Il.* 10.460–6, Verg. *Aen.* 11.5–8 with Horsfall's note, Luc. *BC* 1.137 with Roche's note, and Stat. *Theb.* 2.707–12 with Gervais's note.

382. ense subit, capuloque tenus ferrum impulit ira: *subit* has its usual meaning of "attack," as at *OLD* s.v. 4. Volpilhac-Lenthéric's translation "son épée de par-dessous le surprend" is accordingly *un peu de trop*; Duff's "Scaevola stabbed him" renders the brief phrase far more accurately. The Virgilian phrase *capulo tenus* (*Aen.* 2.553, 10.536) recurs in subsequent poets: see Ov. *Met.* 12.491, Stat. *Theb.* 2.534. For variations on thrusting the sword "to the hilt," see 1.515–16 *sic Poenus pressumque ira simul exigit ensem / qua capuli statuere morae.*

383. uoluitur ille ruens: likely modeled on Verg. *Aen.* 9.414 *uoluitur ille uomens.* For *uoluere* of collapsing in death, see 4.254 *uoluitur ille solo*, Verg. *Aen.* 9.433 *uoluitur Euryalus leto*, *Aen.* 10.590 *excussus curru moribundus uoluitur aruis*, etc.; Verg. *Aen.* 11.640 *uoluitur ille excussus humi*, which Horsfall *ad loc.* traces back to Hom. *Il.* 8.86 κυλινδόμενος περὶ χαλκῷ.

383–4. atque arua hostilia morsu / appetit: Caralis "bites the dust" as he dies. Others who perish this way include Sychaeus at Trasimene (5.526–7 *labitur infelix atque adpetit ore cruento / tellurem expirans*) and Hasdrubal, as remembered by his brother Hannibal: 17.262–3 *et cui fata dedere / Ausoniam extremo tellurem apprendere morsu.* In the present passage, Silius recombines two Virgilian examples of the topos: Verg. *Aen.* 10.489 *terram hostilem moriens petit ore cruento* (Pallas) and *Aen.* 11.418 *procubuit moriens et humum semel ore momordit* (the ideal patriot as described by Turnus). For the latter phrase, see Ov. *Met.* 9.60 *et harenas ore momordi.* The topos of biting the dust originates at Hom. *Il.* 2.417–18 πολέες δ᾽ ἀμφ᾽ αὐτὸν ἑταῖροι / πρηνέες ἐν κονίῃσιν ὀδὰξ λαζοίατο γαῖαν; for the formula ὀδὰξ ἕλον (ἄσπετον) οὖδας, see also *Il.* 11.749, 19.61, 24.738. For discussion, see Augoustakis 2010: 153.

Commentary Lines 384–6   203

For the "hostile fields," see 2.185 *campis deletur Hiberis* with my note, 17.262–3 (quoted above in this note), Verg. *Aen.* 10.489 (quoted above in this note). The motif of dying far from one's homeland originates at Hom. *Il.* 2.162 ἐν Τροίη ἀπόλοντο φίλης ἀπὸ πατρίδος αἴης, *Il.* 11.817 τῆλε φίλων καὶ πατρίδος αἴης, etc.; see Griffin 1980: 106–12.

384. et mortis premit in tellure dolores: perhaps modeled on Verg. *Aen.* 1.209 *premit altum corde dolorem.*

385–91. Gabar loses his right hand to Scaevola ("Lefty"), the man whose legendary ancestor Mucius Scaevola also lost his own right hand by burning it in a fire. The descendant avenges his forefather by cutting off an enemy's right hand. While endeavoring to come to his aid, Siccha trips on the sword still carried by Gabar's severed hand. The pun on Scaevola's name and the bizarre manner of Siccha's wounding make the vignette a characteristic example of Silius' heavy-handed humor.

The scene is a restrained variation on the "Automatismus" topos, where hands severed in battle (387n.) still clutch their weapons (391n.) or even continue to move them. The topos originates for Latin epic with Pallas' severing of Larides' hand, which continues to move: Verg. *Aen.* 10.395–6 *te decisa suum, Laride, dextera quaerit / semianimesque micant digiti ferrumque retractant.* For further examples, see *Pun.* 2.137 with my note, 4.209–12, 4.389–90 *inque suo pressa est non reddens tegmina nisu / infelix manus atque haesit labentibus armis,* 7.659–60, 14.537–8; Enn. *Ann.* 483–4 with Skutsch's lengthy discussion, Ov. *Met.* 6.555–62, Luc. *BC* 3.609–12, Stat. *Theb.* 9.268–9; Dinter 2010.

385–6. nec Gabaris Sicchaeque: the name *Gabar* is otherwise unattested in Latin. It may conceivably be of Celtic origin: see Holder 1896 s.v. *Gabarus* (modern Gave de Pau, a river in southwest France) or *Gaberius,* the name of a Roman knight (Varro *RR* 2.3.10). Spaltenstein's suggestion that the name is Semitic is more likely. The root GBR produces the simple form גָּבַר "be strong, prevail," and the Biblical names Gever (1 *Kings* 4:19) and Gibbar (*Ezra* 2:20). Siccha's name recalls Sicca (modern El Kef, Tunisia), and his bare feet (390n.) further mark him as a North African warrior. Siccha's identity is a further argument for the Semitic origins of Gabar's name, as Silius' warrior comrades tend to be compatriots. I am grateful to Jessica Andruss for discussing this passage with me.

385–6. uirum tenuere furentem / concordi uirtute manus: Siccha's endeavor to rescue his friend (388–9) certifies their concord. It prefigures the *concordia* evinced by the Roman friends Marius and Caper (401–10n.). The point of the epithet is to describe their amity; it does not specify their equality. Accordingly, Duff's translation "united valour" is more accurate than Vinchesi's "di pari valore." Delz's conjecture *furentem* is based on 393 *iuuenis furor.*

204 *Commentary Lines 386–93*

386–7. sed perdidit acer, / dum stat: Gabar stands fast (*dum stat*), in contrast to his friend Siccha who runs (389 *dum...accelerat*). For the topos of pairs of warriors killed in different ways, see 4.175–7, where a sword kills Laurus, while a spear kills Picens. For the initial spondee *dum stat*, see 370n. *stabat*.

387. decisam Gabar inter proelia dextram: for the loss of a hand, see 4.209 *decisaque uulnere dextra*, 4.387 *decidit uulnere laeuam*, 16.66–7 *remeans nam dextera ab ictu / decisa est gladio*, Verg. *Aen.* 10.395 (quoted at 385–91n. above), etc. L reads *densam*; this MS makes the same error at 1.524 *decisae uertice cristae*.

388. at Siccha auxilium magno turbante dolore: for destabilizing grief, see 1.169 *succensa ira turbataque luctu*, Verg. *Aen.* 12.599 *subito mentem turbata dolore*, etc.

389–90. dum temere accelerat, calcato improuidus ense / succidit: for *auxilium...accelerat*, compare phrases such as 7.565 *celeremus opem*, similarly of an effort to rescue comrades threatened in combat. For other contexts, see, e.g., VF *Arg.* 3.251 *supremam celerauit opem*. The enjambement of *succidit* emphasizes the suddenness of Siccha's collapse.

390–1. ac nudae sero uestigia plantae / damnauit: the Carthaginians are similarly described as fighting barefoot in the catalog of Hannibal's forces: 3.235 *uestigia nuda*. Virgil applied the phrase to the unusual outfit of the primitive Praenestines, who wore only one *pero* (Verg. *Aen.* 7.689–90 *uestigia nuda sinistri / instituere pedis*). For *uestigia plantae*, see 7.463, 15.505, Ov. *Fasti* 4.463, etc.

391. dextraque iacet morientis amici: Delz observes "male intellegunt interpretes 'a dextra parte amici'; sensus est 'et sic amicus moriens eum occidit.'" *Dextra* specifics that Gabar's severed hand continues to clutch its weapon and so wounds his friend Siccha, following the "Automatismus" topos discussed in 385–91n. Without this specification, we would envision something like Bibulus' fate during Fabius' rescue of Minucius (7.621–33). He is fatally wounded by a sword that happens to be sticking out of a corpse's guts. Spaltenstein observes that *iacet* does not necessarily signify that Siccha has been killed; he could have been merely wounded in the foot.

392–3. tandem conuertit fatalia tela Nealcae / fulminei gliscens iuuenis furor: for "fatal/fated missiles," see Verg. *Aen.* 12.919 *cunctanti telum Aeneas fatale coruscat*. As Parkes observes, *fulmineus* is "a common meteorological image used to evoke a warrior's power"; see her note on Stat. *Theb.* 4.94 *fulmineus Tydeus*. For *fulmineus* applied to a warrior, see 17.548 *fulmineus ductor*, Verg. *Aen.* 9.812 *fulmineus Mnestheus*, Stat. *Theb.* 2.571 *Dorylas* with Gervais's note. 393 *ardens* extends the image of lightning.

Though the phrasing of *gliscens...furor* echoes Lucr. *DRN* 4.1069 *inque dies gliscit furor*, it more directly evokes the rage of Silius' Hannibal and Virgil's

Turnus. For *gliscere* of anger, see 2.239 *gliscit Elissaeo uiolentior ira tyranno* with my note and Verg. *Aen.* 12.9 *haud secus accenso gliscit uiolentia Turno* with Tarrant's note.

393–4. exsilit ardens / nomine tam claro stimulante ad praemia caedis: famous names make warriors targets for ambitious opponents. Thus, Brutus, himself the bearer of a famous name, wishes to kill Cleadas, a descendant of Cadmus: 7.643–4 *hic auidum pugnae et tam clarum excidere nomen / Brutum exoptantem.* The clausula is unique, but modeled on phrases such as 16.147 *praemia Martis,* Verg. *Aen.* 11.78 *praemia pugnae,* Luc. *BC* 1.341 *praemia belli,* etc.

395–400. Nealces hurls a stone at Scaevola and kills him. Shattering the victim's skull creates a disgusting tableau of blood, brains, and bone. As Lovatt observes, "The beautiful death is thoroughly contaminated and pushed into the background, with the rush of internal fluids in the foreground" (Lovatt 2013: 300). Nealces' action prefigures on the human level what Pallas soon after does on the divine level. She tears off a mountainside and hurls it at Mars (466–9n.).

Stones are conventional battlefield weapons; see 1.488–92, 5.298–301, 10.235–7, 13.231–2, Hom. *Il.* 5.302–10, 12.378–86, 20.285–7, Verg. *Aen.* 10.127–8 *fert ingens toto conixus corpore saxum, / haud partem exiguam montis, Aen.* 12.896–902, VF *Arg.* 6.648–51, Stat. *Theb.* 2.559–69 with Gervais's note, etc. Lines 395–7 feature a careful pattern of repeated consonants: S- in 395, R- in 396–7, T- in 395–7.

395–6. tum silicem scopulo auulsum, quem montibus altis / detulerat torrens: the description of the stone hurled by Nealces recombines three scenes from prior epic:

(a) a Homeric simile comparing Hector's advance against the ships to a river that loosens a boulder: Hom. *Il.* 13.137–9 ὀλοοίτροχος ὣς ἀπὸ πέτρης, / ὅν τε κατὰ στεφάνης ποταμὸς χειμάρροος ὤσῃ / ῥήξας ἀσπέτῳ ὄμβρῳ ἀναιδέος ἔχματα πέτρης;

(b) Virgil's Pallas rallies his troops at the spot where the river has churned up a stone: Verg. *Aen.* 10.362–3 *qua saxa rotantia late / **intulerat torrens**;*

(c) Lucretius' description of erosion: Lucr. *DRN* 5.313 *non ruere **auolsos silices** a montibus altis.*

For similar passages comparing action on the battlefield to a crashing boulder, see 4.520–4, esp. 522 *auulsum montis...latus,* Verg. *Aen.* 12.684–5, Luc. *BC* 3.469–73, Stat. *Theb.* 7.744–9, etc.

396–7. raptum contorquet in ora / turbidus: an effective enjambement of the adjective. For *turbidus,* see 23n.

397. incusso crepuerunt pondere malae: the phrasing evokes Virgil's boxing match: Verg. *Aen.* 5.436 *duro crepitant sub uulnere malae.*

206   *Commentary Lines 398–410*

398. ablatusque uiro uultus: later in the battle, a stone similarly disfigures Paulus' face: 10.237 *compleuit sanguine uultus.* See also VF *Arg.* 4.184–5 *aduerso sub uulnere nulla / iam facies nec nomen erat* with Murgatroyd's note. For *auferre,* see Mart. *Epig.* 11.91–6 *uultus / abstulit.*

398–9. concreta cruento / per nares cerebro sanies fluit: Theron's crushing of Asbyte's skull with his club is described in comparable terms: see 2.200 *disiecto spargit conlisa per ossa cerebro* with my note. For Homeric examples, see Hom. *Il.* 11.97–8 ἀλλὰ δι' αὐτῆς ἦλθε καὶ ὀστέου, ἐγκέφαλος δὲ / ἔνδον ἅπας πεπάλακτο, *Il.* 20.399–400, etc. Virgil adapts the Homeric motif for Halaesus' killing of Thoas with a stone: Verg. *Aen.* 10.415–16 *saxo ferit ora Thoantis / ossaque dispersit cerebro permixta cruento.* Repetition of C- sounds suggests the cracking of bones.

399–400. atraque manant / orbibus elisis et trunca lumina fronte: Lucan's description of the torture of Marius Gratidianus provides a potential model here: Luc. *BC* 2.184–5 *ille cauis euoluit sedibus orbes / ultimaque effodit spectatis lumina membris.* For dark blood, see 153–4n. For *manare* of a wounded eye, see 4.752–3 *manante per ora / perque genas oculo.*

For *elidere* of smashing the face, see 4.242 *elisa incussis amisit calcibus ora.* For *trunca…fronte,* see 4.539 *truncata fronte* (Scipio's combat with a one-eyed opponent), Ov. *Met.* 9.86 *truncaque a fronte* (Hercules rips off Achelous' horn). See *TLL* 9.2.912.73 "de foraminibus oculorum."

Liberman 2006: 22 observes that "*lumina manant* is in itself good but we miss an ablative as in Ov. *Met.* 4.674 *tepido manabant lumina fletu* and *atra,* an epithet which hardly fits *lumina,* calls for *flumina* (cf. Verg. *Geo.* 3.310 *pressis manabunt flumina mammis*)." Silius' characteristic redundancy, however, typically takes the form of synonymy; the noun *flumina* directly after the verb 399 *fluit* would not be characteristic. The ablative found in the Ovidian passage specifies what the eyes are dripping with (tears), whereas the ablatives in the present passage refer to the source of the severed eyes (sockets and face). *Atra* "fits" *lumina* as a typical epithet for bloodshed (*OLD* s.v. 3).

401–10. Symaethus kills the friends Marius and Caper. The passage is an expansion of two proverbial themes: (a) κοινὰ τὰ φίλων and (b) those who are poor in money may yet be rich in friendship. The friends share their homeland, their poverty, their pursuits, their likes and dislikes. Pairs of friends who die together in Roman epic inevitably recall Virgil's Nisus and Euryalus, but these men are similar in age and do not appear to be involved in an erotic relationship. As Zaia observes, the ideal exemplified here is closer to the Ciceronian one: Cic. *Amic.* 32 *sintque pares in amore et aequales.*

The friends' *concordia* and their achieved wish to die at the same moment further recall the ideals of Roman marriage, as in Ovid's story of Baucis and Philemon; see 407–8n. See also Silius' Brutus and Casca at *Pun.* 7.643–60, with

Commentary Lines 401–4 207

Littlewood's note on 7.652 for discussion. This passage is suffused with keywords that emphasize the friends' *concordia*, including 401n. *unanimo*, 403n. *idem, commune duobus*, 405n. *iuncta*, 406–7n., 408n. *unum*, 409n. *iunctam*, 410n. *bina*, etc. Duff 1934: 1.xv–xvi includes this passage as one of four overlooked by "contemptuous critics" that serve "as proofs of Silius' narrative power" and concludes that "the man who wrote these lines was certainly a poet."

Silius' Marius is an example of a character with no known connection to the Second Punic Wars whose name evokes subsequent periods of civil strife at Rome. On this theme in the Cannae episode, see McGuire 1995 and Introduction, section 4b. At Silius' idealized Cannae, even a man named Marius can exemplify the *concordia* of friendship (407n.) in contrast to the *discordia* of civil war.

401. sternitur unanimo Marius succurrere Capro: Silius' other application of the adjective *unanimus* to friendship occurs at 16.250–1, where Scipio asks Syphax *coniunge Latinis / unanimum pectus*; see also Catul. 30.1 *unanimis…sodalibus*, Stat. *Silv.* 5.2.155 *unanimi…amici*, *Theb.* 9.169, etc. Poets more typically apply the adjective *unanimus* to family members, especially siblings. Silius describes Crista's six sons as *unanima…phalanx* (10.98) and Scipio's uncle as *unanimi* with his brother (13.651); see also Catul. 9.4, Verg. *Aen.* 4.8 *unanimam…sororem*, *Aen.* 7.335 *unanimos…fratres*, Stat. *Theb.* 8.669, etc. For application to parents and spouses, see Stat. *Theb.* 4.354–5 *parentem unanimum*, Catul. 66.80 *unanimis…coniugibus*, Sen. *Oed.* 773.

Silius elsewhere follows the example of Verg. *Aen.* 12.264 *uos unanimi densete cateruas* in applying the adjective to collectivities. His Picentines hurl their javelins *unanimo nisu* (*Pun.* 5.214); some of Fabius' men are *unanimi* in their desire to die beneath his gaze (7.620); the example of Crista's sons (10.98, quoted above in this note) creatively bridges the familial and collective senses of the adjective. For collectivities, see also VF *Arg.* 1.615 (the winds), 6.60 *unanimis…milibus*, etc.

Caspro ω reflects 8.414–15 *Bactris nomina ducens / Casperia*; see Ariemma *ad loc.*

402. conatus metuensque uiro superesse cadenti: Spaltenstein explains the present tense of *cadenti* as if it were equivalent to perfect *mortuo* (cf. L-H-S 386) and compares 4.203 *uouentem* and 17.468 *lapsantis…fratris*. Zaia correctly objects that the present "mantiene il valore dinamico," emphasizing that Marius is endeavoring to save his friend at the moment of his death.

403–4. lucis idem auspicium ac patrium et commune duobus / paupertas: for *lux* as life, see 41n. For *auspicium* as "exordium, principium," see *TLL* 2.1548.29. As most of these citations refer to omens of victory (e.g., QCurt. 4.15.27 *uictoriae auspicium*) or death (e.g., Sen. *Tro.* 609 *abominandae mortis auspicium*, Stat. *Theb.* 6.222 *funeris auspicium*), it is possible that Silius may differentiate

208 *Commentary Lines 404–5*

his usage by having it refer to birth. For the motif of virtuous poverty, see 2.102–5 (Mopsus) with my note, 6.76 *paupere Vesta* (Marus), 10.94 *pauperque penatum* (Crista). For the motif of the poor warrior, see Verg. *Aen.* 3.614 *Troiam genitore Adamasto / paupere (mansissetque utinam fortuna!) profectus* (of Achaemenides). These individuals' poverty should be contrasted with that of Silius' viniculturist Falernus, who lives in a mythical "age of poverty" (7.175 *pauperis aeui*) before luxury was invented, and the wealthy senators who voluntarily choose moderation (1.609–10 *castaque beatos / paupertate patres*). For representations of wealth and poverty in Roman epic, see Coffee 2009.

Heinsius proposed *patriae*, but the lack of parallelism between cases does not cause difficulty.

404. sacro iuuenes Praeneste creati: the Praenestine forces historically did not participate in the battle of Cannae because of a tardy levy and so participated instead in the defense of Casilinum. See Livy 23.17.9 *non confecto Praeneste ad diem dilectu.* Silius, however, envisions a Praenestine levy at *Pun.* 8.364–6; see Ariemma's note and Venini 1978: 130. Praeneste evocates a number of potentially relevant associations for these ideal friends. The most likely is that it was the site of the famous oracle of Fortuna Primigenia, which grants the young men's wishes at 409n.; see earlier 8.364–5 *sacrisque dicatum / Fortunae Praeneste iugis* with Ariemma's note. The oracle was active throughout Domitian's reign: see Suet. *Dom.* 15.6 *Praenestina Fortuna, toto imperii spatio annum nouum commendanti laetam eandemque semper sortem dare assueta, extremo tristissimam reddidit nec sine sanguinis mentione.* See Cic. *Div.* 2.85, Strabo 5.3.11, Bona 1998: 145–6.

A second, quite unlikely possibility is that there is a reference to the family of Caeculus, the mythical founder of Praeneste, mentioned in Virgil's catalog of heroes (*Aen.* 7.678–81); see Horsfall's notes and Bona 1998: 145–6. Servius preserves the story of his uncles: Serv. *Aen.* 7.678 *erant etiam illic duo fratres, qui diui appellabantur.* However, Silius' young men are friends, not brothers, and Servius' story focuses on Caeculus rather than any special amity between his uncles. 294n. *Indigetesque dei* would have been a more appropriate place to activate mention of these local gods.

Zaia further suggests that Marius' name and the site of Praeneste may also evoke Marius the Younger, son of the famous Marius, who committed suicide at Praeneste in 82 BC. As Silius' young warriors are neither suicides nor politically connected, the lack of relevant context also makes this association seem quite unlikely.

405. miscuerant studia et iuncta tellure serebant: *miscere studia* is an apparently unique phrase, but likely inspired by *amicitia* themes such as Sen. *Ep.* 3.1.3 *cum amico omnes curas, omnes cogitationes tuas misce.* For the motif of adjoining fields, see 5.302 *coniuncto miscens certamina campo* (there of battlefields).

Commentary Lines 406–9   209

406. uelle ac nolle ambobus idem: for this aspect of *amicitia*, see Cic. *Planc.* 5
uetus est enim lex illa iustae ueraeque amicitiae…ut idem amici semper uelint,
Sall. *BC* 20.4 *nam idem uelle atque idem nolle, ea demum firma amicitia est*;
Otto 1890 s.v. *amicitia* 2. Wills 1996: 453 observes that the *uelle–nolle* complementarity is rare in poetry, and that the present phrase referring to the young
men's "likes and dislikes" should be distinguished from, e.g., Mart. 1.57.1
qualem, Flacce, uelim quaeris nolimue puellam, 8.44.16 *uelis nolis*.

406–7. sociataque toto / mens aeuo: that *socii* have similar mindsets is a basic
idea of ancient friendship. It is notable, however, that Silius elsewhere uses
sociatus exclusively to refer to union among larger groups; see 3.340 *Celtae
sociati nomen Hiberis*, 4.159 *sociata examina*, 11.31 *moenia…sociata*, 11.60
sociato consule, 13.810 *Troiugenas iunxit sociata prole Latinis*, 14.157 *sociataque
bella*, 15.290 *sociatae foedere uires*. This lone application to a pair of friends
accordingly makes their friendship evoke the scale of an alliance between
states. For the interlaced word order of the clausula of 406, similar to that of
6.50–1 *ipsaque diris / frons depasta modis*, see Arribas Hernáez 1990: 250.

407–9. Marius and Caper have enjoyed *concordia* in their friendship, which has
received a far fuller description than that of the Carthaginian friends Gabar
and Siccha; see 386n. *concordi uirtute*. The implication is that Romans express
friendship better than perfidious Carthaginians. In achieving their wish to die
at the same moment, the Roman friends recall Ovid's virtuous couple Philemon
and Baucis: Ov. *Met.* 8.708–9 *et quoniam concordes egimus annos, / auferat hora
duos eadem*. For examples of loved ones dying conjoined deaths in battle, see
Pun. 2.125–47 (Mopsus and his sons; see my notes), 17.471 *iuncta leniuit morte
dolores* (the brothers Herius and Pleminius); for Virgil's Nisus and Euryalus,
see 401–10n.; see 408–9n. for two further examples.

407. ac paruis diues concordia rebus: for the motif that friendship is a more
valuable form of wealth, see Plaut. *Truc.* 885 *ubi amici, ibidem opes*, Quint. *Inst.*
5.11.41; Otto 1890 s.v. *amicus* 2. For praise of virtuous poverty, see 403–4n.

**408–9. occubuere simul, uotisque ex omnibus unum / id Fortuna dedit,
iunctam inter proelia mortem:** Silius' phrasing combines two earlier narratives of conjoined death:

(a) the *iuncta mors* of the lovers Lycabas and Athis: Ov. *Met.* 5.73 *et tulit ad
    manes iunctae solacia mortis*;

(b) the *uotum* of the Thespiads: Stat. *Theb.* 2.642–3 *procubuere pares fatis,
    miserabile uotum / mortis, et alterna clauserunt lumina dextra*; see
    Gervais's notes.

Silius distinguishes the moral value of the deaths of Marius and Caper. They die
on the battlefield during Rome's greatest struggle for survival, not during a

210   *Commentary Lines 410–15*

brawl at a wedding, as in Ovid, or a night raid prompted by a vicious tyrant, as in Statius. These friends have prayed to die simultaneously and received their wish; it is not a matter to grieve, as for Statius' Thespiads.

See 404n. for the *Fortuna* of Praeneste. *Iunctam* echoes 405n. *iuncta tellure.*

410. arma fuere decus uictori bina Symaetho: *Symaetho* appears uniquely here as the name of an individual. It appears elsewhere as the name of a Sicilian river: see 14.231, Verg. *Aen.* 9.584, Ov. *Fasti* 4.472, etc.; *NP* s.v. *Symaethum.* For Silius' use of toponyms as personal names, see 380n.

411–18. The Romans rally after a series of Carthaginian advances, and a series of prominent commanders attempt to resist Hannibal. As Stocks 2014: 183 observes of this passage, "Though the narrator sees the parity between the two, it is Varro who catches Hannibal's attention." Scipio then comes to Varro's aid and engages Hannibal in an abortive solo combat (428–37).

411–12. sed longum tanto laetari munere casus / haud licitum Poenis: *haud licitum* occurs elsewhere as a line opening in poetry only at 4.288, 7.94 and in its Virgilian model, Verg. *Aen.* 10.106. Harrison notes the "grander passive form of the perfect"; cf. L-H-S 1.533. Stat. *Theb.* 5.685 places the phrase in a different *sedes.*

412. aderat terrore minaci: a hypallage for *minax terrore.* Elsewhere *minax* qualifies *terror* only at Luc. *BC* 2.453–4 *pugnatque minaci / cum terrore fides*; cf. *TLL* 8.996.67. The catalog of the preceding book introduces Scipio as a figure that inspires fear: see 8.561 *gratusque inerat uisentibus horror* with Ariemma's note.

413. Scipio conuersae miseratus terga cohortis: Norden on Verg. *Aen.* 6.842 observes "für Silius ist *Scipio* vor Konsonant als Daktylus im nom. (voc.) sg. verwertbar geworden." *Conuertere terga* (i.e., *in fugam*) is an alternative to the more common *dare.* See 2.703 *tergaque uertentem* with my note, 13.677–8 *conuertit...terga* with van der Keur's note, 14.560 *terga fuga celeri Libyae conuertit ad oras*, etc. *Conuersus* can also indicate retreat without further qualification; cf. 10.148 *conuersis*, 15.743–4 *conuersa...agmina.*

414. et cuncti fons Varro mali: the phrase recapitulates the previous narrative that attributes sole responsibility to Varro for the disaster at Cannae; see Ariemma 2010. For the phrase, see Livy 39.15.9 *et is fons mali huiusce fuit*, Gratt. *Cyn.* 1.377 *fontem auerte mali*, etc. For *fons* applied to an individual, see, e.g., Pliny *NH* 17.37 *fons ingeniorum Homerus*; *TLL* 6.1.1025.6–1026.18.

414–15. Curio and Brutus would have rallied the Romans, but Hannibal's sudden assault sets them back. These commanders were introduced in the preceding book's catalog of Roman forces. Neither man has a known connection to the Second Punic War. As with Scaevola (370–9n.) and Marius (401–10n.), Silius has

Commentary Lines 414–21 211

chosen anachronistic names that recall the regal and/or triumviral periods. See Ariemma *ad locc.*, McGuire 1995, Marks 2010c; Introduction, section 4b.

414–15. flauusque comarum / Curio: Brutus is the commander of the Picentine contingents (8.425), and the Romans grieve his death at 10.403–4 *et leto non dignus inerti / Curio deflentur.* Accusative of relation is more common than genitive, e.g., Ov. *Met.* 6.118, 9.307 *flaua comas.*

415. et a primo descendens consule Brutus: Brutus is the commander of the Venetians (8.607). M. Iunius Pera (*NP Iunius* I 26) became dictator after Cannae (Livy 22.57.9), but no Brutus is historiographically attested at Cannae or its aftermath. The narrator draws a similar connection with Scaevola between a contemporary Roman and his ancestor from the regal period; see 373n. *dignum proauo letum.* The Saguntum narrative features a similarly motivated alteration: the historically attested P. Valerius Flaccus (*NP Valerius* I 25) who participated in the embassy to Hannibal becomes a "Publicola" instead. See 2.8 *Publicola, ingentis Volesi Spartana propago* with my note.

416. atque his fulta uiris acies: the phrasing is Livian: Livy 3.60.9 *priusquam totis uiribus fulta constaret hostium acies,* 9.32.9 *quia nullis recentibus subsidiis fulta prima acies fuit.*

416–17. repararet ademptum / mole noua campum: for *adimere* of territory lost in battle, see 2.565 *si terras adimit uictoria Poeni.*

417–18. subito ni turbine Poenus / agmina frenasset iam procurrentia ductor: *Poenus* refers to Hannibal, as 419 *isque* indicates. The phrase *frenare agmina* is unique, as is *frenare acies* (11.264); for the latter, note Cic. *Phil.* 14.26 *sed cum libertatis auida legio effrenatius in aciem hostium inrupisset.* Both are modeled on more common collocations such as *frenare gentes* (Verg. *Aen.* 1.523), *frenare cohortes* (Stat. *Silv.* 4.4.61), etc. For *ductor,* see 24n.

419–27. Hannibal catches sight of Varro and pursues him. Had not the gods rescued Varro, he would have died, as Paulus will die heroically in the next book, and as Flaminius died at Trasimene. Varro's subsequent disgrace will make him wish that Hannibal had killed him; see 644–57n.

419–21. isque ut Varronem procul inter proelia uidit / et iuxta sagulo circumuolitare rubenti / lictorem: line 419 is modeled on Verg. *Aen.* 9.549 *isque ubi se Turni media inter milia uidit.* 420 *iuxta* answers 419 *procul.* For the *sagulum*'s red color, see 4.516–17 *umeroque refulget / sanguinei patrium saguli decus,* [Caes.] *BAfr.* 57.5 *sagulo purpureo.* For other wearers of the *sagulum* in the *Punica,* see 1.248 *insignis sagulo* (Hannibal), 4.517 (quoted above in this note, worn by Sempronius), 17.527 (Scipio).

There may be a subtle *figura etymologica* in Hannibal's ability to recognize the consul's retinue from a distance. Varro relates *paludamentum* to *palam,* as

212   *Commentary Lines 421–25*

it makes the wearer conspicuous: Varro *LL* 7.37 *quae propter quod conspiciuntur qui ea habent ac fiunt palam, paludamenta dicta.* Caesar is similarly recognized at a distance from the color of his cloak: Caes. *BG* 7.88.1 *ex colore uestitus.*

421. nosco pompam atque insignia nosco: for the chiastic arrangement with *redditio,* featuring nouns with a repeated verb, see Flammini 1983: 99.

422. 'Flaminius modo talis' ait: Hannibal confirms the truth of Fabius' words, who observed to Paulus that Varro would likely lead the Romans into the same disaster as Flaminius at Trasimene: 8.309–10 *stat campis acies, expectaturque sub ictu / alter Flaminius*; see Ariemma's note. Paulus expresses this concern during his argument with Varro: see 55n.

422–3. ait. tum feruidus acrem / ingentis clipei tonitru praenuntiat iram: Silius varies the Virgilian phrase *feruidus ira* (*Aen.* 8.230, of Hercules; *Aen.* 9.736, of Pandarus); cf. Stat. *Theb.* 11.253. Claudian nods to Silius' expansion of the Virgilian phrase in deriding the decidedly unheroic Hosius, one of Eutropius' client ministers: Claud. *Eutr.* 2.349 *feruidus, accensam sed qui bene decoquat iram.* Hannibal shakes his arms, as at 2.453–4 *noua tegmina latis / aptat concutiens umeris*; see my note. For the thundering of arms, see 13.10 *armorum tonitru,* Stat. *Theb.* 3.423 *armorum tonitru.* For the chiastic arrangement of nouns and adjectives, see Flammini 1983. This is the only occurrence in this book of the common epic adjective *ingens*; see Introduction, section 5b.

424–30. The narrator observes that Varro would have enjoyed a glorious death at Hannibal's hands, if the gods had not been angry with the hapless Roman commander and sent Scipio to his rescue. Varro accords with the narrator's judgment when he questions which god spared his life (650–1n.). His introduction to the narrative emphasizes that he is no fighter: 8.259–61 *sic debilis arte / belligera Martemque rudis uersare nec ullo / spectatus ferro.*

424. heu miser: *heu miser* occurs as an epic line opening at VF *Arg.* 7.533 and Stat. *Theb.* 9.273. Zaia observes that the phrase "rappresenta uno dei nessi preferiti dalla poesia epica ed elegiaca," as represented, e.g., by Catul. 101.6 *heu miser indigne frater adempte mihi* and *CLE* 1116.2 *heu miser aetatis praemia nulla tuli.*

424. aequari potuisti funere Paulo: Paulus' death in battle (10.260–308) and opulent burial by his enemy Hannibal (10.503–77) form significant episodes in the succeeding book.

425. si tibi non ira superum tunc esset ademptum: Paulus foresaw the gods' anger against the Romans at 47–8n. *dum transit diuum furor et consumitur ira / Fortunae.* The gods' anger is a cliché of Roman epic. Like the *Aeneid,* the *Punica* focuses on Juno's anger; for the anger of collective gods, see 5.588, 8.213 *ira* *deorum*, 8.234–5 *iras / caelicolum*, etc. See 160n. for the rare construction involving *adimere* with an infinitive.

426. Hannibalis cecidisse manu: for the glory of being killed by Hannibal, see 5.562–3 *quisquis es, haud alia decuit te occumbere dextra / ad manis leti perfer decus*. The phrasing echoes the consolation that Virgil's Camilla offers to her victim Tyrrhenus: Verg. *Aen.* 11.688–9 *nomen tamen haud leue patrum / manibus hoc referes, telo cecidisse Camillae*. Aeneas offers similar glory to Lausus as a consolation (Verg. *Aen.* 10.829 *Aeneae magni dextra cadis*); Ovid parodies the motif at Ov. *Met.* 5.191–2 *magna feres tacitas solacia mortis ad umbras, / a tanto cecidisse uiro*. See 140–1n. for the reversal of this topos in the death of Satricus.

426–7. quam saepe querere / Varro, deis, quod Sidonium defugeris ensem: for inglorious retreat as a leitmotif for Varro, see 175n. and 649–50n. For *(de) fugere ensem*, see 558n., *fugerat arma*, Verg. *Aen.* 8.320 *arma...fugiens*, Ov. *Met.* 15.806 *fugerat enses*, Luc. *BC* 8.506 *arma fugit*, etc.

428–30. nam rapido subitam portans in morte salutem / procursu exceptă in sese discrimina uertit / Scipio: numerous suggestions have been proposed for the difficult line 429. I give a fuller version here than in the apparatus:

> procursu α_ς : pro cursu β exceptă in sese *Shackleton Bailey 1959: 174* : incepta sese in ω : incepta sese δ : incepta ad sese Γ^2r1 : coepta sese in b1 : coepta in sese *Livineius* : suscepta ad se *Blass 1867: 24, prob. Thilo 1891: 622* : inceptă, in sese *Bauer 1890, alii* : inceptă *Bauer 1893: 48, prob. Spaltenstein* : certa (*an interea?*) in sese *Summers* : intentă *Watt 1988: 174*

Most modern editors, including Delz, Volpilhac-Lenthéric, Duff, and Bauer, read *inceptă* modifying *morte*, some clarifying with a comma. Bauer 1893: 48 later proposed *inceptă* modifying *discrimina*, which Spaltenstein approves. I have followed Shackleton Bailey 1959: 174, who proposes *exceptă* modifying *discrimina*. He translates "intercepted," "took on himself," and compares Cic. *Prov. Cons.* 23 *subire coegit et excipere* [i.e., *pericula*].

Spaltenstein observes that Shackleton Bailey's conjecture "redoublerait 'vertit' de façon typique pour Sil." Though he prints *incepta* in his text, Delz (app. crit.) comments "recte ut puto" on *exceptă* and compares Scipio's boast before the Senate at *Pun.* 16.650–1 *excepi nubem belli...atque in me omnia uerti*. The chiastic phrase is complete at *procursu*, and corruption to *incepta* was likely prompted by the subsequent preposition *in*.

Watt 1988: 174 objects, however, that *exceptă* "would leave *morte* without a qualifier, and a qualifier is essential because Varro did *not* die at Cannae." Watt would accordingly read *intentă*, perhaps inspired by Verg. *Aen.* 1.91 *intentant omnia mortem*, with parallels such as *Pun.* 17.478 *intento igne*, Epic. *Drus.* 361 *necem intentam*, VF *Arg.* 5.339 *intenta nece*. *OLD* s.v. 7b "to offer as a threat" supports this meaning.

214   *Commentary Lines 430–32*

Watt's objection that Varro survives the battle is not unanswerable, as *mors* can be used for the imminent threat of death. Compare, for example, Catul. 76.18 *extremam iam ipsa in morte tulistis opem*, Cic. *Dom.* 64 *se in medios hostis ad perspicuam mortem pro salute exercitus iniecisse* (the Decii and others who survived suicide runs), Sen. *Contr.* 7.3.8 *mortem, inquit, meam effudit* (the speaker has narrowly escaped an attempt at poisoning), etc. Shackleton Bailey's *exceptā* can be further supported by the enjambement of 430 *Scipio*. The emphasis placed on the name reminds us that he earlier risked death at Ticinus to rescue his father (4.459–71), and thus his later boast recalls both of these instances.

In sese has also attracted attention. The phrase results from Livineius' choice to reverse the order presented in some of the manuscripts and can be supported by 4.458 *conuersa in semet dextra*, 7.8 *in sese cuncta…gerebat*, 8.386–7 *ira / in semet uera*, and 16.651 *in me omnia uerti*. Housman *ad* Manil. *Astr.* 1.245 Add. discussed *sese in* ω as an example of anastrophe; Delz observed that anastrophe of *in* is rare, according to *TLL* 7.1.805.32–7. Finally, Blass proposed *suscepta ad se*, corroborated by Thilo 1891: 622 with the observation that the final syllable of *procursu* may have corrupted the initial syllable of *suscepta*.

430–3. Hannibal eagerly changes the target of his onslaught to Scipio, the victim who earlier eluded him at the Ticinus (4.445–79). The gods interrupt this combat, leaving Hannibal and Scipio to face each other once more in a similarly abortive combat at Zama (17.391–405, 509–80).

430–1. nec Poenum, quamquam est ereptus opimae / caedis honor: if the Roman commander killed the enemy commander in single combat, he could dedicate the *spolia opima* to Jupiter Feretrius (Livy 4.20.6, Cass. Dio 51.24.4). The *Punica* recalls this custom twice:

    (a) The Massylian priestess indirectly praises Marcellus, who killed the commander of the Insubrian Gauls in combat in 222 BC: 1.133 *tertia qui tulerit sublimis opima Tonanti*.

    (b) Before giving battle at Trasimene, Flaminius rallies Orfitus, one of his soldiers: 5.167–8 *quis opima uolenti / dona Ioui portet feretro suspensa cruento*. As Spaltenstein correctly observes of this passage, Silius is not concerned to be precise regarding Orfitus' *imperium*.

In the present passage, Silius makes Hannibal think like a Roman general who would receive the *spolia opima* if he were to kill Varro, who holds *imperium* on the day of Cannae. For a similar analogy of Roman custom to a foreign context, Spaltenstein compares Curtius' description of the battle between Alexander and Darius: QCurt. 3.11.7 *Alexander…opimum decus caeso rege expetens*.

431–2. mutasse piget maiore sub hoste / proelia: for the use of *sub*, see 258n.; the line ending is modeled on Verg. *Aen.* 10.438 *illos sua fata manent maiore sub hoste*.

Commentary Lines 432–7 215

432. et erepti Ticina ad flumina patris: for Scipio's rescue of his father at the Ticinus, see 4.454–79. Jupiter evokes this scene through similar phrasing when promising Juno that Hannibal will survive Zama *ereptus pugnae* (17.377). For *eripere* in its more common sense of the loss of an individual rather than rescue, see, e.g., 1.183 *erepto...ductore*, 15.547–8 *erepto.../ Marcello*, etc.

433. exigere oblato tandem certamine poenas: chiastic structure (see Flammini 1983) emphasizes Hannibal's desire to exact vengeance (*exigere...poenas*) for his unachieved killing of the elder Scipio and how long he has been waiting (*tandem*).

434–7. Men from different parts of the world face one another, equal in combat skills but different in moral qualities. The topos links Cannae to Ticinus and anticipates Zama:

(a) The elder Scipio prepares to meet Hannibal at Ticinus: 4.53–5 *ingentisque duces, pelagi terraeque laborem / diuersum emensos, propiora pericula uallo / iungebant.*

(b) The armies clash at Zama: 17.387–9 *non alio grauiores tempore uidit / aut populos tellus aut, qui patria arma mouerent, / maioris certare duces.*

Topos and phrasing further recombine two moments of Virgil's *Aeneid*:

(a) Latinus watches in amazement as foreign Aeneas and native Turnus face each other in their final duel: Verg. *Aen.* 12.707–9 *stupet ipse Latinus / ingentes, genitos diuersis partibus orbis, / inter se coiisse uiros et cernere ferro.*

(b) Diomedes recalls how both Aeneas and Hector held back the Greeks until the tenth year of the war. Like Scipio, Aeneas was superior in *pietas*: Verg. *Aen.* 11.291–2 *ambo animis, ambo insignes praestantibus armis, / hic pietate prior* ~ *Pun.* 9.436–7.

For full discussion, see Marks 2005: 129–30.

434. stabant educti diuersis orbis in oris: for initial *stare*, see 252n. The phrasing is modeled on Verg. *Aen.* 12.708, quoted at 434–7n. above.

435. quantos non alias uidit concurrere tellus: Livy identifies Scipio and Hannibal as the greatest commanders that the world had seen up to that point in introducing their colloquy before Zama: Livy 30.30.1 *non suae modo aetatis maximi duces sed omnis ante se memoriae omnium gentium cuilibet regum imperatorumue pares*; see also Polyb. 15.9.4. Silius' phrasing recapitulates the preparation for Cannae and anticipates the subsequent battle of Zama: see 8.352–3 *non alias maiore uirum, maiore sub armis / agmine cornipedum concussa est Itala tellus*; 17.387–9, quoted at 434–7n. above. For the earth as a witness to battle, see Luc. *BC* 5.461–2 *prima duces iunctis uidit consistere castris / tellus*; for individuals, see *Pun.* 1.280–1 *haud alium uidit tellus, cui ponere finem / non posset mors una uiro*, 15.451 *te quoque Pyrenes uidit conterrita tellus*.

216   *Commentary Lines 436–41*

Delz supports *alias ω* over *alios* Ch on the model of 8.352 *non alias*.

436. Marte uiri dextraque pares: the assertion of equality in combat recurs at Zama (17.400–5). Few combatants of epic final duels, however, are equally matched. Homer's Hector knows that the semi-divine Achilles outclasses him (Hom. *Il.* 22.131–7), and Virgil's Rutulians similarly recognize that Aeneas is stronger than Turnus and so support Juturna's breaking of the truce (Verg. *Aen.* 12.216–18). Lucan's narrator asserts that his rival leaders are unequal: see Luc. *BC* 1.129 *nec coiere pares* with Roche's note. Statius' dueling brothers are more similar, but Polynices' situation nevertheless gives him an advantage (Stat. *Theb.* 11.541–2 *cui fortior ira nefasque / iustius*).

Marte is used here in its generic sense of "combat," but the appearance of the god Mars himself at 439 lends it further significance. Volpilhac-Lenthéric appears to take *Marte* with *concurrere*: "dans des autres combats livrés au nom de Mars et, pour la valeur de leurs bras, il s'égalaient." I concur with Duff, who takes *Marte…dextraque* as a hendiadys with *pares*: "in prowess they were well matched."

436–7. sed cetera ductor / anteibat Latius, melior pietate fideque: for *ductor*, see 24n. As elsewhere in the *Punica*, Scipio's *pietas* aligns him with Aeneas; see Verg. *Aen.* 11.291–2, quoted at 434–7n. above. Hannibal, meanwhile, is introduced as *fideique sinister* (*Pun.* 1.56); yet his father Hamilcar will celebrate him as a paragon of both virtues during his encounter with Scipio in the Underworld: see 13.749 *o pietas, o sancta fides, o uera propago* with van der Keur's note. For these virtues in the *Punica*, see Ripoll 1998.

438–41. Mars and Pallas descend to earth to support their champions and thereby cause unease among the troops.

438. desiluere caua turbati ad proelia nube: for *desilire* of the gods' descent, Ov. *Met.* 1.674 (Jupiter), VF *Arg.* 2.198 (Venus), Stat. *Theb.* 1.309 (Mercury), etc. Gods typically conceal themselves in cloud; see, e.g., 484n., 1.551 *aduolat obscura circumdata nube*, Ov. *Met.* 5.251–2 *inde caua circumdata nube Seriphon / deserit*, etc. For the similar phrase *caua nubila*, see *Pun.* 3.656, 15.713–14, Verg. *Aen.* 9.671, Ov. *Met.* 9.271, Stat. *Theb.* 2.38 with Gervais's note, etc. For *turbati*, see 1n.

439. Mauors Scipiadae metuens, Tritonia Poeno: the careful arrangement of nominatives and datives helps to convey the image of the opposed gods standing beside their champions. Mars earlier protected Scipio at Ticinus (4.458–60). For *Scipiadae*, see 276n.; for *Tritonia*, see 297n., 479n.

440–1. aduentuque deum intrepidis ductoribus ambae / contremuere acies: the battle lines shake as the gods approach, just as the Earth shook as the gods descended from Olympus; see 300–1n. For the concussive effect of a god's arrival, see 2.544–5 *tremuitque repente / mons circum* with my note, Enn. *Ann.* 554 Skutsch *contremuit templum magum Iouis*, etc. As Zaia observes, Silius reserves the adjective *intrepidus* for Scipio (4.460) and Hannibal (4.783, 11.230). For the

Commentary Lines 441–2 217

fear that divine epiphany typically inspires, see, e.g., Verg. *Aen.* 12.868 *arrectaeque horrore comae et uox faucibus haesit*, VF *Arg.* 6.480–1 *fulsit ab inuita numen procul et pauor artus / protinus atque ingens Aeetida perculit horror*, Stat. *Theb.* 9.155–6 *ille loquentis / extimuit uultus admiraturque timorem*, etc. For *ductor*, see 24n. Silius uses the rare compound *contremiscere* only once more, at Zama (17.406), and thereby associates Cannae once more with the final battle.

441–6. An ekphrasis describes Pallas' appearance and her terrifying effect on observers. Some aspects of the description further align her with her protégé Hannibal. Each character bears arms that either spew flame or appear to (442n.), and each is compared to a comet (444–5n.). The primary models for the passage are:

(a) Virgil's description of Pallas' aegis: Verg. *Aen.* 8.435–8 *aegidaque horriferam, turbatae Palladis arma, / certatim squamis serpentum auroque polibant / conexosque anguis ipsamque in pectore diuae / Gorgona, desecto uertentem lumina collo*;

(b) Virgil's description of Aeneas' helmet and shield, similarly compared to a comet: Verg. *Aen.* 10.270–5 *ardet apex capiti cristisque a uertice flamma / funditur et uastos umbo uomit aureus ignis: / non secus ac liquida si quando nocte cometae / sanguinei lugubre rubent, aut Sirius ardor / ille sitim morbosque ferens mortalibus aegris / nascitur et laeuo contristat lumine caelum*.

441–2. ater, qua pectora flectit / Pallas: note the similar phrasing at the prior mention of Minerva's aegis: 7.459–61 *iam bellica uirgo, / aegide deposita et qua adsuetum casside crinem / inuoluit*. Spaltenstein refers the phrase to "une cuirasse"; Zaia observes more precisely that Silius "possa descrivere genericamente la torsione della dea che, muovendo il corpo, muove anche l'egida."

442. Gorgoneo late micat ignis ab ore: tracing the associations of the shield that spews fire draws closer associations between the gods, their champions, and their Virgilian analogues. Mars' shield spews flame at Ticinus: see 4.431–2 *fulminis atri / spargentem flammas clipeum* and 447–50n. Spaltenstein observes that Minerva's Gorgon spews genuine flame in contrast to Virgil's Chimaera on Turnus' shield, which only spews the image of flame: Verg. *Aen.* 7.785 *galea…Chimaeram / sustinet Aetnaeos efflantem faucibus ignes*. Hannibal, however, similarly flashes terrifying fire even without divine aid, and his shield's reflection causes the Saguntine ranks to flee: see *Pun.* 2.211–14 with my notes. Pacuvius tries to deter his son's attempt to assassinate Hannibal by describing the fire that flashes from the Carthaginian's face: 11.327–8 *uibrabat ab ore / ignis atrox*. Marks 2010: 136 notes a parallel with Luc. *BC* 7.149 *Pallas Gorgoneos diffudit in aegida crines*.

Heinsius suggested *orbe*; Delz (app. crit.) cites Prop. 3.22.8 *sectaque Persea Phorcidos ora manu* and Ov. *Met.* 4.655–6 *Medusae /…squalentia protulit ora* in support of the MSS reading *ore*.

218   *Commentary Lines 443–7*

443. sibilaque horrificis torquet serpentibus aegis: the run of sibilants suggests the serpents' hissing. The structure and phrasing of the line recall Crixus at Trebia: 4.277–8 *murmur / torquet et horrisonis ululatibus erigit iras*. For *torquere* applied to sibilants, see 7.424 *sibila torsit*, Prop. *Eleg.* 4.8.8 *sibila torquet*, VF *Arg.* 7.525–6 *torsit / sibila*; La Penna 1979. For *torquere* applied to other noises, see, e.g., 3.465 *torsit…minitantia murmura*, 10.245 *murmura torquens*, 11.340–1, etc.

444–5. fulgent sanguinei, geminum uibrare cometem / ut credas, oculi: Minerva's bloody eyes evoke numerous Virgilian figures, including the serpents she sent to kill Laocoön and his sons (Verg. *Aen.* 2.210 *ardentisque oculos suffecti sanguine*), as well as the raging Dido (*Aen.* 4.643 *sanguineam uoluens aciem*) and Amata (*Aen.* 7.399 *sanguineam torquens aciem*); see also VF *Arg.* 4.235. Hannibal's cheeks blaze with anger (562–3n.), and his terrifying crest is similarly compared at *Pun.* 1.460–4 to a comet that trails bloody fire.

For the comet as an ill omen for leaders, see, e.g., 8.636–7 *non unus crine corusco, / regnorum euersor, rubuit letale cometes*, Luc. *BC* 1.528–9, [Sen.] *Oct.* 232, etc. For *uibrare* of light, see 2.663–4 with my note, 14.565–6, etc. The proximity of *ut credas* to the ekphrasis of the aegis evokes the frequent topos that the viewer would believe that ekphrastic figures live and move; on which, see 2.430 with my note and Laird 1993.

445–6. summaque in casside largus / undantes uoluit flammas ad sidera uertex: the hyperbolic description attributes the power to emit consuming fire to the helmet. The phrasing evokes passages such as the burning of Saguntum (see 2.658–9 *erigit atro / nigrantem fumo rogus alta ad sidera nubem* with my note) or Virgil's Latin capital (Verg. *Aen.* 12.672–3 *flammis inter tabulata uolutus / ad caelum undabat uertex*). Other helmets' brilliant crests only appear to emit flame; see, e.g., 10.107 *aut quae flagrarent galea exhorrescere flammas*, 17.398 *flammam ingentem frons alta uomebat*, Verg. *Aen.* 10.270–1 *ardet apex capiti cristisque a uertice flamma / funditur et uastos umbo uomit aureus ignis*; contrast the more mundane description of Fabius' helmet at *Pun.* 7.592–3 *altae / scintillant cristae*.

447–50. A briefer description of Pallas' adversary Mars features similar motifs: the immense god's armor emits flame, and his crest strikes the sky. See 300–1n. for the tradition of the gods' massive size and weight. This passage also evokes aspects of the much longer description of Mars' earlier appearance at Ticinus (4.430–9).

447. at Mauors moto proturbans aera telo: the opening phrase *at Mauors* begins the evocation of Mars' appearance at Ticinus (4.430). These are the only two occurences of the phrase *at Mauors* in Latin poetry. This repetition may accordingly be the signal for an intratextual link, even though these phrases are in different *sedes*. On intratextuality, see Sharrock 2000. Mars' spear shakes the

Commentary Lines 448–53   219

air all by itself, as at Ticinus: 4.434–5 *quassatque per auras . . . / hastam*. At Zama, by contrast, the same effect requires massed armies: 17.406–7 *contremuere aurae, rapido uibrantibus hastis / turbine*. For *proturbans*, see 5.604, Verg. *Aen.* 9.441, 10.801, Ov. *Met.* 3.80, etc.

448. et clipeo campum inuoluens: Mars' massive shield covers the battlefield, as his chariot filled the field at Ticinus: 4.436 *atque implet curru campos*. Elsewhere in the epic, the verb *inuoluere campum* in the sense "fere i. q. operire" (*TLL* 7.2.262.42) refers to overflowing rivers: 6.143 *et stagnante uado patulos inuoluere campos*, 12.621–2 *atque omnes circa campos spumantibus undis / inuoluit*.

448–9. Aetnaea Cyclopum / munere fundentem loricam incendia gestat: Mars' breastplate emits fire to match Pallas' arms (441–6n.), and he offers Scipio a sword forged in Aetna (458–9n.), presumably by the Cyclopes. At Ticinus, Mars similarly wields arms fashioned by the Cyclopes that emit flame: 4.431–4 *tum fulminis atri / spargentem flammas clipeum galeamque deorum / haud ulli facilem multoque labore Cyclopum / sudatum thoraca*. See further 458–9n. *TLL* 7.1.861.47 lists this as the sole instance of *incendium* "de fulgore metalli." Vulturnus similarly heats up in Aetna before attacking the Roman forces: see 497n.

450. ac pulsat fulua consurgens aethera crista: a recollection of Homer's Eris, the companion of Ares, whose head strikes the sky as battle swells: Hom. *Il.* 4.442–3 ἥ τ' ὀλίγη μὲν πρῶτα κορύσσεται, αὐτὰρ ἔπειτα / οὐρανῷ ἐστήριξε κάρη καὶ ἐπὶ χθονὶ βαίνει. Silius' Hercules does the same in the Gigantomachy (*Pun.* 17.650 *incessit campis tangens Tirynthius astra*), as does Valerius' Giant Amycus (VF *Arg.* 4.149 *uasto qui uertice nubila pulset*). More commonly, the noise of battle strikes heaven: 5.393–4 *clamor . . . / fert belli rabiem ad superos et sidera pulsat*, Luc. *BC* 6.225–6 *laetus fragor aethera pulsat / uictorum*, etc. Spaltenstein specifies that *consurgens* represents a different use of the *surgere* stem than 1.400–1 *et ferit alte / insurgens gladio*, where Hannibal rises to deal a killing blow. For the golden crest, see Verg. *Aen.* 8.445.

451–4. Hannibal and Scipio prepare to fight, pleased that the gods are observing them. Virgil's Venus and Juno similarly observe the combat between Aeneas and Mezentius: Verg. *Aen.* 10.760 *hic Venus, hic contra spectat Saturnia Iuno*.

451–2. ductores pugnae intenti, quantumque uicissim / auderent, propius mensi: the choppy phrases suggest men circling each other as they close in battle. For *ductores*, see 24n. *Intentus pugnae* is a historiographical phrase: see 518n., Caes. *BG* 3.26.2, Livy 22.5.8, Tac. *Hist.* 1.79, etc. For *quantum*, Zaia compares Stat. *Theb.* 11.347 *et metire quod audes*. For Spaltenstein, Duff's translation "what he could dare to do" is "de trop."

452–3. tamen arma ferentes / sensere aduenisse deos: my translation follows both Duff and Volpilhac-Lenthéric, who oppose *intenti* with *tamen* and connect

220 *Commentary Lines 453–9*

accusative *ferentes* with *deos*: "that gods had come down bearing arms"; "ressentirent pourtant l'arrivée des dieux en armes." The word order of the phrase, with a subject phrase placed before finite *sensere*, supports this reading. Zaia similarly supports this interpretation.

Spaltenstein objects, however, that Scipio and Hannibal "ne s'aperçoivent de la présence des dieux qu'ensuite," and so makes *ferentes* nominative ("mais pourtant ['tamen'] n'abandonnent pas le combat"). Contra Spaltenstein, the gods can often observe the epic battlefield without intervening in arms. An accusative phrase emphasizes that a theomachy, an atypical moment, is imminent. 451 *pugnae intenti*, meanwhile, reminds us that this confrontation is the rematch awaited from the moment when Scipio rescued his father at the Ticinus. Men as eager for each other's blood as Hannibal and Scipio are not about to put down their arms just because the gods have decided to join in. It would be otiose to recall that the human fighters are still bearing their weapons, but meaningful to specify that the gods are armed.

453–4. et laetus uterque / spectari superis addebant mentibus iras: commanders inspire their men by promising to observe them in combat; here observation by the gods increases the duelists' pride. As in the rest of the theomachy episode, this passage offers a *Steigerung* of a typical feature of human combat; see 247–8n. and Introduction, section 3e. There is also an evocation of Virgil's Nisus and Euryalus episode, in which Nisus asks Euryalus *dine hunc ardorem mentibus addunt, / Euryale, an sua cuique deus fit dira cupido?* (Verg. *Aen.* 9.184–5). Here the answer is made clear: the gods are unambiguous in their support for a patriotic combat rather than a failed night raid. For *laetus* governing an infinitive, see, e.g., 3.575 *laeta domare labores*, 6.482 *astu fallere laeta*, 8.615 *laetos cingere ferrum*, etc.; *TLL* 7.2.885.83.

455–9. Pallas rescues Hannibal from a spear thrown by Scipio. Mars offers Scipio a divinely forged weapon and encourages him to greater combat. Pallas' actions recombine two scenes featuring her Iliadic counterpart. Homer's Athene blows a spear thrown by Hector away from Achilles (*Il.* 20.438–40), prompting Apollo to come to his rescue; earlier she saves Diomedes from Ares' spear (*Il.* 5.853–4). As often, Silius redistributes elements of the Homeric scenes across several of his own scenes. Here he matches Minerva and Mars around the principal champions and later sends Apollo to prevent Hostus from killing his beloved poet Ennius: *Pun.* 12.406 *et telum procul in uentos dimisit Apollo*. The recombination more closely resembles the Homeric scenes rather than the comparable scenes of Roman epic: Virgil's Juno turns a spear thrown by Pandarus away from Turnus (Verg. *Aen.* 9.745–6 *uulnus Saturnia Iuno / detorsit ueniens*), while Valerius' Minerva defends Perses (VF *Arg.* 6.746 *stridentesque uiri circum caput amouet hastas*).

A series of temporal adverbs in this passage and the following one emphasize the speed of the gods' actions: 455 *iamque*, 458 *protinus*; see further 460–9n.

Commentary Lines 455–65   221

455–6. iamque ictu ualido libratam a pectore Poeni / Pallas in obliquum dextra detorserat hastam: triple alliteration and enjambement both emphasize the suddenness of Minerva's intervention, while the lengthy separation of *libratam* from *hastam* encloses the narrative unit. *Ictu ualido* originates in Cic. *Arat.* 431; see also Verg. *Aen.* 8.419, Ov. *Met.* 3.64, etc. For *librare* of a missile, see 1.317 *librat stridentia saxa*, 1.523 *librataque pondera plumbi*, etc. The phrase *dextra detorserat* reflects Verg. *Aen.* 12.373 *dextra detorsit*, but the closer Virgilian context is *Aen.* 9.745–6 *uulnus... detorsit*, quoted above at 455–9n.

457–8. et Gradiuus opem diuae portare ferocis / exemplo doctus: *ferox* is a typical epithet for Minerva: [Sen.] *Oct.* 546 *ferox armis dea*, Stat. *Ach.* 1.825–6 *feroxque / Pallas*, Mart. *Epig.* 14.179.1 *uirgo ferox*, etc. For *doctus* governing an infinitive, see 1.412 *doctus... sopire*, 10.187 *fallere doctos*, 14.137 *pati docta*, etc.; *TLL* 5.1.1760.31.

458–9. porgebat protinus ensem / Aetnaeum: see 448–9n. for Aetna as the site where the Cyclopes produce weapons for the gods. Scipio's acquisition of a weapon forged in Aetna both aligns him further with Jupiter in the Gigantomachy and recalls Lucan's Gigantomachic simile at Pharsalus: Luc. *BC* 7.144–6 *si liceat superis hominum conferre labores, / non aliter Phlegra rabidos tollente Gigantas / Martius incaluit Siculis incudibus ensis*. The verb form *porgebat* replaces the metrically impossible *porrigebat*. Forms of *porgere* are far less common in epic than *porrigere*; it is found only at Verg. *Aen.* 8.274, VF *Arg.* 2.655, and Stat. *Theb.* 8.754.

459. in pugnas iuueni ac maiora iubebat: Mars recapitulates the encouragement he offered when he helped Scipio rescue his father at Ticinus: 4.476–7 *et adhuc maiora supersunt, / sed nequeunt meliora dari*. The meaning in the present passage is accordingly not "greater than Hannibal's effort," but "greater deeds." Mars' words in these two passages of Silius accordingly reserve the most "epic" deeds of the *Punica* for Scipio. The motif continues in the omen scene of the funeral games (16.590 *ad maiora iubent praesagi tendere uates*) predicting Zama. The repetition thereby creates an arc linking Scipio's most significant battles. At Liternum, Hannibal unsuccessfully attempts to appropriate the *maiora* motif for himself and Carthage: 6.711 *et adhuc maiora dabuntur*. See Marks 2005: 168–9.

Maior signifies the subject matter of martial epic, beginning most famously in the "proem in the middle" to Virgil's *Aeneid*: Verg. *Aen.* 7.44–5 *maior rerum mihi nascitur ordo, / maius opus moueo*. See Conte 2007: 219–31.

460–5. Pallas' rage causes Mars to step back. Silius thereby evokes the climax of Homer's first theomachy, in which Ares retreats after being wounded by Diomedes and Athene conjointly. Ares rushes up to Olympus like a whirlwind (Hom. *Il.* 5.864–7), where Zeus rebukes him for his cowardice and propensity for strife. Silius emphasizes the difference of his brave and patriotic Mars, who

222　　　　　　　*Commentary Lines 460–2*

only gives ground *sensim* (465n.) and thereby makes Homer's Ares look trivial in comparison.

Scipio recalls Pallas' rage when dealing with the deserters after Cannae: see 10.434–5 *tuque aspera pectus / aegide Gorgoneos uirgo succincta furores*. The run of temporal adverbs emphasizing the speed of the gods' actions continues from 455–9n. In this passage, see 460 *tum . . . repente*, 465 *sensim*.

460. tum Virgo ignescens penitus: as Athene Parthenos, Pallas is *Virgo* again at 479n. and 526n.; see also 7.459 *bellica uirgo*, 10.435, 13.57, etc. For *ignescere* of emotions, see 13.180 *ignescunt animi*, Verg. *Aen.* 9.66 *ignescunt irae*, VF *Arg.* 5.520 *furiis ignescit opertis*, etc. For *penitus* of emotions, see 1.59–60 *penitusque medullis / sanguinis humani flagrat sitis* (Hannibal), Catul. *Carm.* 66.23 *quam penitus maestas exedit cura medullas*, Ov. *Her.* 19.156 *o penitus toto corde recepte mihi*, etc.

460–1. uiolenta repente / suffudit flammis ora: *suffudit flammis* varies 460n. *ignescens*. Ruperti's note compares Appius' rage at 5.275–6 *uiolentaque lumina flammis / exarsere nouis*. Spaltenstein objects, however, that the earlier passage describes only the eyes rather than the whole face, while 461–2 in the present passage proceed to describe Pallas' eyes. The same movement from face to eyes occurs when Hannibal rages at Decius: 11.218–19 *suffuderat ora / sanguis et a toruo surgebant lumine flammae*. *TLL* 6.1.866.83. reflects usages applied to eyes and metal, not to faces, and so Spaltenstein characterizes the usage in the present passage as "inattendu, et donc suggestif." It seems to be modeled, however, on phrases describing high emotion, whether blushing, as at Ov. *Met.* 1.484 *pulchra uerecundo suffuderat ora rubore*, or murder, as at [Quint.] *DM* 17.18 *uultus parricidali ardore suffusos*.

461–2. atque obliqua retorquens / lumina turbato superauit Gorgona uultu: the phrasing evokes an earlier exploit of the elder Scipio at Ticinus, who braves Larus' fierce gaze to kill him: 4.234 *Gorgoneoque Larum torquentem lumina uultu*. The present passage accordingly represents a *Steigerung*: Pallas' gaze is more terrifying than the Gorgon's, as Cannae is a greater battle than Ticinus, and as the younger Scipio is a greater leader than his father. He will not be able, however, to directly attack the goddess, let alone kill her.

Pallas' eyes were earlier described as bloodshot: see 444–5n. The Gorgon's face typically includes twisting eyes: see Verg. *Aen.* 8.438 *Gorgona desecto uertentem lumina collo*. Pallas' disturbed face, more terrifying than the Gorgon image, is a further recollection of the Virgilian passage: *turbato . . . uultu* evokes *Aen.* 8.435 *turbatae Palladis arma*. Fiery, twisting eyes are an attribute that adds to the terror of Virgil's Fury (Verg. *Aen.* 7.448–9 *flammea torquens / lumina*) and Valerius' Venus as she incites the Lemnian women to murder (VF *Arg.* 2.184–5 *ignea torquens / lumina*). From a different perspective, Marks 2010a: 136 also notes the evocation of Lucan's Caesar, compared to a lightning bolt: Luc. *BC* 1.154 *terruit obliqua praestringens lumina flamma*.

Commentary Lines 463–7 223

Obliqua is a proleptic adjective that describes the result of *retorquens* in Silius' typically repetitive style. A similar pairing occurs at 2.170 *obliquos detorquet equos* (Asbyte wheels her horses around); see my note. The sidelong gaze typically connotes threatening or hostile body language, as at Hor. *Epist.* 1.14.37–8 *non istic obliquo oculo mea commoda quisquam / limat, non odio obscuro morsuque uenenat*, Petr. *Sat.* 113.6 *sed obliquis trucibusque oculis utrumque spectabam*, Stat. *Theb.* 3.377 *respectentue truces obliquo limine matres*, etc.; see *TLL* 9.2.101.51–4. Sil. *Pun.* 2.621 *obliquos... uisus*, by contrast, refers to a man who attempts to avert his eyes from the crime he is about to commit; see my note.

463. erexere omnes immania membra chelydri: for *immania membra*, see 4.149, 5.306, 13.239, 17.414. Silius uses *chelydrus* six times; his predecessors were far more sparing with the Greek term (Verg. *Geo.* two times, *Aen.* zero times, Ov. *Met.* one time, Luc. *BC* one time; not in Statius or Valerius) and did not apply it to the Gorgon.

464. aegide commota, primique furoris ad ictus: Spaltenstein criticizes Duff's translation "first furious onset." For him, it is "la prime colère, dans tout son éclat initial," which I have attempted to render with "rage's initial blows." *TLL* 7.1.165.15 characterizes this sense of *ictus* as "poetice pro hominibus impetus animi ponitur"; cf. Sen. *Phoen.* 530 *sceleris sub ictu*. Spaltenstein would refer the usage instead to *TLL* 7.1.168.11 "de motu animi, impulsu cupiditatum."

465. rettulit ipse pedem sensim a certamine Mauors: for the prosaic *referre pedem*, see 10.238, Verg. *Aen.* 10.794, Ov. *Met.* 2.439, etc. Poets often choose the alternatives *uestigia* (Verg. *Aen.* 9.797), *gradum* (Ov. *Fasti* 2.502), etc.; see *OLD* s.v. *refero* 2b. See 460–5n. for the significance of *sensim* as a contrast to Homer's Ares; for its register, see 179n.

466–9. Pallas tears away the side of a mountain and hurls it at Mars. Her action recapitulates Nealces' earlier casting of a stone at Scaevola (395–400n.), as well as the Homeric Athene's casting of a boundary stone at Ares: *Il.* 21.403–6 ἣ δ' ἀναχασσαμένη λίθον εἵλετο χειρὶ παχείῃ / κείμενον ἐν πεδίῳ μέλανα τρηχύν τε μέγαν τε, / τόν ῥ' ἄνδρες πρότεροι θέσαν ἔμμεναι οὖρον ἀρούρης· / τῷ βάλε θοῦρον Ἄρηα κατ' αὐχένα, λῦσε δὲ γυῖα. Silius emphasizes the scale of his theomachy by replacing these earlier stones with a mountainside.

Marsus identified the mountain torn apart by Pallas as Garganus, which is both a needless attempt at precision and likely too far away (80 km; 33–4n.) to be described as *uicini* (467n.). For the Gigantomachic connotations of this feat, Zaia appositely compares Ov. *Met.* 14.181–4 *uidi, cum monte reuulsum / immanem scopulum medias permisit in undas; / uidi iterum, ueluti tormenti uiribus acta, / uasta Giganteo iaculantem saxa lacerto*.

466–7. hic dea conuulsam rapido conamine partem / uicini montis scopulisque horrentia saxa: *rapido* continues the run of temporal markers (see

224 *Commentary Lines 468–72*

455–9n. and 460–5n.) and contrasts with Mars' slow retreat (465n. *sensim*). For *horrentia saxa,* see 4.741 *horrebat glacie saxa,* Verg. *Aen.* 7.713 *horrentis rupes,* Ov. *Met.* 4.778 *horrentia saxa,* etc.

468. in Martem furibunda iacit: for adjectives in *-bundus,* see 143–4n. Silius uses *furibundus* more frequently (ten times) than the other epic poets (Verg. *Aen.* two times, Ov. *Met.* six times, Luc. *BC* zero times, VF *Arg.* one time, Stat. *Theb.* five times).

468–9. longeque relatos / expauit sonitus tremefacto litore Sason: *expauit… tremefacto* reflects Silius' typically repetitive style. The motif recalls two earlier moments from Trasimene:

(a) a simile describing the noise of combat compared to a storm at sea that distant lands hear; Sason similarly hears the impact of the mountain hurled by Pallas: 5.399–400 *audit Tartessos latis distermina terris, / audit non paruo diuisus gurgite Lixus.*

(b) the earthquake that actually shakes the mountains, like Sason's shaken beach: 5.612–13 *colles et summa cacumina totis / intremuere iugis.*

For the island Sason (modern Sazan Island, Albania; Saseno in Italian), see 7.480 with Littlewood's note. Lucan brings the island into Latin poetry: see Luc. *BC* 2.625 *Calaber… Sason* and 5.650 *non humilem Sasona uadis.* Pliny *NH* 3.152 comments *piratica statione nota.* Strabo *Geog.* 6.3.5 inaccurately locates it midway between Epirus and Brundisium, which, if true, would have conferred a far less impressive meaning on *longe.* Sason is, in fact, located in the harbor of Vlorë, 278 km from the battlefield of Cannae. Proteus displays his typical foresight and obscurity in predicting Pallas' remarkable feat (*Pun.* 7.480 *Hadriaci fugite infaustas Sasonis harenas*).

470–8. Jupiter sends Iris to halt the combat, in the tradition of the *Iliad* and *Aeneid.* Homer's Zeus sends Iris to stop Poseidon from aiding the Achaeans (*Il.* 15.157–67). Virgil's Jupiter sends Iris to stop Juno from aiding Turnus in the Trojan camp: Verg. *Aen.* 9.803–4 *aëriam caelo nam Iuppiter Irim / demisit germanae haud mollia iussa ferentem.*

470–1. at non haec superum fallebant proelia regem / demittit propere succinctam nubibus Irim: Iris, the rainbow, is typically associated with clouds, rain, and sunlight: Verg. *Aen.* 4.700 *Iris croceis per caelum roscida pennis,* VF *Arg.* 4.77 *uelocem roseis demittit nubibus Irin* (perhaps a model for the present line).

472. quae nimios frenet motus: the characterization of the abortive theomachy as "excessive" is likely focalized through Jupiter, whose Homeric and Virgilian analogues also tried (unsuccessfully) to forbid divine intervention on the battlefield. In addition to 470–8n., see, e.g., Verg. *Aen.* 10.9 *quae contra uetitum discordia?* with Harrison's note.

Commentary Lines 472–7 225

472. ac talia fatur: a common Virgilian clausula (twelve times in the *Aeneid*); see Verg. *Aen.* 7.330 with Horsfall's note. Subsequent epic poets generally avoid it, however; after Virgil, it is only found here, at 12.636, and at VF *Arg.* 7.197.

473. i, dea, et Oenotris uelox allabere terris: Silius frequently refers to Italy as *Oenotria*, thereby associating the Romans with the aboriginal inhabitants of Italy; cf. Verg. *Aen.* 7.85 with Horsfall's note, D.H. *Ant. Rom.* 1.23. See *Pun.* 2.57 with my note, 8.46, 8.220, etc. For Iris' characteristic swiftness, see Hom. *Il.* 2.786 ποδήνεμος ὠκέα Ἶρις, *Il.* 24.77 Ἶρις ἀελλόπος, etc. *Allabi* is a typical verb for divine descent from Olympus; see 10.353 *allapsus* (*Somnus*), 15.21 *allapsae* (*Virtus* and *Voluptas*), Verg. *Aen.* 4.233 *labere pennis* (Mercury), Stat. *Theb.* 2.90 *allapsus* (Mercury) with Gervais's note, etc.

474. germanoque truces, dic, Pallas mitiget iras: Pallas is Mars' half-brother, according to the traditional narrative that makes both children of Jupiter. As an alternative to springing from Jupiter's head, Silius also makes her arise from Lake Tritonis: see 297n. and 3.322–3 *qui stagna colunt Tritonidos alta paludis, / qua uirgo, ut fama est, bellatrix edita lympha.* The phrasing reflects Ov. *Trist.* 4.6.15 *saeuas paulatim mitigat iras,* an alternative to the more common *temperare iras.*

475. nec speret fixas Parcarum uertere leges: use of the maximum number of spondees emphasizes the solemnity of the Fates' laws. *Fixas... leges* gestures toward the historical reality that structures the narrative. Were the combat to continue, Scipio would doubtless kill Hannibal (484–5n.). Accordingly, Hannibal must be rescued here, as he is once more at Zama, where Juno supplicates Jupiter on his behalf. She concedes that Carthage's defeat has been foreordained by Fate (17.358 *fixa dies*; 17.361–2 *nil fila sororum / aduersus posco*) but persuades Jupiter to allow Hannibal to escape (17.365–7). The motif recalls the tradition of Homer's Poseidon, who similarly observes that he is rescuing Aeneas from Troy's destruction in accordance with Fate: Hom. *Il.* 20.302 μόρσιμον δέ οἵ ἐστ' ἀλέασθαι. For Fate's laws, see 10.643–4 *infixum est Aeneia regna / Parcarum in leges quacumque reducere dextra,* [Tib.] 3.4.47 *fatorum leges,* Luc. *BC* 8.568 *fatorum leges,* Stat. *Ach.* 1.685 *certas fatorum... leges,* etc.; for *figere,* see *TLL* 7.2.1254.60.

476–7. dic etiam: ni desistis (nam uirus et aestus / flammiferae noui mentis): for the figurative sense of *uirus* as arrogance (*OLD* 1d), see 2.288 *ingenitum noscens uirus* with my note, 11.557 *uirus futtile linguae.* *TLL* 6.1.873.4 cites this line for *flammifer* in the sense of "alacer, acer." Spaltenstein correctly rejects this classification as "abusive" and compares 11.412 *flammiferas... pennas* (of the Cupids). For compounds in *-fer* and *-ger*, see 37n.

477. nec colligis iram: *colligis* is used in the sense of *cohibere,* as at 6.399 *collegit gressum,* 7.695 *collegisse gradum,* Ov. *Met.* 2.398–9 *colligit amentes.../ Phoebus*

226   *Commentary Lines 478–83*

equos, VF *Arg.* 7.335 *colligit iras*, etc.; see *TLL* 3.1616.59–67 and VF *Arg.* 7.335 with Langen's note. The sense of *redigere*, *conflare* represents the more typical poetic usage of this phrase; see Verg. *Aen.* 9.63–4 *collecta fatigat edendi / ex longo rabies*, Ov. *Met.* 1.234 *colligit os rabiem*, Luc. *BC* 1.207 *totam dum colligit iram*, *TLL* 3.1613.47–84, etc.

478. aegide praecellant quantum horrida fulmina nosces: Drakenborch found the correction *aegida* in a copy of the Roman *editio princeps*. The dative with *praecello* is better attested; see, e.g., 15.74 *praecellunt cunctis*. For this ablative usage, see *TLL* 10.2.408.76.

Spaltenstein compares 4.179–80 *hasta . . . horrida* for this use of the adjective, but it is also worth noting its application to storms: Sen. *Contr.* 7.1.4 *emicabant densis undique nubibus fulmina et tempestates horridae absconderant diem*, Sen. *NQ* 6.32.4 *securus aspiciet fulminantis caeli trucem atque horridam faciem*. The extension of *horridus* from the sky to the thunderbolts sent from it is accordingly plausible.

479–85. Pallas, nevertheless, persists, at least initially, but ultimately follows Jupiter's command. She consoles herself that he cannot prevent the gods from witnessing the slaughter at Cannae. Pallas then rescues Hannibal from an unequal contest by concealing him in a hollow cloud. The Homeric and Virgilian gods similarly intervene to rescue their favorites in hollow clouds (484–5n.). Juno similarly rescues Hannibal at Zama: see 475n. Frequent repetition of initial A- and C- throughout the passage helps to emphasize Pallas' growing rage.

479. quae postquam accepit dubitans Tritonia uirgo: for *Tritonia*, see 297n., 439n.; for *uirgo*, see 460n. The clausula recurs at 13.57.

480. nec sat certa diu, patriis an cederet armis: Pallas meditates *diu* on the possibility of taking up arms against her father Jupiter. The image of the potentially rebellious daughter strongly contrasts with Scipio, the epic's paragon of filial *pietas*.

Silius used comparable phrasing to describe disbelief as the news of Trasimene reached Rome: 6.566 *nec laetis sat certa fides, iterumque morantur*. For *cedere armis*, see 13.43–4 *Therapnaeis Ilion armis / cessurum*.

481. 'absistemus' ait 'campo. sed Pallade pulsa': *absistere campo* is a unique phrase, modeled on the far more common *absistere bello* (2.325 with my note, Hor. *Sat.* 1.3.104, VF *Arg.* 3.451, etc.). Corippus may have adapted Silius' phrasing at *Ioh.* 4.51 and 6.619 *campis desistere*. The resonant clausula, featuring alliteration and similar vowels, emphasizes Pallas' rage at her thwarted intention.

482–3. num fata auertet caeloque arcebit ab alto / cernere: Pallas sarcastically envisions a similar situation to that of the brothers' duel in Statius'

Commentary Lines 483–90 227

Thebaid, where Jupiter commands the gods *auferte oculos* (Stat. *Theb.* 11.126) to avoid seeing the act of *impietas* inspired by the Furies. For discussion of that scene, see Lovatt 2013: 246 and Bernstein 2004. For *arcere* with the infinitive, see 5.51 *remeare... arcet*, 13.341–2 *inferuescere... arcet*, Ov. *Met.* 3.88 *sedere... arcebat*, etc.; *TLL* 2.446.46–73. A second alliterative clausula binds this line to the preceding one. Ruperti interpreted *arcebit* as *prohibebit me*, which is unnecessarily limiting; others may join Pallas in seeing the Roman defeat. I have accordingly followed Spaltenstein's "empêchera-t-il de voir"; though Spaltenstein comments that Duff "justement" translates "avoid," if "en soi trop approximatif."

483. Gargani feruentia caedibus arua: for Garganus as a metonym for Cannae and Apulia, see 33–4n. *Feruentia caedibus* indicates a battlefield seething with slaughter, a different image from that of 243n. *feruere campo*, where the field seethes with masses of men. Phrases similar to the present passage occur at 10.334 *feruet cruor et perfusae caede cohortes*, 17.488–9 *Geticas soluit feruenti sanguine Mauors / laetus caede niues*, Verg. *Aen.* 9.692–3 *hostem / feruere caede noua*, etc. Blass proposed *sternere*, but Delz (app. crit.) observes that this is unnecessary, as *cernere* may be construed with 482 *caelo... ab alto*.

484–5. haec effata caua Poenum in certamina nube / sublatum diuersa tulit terrasque reliquit: hollow clouds are the gods' preferred method of rescuing their favorites. The formula ἐκάλυψε δ᾽ ἄρ᾽ ἠέρι πολλῇ occurs at Hom. *Il.* 3.381 (Aphrodite rescues Paris), 20.444 (Apollo rescues Hector), 21.597 (Apollo rescues Agenor); see also 11.752 καλύψας ἠέρι πολλῇ (Poseidon rescues the Moliones). Virgil's Venus recalls how she similarly rescued Aeneas at Troy (*Aen.* 5.809–10 *Aenean.../ nube caua rapui*), as his Diana promises to rescue Camilla's corpse (*Aen.* 11.593–4 *nube caua miserandae corpus.../ feram*). For the hollow cloud from which the gods watch human combats, see 438n.

Juno rescues Hannibal at Zama through the different method of creating an illusory Scipio for him to pursue off the battlefield. The phrasing of the present passage, however, further anticipates that rescue: 17.545–7 *donec longinquo frustratum duxit in arua / diuersa spatio procul a certamine pugnae; / tum fallax subito simulacrum in nubila cessit.*

For the speech formula *haec effatus/a*, see 13.776, Verg. *Aen.* 7.274 with Horsfall's note, *Aen.* 11.741, etc. For the clausula of 485, see Man. *Astr.* 2.595, Luc. *BC* 9.304, Stat. *Theb.* 11.692, etc.

486–90. Mars rallies the Roman forces, while concealed in mist in the gods' typical fashion (438n., 484–5n.). He pushes the wavering soldiers forward with his massive hand. The motif of gods propelling mortals forward originates at Hom. *Il.* 15.694–5 τὸν δὲ Ζεὺς ὦσεν ὄπισθε / χειρὶ μάλα μεγάλῃ, ὄτρυνε δὲ λαὸν ἅμ᾽ αὐτῷ. On the divine level, Juno sends the Fury against the walls of Saguntum by pushing her forward and asks her to use her hands against the walls: see *Pun.*

228   *Commentary Lines 486–90*

2.532 *hos muros impelle manu*, 2.543–4 *dextra dea concita saeuam / Eumenida incussit muris* with my notes.

486. at Gradiuus atrox remeantis in aethera diuae: for the epithet *atrox*, compare 3.702 *Gradiuumque trucem*. Silius elsewhere applies it to human beings; see 222n. *Maurus atrox*. Marks 2010a: 136 detects an allusion to Luc. *BC* 1.391 *fit sonus aut rursus redeuntis in aethera siluae*, but the contexts are somewhat different.

487. abscessu reuocat mentes fusosque per aequor: *abscessu* is a hapax in Silius, as it is at Verg. *Aen.* 10.445 and VF *Arg.* 3.9; the noun does not appear elsewhere in poetry until late antiquity. Harrison on Verg. *Aen.* 10.445 observes that *abscessu* appears to recapitulate *cesserunt* of the previous line. Silius may accordingly be "correcting" Virgil by choosing words from different stems.

Duff's translation "Mars... renewed his purpose" is inaccurate. The *mentes* belong to the Roman forces, the routed soldiers (*fusos*) whom he restores to the battle. For the phrasing, see 1.622 *fusaque per aequora*; the only other occurrence is Man. *Astr.* 4.782 *fusasque per aequora*. Some early editors (*edd. a* l) adopted *fusamque* Γ^2 with the alternative reading 489 *pugnam* $F^2\beta$.

488–9. ipse manu magna nebulam circumdatus acri / restituit pugnae: for Mars' massive size, see 447–50n. For the gods using their large hands to push people, walls, and ships, see 2.532 and Hom. *Il.* 15.694–5, both quoted at 486–90n. above, as well as Enn. *Ann.* 581 Skutsch *atque manu magna Romanos impulit amnis* with Skutsch's note, Verg. *Aen.* 5.241–2 *et pater ipse manu magna Portunus euntem / impulit*, etc. A cloud conceals Mars, as at 438n.

For *circumdatus* of gods veiled in cloud, see 1.551 *aduolat obscura circumdata nube per auras* (Juno), Ov. *Met.* 5.251–2 *inde caua circumdata nube Seriphon / deserit* (Minerva). For *acri... pugnae*, see, e.g., 3.92 *sudatus labor et, bellis labor acrior, Alpes*, Caes. *BG* 1.26.1 *acriter pugnatum*, Ov. *Ibis* 644 *acria bella*, etc. Spaltenstein observes that the grammatical structure *fusos... restituit pugnae* permits "une variation ingénieuse" on the more common phrases *restituere pugnam* (Livy 2.19.10, 4.40.7, 10.29.5, etc.) or *restituta pugna* (Livy 3.63.1, 10.36.12, 30.18.15, etc.)

489–90. conuertunt signa nouamque / instaurant Itali uersa formidine caedem: the alliteration of I-, the penthemimeral caesura, and the separation of adjective *nouam* and noun *caedem* emphasize the word *Itali*. For the fantasy of political unity throughout the Italian peninsula at Cannae, see Introduction, section 3c. For *conuertere signa*, see 12.173–4, 16.641, etc.

The complementary pairs *conuertunt... uersa* and *nouamque instaurant* reflect Silius' typically abundant style. For *instaurare* with a complementary word meaning "anew," see also 1.35 *iterum instaurata capessens*, 13.878 *rursus bella uolet Macetum instaurare sub armis*, or with the adjective *nouus* at Livy 37.19.5 *instauremus nouum de integro bellum*, etc. For *Itali*, see 76n.

Commentary Lines 491–94   229

491–523. The historiographical tradition claimed that the Vulturnus wind impaired the Roman troops' performance at Cannae. The *Punica* combines the historical event with the tradition of the epic storm. Silius' Aeolus obeys Juno in sending a storm on Aeneas' descendants, thereby evoking the storm of Virgil *Aeneid* 1. This storm further links the epic's beginning, middle, and end, as represented by the Saguntum, Cannae, and Zama episodes. The Saguntine ambassadors endure Boreas on their voyage to Rome (1.584–94); the Vulturnus wind assaults the Romans twice at Cannae, returning to harass the Romans further at the climax of the battle (10.202–4); and a storm assaults Hannibal's fleet as he departs from Italy (17.236–91).

491–6. Aeolus, king of the winds, lets loose the Vulturnus wind at Juno's request.

491–2. cum uentis positus custos, cui flamina carcer / imperio compressa tenet caelumque ruentes: Aeolus' prison for the winds appears elsewhere at 3.658–9 *uel si perfracto populatus carcere terras / Africus*, 12.188 *ut rupto terras inuadunt carcere uenti*. Motifs and language in the present passage vary Virgil's description of Aeolus' kingdom. *Positus* reflects Verg. *Aen.* 1.62 *imposuit*, while *flamina carcer / imperio compressa* adapts Verg. *Aen.* 1.53–4 *luctantis uentos tempestatesque sonoras / imperio premit ac uinclis et carcere frenat*.

After Virgil, the winds' prison becomes a traditional motif for subsequent Roman poets: Ov. *Met.* 4.663 *clauserat Hippotades Aetnaeo carcere uentos*, Luc. *BC* 5.608–9 *non Euri cessasse minas, non imbribus atrum / Aeolii iacuisse Notum sub carcere saxi*, VF *Arg.* 1.602 with Zissos' note, Stat. *Theb.* 3.432, etc. For *caelumque ruentes*, see 17.252 *ruere caelum* and for the common phrase *caeli ruina*, see Lucr. *DRN* 1.1107, Verg. *Aen.* 1.129, [Sen.] *Oct.* 394, etc.

493. Eurique et Boreae parent Corique Notique: the polysyndetic list of winds is an adaptation of Hom. *Il.* 2.145 Εὖρός τε Νότος τε, *Od.* 5.295–6 σὺν δ' Εὖρός τε Νότος τ' ἔπεσον Ζέφυρός τε δυσαὴς / καὶ Βορέης αἰθρηγενέτης, Verg. *Aen.* 1.85–6 *una Eurusque Notusque ruunt creberque procellis / Africus*. For similar polysyndeton, see Stat. *Silv.* 3.2.45 *Borean Eurumque Notumque*. For further examples of repeated *–que* in lists of winds, see Wills 1996: 373–4. For the identification of the Vulturnus wind with Eurus, see Sen. *NQ* 5.16.4 *ab oriente hiberno Eurus exit, quem nostri uocauere Vulturnum, —T. Liuius hoc illum nomine appellat*, Florus 1.22.

494. Iunonis precibus promissa haud parua ferentis: the Trebia similarly raises its waves to drown the Romans *precibus Iunonis* (4.574). The present scene evokes the opening of Virgil's *Aeneid*, in which Juno bribes Aeolus to cause the storm with the promise of marriage to the nymph Deiopea: Verg. *Aen.* 1.65–75. Similar phrasing occurs at *Pun.* 4.828 *namque haud parua deus promissis spondet apertis*, where Hannibal tells his commanders that the god of Trasimene has promised him victory.

230   *Commentary Lines 495–8*

495–6. regnantem Aetolis Vulturnum in proelia campis / effrenat: for southern Italy as Diomedes' Aetolian land, see 99n. The erroneous alternative *(a)
eoliis* F²Γ²s was likely prompted by a gloss identifying the unnamed *custos* of
line 491 or memories of Virgil's Aeolus scene. *Regnantem* adds an additional
level of hierarchy to Virgil's wind scene, in which Aeolus is *rex* of the winds
(Verg. *Aen.* 1.62 *regem*), but the winds are not themselves *reges* in turn. The
emphatic enjambement of *effrenat* evokes Verg. *Aen.* 1.54 *carcere frenat*, quoted
at 491–2n. above.

496. placet hic irae exitiabilis ultor: as the agent of Juno's revenge on the
Romans, Vulturnus evokes Virgil's Hannibal, whose career Dido predicts in her
dying curse on the Aeneadae: Verg. *Aen.* 4.625–6 *exoriare aliquis nostris ex
ossibus ultor / qui face Dardanios ferroque sequare colonos.* The wind may also
be avenging the relatively recent domination of his region by the Romans. After
Cannae, Capua and other southern Italian cities defect to Hannibal (11.1–54),
providing a clear indication that earlier conquest did not immediately create
loyalty to Rome. See Fucecchi 2019 and Biggs 2019. Silius uses the adjective
exitiabilis four times; it appears elsewhere in poetry only at Plaut. *Epid.* 605, Ov.
Met. 6.257, 8.425, and Stat. *Theb.* 1.395.

497–504. Vulturnus heats his winds in Mount Aetna's volcanic fires and then
blinds the Roman soldiers with his dust. For the wind's dryness and heat, see
Livy 22.43.10 *Hannibal castra posuerat auersa a Volturno uento, qui campis torridis siccitate nubes pulueris uehit.* In his discussion of winds, Seneca recalls
Vulturnus as an important aspect of Cannae: Sen. *NQ* 5.16.4 *Hannibal et contra
solem orientem exercitum nostrum et contra uentum constitutum uenti adiuto-
rio ac fulgoris praestringentis oculos hostium uicit.* There may also be a recollection of Pompey's assault in Lucan's Dyrrachium episode, which employs a
simile involving Aetna's volcanic activity to describe the soldiers' fear as they
are conquered by the dust: Luc. *BC* 6.293–7 *non sic Hennaeis habitans in uallibus horret / Enceladum spirante Noto, cum tota cauernas / egerit et torrens in
campos defluit Aetna, / Caesaris ut miles glomerato puluere uictus / ante aciem
caeci trepidus.*

497. qui, se postquam Aetnae mersit candente barathro: Mars similarly carries arms forged in Aetna's fires; see 448–9n. *TLL* 3.235.30 cites this passage for
candens in the sense of "albus," but the sense is clearly "ardens, fervens" (*TLL*
3.235.46). Vulturnus proceeds to hurl *candentes...globos* at the Romans: 502–3n.
The wind similarly carries burning sands on his next appearance: 10.203–4
sublatum puluere campum / Vulturnus rotat et candentis torquet harenas.
Describing Aetna's interior as a *barathrum* evokes the noun's application to the
Underworld; see, e.g., Lucr. *DRN* 3.966, VF *Arg.* 2.86, etc.

498. concepitque ignes et flammea protulit ora: *concipere ignes* is more commonly used metaphorically of rage or desire in poetry; see, e.g., Ov. *Met.* 9.520,

Commentary Lines 499–504   231

VF *Arg.* 1.48, etc. For literal application to fire, see Lucr. *DRN* 6.308, Ov. *Met.* 7.108, *Met.* 15.348 (describing Aetna, as here), etc. For the clausula, see Ov. *Met.* 4.656, *Trist.* 3.10.9.

499. euolat horrendo stridore ac Daunia regna: references to Vulturnus' tremendous noise occur throughout the subsequent lines: see 510n. *stridulus*, 515n. *stridentibus*, 516n. *clamante*, 517n. *insibilat*, 522n. *mugitibus*. At his next appearance, Vulturnus is described as *stridens immane procella* (10.205), which evokes Verg. *Aen.* 1.102 *stridens Aquilone procella*. This is the only occurrence of *horrendo stridore* in poetry, but the phrase occurs in prose at Livy 44.5.2, QCurt. 8.13.10, Pliny *NH* 7.24, etc. For Daunus, see 212n.; for the clausula, see 4.125, 8.357, 14.3, etc.; see also the alternative *Daunia tellus*, 13.9, 13.59, 17.220, etc.

500. perflat agens caecam glomerato puluere nubem: *perflat* evokes the action of the winds in Virgil's Aeolus scene: Verg. *Aen.* 1.83 *terras turbine perflant.* For *perflare* in Silius, see 5.456, 11.579, 14.259. The line ending recurs in the description of Claudius' ride as he advances to the single combat with Taurea: 13.158 *erigit undantem glomerato puluere nubem*. The line ending is an evocation of the Latins' advance: Verg. *Aen.* 9.33 *subitam nigro glomerari puluere nubem*; see also Luc. *BC* 6.296, quoted at 497–504n. For blinding dust, see Verg. *Aen.* 12.444 *caeco puluere*.

501. eripuere oculos aurae uocemque manusque: a hyperbolic description of Vulturnus' assault, which removes (the use of) the soldiers' eyes, voices, and hands. Word order and sentence structure again evoke Virgil's Aeolus scene: Verg. *Aen.* 1.88–9 *eripiunt subito nubes caelumque diemque / Teucrorum ex oculis*. For the clausula, see 6.458 *uoce manuque*.

502–3. uertice harenoso candentes, flebile dictu, / torquet in ora globos Italum: *harenoso* varies 500n. *puluere*. For *candentes,* see 497n. The previous mention of Aetna (497n.) likely inspired a memory of Virgil's volcano, which smokes with *candente fauilla* and spews *globos flammarum* (Verg. *Aen.* 3.573–4). Silius earlier described the hot Spanish sun as *candentique globo* (*Pun.* 1.258). For parenthetical *flebile*, see 631n. and 7.648.

Globos recapitulates 500n. *glomerato*. The phrasing reflects the storm at Ticinus, which similarly hurls dark masses (of cloud): 4.441 *nigrantisque globos et turbida nubila torquens*. Mars similarly descends to the battlefield in that earlier passage; there may accordingly be an intratextual link between the god's two appearances. For similar storm descriptions, see also 5.535 *it globus intorquens nigranti turbine nubem*, 6.321–2 *sic ubi nigrantem torquens stridentibus Austris / portat turbo globum*.

503–4. et bellare maniplis / iussa laetatur rabie: *iussa* recapitulates 494n. *Iunonis precibus*. Vulturnus' joy in his maddened rage is a typical motif in martial epic, inspired by the tradition of Virgil's *gaudens... Discordia* (Verg. *Aen.*

232 *Commentary Lines 504–7*

8.702). See *Pun.* 17.489 *laetus caede*, Stat. *Theb.* 7.52 *laetusque Furor* with Smolenaars' note, etc.

504–11. Vulturnus knocks the Roman soldiers backwards, disrupts their missiles in flight, and speeds on the Carthaginian missiles. This aspect of Cannae only appears elsewhere at App. *Hann.* 22 τά τε βέλη Ῥωμαίοις μὲν πάντα ἀμβλύτερα διὰ τὴν ἀντίπνοιαν ἦν, τοῖς δὲ ἐχθροῖς ἐπιτυχῆ, τοῦ πνεύματος τὴν βολὴν συνωθοῦντος. Spaltenstein suggests that the later author "peut penser à Sil.," but it is improbable that the Greek historian consulted any Roman epic except possibly the *Aeneid*. Rather, both authors likely drew on a tradition that most other narratives (Polybius, Livy, Seneca, Florus, etc.) did not follow. See Introduction, section 3e.

Claudian's description of the miraculous wind that intervened on Theodosius' behalf at the Frigidus employs a similar motif: Claud. *III Cos. Hon.* 93–5 *te propter gelidis Aquilo de monte procellis / obruit aduersas acies reuolutaque tela / uertit in auctores et turbine reppulit hastas.* As Cameron 2011: 116 observes, "Claudian undoubtedly knew Silius, and it makes a neat reversal to turn the wind responsible for Rome's most infamous defeat into the wind that gave Theodosius his greatest victory."

504–5. tum mole ruinae / sternuntur tellure et miles et arma tubaeque: *mole* and *sternuntur* help to specify that *ruinae* refers to the Roman soldiers' collapse, as at 4.584 *occumbunt seseque sua pressere ruina* and 17.424 *mole ruinae*. The phrase does not refer to "the ruin of the sky" at 492n. The clausula of 504 is common; see Ov. *Trist.* 5.12.13, Luc. *BC* 2.187, Stat. *Theb.* 6.715, etc. For *sternere tellure*, see 39n., 10.459 *sternit tellure*, Verg. *Aen.* 3.509.

The *tubae* are an unexpected inclusion in the catalog of Vulturnus' victims. The clausula may be modeled on Stat. *Theb.* 7.11–12 [Mauors] *arma tubasque / insatiatus habet*, *Theb.* 10.233–4 *quis in arma tubasque / natus*; see also VF *Arg.* 5.252 *arma tubaeque sonent.* Each of these passages, however, represents a metonymy for warfare itself rather than a catalog of losses. Nevertheless, Livineius' *iubaeque* may be banalizing, as it is easier to visualize the wind knocking crests to the ground. For the collocation, cf. Stat. *Theb.* 10.754–5 *arma furentis / terribilesque iubas*, 11.406 *arma manu mixtisque iubas serpentibus.*

Delz (app. crit.) is correct, however, that both *iubae* and *tubae* are "ineptum." *Tubae* may be an intrusion on the example of the Statius citations given immediately above. Delz conjectures *tellure <equitesque> et miles et arma [tubaeque]* on the example of Livy 23.15.13 *utique Cannensi proelio non prius pugna abstiterit quam prope exsanguis ruina superincidentium uirorum equorum armorumque sit oppressus.* While this conjecture does reflect the Livian text more closely, it also involves extensive change to the paradosis.

506–7. atque omnis retro flatu occursante refertur / lancea: for *retro* paired with *referre*, see 10.17–18 *abscessere retro pauidique in terga relatos / abduxere*

Commentary Lines 507–11   233

gradus, Verg. *Geo.* 1.200, *Aen.* 2.169 *retro sublapsa referri*, where Horsfall compares *Aen.* 2.378 *retro...repressit* and *Aen.* 9.797–8 *retro...refert*.

507. et in tergum Rutulis cadit irritus ictus: Barth's *in tergum*, accepted by most modern editors, is a better choice than the manuscripts' *interdum*, accepted by Volpilhac-Lenthéric. The emphasis is on the trajectory of the spears. *Interdum* may have been an eye-skip from 518 and would not cohere well with *omnis*. 4.315 *nunc Itali in tergum uersis referentur habenis* is an adequate parallel for the phrasing; cf. 506n. *refertur*. Silius frequently uses *Rutuli* to refer to the Romans and thereby embeds his historical narrative in Rome's mythological past. For *Rutuli* applied to the Romans rather than the Saguntines, see, e.g., 8.357 with Ariemma's note, 10.449, 11.565, etc. For missiles that fall without effect, see Stat. *Theb.* 2.652–3 *sic inrita nobis / tela cadant* with Gervais's note.

508. atque idem flatus Poenorum tela secundant: *flatus* recapitulates 506n. For *secundare* with wind, see Lucr. *DRN* 5.1230 *uentorum pauidus paces animasque secundas*, Prop. *Eleg.* 3.21.14 *aura secundat*, Tac. *Ann.* 2.24 *secundante uento*.

509. et uelut ammento contorta hastilia turbo: the wind's force provides impetus to the spears, as if they had been hurled from a leather thong. For the *ammentum*, see 1.318 *huic impulsa leui torquetur lancea nodo*, 4.14–15 *hasta iuuatur / ammento*, 13.159 *opem ammenti*. Van der Keur on 13.159 notes that the *ammentum* may not have been in use during the Second Punic War. Silius extends the idea metaphorically in the battle in the Syracusan harbor, where the wind spreads the fire that Corbulo hurls on the Carthaginian ships: 14.422 *ammentante Noto*.

The collocation *contorta hastilia* adapts Verg. *Aen.* 11.561 *contortum hastile*. Describing Vulturnus as a *turbo* ("whirlwind") provides the climax to the wind's earlier identifications as 501n. *aurae* and 508n. *flatus*.

510. adiuuat ac Tyrias impellit stridulus hastas: missiles are conventionally *stridens* (see 247n.), but here it is the wind Vulturnus, with its *horrendo stridore* (499n.), that produces the sound as it hurls the Carthaginian spears forward. *Tyrias...hastas* recapitulates both *hastilia* of the preceding line and 508n. *Poenorum tela*.

511–20. Vulturnus chokes the Romans with dust, a frequent motif in descriptions of Cannae. More hyperbolically, the wind also rips the weapons from their hands. Earlier commentators adduced Livy 22.51.8 *inuenti quidam sunt mersis in effossam terram capitibus, quos sibi ipsos fecisse foueas obruentesque ora superiecta humo interclusisse spiritum apparebat*. Spaltenstein correctly observes that this passage refers to soldiers committing suicide, not to the effects or consequences of the Vulturnus wind.

511. tum denso fauces praeclusus puluere miles: *denso...puluere* recapitulates 500n. *glomerato puluere*. Spaltenstein observes that this is the only example

234   *Commentary Lines 512–15*

of *praecludi* with an accusative of relation. For more typical usage, see, e.g., Sen. *Thy.* 781–2 *praeclusae...fauces*. O's reading *perculsus* is the result of a typical confusion; see *TLL* 10.2.492.10–15 for examples.

512. ignauam mortem compresso maeret hiatu: the Romans fear that their deaths will be dishonorable, as nature rather than their enemies on the battlefield would be the cause. 521n. *foedare* resumes this idea. In his subsequent assault on the Romans, Vulturnus causes Curio's death by drowning in the Aufidus, which elicits the following judgments from the narrator: 10.209 *tacito, non felix Curio, leto*, 10.403–4 *leto non dignus inerti / Curio*. The narrator comments *miserabile* (4.571) as Hannibal herds the Roman soldiers to drown in the Trebia, and Fibrenus objects to dying in this dishonorable way: 4.605–6 *namque inhonoratam Fibrenus perdere mortem / et famae nudam impatiens*. The plague at Syracuse elicits similar comment: 14.606–7 *heu dolor! insignis notis bellator in armis / ignauo rapitur leto*. For the motif, see Stat. *Theb.* 9.506–10 with Dewar's notes.

Duff renders *compresso...hiatu* as "shut their mouths tight". I have taken the phrase, with Spaltenstein, as a doublet of *fauces praeclusus* and accordingly translated "as their windpipes shut."

513–14. ipse caput flauum caligine conditus atra / Vulturnus multaque comam perfusus harena: the adjectives *flauum* and *atra* create an effective visual contrast; Vulturnus carries dark cloud and volcanic smoke along with light-colored sand, as at 500n. The couplet offers a learned evocation of earlier poetic winds. For the collocation *condere caligine*, see 2.611 *caligine condit* with my note, Verg. *Aen.* 11.187 *conditur in tenebras altum caligine caelum*, Sen. *HF* 92 *in alta conditam caligine*. Silius varies Ovid's description of Notus (*Met.* 1.265 *terribilem picea tectus caligine uultum*) and his own description of fire (*Pun.* 4.306 *nigranti piceus sensim caligine uertex*). Sandstorms typically block out the sunlight; Marks 2010a: 135 accordingly notes the correspondence with Lucan's description of a solar eclipse: Luc. *BC* 1.540–1 *ipse caput medio Titan cum ferret Olympo / condidit ardentis atra caligine currus*. The *caligo* derives from Aetna's volcanic fires (see 497n.), but winds are also conventionally dark because they carry cloud: see, e.g., 3.524 *fuscis... alis* (Corus).

Line 514 likely expands VF *Arg.* 1.613 *multa flauus caput Eurus harena*; see 493n. for the assimilation of Vulturnus to Eurus. Winds typically carry *harena*, which is conventionally *flaua* or *fulua*, and so Vulturnus' hair turns *flauum* as well. Examples include 4.241 *fulua...harena*, Verg. *Geo.* 3.350 *flauentis...harenas*, Ov. *Met.* 14.448 *flaua...harena*, etc. Statius attributes a *flauum caput* to the silty river Vulturnus (Stat. *Silv.* 4.3.67); see Coleman's note.

515. nunc uersos agit a tergo stridentibus alis: the repeated temporal markers *nunc..., nunc...*(516), and *interdum...iam iamque* (518) emphasize the speed and multiplicity of Vulturnus' assault. The winds' wings are conventionally strident: see 499n., 1.589, 14.124, Verg. *Aen.* 1.397, Ov. *Met.* 4.616, etc.

Commentary Lines 516–22

516. nunc mediam in frontem ueniens clamante procella: storms convention-ally shriek; see 499n., 6.177 *mixtam stridore procellam*, Prop. 3.7.47 *stridorem...procellae*, Verg. *Aen.* 1.102 *stridens...procella*, etc. Apuleius offers a (false) etymology on this point: Apul. *Mund.* 13 βορέαν *uero* ἀπὸ τῆς βοῆς *quod non sine clamore soleat intonare.*

517. obuius arma quatit patuloque insibilat ore: the wind's impact shakes the men's arms, as Hannibal's spear shakes Paulus' armor at 642n. *quatiun-tur...arma*; see also Livy 21.40.9 *quassata fractaeque arma*. For *insibilat*, see 499n. and 2.626 *atros insibilat ore timores*. Most translators, including me, take *ore* with the wind. Spaltenstein observes that, according to *TLL* 9.2.1089.47, this is the sole attribution of *os* to a wind. Heinsius proposed *ori* (i.e., *militum*), but it is difficult to see why any of the soldiers would still have their mouths open at this point in Vulturnus' assault.

518. interdum intentos pugnae: for *intentos pugnae*, see 451n. The Romans reprise the aborted duel of Scipio and Hannibal on a larger scale.

518–19. et iam iamque ferentes / hostili iugulo ferrum conamine et ictu: for gemination of *iam*, see 120n. *Ferre* is *simplex pro composito* for *inferre*, as also at 544n. Thus, Heinsius' conjecture *prementes*, adopted by Håkanson, is needless on grammatical grounds. For *ferentes...ferrum*, see Verg. *Aen.* 9.37 *ferte citi ferrum*, Ov. *Met.* 13.91 *ferunt Troes ferrumque*; see Michalopoulos 2001: 80–1 on the *figura etymologica*. *Conamen* and *ictus* function elsewhere as near syn-onyms at 5.294–5 and Stat. *Theb.* 9.773–4 *modo derigit ictus, / nunc latere alterno dubius conamina mutat*, but are used in different senses at Luc. *BC* 4.286–7 *dum dolor est ictusque recens et mobile neruis / conamen calidus praebet cruor.*

520. auertit dextramque ipso de uulnere uellit: for *auertere* without an accom-panying preposition, see 344n. and 548n. The run of temporal markers con-cludes with *ipso*: the Romans are on the very point of wounding their enemies when Vulturnus wrenches their hands away.

521–3. Vulturnus attacks Mars as the climax of his assault.

521. nec satis Ausonias passim foedare cohortes: Vulturnus moves on from human victims to divine. The phrase *nec satis* indicates this *Steigerung*, as also at 570n. *Foedare* combines the physical image of covering the Romans in dust with the moral image of dishonoring them; see 511–12n.

522. in Martem uomit immixtas mugitibus auras: the personified wind is imagined as emitting air from its mouth. To illustrate the metaphor, Ruperti adduced passages such as Verg. *Geo.* 2.462 *salutantum...uomit...undam* (the doors of a noble house), *Aen.* 8.680–1 *flammas...uomunt* (Augustus' temples). *Mugitibus* is also a metaphorical word similar to 6.177 *mixtam stri-dore procellam*, as "shriekings" are not a tangible substance like hail, sand, or

236   *Commentary Lines 523–8*

smoke. For air "mixed" with other substances, see Lucr. *DRN* 6.1129 *mixtas… auras,* Ov. *Fasti* 4.626 *uentus… grandine mixtus.* The "shriekings" continue the frequent references to Vulturnus' tremendous noise, on which, see 499n. Ch adopted D. Heinsius' conjecture *iras,* but it is unlikely as the clausula of 525 already has *iras.*

523. bisque dei summas uibrauit turbine cristas: the crest of Mars' helmet struck the sky at 450n.; Vulturnus' winds now strike the crest. The detail emphasizes the contrast between divine and human experience: the wind can choke the Romans, but only manages to make the god's crest flutter. Van Veen argued for *librauit β,* following Drakenborch.

524–7. Pallas, supported by Juno, complains to Jupiter about Mars' intervention. The scene recalls Hom. *Il.* 4.20–4, where Hera, supported by Athene, makes a similar complaint to Zeus about Aphrodite's intervention in the duel between Paris and Menelaus.

524. quae dum Romuleis exercet proelia turmis: reference to the Romans as *Romulei* is common in Silius; see 3.618, 7.485, 11.75, etc. Here it recalls Romulus' descent from Mars and thus the god's predisposition to aid Scipio and the Roman people. For the clausula, see 6.241, Prop. *Eleg.* 2.10.3.

525. Aeolius furor et Martem succendit in iras: Vulturnus can be described as "Aeolian" thanks to his king, as at Mart. *Epig.* 5.71.4 *Aeolio… Noto.*

526. affatur Virgo, socia Iunone, parentem: for Pallas as *Virgo,* see 460n. For *socia Iunone,* see VF *Arg.* 1.73 *socia Iunone et Pallade.*

527–34. Pallas protests that she does not intend to destroy the Romans, who she refers to in this mythologized context as Trojans (as at 524n., where the Romans are *Romulei*). Her goal is to keep Hannibal, her fellow African, alive so he can fulfill the destiny already evinced by his *primordia.*

527–8. quantos Gradiuus fluctus in Punica castra, / respice, agit: Juno similarly asks Hannibal to look at the gods' activity as he tries to attack Rome: 12.719–21 *sed enim* **aspice, quantus** / *aegida commoueat nimbos flammasque uomentem /* **Iuppiter** *et* **quantis** *pascat ferus ignibus iras.* For *fluctus* as a metaphor for war, see, e.g., Acc. *Trag.* 608 *non uides… quantos belli fluctus concites?,* Lucr. *DRN* 5.1289 *belli / miscebant fluctus,* Cic. *Phil.* 13.20 *belli fluctibus circumiri,* etc.; *TLL* 6.1.947.55.

    The phrase *Punica castra* occurs six times in Silius. Servius on Verg. *Aen.* 2.27 *Dorica castra* argued that the repetition of *ca ca* produces a *cacemphaton;* see 34n. Yet Silius has adequate precedent from Virgil (*Aen.* five times) and the subsequent tradition of Ov. *Her.* 16.372 and Luc. *BC* 8.14. Silius uses the epithet *Punicus* less frequently (seventeen times) than others describing the Carthaginians, e.g., *Sidonius* sixty-nine times, *Tyrius* eighty-five times.

Commentary Lines 528–33 237

528. quantisque furens se caedibus implet: an evocation of Aeneas' threat: Verg. *Aen.* 8.537 *heu quantae miseris caedes Laurentibus instant.* "Mad with slaughter" is a typical poetic collocation: see 5.172–3 *uideoque furentem / iam Tyria te caede*, Verg. *Aen.* 2.499 *uidi ipse furentem / caede Neoptolemum*, Sen. *Tro.* 446 *nec caede multa qualis in Danaos furens*, etc. For *se implere*, see 13.736 *sitiens se impleuit imago*, Verg. *Aen.* 1.215 *implentur ueteris Bacchi*, Luc. *BC* 9.11–12 *se lumine uero / inpleuit*, etc.; *TLL* 7.1.632.80–633.11.

529. nunc, quaeso, terris descendere non placet Irim: for Iris' descent, see 470n. For the 1+2+2 clausula, see 128n. Spaltenstein observes that *descendere* rarely governs a dative: 13.708 *descendere nocti*, 13.759 *descendisse Erebo*, *Carm. De Bell. Aeg.* 52 *solio descendit*, Stat. *Theb.* 11.464 *descensuram Erebo*; *TLL* 5.1.644.26.

530–1. quamquam ego non Teucros (nostro cum pignore regnet / Roma, et Palladio sedes hac urbe locarim): Dasius relates the myth of the Palladium at 13.30–81, where, see van der Keur's notes. Spaltenstein suggests that *pignore* implies the *Palladium*, since the Palladium was the *pignus imperii* (Cic. *Scaur.* 48, Livy 5.52.7, 26.27.14, etc.), and/or "avec ma garantie (de paix)," which I have opted for. For the phrase *locare sedes*, see Lucr. *DRN* 5.1188 *in caeloque deum sedis et templa locarunt*, Verg. *Aen.* 1.247–8 *sedesque locauit / Teucrorum*, etc.

532. non Teucros delere aderam: the phrasing evokes Aletes' prayer right before the disastrous night raid of Nisus and Euryalus: Verg. *Aen.* 9.247–8 *di patrii, quorum semper sub numine Troiast, / non tamen omnino Teucros delere paratis.* The allusion suggests how both moments seem like the end for the Aeneadae, whether for the Virgilian Trojans confined in their camp or for Silius' Romans currently being massacred at Cannae.

Wills 1996: 67 identifies the repetition of *non Teucros* as a "resumption," which he attributes to "a rise in the use of the parenthesis" in Silver Latin poetry, as at 2.338–9 *mortalem, mihi crede, licet formidine turpi / frigida corda premant, mortalem sumimus hostem* (with my note), 3.425–6 *letique deus, si credere fas est, / causa fuit leti miserae deus*, 16.73–4 *ecce trahebatur lucemque (heu dulcia caeli / lumina!) captiuus lucem inter uincla petebat.* See 39n. for *delere* of death in battle. *TLL* 2.916.49 lists only Tert. *Apol.* 22 for *adesse* with an infinitive of goal.

532–3. sed lumen alumnae / Hannibalem Libyae: for a hero as a *lumen* that can be extinguished (534n.), see 6.129–30 *donec dis Italae uisum est exstinguere lumen / gentis* (Regulus), Cic. *Phil.* 5.39 *imperi populi Romani lumen*, Val. Max. 5.8.4 *lumen ac decus patriae*, Vell. 2.52.3 *alterum Romani imperii lumen*, etc. Spaltenstein suggests interpreting *alumnae…Libyae* with Marsus as "quae me aluit," as if an equivalent of 11.182 *Marmarico…alumno*. *TLL* 1.1798.51 offers this sense ("nutrix, patrona"), but only lists late ancient texts as examples. Libya is the birthplace of both Hannibal and Pallas, who was born from Lake Tritonis

238 *Commentary Lines 533–8*

(439n.). Another possible interpretation, then, would be viewing Libya as Pallas' protégée, like Delos for Apollo.

533–4. pelli florentibus annis / uita: for "flourishing years," see 15.69–70, 16.669; Stat. *Silv.* 3.3.127, 3.5.23, etc.

534. atque extingui primordia tanta negabam: *extingui* resumes the image suggested by 532n. *lumen*, as at 6.129–30 (quoted at 532–3n. above).

535–41. Juno resumes and amplifies Minerva's complaint: Jupiter should show the other gods his power by destroying Carthage with his thunderbolt. Spaltenstein observes that Juno is "ironique et amère," like the Iliadic Hera, who makes a similarly sarcastic offer to Zeus to destroy her three beloved Greek cities so long as he permits the destruction of Troy (Hom. *Il.* 4.50–67). Statius' Juno makes a similar offer at *Theb.* 1.260–2. Silius' Juno does not abandon her resistance until forced to at 17.357–69, whereupon Jupiter graciously concedes *do spatium muris, ut uis, Carthaginis altae* (17.371).

535. excipit hinc Iuno longique laboris ab ira: Delz's certain correction *hinc* (*haec ω, hic Γ²O*) is drawn from 6.430 *excipit inde* and VF *Arg.* 5.672 *excipit hinc*. Note also Caes. *BG* 7.3.2 *hinc alii deinceps excipiunt et proximis tradunt* and (in a non-speech context) Verg. *Aen.* 9.762–3 *Gygen…excipit, hinc…ingerit hastas.* As part of a speech formula, see also Verg. *Aen.* 4.114 *tum sic excepit regia Iuno.*

"Long labor" is a common poetic phrase (5.579, 15.718) which often serves as a generic reference to the subject matter of epic, and/or Juno's anger in particular. See Silius' reference to Hannibal's future deeds (1.139 *latent casus longique labores*) or Dido's memory of Aeneas' recollection of his wanderings (8.138 *narrantem longos se peruigilante labores*); 5.579 refers to the veteran Labicus' advanced age. Compare also the long journey of Virgil's Aeneadae (Verg. *Aen.* 3.160 *longumque fugae ne linque laborem*) or Statius' praise of his wife's patience with his epic composition: Stat. *Silv.* 3.5.35–6 *longi tu sola laboris / conscia.* For Juno's programmatic *ira*, the cause of the *Punica*, as of the *Aeneid*, see 1.38–9 *iamque deae cunctas sibi belliger induit iras / Hannibal.*

536. 'immo,' ait 'ut noscant gentes, immania quantum / regna Iouis ualeant': Juno sarcastically echoes the words that Jupiter used to threaten Pallas at 478n. *aegide praecellant quantum horrida fulmina nosces.* The phrasing may also evoke Statius' minor theomachy between Hippomedon and the river Ismenus: Stat. *Theb.* 9.484–5 *quantum ira deusque ualebat, / impulit adsurgens.*

537–8. cunctisque potentia quantum / antistet, coniunx, superis tua: an elegant periphrasis in synchysis for the prosaic phrase *quantum posse*; contrast, e.g., 5.92–3 *improba quantum / hoc possit Fortuna loco*, 12.512 *et quantum humani possunt se tendere passus.* The repetition of the ending *-ia quantum* in 536 and 537 does not attract the attention of Wills 1996. The echo of similar sounds emphasizes the familiarity and repetitiveness of Juno's complaints throughout

Commentary Lines 538–41   239

the epic tradition. The verb *antistare* does not occur in poetry before Silius; see also 11.65 *antistat cunctis praecellens Virrius ore.* Juno addresses her brother and husband as *coniunx,* and he will address her similarly at 547n.

538–9. disice telo / flagranti (nil oramus) Carthaginis arces: Juno sarcastically goads Jupiter to raze her beloved Carthage; Jupiter instead sends his thunderbolts against Hannibal in order to deter him from conquering Rome after victory at Cannae. Hannibal visualizes Jupiter's thunder first in a dream immediately after the battle: 10.360–2 *ipse refulgebat Tarpeiae culmine rupis / elata torquens flagrantia fulmina dextra / Iuppiter, et lati fumabant sulphure campi.* When he actually approaches Rome, Jupiter sends a massive thunderstorm and strikes Hannibal's shield with his lightning bolt (12.622–6); see Chaudhuri 2014: 245–6. *Telo / flagranti* is an evocation of the Virgilian Jupiter's characteristic behavior during thunderstorms: Verg. *Geo.* 1.331–3 *ille flagranti / aut Atho aut Rhodopen aut alta Ceraunia telo / deicit;* cf. Germ. *Arat.* frg. 4.106 *flagrantis teli mortalia lumina uincet.*

Interpreters differ on the force of *nil.* My translation "We beg you for nothing" substantially follows Duff's "I beg for no mercy." Volpilhac-Lenthéric's "Ma prière n'est rien" and Spaltenstein's "Ce que je demande n'est qu'une bagatelle" offer different emphasis. The clausula of 539 appears in this form twelve times in Silius (1.693, 2.406 with my note, 3.138, 4.472, etc.); see Manil. *Astr.* 4.40, Ov. *Fasti* 6.45, Luc. *BC* 4.585, Claud. *Cons. Stil.* 1.343, etc.

540–1. Sidoniamque aciem uasto telluris hiatu / Tartareis immerge uadis: defeated soldiers at Trebia long to be swallowed up in "a chasm of the earth" (4.330 *terraeque optantur hiatus*) to avoid cowardly deaths. The chasm is common in epic: 12.128 *laxat et horrendos aperit telluris hiatus,* 14.239 *hic specus ingentem laxans telluris hiatum,* Ov. *Her.* 3.63, Luc. *BC* 5.82, Petr. *Sat.* 121.101 *conatus rupto tellurem soluit hiatu,* VF *Arg.* 7.604, Stat. *Theb.* 11.175 *telluris hiatus,* etc. For the chasm's path to Tartarus, see Sen. *Tro.* 179–80 *et hiatus Erebi peruium ad superos iter / tellure fracta praebet,* [Sen.] *Oct.* 593 *tellure rupta Tartaro gressum extuli,* Stat. *Theb.* 8.19–20 *telluris hiatu / Tartara,* etc. The motif's ubiquity accordingly suggests the unlikelihood of any specific connection with Stat. *Theb.* 1.184 *fraternasque acies fetae telluris hiatu* or with the particular fate of Statius' Amphiaraus.

541. aut obrue ponto: a comparable fate destroyed the Carthaginian victims of the First Punic War: 4.79–80 *quae mersa sub aequor / Aegatis inter uasto iacet obruta ponto.* Spaltenstein suggests that the present reference to drowning in the ocean is either:

(a) the poet's typical geographic license ("Cannes est, pour un poète tout au moins, proche de la mer"), as at, e.g., 468–9n.

(b) part of an opposition "mécanique" between earth and sea.

240 *Commentary Lines 542–6*

I would suggest that the point is rather a continuation of the Vulturnus episode's adaptation of Virgil's Aeolus scene. Virgil's Juno uses similar language as she instructs Aeolus to drown the Aeneadae: Verg. *Aen.* 1.69–70 *submersasque obrue puppis / aut age diuersos et dissice corpora ponto.*

542–50. Jupiter keeps calm and informs the emotionally disturbed goddesses that they are fighting uselessly against Fate. Scipio will soon triumph, and Hannibal will wish he had not crossed the Alps. The speech is an adaptation of the Virgilian *parce metu* type scene, discussed by Hershkowitz 1997.

542. contra quae miti respondet Iuppiter ore: the stately spondees of the first four feet emphasize Jupiter's characteristic serenity. The multiple caesurae coinciding with the foot boundaries further slow the line. See Verg. *Aen.* 1.255 *uultu, quo caelum tempestatesque serenat,* Ov. *Met.* 8.703 *talia tum placido Saturnius edidit ore,* Stat. *Theb.* 1.202 *placido quatiens tamen omnia uultu,* etc.

543. certatis fatis et spes extenditis aegras: when sending Iris to restrain Pallas, Jupiter observes that the gods cannot fight against fate: see 475n. *nec speret fixas Parcarum uertere leges.* For the motif, see 5.76 *heu fatis superi certare minores.* Statius' Jupiter berates the gods in a comparable scene (Stat. *Theb.* 3.239–43). He accuses them of competing (*Theb.* 3.241 *certetis*) to persuade him and reminds them the war's fate has been fixed: 3.242–3 *manet haec ab origine mundi / fixa dies bello.*

Spaltenstein correctly observes that *TLL* 5.2.1979.24 has classified this sense of *extendere* incorrectly as "facere, ut…spes…in longum tempus spectet," along with Verg. *Geo.* 2.405 *curas uenientem extendit in annum.* It is rather in the sense of "prolonger," and the goddesses "entretiennent un espoir vain." The phrase *spes aegrae* does not occur before Silius and then not again till Claud. *Hon. nupt.* 14 *incusat spes aegra moras;* see *TLL* 1.942.7. It is a variation of more common phrases such as *mens aegra* (6.205, 7.726, 11.120, etc.) or *animus aeger* (8.108, Ov. *Rem.* 129, Stat. *Theb.* 8.531, etc).

544. ille, o nata, libens cui tela inimica ferebas: *ferre* is *simplex pro composito* for *inferre,* as also at 518n.; see *TLL* 6.1.1541.49. *Tela inimica* is a Virgilian phrase: Verg. *Aen.* 8.117, 11.809.

545–6. contundet iuuenis Tyrios ac nomina gentis / induet: Jupiter foretells that his son Scipio will acquire the cognomen *Africanus* from the present war. The pairing recapitulates Proteus' prophecy: 7.491 *huic Carthago armis, huic Africa nomine cedet.* See also 17.626 *deuictae referens primus cognomina terrae,* Livy 30.45.6 *Africani cognomen militaris.* The evocation of Verg. *Aen.* 1.263–4 *populosque ferocis / contundet* aligns Scipio with Aeneas. For "smashing" peoples, see also 4.706 *contundere gentem.* The clausula is common; it appears in this form at Ov. *Met.* 13.33, Mart. 7.32.1; in varied cases at *Pun.* 17.609, Verg. *Aen.* 1.533, 3.166, etc. For *induere* of acquiring a name, see Livy 6.18.14 *ego me* *patronum profiteor plebis, quod mihi cura mea et fides nomen induit,* Flor. *Epit.* 1.5 *ut captum oppidum Gnaeus Marcius Coriolanus quasi Numantiam aut Africam nomini indueret.*

Delz accepts Bothe's conjecture for the present word order *iuuenis Tyrios.* ω read *Tyrios iuuenis,* which would require lengthening of the final short syllable of nominative *iuuenĭs.* Müller 1861: 332 observes that Silius has license for this lengthening *in arsi* before a caesura from over fifty examples in Virgil. See, e.g., Austin on Verg. *Aen.* 4.64, Norden 1903: 439–41. Courtney 1989: 53 countered that "since Silius goes out of his way to avoid such lengthening by morphological innovation at 3.405 [*Palladio Baetēs umbratus cornua ramo*], it should probably not be accepted" here. The same lengthening *in arsi* occurs, however, at 2.70 *manus,* 16.543 *mucro.*

546. et Libycam feret in Capitolia laurum: Jupiter completes a *tricolon abundans* narrating the deeds that Scipio will complete in the course of the *Punica.* For Scipio's victory laurel, see Virtus' prophecy: 15.119–20 *superare manu laurumque superbam / in gremio Iouis excisis deponere Poenis.* The line again recapitulates Proteus' prophecy: see 7.493 *et cinerem Libyae ferat in Capitolia uictor.* For the clausula, see Luc. *BC* 1.287 *aut sacras poscunt Capitolia laurus.* For laurels named for foreign victories, see Tib. *Eleg.*1.7.7 *uictrices laurus,* Ov. *Am.* 2.12.1 *triumphales...laurus,* Mart. *Epig.* 7.6.10 *Sarmaticae laurus,* Stat. *Silv.* 4.1.41 *Indica laurus,* etc.

547. at, cui tu, coniunx, cui das animosque decusque: Jupiter returns his wife's address as *coniunx* at 537n. The same exchange of addresses occurs when these gods discuss Carthage's ultimate fate. Jupiter asks *da noscere, coniunx* (17.344) and Juno replies *et soror et coniunx oro* (17.365). In a better mood, though still endeavoring to restrain Hannibal, Jupiter also recalls that Juno is his sister as well as his wife: 12.693–4 *coniunxque sororque / cara mihi.*

For the repetition of the relative pronoun, see 15.508 *quos Roma, inquit, quos altius* and Wills 1996: 87. For *animum dare,* see 10.218, 17.112–13, Verg. *Aen.* 9.144, Ov. *Met.* 5.47, etc.; for *decus dare,* see 1.3 *da, Musa, decus memorare laborum,* 12.363–4, Verg. *Aen.* 12.83, Ov. *Fasti* 3.86, etc.; *TLL* 5.1.246.43–6.

548. (fata cano) auertet populis Laurentibus arma: Jupiter's words are identical to those of Paulus at 61n. and so create a strong contrast between the god's authority and the human being's effort at irony. It is noteworthy that Jupiter has returned to *singing* oral *fata* ("that which has been spoken") rather than unrolling its written scrolls, as at Verg. *Aen.* 1.262 *et uoluens fatorum arcana mouebo,* or consulting it in a *tabularium,* as at Ov. *Met.* 15.807–15. Jupiter earlier foretold Hannibal's downfall at 3.590–2. In this respect he resembles his Homeric counterpart more closely than his Roman predecessors.

For *auertere* without accompanying preposition, see 344n., 520n. Spaltenstein suggests that *populis* could be a dative, as at 13.457–8 *fesso mihi.../ lux...equos auertit.* For *populis Laurentibus,* see 16.255, 16.678, Verg. *Aen.* 6.891.

242   *Commentary Lines 549–55*

549. nec longe cladis metae: Spaltenstein's remark on the originality of this phrase is apposite: "Sil. a condensé deux idées, celle de la carrière achevée (pour quoi 'meta' est habituel) et celle du désastre pour obtenir cette tournure inattendue." In the context of fate, it recalls phrases such as 5.406–7 *sed non augurio Parcarum impellere metas / concessum cuiquam*, Verg. *Aen.* 12.546 *mortis… metae*; it further reverses Ov. *Met.* 10.664 *metaque erat longe*. The phrase also has a metapoetic dimension: the *Punica* establishes Cannae as the *meta* between Saguntum and Zama; see Introduction, section 4a.

549. uenit hora diesque: *uenit dies* derives from the Virgilian episode in which Panthus announces the fall of Troy to Aeneas: Verg. *Aen.* 2.324–5 *uenit summa dies et ineluctabile tempus / Dardaniae*. This narrative moment fulfills the predictions of Homer's Agamemnon and Hector: *Il.* 4.164–5, 6.448–9 ἔσσεται ἦμαρ ὅταν ποτ᾽ ὀλώλῃ Ἴλιος ἱρὴ / καὶ Πρίαμος καὶ λαὸς ἐυμμελίω Πριάμοιο. Lucan adapts the phrase for the battle of Pharsalus, his epic's equivalent of the fall of Troy; an unnamed augur reports *uenit summa dies, geritur res maxima* (Luc. *BC* 7.195).

Silius unites epic and historiographical tradition brilliantly by attributing *uenit dies* to Jupiter in the context of Scipio's fate at Cannae, Rome's worst moment. Polybius reports that Scipio Aemilianus quoted the Iliadic lines to him upon witnessing the destruction of Carthage in 146 BC (Polybius 38.22 = App. *Pun.* 132). Silius restores the words to a more authoritative speaker than a human prophet and makes them pertain to Carthage, as they did for Polybius.

550. qua nullas umquam transisse optauerit Alpes: at Virgil's divine council, Jupiter similarly tries to restrain the gods from interfering on the battlefield. He tells them that the Punic Wars will be their appropriate moment for involvement: Verg. *Aen.* 10.11–14 *adueniet iustum pugnae (ne arcessite) tempus, / cum fera Karthago Romanis arcibus olim / exitium magnum atque Alpis immittet apertas: / tum certare odiis, tum res rapuisse licebit*. Silius' Jupiter now presents an ironic reversal of the Virgilian Jupiter's words. We appear to have arrived at the *iustum pugnae… tempus* predicted in the *Aeneid*; yet Jupiter is still telling Juno and Pallas to hold off, and that Hannibal will regret his crossing of the Alps.

551–5. Jupiter sends Iris again, this time to recall Mars. Spaltenstein asks a pertinent question: "Pourquoi Jupiter intervient-il seulement maintenant et non plus tôt, aux vers 470 sqq.?" We should not default, as Spaltenstein does, to the assumption of compositional ineptitude. The two dispatches of Iris reflect the balanced focus that the episode has maintained upon the two champions, Hannibal and Scipio. They also serve to characterize Silius' Jupiter and the relationship between epic and history. Jupiter is concerned to keep fate on its destined path by keeping Hannibal safe from Scipio and Scipio safe from Vulturnus, while still making sure that the Romans experience a massive defeat at Cannae.

Commentary Lines 551–60 243

551–2. sic ait atque Irim propere demittit Olympo / quae reuocet Martem iubeatque abscedere pugna: the phrasing deliberately recapitulates 471–2n. *demittit propere succinctam nubibus Irim, / quae... frenet* in order to emphasize the parallel between Jupiter's two dispatches of Iris. *Abscedere pugna* varies the more frequent *excedere pugna*.

553–4. nec uetitis luctatus abit Gradiuus in altas / cum fremitu nubes: the parallelism with Iris' earlier mission emphasizes the contrast in behavior of Mars and Pallas. Pallas initially rejected Iris' command (479–80n. *dubitans... / nec sat certa diu... an cederet*). Mars, on the other hand, obeys his father promptly, and thereby exemplifies the *pietas* that characterizes his children, the Roman people. *Cum fremitu* accordingly refers, as Zaia observes, to Mars' traditional battle cry rather than a cry of protest. Thus, Duff's translation "loudly protesting" and Volpilhac-Lentheric's "grommelant" should be rejected. *Altae* is a traditional epithet of *nubes*: 5.482, Lucr. *DRN* 6.479–80, Verg. *Geo.* 1.364, *TLL* 1.1774.53, etc.

554–5. quamquam lituique tubaeque / uulneraque et sanguis et clamor et arma iuuarent: Mars is traditionally obsessed with war, and his name itself is a metonym for combat (*OLD* s.v. 2). The battle polysyndeton continues at 559–60n. and evokes an earlier description of Mars' "insane work"; see 6.6–10 *insani Mauortis opus: simul arma uirique / ac mixtus sonipes dextraeque in uulnere caesi / haerentes hostis, passim clipeique iubaeque / atque artus trunci capitum fractusque iacebat / ossibus in duris ensis.* The naval battle at Syracuse features similar polysyndeton: 14.557–8 *hinc clamor, gemitus illinc mortesque fugaeque / remorumque fragor flictuque sonantia rostra.* See also Hor. *Carm.* 1.2.38 *quem iuuat clamor galeaeque leues* with Nisbet and Hubbard's note, and VF *Arg.* 3.84 *ingentes animae clamorque tubaeque.*

556–60. Hannibal rallies his troops as Mars departs the field.

556–7. ut patuit liber superum certamine tandem / laxatusque deo campus: the field is relieved from the gods' tremendous weight, on which, see 447–50n. The collocation of *patuit, liber,* and *laxatus* represents Silius' characteristically abundant style. Silius adds the further term *liber* to collocations of *laxare* and *patere* introduced to poetry by Seneca: see Sen. *Med.* 376–7 *Oceanus uincula rerum / laxet et ingens pateat tellus, Oed.* 582–3 *subito dehiscit terra et immenso sinu / laxata patuit.*

The phrase *patere campus* encloses a lengthy unit. Appearing again at 12.382, it is a Virgilian phrase (Verg. *Geo.* 4.77, *Aen.* 5.552, 12.710) that later poets adapt: Ov. *Met.* 6.218, Luc. *BC* 4.19, Stat. *Theb.* 4.434, Claud. *Mall. Theod.* 262, etc. For *laxare campum,* see 6.319 *laxabat ferro campum.*

557–8. ruit aequore ab imo / Poenus, quo sensim caelestia fugerat arma: the initial phrase adapts Verg. *Aen.* 12.614 *interea extremo bellator in aequore*

244   *Commentary Lines 559–63*

Turnus and thereby evokes Juturna's rescue of her brother Turnus from a potentially fatal combat. *TLL* 7.1.1402.61 "de regionibus" similarly interprets *imo* as *extremo*, as at [Ov.] *Nux* 62 *imus...fundus*. *OLD* s.v. *sensim* offers "slowly" or "cautiously," as reflected in Duff's translation "step by step" and Vinchesi's "lentamente;" Volpilhac-Lentheric's "sans qu'on s'en fût aperçu" is accordingly excessive. For *fugerat arma,* see 426–7n. Spaltenstein finds *fugerat* extravagant, as "Sil. dit seulement qu'Annibal avait reculé pas à pas," and a further "incohérence," because Hannibal did not actually run but was divinely transported by Pallas. As Zaia observes, such imprecisions are characteristic of epic and part of Silius' goal of "efficacia scenica e narrativa." For the collocation *caelestia arma,* see Ov. *Fasti* 3.259–60, similarly referring to Mars.

559–60. These lines survey the four components of Hannibal's army: cavalry, infantry, elephants, and artillery.

559. magna uoce trahens equitemque uirosque feraeque: for the battle polysyndeton, see 554–5n. For *uiros* as *pedites* to be distinguished from *equites,* see Hor. *Carm.* 1.15.9–10 *quantus equis, quantus adest uiris / sudor,* Livy 21.27.1 *equites uirique,* Cic. *Off.* 3.116 *uiris equisque.*

560. turrigerae molem tormentorumque labores: a four-word line that does not feature a lengthy Greek adjective or patronymic. The final two words' repetition of *-ōr-,* emphasized by the coincidence of ictus and accent, adds further resonance. For the elephant as a *moles* and for its turrets, see 239–40n. Plurals such as 571n. *monstris,* 573n. *boues* show that Silius anachronistically envisions a force of several elephants. *Molem* accordingly is a collective noun, as at 17.649 *confecta mole Gigantum.*

561–9. Before killing him, Hannibal taunts Minucius with his rescue by Fabius at Gerunium, the result of his foolhardy assault (7.515–750). Livy lists Minucius among the fatalities at Cannae (Livy 22.49.16). Through this invented scene of confrontation with Hannibal, Silius strengthens the intratextual relationship with the Gerunium episode. Varro makes an even more destructive decision to give battle at Cannae, despite the earlier examples of Flaminius and Minucius, and warnings from Fabius and Paulus. At Cannae, however, Fabius will not be around to save Minucius, and so he perishes along with the entire Roman army. See Introduction, section 4b.

561–2. atque ubi turbantem leuiores ense cateruas / agnouit iuuenem: for the chiastic word order, see Flammini 1983. For *cateruas,* see 77n.

562–3. scintillauitque cruentis / ira genis: the description of Hannibal's anger evokes Pallas' blood-red eyes: see 444n. For Hannibal's superhuman facial expressions, see 5.603 *sic memorans torquet fumantem ex ore uaporem.* The phrasing evokes Virgil's ekphrasis of Turnus' rage: Verg. *Aen.* 12.101–2 *totoque*

Commentary Lines 563–9   245

ardentis ab ore / scintillae obsistunt, oculis micat acribus ignis. For flashing eyes as a sign of rage, see Sen. *Ira* 1.1.4 *flagrant ac micant oculi*, Persius 3.117 *ira / scintillant oculi*, etc.

563–4. quaenam Furiae quisue egit in hostem, / en, Minuci, deus: Hannibal's taunt echoes the derisive comments that others have earlier aimed at him. As he assaults Saguntum, Daunus asks: 1.443–4 *quaenam te, Poene, paternae / huc adigunt Furiae?* At the Carthaginian council, Hanno similarly accuses Hannibal of being goaded by his father's Furies: see 2.296 *exagitant manes iuuenem Furiaeque paternae* with my note.

564–5. 'ut rursus te credere nobis / auderes?' inquit: for *credere audere* in the context of combat, see Verg. *Aen.* 5.383 *si nemo audet se credere pugnae, Aen.* 9.42 *neu struere auderent aciem neu credere campo*, etc.

565–6. genitor tibi natus ab armis / ille meis ubi nunc Fabius?: Minucius and his troops hailed Fabius as their father after their rescue at Gerunium: see 7.737 *sancte…genitor*, 7.734–5 *ibat ouans Fabiumque decus Fabiumque salutem / certatim et magna memorabant uoce parentem* with Littlewood's notes, and 8.2–3 *Romana parentem / solum castra uocant* with Ariemma's note. Spaltenstein correctly objects to Duff's "saved you" as "fantaisiste." For use of *ille* as part of a contrast with a prior state of being, see 126n.

566–7. semel, improbe, nostras / sit satis euasisse manus: *semel* recapitulates the point of 564 *rursus*, and *improbe*, in its meanings of "immoderate" or "shameless" (*OLD* s.v. 5a, 7), reinforces the point. To have once escaped from Hannibal and live is more than Minucius or anyone could have hoped for, and to face him again appears to show unreasonable arrogance. There is an implicit contrast with Scipio, who faced Hannibal once before at Ticinus and will face him again at Zama. For *euasisse manus,* see 113–14n.

567–8. atque inde superbis / hasta comes dictis: for warriors who accompany their words with their missiles, see 4.134–5 *tum dictis comitem contorquet primus in hostis /…hastam*, 4.281–3 *inquit et una / contorquet…/ trabem*, Verg. *Aen.* 12.266 *dixit, et aduersos telum contorsit in hostis*, Ov. *Met.* 8.408 *dixit et aerata torsit graue cuspide cornum*, etc.

568–9. murali turbine pectus / transforat et uoces uenturas occupat ictu: Hannibal throws his javelin with the force of a ballista. The motif recalls Virgil's comparison of Aeneas' cast in the final duel of the *Aeneid* to a ballista: Verg. *Aen.* 12.921–3 *murali concita numquam / tormento sic saxa fremunt nec fulmine tanti / dissultant crepitus.* For the ballista in the *Punica*, see 6.269 *donec murali ballista coercuit ictu*, 10.511–12 *perfracti turbine dentes / muralis saxi*, 14.433, etc. *Transforare* occurs only here in poetry; it is presumably an alternative to the far more common *transuerberare* of 593. The clausula of 569 recurs at 10.197.

246 *Commentary Lines 570–5*

570–6. After rallying his other forces, Hannibal sends the elephants into combat. The mahouts goad them swiftly toward engagement with the Roman forces. The elephants were anachronistically introduced during the disposition of Carthaginian forces (237–43n.).

570. nec ferro saeuire sat est: as at 521n., *nec…sat* marks a *Steigerung* in the narrative; the Romans now must face strange monsters and a new mode of combat. For *ferro saeuire*, see, e.g., Verg. *Aen.* 7.461 *saeuit amor ferri*, Sen. *Thy.* 573 *iam minae saeui cecidere ferri*.

570–1. appellitur atra / mole fera: the elephants were described similarly during the crossing of the Rhône: 3.463–4 *territus atras / expauit moles Rhodanus*. For their dark backs, see 240n. Silius plays on the opposition between the animals' dark skin and white tusks (577n. *liuenti*, 581n. *niueis*).

571. et monstris componitur Itala pubes: for the elephants as monsters, see 599n. and 628n. The phrasing evokes Regulus' exhortation to his men in the battle with another massive, terrifying animal, the Bagrada serpent: 6.246–7 *ibo alacer solusque manus componere monstro / sufficiam*. The phrase *componere monstro/is* does not appear before Silius. Prudentius appears to have adapted the phrase from Silius in his poem against Symmachus: Prud. *Symm.* 2.40 *iure poetarum numen componere monstris*. For *pubes,* see 317–18n.

572–3. nam praeuectus equo moderantem cuspide Lucas / Maurum in bella boues stimulis maioribus ire: the phrase *praeuectus equo* occurs four times in Silius; Verg. *Aen.* 7.166, Luc. *BC* 7.342, Livy 10.36.6, 24.44.10, etc. The Romans nicknamed elephants "Lucanian cattle" after encountering them in the war against Pyrrhus: Pliny *NH* 8.16 *elephantos Italia primum uidit Pyrri regis bello et boues Lucas appellauit in Lucanis uisos anno urbis CCCCLXXII*. For the phrase in poetry, see Naev. *carm. frg.* 55.2 Blänsdorf = Varro *LL* 7.39 *prius pariet / lucusta Lucam bouem*, Plaut. *Cas.* 845, Lucr. *DRN* 5.1302, Sen. *Phaed.* 352, etc. "Greater stimuli" refers here literally to the goads employed by the mahouts, but also registers the battle's rising fury. Silius' North African ethnonyms are typically generic; see 10–11n. For the phrase, see Luc. *BC* 4.174–5 *stimulis maioribus ardens /…amor*, Stat. *Theb.* 11.497 *accensae stimulis maioribus irae*, etc.

574. ac raptare iubet Libycarum armenta ferarum: *raptare* functions as a poetic alternative for *rapere*; see Bömer's note on Ov. *Met.* 12.223. The clausula adapts Lucretius' frequent clausula *armenta feraeque*: Lucr. *DRN* 2.343, 2.922, 4.1197, etc.

575. immane stridens agitur: the adverbial use of *immane* typically occurs, as here, in poetic contexts referring to loud sounds: 4.297 *immane sonans*, 10.205 *stridens immane*, 11.244–5 *immane…infremuit*, etc.; Verg. *Geo.* 3.239 *immane sonat*, etc.; *TLL* 7.1.441.58. Lengthenings before a double consonant (*immanē stridens*) are relatively rare in post-Augustan poetry; see Courtney 1980: 53.

Commentary Lines 575–82   247

Compare 10.205 *immanē procella*, 12.209 *ne quā spes*, 17.546 *diuersā spatio*; cf.
Luc. *BC* 5.118 *quippē stimulis*, Stat. *Theb.* 6.551 *agilē studium*; see Müller 1861:
320 for lists. These parallels provide adequate justification for modern editors
to reject the conjectures of Livineius (*immani*) and Blass (*immanis*).

575–6. crebroque coacta / uulnere bellatrix properos fert belua gressus: as at
572 *moderantem cuspide* and 573 *stimulis*, the mahout goads the elephant with
his spear to make it run faster. For *bellatrix*, see 221n. For *properos…gressus*,
see Sen. *Oed.* 202 *propero…gressu*, VF *Arg.* 4.176, etc.

577–83. As the elephants advance, their riders hurl missiles at the Roman
ranks. Spears fastened to the elephants' tusks further threaten the Romans.

577–8. liuenti dorso turris flammaque uirisque / et iaculis armata sedet: for
the elephants' turrets, see 239n. *Liuenti* resumes 570n. *atra*. Liberman 2006: 22
objects to 579 *arma* immediately after *armata* and proposes *aptata* in its place.
Such redundancy may have been licensed, however, by passages in earlier
poetry such as Ov. *Met.* 5.197–9 *'et prosternite humi iuuenem magica arma
mouentem!' / incursurus erat: tenuit uestigia tellus, / inmotusque silex armataque
mansit imago*, Sen. *Phaed.* 545–7 *et ramos rudes / uertere in arma: non erat
gracili leuis / armata ferro cornus*. Similar examples can be found in prose: Cic.
Sest. 35 *arma essent in templis, armati in foro*, Livy 9.12.8, 24.10.11, etc.

578–9. procul aspera grando / saxorum super arma ruit: the "hailstorm of
missiles" motif appeared earlier in the assault on Saguntum: see 2.38 *et densa
resonant saxorum grandine turres* with my note. Battlefield missiles are often
compared to a storm; examples include Hom. *Il.* 12.154–61, 278–89, Enn. *Ann.*
266 Skutsch *fit ferreus imber*. Virgil compares the missiles aimed at Aeneas
during his rampage to a shower of hail: Verg. *Aen.* 10.803–4 *si quando grandine
nimbi / praecipitant*.

579–80. passimque uolanti / celsus telorum fundit Libys aggere nimbum:
Van Veen remarks "elephantos passim volare absurdius mihi videtur," and proposed *uolantem*; cf. 2.125 *illa* [i.e., *cornus*] *uolans*, 17.134 *hasta uolans*. Silius
uses *uolanti*, however, in the same deliberately oxymoronic sense as 240n.
mobilis agger, as neither elephants nor ramparts move quickly. For the "cloud of
missiles" motif, see 11–12n.

581–2. stat niueis longum stipata per agmina uallum / dentibus: Silius adapts
Lucretius' famous image of the palisade of elephant tusks: Lucr. *DRN* 2.537–8
India…/ uallo munitur eburno; see Brown 1991. He combines this passage with
Virgil's description of a line of armed men: Verg. *Aen.* 2.333–4 *stat ferri acies
mucrone corusco / stricta*. Meurig Davies 1951: 155 envisions that "the Ivory
Vallum (cf. 'the thin red line') for the elephants ranged in battle-line may have
been proverbial in Roman military lore since the wars against Pyrrhus and
Carthage," but this is fanciful.

248　　　　　　　　　*Commentary Lines 582–5*

For initial *stare*, see 252n. *Dens* is the normal word for elephant tusk: 16.205 *niuei nunc munera dentis*, Luc. *BC* 10.144 *dentibus... niueis*; *TLL* 5.1.538.44. For the chiastic word order, see Introduction, section 5c and Flammini 1983.

582–3. atque ebori praefixa comminus hasta / fulget ab incuruo derecta cacumine cuspis: Arrian describes the practice of attaching lances to the war elephant's tusks: Arr. *Tact.* 2.4 τῶν δὲ καὶ οἱ ὀδόντες σιδήρῳ ὀξεῖ ὡπλισμένοι ἦσαν. 585n. *sceleratum... dentem* and 589n. *spicula dentis* continue the reference to this combination. See *TLL* 5.2.19.36 for classification of this usage of *ebori* "de... elephanti dente vivo"; cf. Cic. *Verr.* 2.5.103 *dentes eburneos*, Livy 37.59.3, etc.

Cellarius argued that lances were attached to the elephants' turrets ("machinae, quam elephas portabat") and that *incuruo... cacumine* accordingly referred to the elephants' curved backs. Thilo 1891: 623 correctly dismissed this image, but conjectured *utque* to suggest that the tusks themselves acted like a curved lance. Summers 1900: 305, followed by Meurig Davies 1951: 154, observed that the reading *atque* is correct, as the lances were affixed to the elephants' tusks "so that what the tusks failed to pierce, the spear might reach."

For the clausula *comminus hasta*, see VF *Arg.* 6.347, 6.518, Coripp. *Ioh.* 5.114, 5.340. For *fulgere* of an elephant's tusks, see Flor. *Epit.* 1.24.16 *elephantis..., auro purpura argento et suo ebore fulgentibus, aciem utrimque uallauerat*, Amm. Marc. 25.1.14 *post hos elephantorum fulgentium formidandam speciem et truculentus hiatus*. Zaia observes that *fulgere* may also suggest a *figura etymologica* on the phrase *Lucas bos* (on which, see 572–3n.). Varro derives *Lucas* from *lux*: *LL* 7.40 *quare ego arbitror potius lucas ab luce, quod longe relucebant propter inauratos regios clupeos, quibus eorum tum ornatae erant turres.*

584–6. An elephant hoists Ufens on its tusks.

584. hic, inter trepidos rerum, per membra, per arma: Silius previously used the phrase *trepidi rerum* to describe the Saguntines' terror at Hannibal's solo approach to the walls. See 2.234 *dum pauitant trepidi rerum fessique salutis* with my note, and Verg. *Aen.* 12.589 *trepidae rerum*. The unfamiliar elephants cause similar terror. For the clausula, see similar collocations at 15.686 *transfixum telo per membra, per arma*, Stat. *Theb.* 10.476 *per et arma et membra iacentum*, etc.

585. exigit Vfentis sceleratum belua dentem: Hannibal earlier killed another Ufens at the Trebia (4.337–42). The name evokes the Ufens, a river in the Volscian territory (8.381–2 *turbidus.../ Vfens*). Silius' usages reflect Virgil's, who similarly mentions both the warrior (*Aen.* 7.745 *Vfens, insignem fama et felicibus armis*) and the river (*Aen.* 7.801–2 *gelidus.../ Vfens*).

Silius names many characters after rivers; see 1.152 *Tagum*, 1.407 *Bagrada*, 1.438 *Galaesum*, 2.112 *Lixum* with my note, etc. See Spaltenstein's note to 1.152 for a complete list, and for discussion, see Cowan 2009 and Jones 2005. For Silius' other uses of toponyms as personal names, see 380n. For *exigere* "de armis adigendis," see 1.307, 1.515 *exigit ensem*, 5.294 *exigit ictum*, Verg. *Aen.* 10.682, etc.; *TLL* 5.2.1451.52. For *sceleratum...dentem*, see 582–3n.

586. clamantemque ferens calcata per agmina portat: the combination of *ferens* and *portat* is characteristic of Silius' abundant style, as at 12.443 *tulit portatas...carinas*.

587–90. An elephant's tusk pierces Tadius' armor and hoists him upward. A turreted elephant carrying two soldiers, which has picked up a man with its trunk, appears on an engraved gem, now in the Cabinet de Médailles, Bibliothèque Nationale, Paris. See Charles 2008: 357, Scullard 1974: 245, fig. 245.

587. nec leuius Tadio letum: for the litotes, see, e.g., 3.70 *nec Aeneadum leuior metus*, 4.542, Ov. *Met.* 11.554, etc. Some older editors, such as Drakenborch, adopted the reading *l(a)euum Γ²* and construed it with 588 *latus*.

587–8. qua tegmine thorax / multiplicis lini claudit latus: for linen armor, see 3.271–2 *tempora multiplici mos est defendere lino / et lino munire latus*, 4.291 *multiplicis lini*, Hom. *Il.* 2.529 λινοθώραξ, VF *Arg.* 6.225 *tenuia non illum candentis carbasa lini*, Stat. *Theb.* 9.241 with Dewar's note, etc.

588–9. improba sensim / corpore non laeso penetrarunt spicula dentis: vulnerable Tadius proves his valor in the face of mortal danger. *Improba* resumes the idea of 585n. *sceleratum...dentem*. Spaltenstein suggests the sense "méchante" is preferable to Duff's "persistent." For *improbus* applied to weapons, see 4.386 *improbus ensis*, VF *Arg.* 3.587–8 *improba Mauri / lancea*, Stat. *Theb.* 9.126 *improba* [i.e., *trabes*]; *TLL* 7.1.692.15. *Sensim* increases the sense of terror at the unfamiliar assault. *Corpore non laeso* echoes Ovid's description of the invulnerable Caeneus (Ov. *Met.* 12.172). *Spicula...dentis* refers to the metal points of the lances affixed to the tusks; see 582–3n.

590. et sublime uirum clipeo resonante tulerunt: *sublime...tulerunt* echoes another of the epic's monsters, the serpent of the Bagrada River: 6.235 *nunc sublime rapit* with Fröhlich's note. In a similar example of combat above the human scale, a grappling hook at Syracuse lofts a ship: 14.329 *sustulerant sublime ratem*. For the resonant shield, see Enn. *Ann.* 355 Skutsch *clipei resonunt*.

591–3. Tadius bravely fights back by striking at the elephant's eye. In facing the elephants earlier at Trebia, Fibrenus similarly overcomes fear and displays his *uirtus* in a difficult situation: 4.603–4 *perque aspera duro / nititur ad laudem uirtus interrita cliuo*. He also attacks the elephant's vulnerable eye: 4.610–11 *tum iacit adsurgens dextroque in lumine sistit / spicula saeua ferae telumque in uulnere linquit*.

591. haud excussa noui uirtus terrore pericli: the litotes *haud excussa* resumes 587n. *nec leuius*. There is a possible *figura etymologica* linking *uirtus* to the

250

etymologically related *uirum* of the preceding line. Compare 7.51–2 *numera-rique aspera uirtus / haud est passa uiros*, Verg. *Aen.* 1.566 *uirtutesque uirosque*, Stat. *Theb.* 6.295 *praestantesque uiros uocat ad sua praemia uirtus*, Coripp. *Ioh.* 5.174 *o uirtus, o corda uirum!*, etc. *Noui* recalls the fear caused by the unfamiliar elephants at Trebia: 4.601–2 *Trebiamque insueta timentem / prae se pectore agit*. For the clausula, see 15.135–6 *tacitus tamen aegra pericli / pectora surrepit terror*.

592. utitur ad laudem casu: the Stoic idea that misfortune creates an opportunity to display *uirtus* forms a major theme of the Cannae episode, and of Roman and allied defeat generally in the *Punica*. For the concept, see Stat. *Theb.* 8.421 *casus agit uirtutis opus* with Augoustakis' note.

592–3. geminumque citato / uicinus fronti lumen transuerberat ense: for *citato… ense*, see 4.536 *citat improbus hastam*, 5.284–5 *citato / ense*, 14.436–7 *citatum / missile*, VF *Arg.* 6.198 *aere citato*, etc. For *transuerberat*, see 2.125 with my note.

594–8. The wounded elephant rears and throws its howdah and mahouts to the ground. There is a further echo of the Fibrenus scene, which concludes with a similar collapse: 4.621 *concidit et clausit magna uada pressa ruina*. Silius adapts a moment from a Virgilian battle scene in which a horse rears and throws its rider after a spear wounds it in the temples: Verg. *Aen.* 10.892–4 *tollit se arrectum quadrupes et calcibus auras / uerberat, effusumque equitem super ipse secutus / implicat eiectoque incumbit cernuus armo*. Silius employs the motif once more at Zama, in a scene involving a wounded horse: 17.133–7 *prima in cornipedis sedit spirantibus ignem / naribus hasta uolans erexitque ore cruento / quadrupedem elatis pulsantem calcibus auras. / corruit asper equus confixaque cuspide membra / huc illuc iactans rectorem prodidit hosti*.

594–5. exstimulata graui sese fera tollit ad auras / uulnere et erectis excussam cruribus alte: for the clausula of 594, see Verg. *Aen.* 2.699, 11.455. The description of rearing and throwing the riders employs phrasing typically applied to horses: see 17.134–5 (quoted at 594–8n. above), Verg. *Aen.* 11.639–40 *uulneris impatiens arrecto pectore crura, / uoluitur ille excussus humi*, Livy 8.7.10 *cum equus prioribus pedibus erectis magna ui caput quateret, excussit equitem*, etc.

596. pone iacit uoluens reflexo pondere turrim: for similar language applied to rearing horses, see 2.196 *quadrupedes iactant resupino pondere currum* with my note. *Voluens* evokes Verg. *Aen.* 9.512 *infesto uoluebant pondere*. For the elephant's turrets, see 239n.

597. arma uirique simul spoliataque belua uisu: for the collocation of *arma* and *uir*, see 100n. The similarity of 596–7 to VF *Arg.* 3.442–3 *arma simul uestesque* **uirum** *lustramina ponto /* **pone iacit** is likely the result of recollection of

Commentary Lines 598–603 251

sound patterns, as there is no apparent connection between the narrative contexts.

598. sternuntur subita, miserandum, mixta ruina: a studied combination of alliteration and disrupted rhythms helps the listener to visualize the elephant's ungainly collapse. For *subita ruina*, see 5.550, Ov. *Met.* 1.202, Luc. *BC* 3.579, etc. For exclamatory *miserandum*, see 14.484, 15.246, 17.275. For the clausula, see 10.504 *permixta ruina*, [Verg.] *Aetna* 202 *mixta ruina*, Luc. *BC* 7.655 *miscere ruinae*, etc.

599–604. Varro orders his men to attack the elephants with fire. Florus reports a similar stratagem at Beneventum in the war against Pyrrhus: Flor. *Epit.* 1.18.10 *et in turres uibratae faces tota hostium agmina ardentibus ruinis operuerunt.*

599. spargi flagrantes contra bellantia monstra: the collocation *flagrans/-are* + *taedas* gestures at the scale of the elephant combat. Silius elsewhere applies the collocation to the burning of walls (10.440–1), ships (14.564–5), and Carthage (17.223). It appears elsewhere in poetry only at [Verg.] *Culex* 216. For the elephants as monsters, see 571n.

600. Dardanius taedas ductor iubet et facis atrae: Duff and Delz adopt Barth's suggestion *ductor* in place of *uictor* ω, based on 7.585 *Dardanius…ductor*, 15.242 *ductor Dardanius*, 16.239 *Dardanium…ductorem*, Verg. *Aen.* 10.602–3 *ductor / Dardanius*, etc. See 199n. for the frequent manuscript confusion of *ductor* and *uictor*. Other modern editors (Bauer, Volpilhac-Lenthéric) preserve the manuscript reading *uictor*, whom Volpilhac-Lenthéric identifies as Varro and Ernesti as Tadius. Neither man can accurately be described as a *uictor*, and Tadius is not qualified to give orders. For *ductor*, see 24n. See 128n. for the 1+2+2 clausula.

601. quos fera circumfert, compleri sulphure muros: for the elephants' turrets as *muros*, see 241n. Van Veen objected that *compleri* was "languidissima" and proposed *conspergi* or *comburi*. For sulfur and bitumen (cf. 609n. *bitumine*) as ingredients of fire, see 12.133–5 *tum sulphure et igni / semper anhelantes coctoque bitumine campos / ostentant*, [Verg.] *Aetna* 514 *commixtum lento flagrare bitumine sulphur*, Claud. *VI Cos. Hon.* 325 *sulphure caeruleo nigroque bitumine fumat*, etc.

602. nec iusso mora: for the phrasing, see 13.855–6 *nec Sulla morari / iussa potest*, Verg. *Aen.* 5.749 *haud mora consiliis, nec iussa recusat Acestes*, [Sen.] *Oct.* 439 *iussa haud morabor*, etc.

602–3. collectis fumantia lucent / terga elephantorum flammis: for the chiastic arrangement of nouns and adjectives, see Flammini 1983. For *collectis…flammis*, see 4.305 *dum tacitas uires et flammam colligit ignis*, 17.92–3 *collecti rapidam diffundere pestem / coeperunt ignes*, Juv. 13.146 *colligit ignes*,

252   *Commentary Lines 603–6*

etc.; *TLL* 3.1609.72. Calderini proposed *coniectis* in *Γ*, supported by Heinsius; the cited passages, however, show that the collocation is well attested. *Terga* most likely refers to the elephants' actual backs, rather than functioning as an epic periphrasis like *terga ferarum* (4.561, Verg. *Aen.* 7.20, Ov. *Met.* 14.66, Stat. *Ach.* 1.115, etc.).

603–4. pastusque sonoro / ignis edax uento per propugnacula fertur: Summers argued for *raptus*: "sed pascitur seu nutritur ignis ea re quam consumit." In defense of *pastus*, Delz (app. crit.) compares 14.307 *pascitur adiutus Vulcanus turbine uenti*, Ov. *Rem.* 808 *nutritur uento, uento restinguitur ignis*; a further example would be *Pun.* 17.504–6 *haud secus ac tectis urbis Vulcania pestis / cum sese infudit, rapidusque incendia flatus / uentilat et uolucris spargit per culmina flammas.* Accordingly, *uento* most likely refers to the drafts such as these that characteristically nourish fires; further examples include, e.g., Luc. *BC* 3.501 *rapiensque incendia uentus.* A wind as powerful and malevolent as Vulturnus would blow the Romans' torches out instead.

   For *ignis edax*, see Verg. *Aen.* 2.758, Ov. *Met.* 9.202, 14.541, etc.; for the motif, see Lucr. *DRN* 5.1252–3 *flammeus ardor / … siluas exederat.* See 239n. on *propugnacula.*

605–8. A simile compares the spread of fire to a shepherd setting fires on a mountainside. Silius earlier used the motif to describe Hannibal's ruse at Gerunium: 7.364–6 *feruoribus atris / cum Calabros urunt ad pinguia pabula saltus, / uertice Gargani residens incendia pastor.* The Virgilian model is a simile describing how Pallas' troops combine to support him: *Aen.* 10.405–9 *ac uelut optato uentis aestate coortis / dispersa immittit siluis incendia pastor, / correptis subito mediis extenditur una / horrida per latos acies Volcania campos, / ille sedens uictor flammas despectat ouantis.* The mountainsides ignited by Silius' shepherd evoke the tall elephants, in contrast to Virgil's shepherd, who sets fire to broad fields that more closely resemble the battlefield. See Barchfeld 1880: 23.

605–6. non aliter, Pindo Rhodopeue incendia pastor / cum iacit: for the collocation of Pindus and Rhodope, see 12.658 *et Rhodope Taurusque et Pindus et Atlas.* The mountains occur together in the catalog at Ov. *Met.* 2.222–5, also of a fire (ignited by Phaethon). For these mountains as part of a northern Greek poetic geography, see 2.73 with my note, 3.494, 4.520, 15.771, etc. For the clausula of 605, see the passages quoted at 605–8n. above. For *incendia iacere/ iactare*, see 7.317 *incendia lucent*, Ov. *Met.* 14.539 *iactas incendia*, etc.

606. et siluis spatiatur feruida pestis: the clausula derives from Luc. *BC* 4.370, in a context referring to thirst; see also *BC* 6.96–7, referring to fever. Silius reassigns the phrase to refer to fire. Elsewhere, he characteristically refers to fire as *Vulcania pestis*: see 7.360 (quoted at 607–8n. below), 17.504 (quoted at 603–4n. above), 14.423 *pestis Vulcania*, 17.594. In this passage, he has reassigned the epithet *Vulcanius* to create a different clausula at 608n. *Vulcanius ardor.*

Commentary Lines 607–13   253

607. frondosi ignescunt scopuli: *frondosi scopuli* is a unique collocation, similar to 3.415 *frondosa cacumina montis*, 7.468 *frondosis rupibus*, 10.530 *frondosis... iugis*, etc. The phrasing continues the run of -S- sounds from 606.

607–8. subitoque per alta / collucet iuga dissultans Vulcanius ardor: the phrasing again recalls Gerunium: 7.360 *per iuga, per uallis errat Vulcania pestis*. For *collucere* of fire, see 5.510–11 *contermina taedis / collucet*, Verg. *Aen.* 4.567 *collucere faces, iam feruere litora flammis*. The clausula of 608 derives from VF *Arg.* 4.686 *Vulcanius ardor*; Silius has varied his characteristic phrase *Vulcania pestis* (606n.).

609–19. The burning elephant rushes to the river to put out the flames.

609. it fera candenti torrente bitumine corpus: *it* appears as an initial word fifteen times in the *Punica*. "Semantically strong monosyllables" are typically placed at the beginning of the line; see 2.441 with my note and Skutsch's note on Enn. *Ann.* 431. *Candens* + *corpus* typically refers to a shining white animal: see, e.g., Varro *Men.* 203.1 *candens corpore taurus*, Verg. *Aen.* 9.563 *candenti corpore cycnum*, etc. Silius has adapted the phrase to describe the shining bitumen burning the dark animal. For burning bodies, see 14.213 *ille ubi torreret subiectis corpora flammis*, Ov. *Met.* 12.155 *corpora tosta*, etc. For *bitumine*, see 601n.

610. amens et laxo diducit limite turmas: the inflamed cattle at Gerunium are similarly driven out of their minds: 7.316 *ut passim exsultent stimulante dolore iuuenci*. For *limes* "per multitudinem obstantem," see 1.267 *latus rubet aequore limes*, 4.461–2 *latusque repente / apparet campo limes*, Verg. *Aen.* 10.513–14 *latumque per agmen / ardens limitem agit ferro*, etc.; *TLL* 7.2.1410.74.

611. nec cuiquam uirtus propiora capessere bella: the line is modeled on Verg. *Aen.* 10.712–13 *nec cuiquam irasci propiusue accedere uirtus, / sed iaculis tutisque procul clamoribus instant*. The Virgilian passage also licenses the rare construction of *uirtus* governing an infinitive. Silius adapts other elements of the passage at 5.442–4 *adspirare uiro propioremque addere Martem / haud ausum cuiquam.../ incessebatur tutis ex agmine telis*. The Homeric tradition characteristically suggests that there is less *uirtus* in using ranged weapons, as at Hom. *Il.* 4.105–13, 11.384–95, 13.713 οὐ γάρ σφι σταδίη ὑσμίνη μίμνε φίλον κῆρ, etc.

612. longinquis audent iaculis et harundinis ictu: *longinquis* contrasts with *propiora* of the previous line. The adjective is used differently here from 329n. *contorum longo... ictu*. The *iaculum* is meant to be thrown and so delivers its blow "from far off," while the cavalry lance (*contus*) is not a ranged weapon. The passage recalls Luc. *BC* 3.479 *longinqua ad tela parati / tormenti*. See *TLL* 7.2.1627.26. Silius similarly pairs *iaculum* and *harundo* at 14.520–1 *nec iaculo aut longe certatur harundine fusa / comminus*.

613. uritur impatiens: the adjective *impatiens* can be applied to other yoke animals which attempt to throw off their burdens, like the elephant which

254   *Commentary Lines 614–19*

throws its riders. See Ov. *Met.* 7.211 *impatiens oneris collum pressistis aratro*, Sen. *Phaed.* 117 *impatiens iugi*, Prud. *psych.* 191 *impatiens madidis frenarier ora lupatis*, etc.

614–16. The rhythm of these lines skillfully suggests the action. Use of the maximum number of spondees in 614–15 emphasizes the slow-moving elephant's tortured progression to the river, while the dactyls of 616 indicate its sudden relief at reaching the water.

613–14. et magni corporis aestu / huc atque huc iactas accendit belua flammas: *aestu* combines both the heat of the fire and the heaving of the elephants' bodies as they try to escape the heat. Ruperti overinterprets *aestu* as *fluctu*; Spaltenstein understands *ardore* correctly as "à cause de la chaleur." *Iactas…flammas* resumes 605–6n. *incendia…/ iacit*.

615–16. donec uicini tandem se fluminis undis / praecipitem dedit: for the Aufidus River, see 227n. The phrasing recalls Verg. *Aen.* 2.719–20 *donec me flumine uiuo / abluero*, Ov. *Met.* 11.139 *donec uenias ad fluminis ortus*, etc. As is typical with related words, the clausula of 615 is very common: Silius three times, Virgil three times, Ovid once, Lucan once, etc. For *se praeceps + dare* and equivalents, see 2.145–6 *uastae se culmine turris / praecipitem iacit* with my note, 17.411 *primis se praecipitem tulit obuia telis*, Hor. *Sat.* 1.2.41 *hic se praecipitem tecto dedit*, etc.

616. et tenui decepta liquore: the notion is probably that the elephants tower high above the river and so cannot get an adequate supply on their backs. It seems unlikely that the Aufidus would suddenly run dry, even after Vulturnus' assault. Other uses of *tenuis liquor* refer to the thinness of liquid rather than its scarcity: see, e.g., Man. *Astr.* 1.157, 1.161, Colum. *RR* 7.8.1 (low-fat milk), Prud. *Symm.* 2.927, etc.

617–18. stagnantis per plana uadi tulit incita longis / exstantem ripis flammam: for *stagnantis* applied to the Aufidus, see 227–8n. *Vadi* provides a further connection to the Bagrada, although the vocabulary is typical: 6.143 *stagnante uado*. Use of the adjective *longis* is hypallage for *longe*, as at 3.409 *longaque umbram tellure trahebat*, 6.280–1 *longoque resoluens / aggere*, etc. Håkanson 1976: 36 understands *ripis* as *aquis*, as at 14.189 *Eridani stagnis ripaue Caystri*. While Spaltenstein commends this reading as "ingénieux," I have followed Zaia. She observes, "è più probabile che Silio…voglia alludere propriamente alle rive del fiume," as in the translations of Duff ("along the banks") and Volpilhac-Lenthéric ("le long des rives"). See further 231n.

618–19. tum denique sese / gurgitis immersit molem capiente profundo: Spaltenstein explains *profundo* as "the deep part of the river," a different usage from 7.378 *Tusci post stagna profundi*. The participle *capiente* explains the sense: this part of the river is deep enough to contain the elephant (*OLD* s.v. *capio* 25).

Commentary Lines 620–5   255

Van Veen observed that the genitive *gurgitis* is difficult to construe and so proposed *gurgitibus mersit*; cf. Verg. *Aen.* 10.599 *gurgite mersum*, or *gurgite summersit*; cf. Verg. *Aen.* 1.40 *summergere ponto*. Delz (app. crit.) observed that *immersit* is already construed with ablative *profundo*. Verg. *Aen.* 6.174 *inter saxa uirum spumosa immerserat unda* is a comparable construction.

620–4. The Roman forces attack other elephants with a variety of missiles. The narrator compares them to soldiers attacking fortified positions on hilltops.

620–1. at qua pugna datur necdum Maurusia pestis / igne calet: the elephants have Moorish riders at 573n., but are "Libyan beasts" at 574n. Silius typically uses North African ethynonyms generically; see 10–11n. The fire that the Romans used to attack the elephants is a *pestis* at 606n.; here Silius applies the term to the elephant itself. The clausula of 620 is a unique phrase, likely inspired by Verg. *Aen.* 4.206 *Maurusia pictis*; see also *Pun.* 4.567 *Maurusia taxus.*

621. circumfusi Rhoeteia pubes: Silius is the only poet to use the epithet *Rhoete(i)us* to mean "Roman," as at 7.431, 14.487, 17.196, etc.; contrast, e.g., Luc. *BC* 6.351 *Rhoeteia litora*, 9.962–3 *Graio nobile busto / Rhoetion*. See 71–2n. for the "Trojan" connotations of the epithet *Rhoete(i)us* and 2.51 with my note. For *pubes,* see 317–18n.

622–3. nunc iaculis, nunc et saxis, nunc alite plumbo / eminus incessunt: for a similar repetition of *nunc* in a more effective *tricolon abundans*, see 1.321 *nunc sude, nunc iaculo, nunc saxis impiger instat.* For other examples of multiple anaphora in the same line, see 5.198 *hinc pariter rupes, lacus hinc, hinc arma simulque*, 12.617, 15.712–13, Verg. *Aen.* 3.490 *sic oculos, sic ille manus, sic ora ferebat,* etc.; Wills 1996: 369–71. For the clausula of 622, see 3.365 *funda bella ferens Baliaris et alite plumbo.* For the slingshot, see 1.314 *hic crebram fundit Baliari uerbere glandem,* 1.523 *librataque pondera plumbi,* etc.

623–4. ut qui castella per altos / oppugnat munita locos atque adsidet arces: earlier comparisons likened the elephants to other fortifications such as the *agger* or the *uallum* (580–1n.). Their turrets likely prompt the comparison to castles placed on heights. The comparison also evokes Virgil's boxing match, where the smaller Dares attempts to strike his massive opponent Entellus: Verg. *Aen.* 5.439–42 *ille, uelut celsam oppugnat qui molibus urbem / aut montana sedet circum castella sub armis, / nunc hos, nunc illos aditus, omnemque pererrat / arte locum et uariis adsultibus inritus urget.*

625–31. While the other Romans attack the elephants with missiles, Mincius bravely fights one single-handedly. The elephant lifts the unfortunate warrior with his trunk and dashes him to the ground.

625. ausus digna uiro, fortuna digna secunda: for *ausus,* see 627n. For repetition of *dignus*, see 5.595–6 *dignus Carthagine, dignus / Hasdrubale ad manes*

256   *Commentary Lines 626–30*

ibis, 15.645 *digna uiro, digna, obtestor, spectacula*. Silius adapts a pattern favored by Ovid: see Ov. *Met.* 3.421, 5.345, *Trist.* 5.12.36, etc. For Fortune's typical injustice, see, e.g., 2.5 *Fors non aequa labori* with my note. For the chiastic arrangement with *redditio*, featuring nouns with a repeated adjective, see Flammini 1983: 96. *Digna fortuna* likely recalls Verg. *Aen.* 3.318 *aut quae digna satis fortuna reuisit*, adapted also at Coripp. *Ioh.* 3.22 *aut quae digna uirum fortuna secuta est*; see also Stat. *Silv.* 4.6.59. For *fortuna secunda*, see Verg. *Aen.* 9.282, Ov. *Pont.* 2.3.23, etc. Statius employs a similar clausula in Eteocles' exhortation to the Thebans: Stat. *Theb.* 10.23–4 *digna secundis / pectora ferte deis*.

626. extulerat dextram atque aduersum comminus ensem: Spaltenstein observes that *extulerat* offers "la précision suggestive," as at VF *Arg.* 5.613 *elata…securi*. For *aduersum*, see 4.207 *aduersumque uiro rotat obuius ensem*, 17.537 *et iacit aduersam properati turbinis hastam*, Verg. *Aen.* 11.612–13 *aduersis…/ hastis*, etc.; *TLL* 1.866.75.

627. Mincius infelix ausi: the Mincius, modern Mincio, is a river of Lombardy which flows from Lake Garda through Mantua into the Po. Virgil praises his hometown's river in each of his works: *Ecl.* 7.13, *Georg.* 3.15, *Aen.* 10.206. For characters named after rivers, see 585n. For *infelix* with the genitive, see 2.682 *infelix obitus* with my note, 4.506 *animae*, 8.119 *tori*, 10.630 *culpae*, 12.432 *fidei*; Verg. *Geo.* 3.498 *studiorum*, *Aen.* 4.529 *animi*, etc.; *TLL* 7.1.1365.5–8. *Ausi* repeats 625 *ausus*; Delz accordingly suspected corruption and conjectured *infelix, saeui*. As Zaia observes, however, such repetition is common in Silius.

627–8. sed stridula anhelum / feruorem effundens monstri manus: for the elephant's trumpeting, see 575n. Its breath is hot like a war horse's; see 6.232 *exspirat naribus ignes*, 17.133–4 *spirantibus ignem / naribus*, Verg. *Aen.* 7.281. For the elephants as monsters, see 571n. For the elephant's trunk as its *manus*, see Pliny *NH* 8.29 *haut inproprie appellata manu*; *TLL* 8.366.25–8. Lucretius thought of the elephant's "hand" as a snake: Lucr. *DRN* 2.537 *anguimanus elephantos*, 5.1303.

628–9. abstulit acri / implicitum nexu diroque ligamine torsit: Zaia observes the similarity of the phrasing to that in Neptune's assault on Typhoeus at VF *Arg.* 2.26–7 *prensum ipse comis Neptunus in altum / abstulit implicuitque uadis*. Liberman 2006: 22 proposes *arto* in place of *acri*, on the examples of Ov. *Met.* 6.242 *arto luctantia nexu*, Stat. *Theb.* 4.730–1 *artos / thoracum nexus*. The phrase *acri…nexu* is indeed unparalleled; see *TLL* 1.361.84. Its description of the elephant's deadly clasp is fully comprehensible, however, and it is unlikely that a more conventional word would have been corrupted to *acri*.

630. et superas alte miserum iaculata per auras: *superas* is a conventional epithet for *auras*, as at 3.712, Verg. *Geo.* 4.486, *Aen.* 5.427, etc.; *TLL* 2.1478.56. Spaltenstein associates this usage with 10.577 *aetherias*, as opposed to 3.712, where it is opposed to *inferas*.

Commentary Lines 631–6 257

631. telluri elisis adflixit, flebile, membris: for smashed limbs, see 5.509 *elisitque uirum spatiosa membra ruina* (caused by a collapsing tree). Livy's elephants similarly trample victims: Livy 44.42.6 *elephanti…obterebant elidebantque.* For parenthetical *flebile*, see 502n.

632–9. Paulus rebukes Varro for his folly in giving battle, despite having been warned. Their brief interaction complements the book's opening through ring composition. 633 *increpitans* recalls Varro's abuse at 6n. *segnitiae Paulum increpitare.* See Introduction, section 3f.

632–3. has inter clades uiso Varrone sub armis / increpitans Paulus: Silius is the first poet to employ the prosaic phrase *inter clades*; cf. Livy 22.7.1, 30.10.20 *inter adsiduas clades.* Sidonius then adapts the phrasing at Sidon. *Carm.* 7.537 *has nobis inter clades.* Spaltenstein, followed by Zaia, favors Duff's translation "on the field" for *sub armis* rather than "en armes," "qui serait trivial." To specify that Varro is on the field is equally banal; where else would he be? Furthermore, Corvinus' assertion at 5.100 *bellandum est astu. leuior laus in duce dextrae* shows that it is not a foregone conclusion that the commander fights hand to hand.

633–4. 'quin imus comminus' inquit / 'ductori Tyrio': *quin imus* reflects the lexical register of Roman comedy (cf. Plaut. *Cas.* 854, *Merc.* 582); Paulus' ironic suggestion is coarse phrasing for epic. For *ductori*, see 24n.

634–5. quem uinctum colla catenis / staturum ante tuos currus promisimus urbi: Varro earlier promised the Roman people to bring Hannibal to Rome as a captive in chains: 8.276–7 *Latia deuinctum colla catena / Hannibalem Fabio ducam spectante per urbem.* Paulus now recalls his words ironically for him. Fulvius angrily repeats the key phrase when ejecting the Capuan envoys from the Roman Senate: 11.117 *ductorem uestris deuinctum colla catenis.* For *uincire* with the accusative of relation, see, e.g., Catul. 64.65 *non tereti strophio lactentes uincta papillas*, Prop. 3.24.14 *uinctus eram uersas in mea terga munus*, Ov. *Met.* 7.429 *colla torosa boum uinctorum cornua uittis*, etc. For *colla catenis*, see 4.359 *iniectus Spartanis colla catenis* (Regulus), 6.505 (Regulus), 7.32 (Cilnius), 15.246–7 *uicta catenis / Poenus colla dedit* (Aris), Claud. *Stil.* 2.374 *barbara ferratis innectunt colla catenis*, etc.

636. heu patria, heu plebes scelerata et praua fauoris: for the people's folly in general, see 6.614 *inuidia aut blando popularis gloria fuco*; for their hostility to Paulus and election of Varro, see 8.286–7 *mobilis ira est / turbati uulgi.* The collocation *praua fauoris* aligns with the narrator's judgment of Varro: 8.259 *prauusque togae.* For *prauus* with the genitive, see 3.253 *Battiadas prauos fidei*, 12.464 *audendi prauus.* For Varro's cultivation of the *fauor plebis*, see 8.249 *infima dum uulgi fouet.* Paulus dies rebuking the foolishness of the plebs: 10.283–5 *amplius acta / quid superest uita, nisi caecae ostendere plebi / Paulum scire mori?* For discussion, see Ariemma 2010.

258 *Commentary Lines 637–51*

637. haud umquam expedies tam dura sorte malorum: for the clausula, see Luc. *BC* 9.491, Drac. *Orest.* 765; see Ov. *Met.* 13.485, Luc. *BC* 9.66–7 for use of the phrase in other *sedes*.

638–9. quem tibi non nasci fuerit per uota petendum, / Varronem Hannibalemne, magis: for the motif that Varro was as much a threat to the Romans as Hannibal, see 8.332–3 *sed quaenam ira deum? consul datus alter, opinor, / Ausoniae est, alter Poenis*, Livy 22.39.4 *nescio an infestior hic aduersarius* (i.e., Varro) *quam ille hostes maneat*.

639–43. Hannibal drives on the fleeing Romans as Paulus rebukes Varro. Carthaginian missiles strike Paulus' armor, and he proceeds against the enemy ranks.

639–40. dum talia Paulus, / urget praecipitis Libys atque in terga ruentum: for the conclusion of Cannae in a Roman rout, see Livy 22.49.13 *tum undique effuse fugiunt*. Silius varies the phrasing of these lines to describe the sneak attack by the sham deserters at 10.191–2 *in terga ruentes / praecipitant*.

641. ante oculos cunctas ductoris concitat hastas: for *ductoris*, see 24n. For *concitat*, see 13.209 *concitat intortam furiatis uiribus hastam*, VF *Arg.* 6.340 *missile… concitat*; *TLL* 4.64.51. As *concitare* more often means "shake" than "hurl," it is possible that Silius' usage alludes to Valerius.

642. pulsatur galea et quatiuntur consulis arma: for Silius' typically abundant style, see Introduction, section 5b. For *quatiuntur… arma*, see 517n.

643. acrius hoc Paulus medios ruit asper in hostis: Paulus rushes against the enemy (*ruit*), while other Roman soldiers rush to flee (640 *ruentum*). The opening of the subsequent book recapitulates Paulus' charge against the enemy: 10.4 *in medios fert arma*, 10.42 *per medios agitur*, 10.72 *mediosque aufertur in hostes*.

644–51. Varro concludes the book with a soliloquy in which he contemplates suicide, but claims to be prevented by an unknown god. Suicide would avert the shame of his return to Rome, narrated at 10.605–14. The scene complements Solymus' achieved suicide, as his flight from the battlefield fulfills Solymus' warning (173–7n.). The motif also establishes Varro as a failed Scipio. Mars earlier prevented Scipio from committing suicide at Ticinus and sent him to rescue his father. After the young hero's success, the god comments 4.476–7 *et adhuc maiora supersunt, / sed nequeunt meliora dari*. Varro experiences *grauiora* (651n.) while Paulus, the symbolic father of the Roman state, dies on the battlefield; by contrast, Scipio will rescue his father and go on to a future of *maiora* as he conquers the Carthaginians.

Varro claims that some god has spared him for worse (651n.), recapitulating thereby the narrator's earlier judgment (424–7n.) that he was saved *ira superum*.

Commentary Lines 644–9   259

Juno in the guise of Metellus tendentiously reports to Paulus on Varro's deci-sion to flee: 10.56 *euasit Varro ac sese ad meliora reseruat*. The echo suggests "the unknown god" is indeed Juno and confirms that the events from Varro's election to the final disaster of Cannae have been under her control.

For the speech's contribution to a pattern of civil war motifs, see Marks 2010a: 132. See Introduction, section 3f for discussion of this passage's adapta-tion of Pompey's flight in Lucan's Pharsalus episode.

644. tum uero excussus mentem: Varro's lack of mental stability has been a major theme of this book; see 23n. Here he abandons his eagerness to give battle and turns instead to fear. The phrasing aligns him with Flaminius imme-diately before Trasimene: 5.54 *excussus consul fatorum turbine mentem*. The evocation of the earlier commander recalls that Varro has made the same destructive mistake, but unlike his predecessor will survive the battle. He also evokes the Saguntines at their moment of greatest despair: see 2.592 *tum uero excussae mentes* with my note. The Saguntines soon follow through on suicide, which Varro contemplates. For *excutere mentem*, see further Luc. *BC* 4.536, Stat. *Theb.* 3.92, etc.

644–5. in certamina Paulo / auia diducto: Varro watches Paulus plunge into battle, but lacks the courage to follow him.

645–6. conuertit Varro manuque / cornipedem inflectens: Juno's report on Varro's flight to Paulus recapitulates the phrasing of the present lines: 10.55–6 *et iam conuersis (uidi nam flectere) habenis / euasit Varro*.

646. 'das,' inquit 'patria, poenas': Varro's words recall those of Fabius' son as he attempts to persuade his father not to rescue Minucius: 7.539–41 *'dabit impro-bus,' inquit / 'quas dignum est, poenas, qui per suffragia caeca / inuasit nostros haec ad discrimina fasces*. As with Minucius, reckless voting similarly put Varro in a position to harm Rome.

647. quae Fabio incolumi Varronem ad bella uocasti: Varro earlier rebuked Fabius for pursuing what he perceived as a cowardly strategy; see 53n. The account of the 300 Fabii at the Cremera introduced the motif of entrusting war to someone other than a Fabius; see 7.59 *Fabia gente incolumi*.

648–9. quaenam autem mentis uel quae discordia fati? / Parcarumne latens fraus est?: for Varro's mental disturbance, see 22n. and 644n. For *discordia mentis*, see Ov. *Met.* 9.630, 10.44; Sen. *Ben.* 3.28.6 *quae est tanta animi discor-dia?* See 288n. for the appearance of personified *Discordia*.

The paradosis reads *quaenam autem mentis uel quae discordia fati? / Parcarumque latens fraus est?* "What conflict was this in your mind or with fate? Is this a hidden deception by the Parcae?" Varro's *discordia mentis* has been reiterated since his introduction into the narrative, but *discordia fati* has given difficulty. Duff's "this change of fortune" is not accurate. More recent translators

260   *Commentary Lines 649–51*

have rendered the contrast correctly: "Mais quelle est cette révolte contre la raison ou bien contre le destin?" (Volpilhac-Lenthéric); "questa ribellione contro la ragione o contro il destino?" (Vinchesi). Lefebvre objected to the linkage of the questions with *–que,* which leaves the latter question without a question word or particle. He proposed *Parcarumne,* which I have adopted, along with Volpilhac-Lenthéric.

More recent critics have proposed more radical textual intervention. Gärtner 2009: 84 proposed: *quidnam autem mentis uult haec discordia? fati…* "What moreover does this your mental disturbance want? Is there a hidden deception of fate or the Parcae?" Liberman 2006: 22 observes that he reviewed Gärtner's proposal in advance of its publication and found that these changes were too radical. He proposes *quaenam autem <tantast> mentis discordia? fati* "What moreover is this such great disturbance of mind? Is there…" Liberman defends the prodelision before the caesura on the examples of 1.573, 1.632, etc. These solutions resolve the apparent difficulty of *discordia fati* but involve considerable change to the paradosis. Starting a new sentence in the sixth foot is not unparalleled but quite rare.

649–50. abrumpere cuncta / iamdudum cum luce libet: *cum luce* specifies that Varro wants to take his own life in addition to breaking off all his affairs. 8.433 *quique Truentinas seruant cum flumine turris* is a parallel example of *cum* replacing an inflected form.

650–1. sed comprimit ensem / nescio qui deus: for *comprimere,* see 13.165 *comprimit hastam,* Stat. *Theb.* 11.363 *comprime tela manu.*

651. et meme ad grauiora reseruat: Fate's *fraus* (649n.) was to keep Varro alive to bring a worse outcome for himself and Rome. Volpilhac-Lenthéric's translation of *grauiora* "un rôle plus noble" is "fantaisiste."

The emphatic form *meme* has attracted editorial suspicion. Delz (app. crit.) argues that this form does not occur. Priscian recognizes its existence: Prisc. *Gramm.* 2.592.6 *'tētē' utraque producta accusatiuus esse geminatus ostenditur uel ablatiuus, quod et in prima et in tertia solet fieri persona, ut 'meme', 'sese'; composita tamen ostenduntur accentu paenultimo acuto.* Housman 1903: lxi–lxii lists this line and *AA* 2.690 *quaeque murer meme sustineamque rogent* as examples of the occurrence of *meme* (as well as his own conjecture for Ov. *Trist.* 5.7b.65).

To change the word *meme* would disrupt the careful parallelism with 10.56 *euasit Varro ac sese ad meliora reseruat.* Wills 1996: 81 observes that repetition of the nominal form *me, me* would evoke comparable scenes of desire for suicide and its frustration. The form occurs in speeches by Imilce (4.498 *me, me, quae genui, uestris absumite uotis*), Virgil's mother of Euryalus (Verg. *Aen.* 9.427 *me, me…in me conuertite ferrum*), and Juturna's lament regarding her unachievable suicide: Verg. *Aen.* 12.260–1 *me, me duce ferrum / corripite o miseri.* Silius may have interpreted some of Virgil's instances of *me, me* as single words, emphatic forms of the pronoun *meme*. For repetition of the pronoun, see 2.362 *nos, nos* with my note.

Other suggestions include the following:

Watt 1985: 277: *et mala me,* on the model of Sen. *Oed.* 31 *cui reseruamur malo.*

Shackleton Bailey 1959: 174: *nece me,* "for a fate worse than death"

Summers 1900: 305: *deus. at quae me* on the example of Dido's question *nam quid dissimulo aut quae me ad maiora reseruo?* (Verg. *Aen.* 4.368).

Bothe 1855: 335: *... ensem / nescio qui. deus est? mene ad graviora...*

652–7. Varro contemplates his shame upon returning to Rome alive, and then rides away from the battlefield. Livy reports Varro's escape: Livy 22.49.14 *consul alter, seu forte seu consilio nulli fugientium insertus agmini, cum quinquaginta fere equitibus Venusiam perfugit.* For Varro's flight as a theme of this book, see Introduction, section 2. See 426–7n. on his survivor guilt. In the event, however, the Romans forgive Varro: see 10.627–9 *magnaque actum se credere mente / testantur, quod fisus auis sceptrisque superbis / Laomedontiadum non desperauerit urbi.*

652–3. uiuamne et fractos sparsosque cruore meorum / hos referam populo fasces: the consular fasces have indeed become sprinkled with blood, as predicted in the soldier's prophecy: 8.671–2 *gestat Agenoreus nostro de more secures / consulis et sparsos lictor fert sanguine fasces.* Gärtner 2009: 82–3 persuasively argues for replacing 8.672 *lictor fert* with *lictorum.*

653–4. atque ora per urbes / iratas spectanda dabo: Fabius will calm the angry crowd as Varro returns to Rome: see 10.605–29. The indefinite *per urbes* soon focuses to 655 *Roma,* where Varro's shame will be greatest.

654–5. et, quo saeuius ipse / Hannibal haud poscat, fugiam et te, Roma, uidebo: Hannibal will indeed offer no objection to Varro's undignified retreat, so long as Paulus is dead: see 10.514–15 *'fuge, Varro,' inquit 'fuge, Varro, superstes, / dum iaceat Paulus.'* By fleeing, Varro has also fulfilled Solymus' warning; see 175n.

656–7. plura indignantem telis propioribus hostes / egere et sonipes rapuit laxatus habenas: Varro rides away from the battlefield. *Laxatus* represents a unique hypallage according to *TLL* 7.2.1071.79. The accusative of respect more typically occurs with *fundere*; see, e.g., 4.137 *fusus habenas,* Man. *Astr.* 3.372 *laxas effusus habenas,* etc. For the phrase in the ablative absolute, see 4.210 *laxatis...habenas,* QCurt. 4.9.24.

Bibliography

Abbreviations

ALL: *Archiv für lateinische Lexikographie und Grammatik mit Einschluss des älteren Mittellateins* (1884–1902). Leipzig: B. G. Teubner.

K-S: Kühner, Raphael, and Stegmann, Karl. 1912. *Ausführliche Grammatik der lateinischen Sprache.* Hanover: Hahn.

L&S: Lewis, Charlton T., and Short, Charles. 1963. *A Latin Dictionary.* Oxford: Oxford University Press.

L-H-S: Leumann, M., Hofmann, J. B., and Szantyr, Anton. 1965. *Lateinische Grammatik.* Munich: Beck.

LSJ: Liddell, Henry George, and Scott, Robert. 1996. *A Greek–English Lexicon,* rev. Sir Henry Stuart Jones. Oxford: Oxford University Press.

NP: Cancik, Hubert, and Schneider, Helmuth. 2002–9. *Brill's New Pauly: Encyclopaedia of the Ancient World.* Leiden: Brill.

OLD: Glare, P. G. W. 1982. *Oxford Latin Dictionary.* Oxford: Oxford University Press.

PHI: Packard Humanities Institute Classical Latin Texts. http://latin.packhum.org/.

TLL: *Thesaurus Linguae Latinae.* 1900–. Leipzig: Teubner.

Works cited

Ahl, F. M., Davis, M. A., and Pomeroy, A. 1986. "Silius Italicus." *ANRW* 2.32.4: 2492–561.

Albrecht, Michael von. 1963. "Gleichnis und Innenwelt in Silius' *Punica.*" *Hermes* 91: 352–74.

Albrecht, Michael von. 1964. *Silius Italicus: Freiheit und Gebundenheit römischer Epik.* Amsterdam: P. Schippers.

Arens, J. C. 1950. "-fer and -ger: Their Extraordinary Preponderance among Compounds in Roman Poetry." *Mnemosyne* 4th. ser, 3(3): 241–62.

Ariemma, Enrico Maria. 2000. *Alla vigilia di Canne: Commentario al libro VIII dei Punica di Silio Italico.* Naples: Loffredo.

Ariemma, Enrico Maria. 2010. "*Fons cuncti Varro mali*: The Demagogue Varro in *Punica* 8–10." In *Brill's Companion to Silius Italicus,* ed. Antony Augoustakis, 241–76. Leiden: Brill.

Arribas Hernáez, M. L. 1990. "Las cláusulas anómalas en la obra de Silio Itálico: Estudio métrico y estilístico." *Emerita* 58(2): 231–54.

Asso, Paolo. 2009. *A Commentary on Lucan De bello civili IV.* Berlin: De Gruyter.

Augoustakis, Antony. 2003a. "*Lugendam Formae sine Virginitate Reliquit*: Reading Pyrene and the Transformation of Landscape in Silius' *Punica* 3." *AJPh* 124(2): 235–57.

Augoustakis, Antony. 2003b. "'*Rapit infidum victor caput*': Ekphrasis and Gender-Role Reversal in Silius Italicus' *Punica* 15." In *Being There Together: Essays in Honor of*

Michael C.J. Putnam on the Occasion of His Seventieth Birthday, ed. P. Thibodeau and H. Haskell, 110–27. Afton, MN: Afton Historical Society Press.

Augoustakis, Antony. 2005. "Two Greek Names in Silius Italicus' *Punica*." *RhM* 148: 222–4.

Augoustakis, Antony, ed. 2010a. *Brill's Companion to Silius Italicus*. Leiden: Brill.

Augoustakis, Antony. 2010b. "Silius Italicus, A Flavian Poet." In *Brill's Companion to Silius Italicus*, ed. Antony Augoustakis, 3–23. Leiden: Brill.

Augoustakis, Antony. 2010c. *Motherhood and the Other: Fashioning Female Power in Flavian Epic*. Oxford: Oxford University Press.

Augoustakis, Antony, ed. 2013. *Ritual and Religion in Flavian Epic*. Oxford: Oxford University Press.

Augoustakis, Antony. 2014. "Valerius Flaccus in Silius Italicus." In *Brill's Companion to Valerius Flaccus*, ed. Mark Heerink and Gesine Manuwald, 340–58. Leiden: Brill.

Augoustakis, Antony. 2016. *Statius, Thebaid 8*. Oxford: Oxford University Press.

Augoustakis, Antony, and Bernstein, Neil W. 2021. *Silius Italicus' Punica: Rome's War with Hannibal*. London: Routledge.

Austin, R. G. 1963. *P. Vergili Maronis Aeneidos Liber Quartus*. Oxford: Clarendon Press.

Austin, R. G. 1964. *P. Vergili Maronis Aeneidos Liber Secundus*. Oxford: Clarendon Press.

Austin, R. G. 1971. *P. Vergili Maronis Aeneidos Liber Primus*. Oxford: Clarendon Press.

Auverlot, Daniel. 1992. "Le Catalogue des armées alliées de Carthage dans les *Punica* de Silius Italicus: Construction et fonction (Livre III, vers 222 à 414)." *IL* 44(2): 3–11.

Axelson, Bertil. 1945. *Unpoetische Wörter, ein Beitrag zur Kenntnis der lateinischen Dichtersprache*. Lund: H. Ohlssons.

Babnis, Tomasz. 2019. "The River Araxes in Roman Poetry." *Classica Cracoviensia* 22: 7–46.

Baehrens, Emil. 1872. "Kritische Satura." *Neue Jahrbücher für Philologie und Pädagogik* 105: 621–38.

Bailey, Cyril. 1950. *Titi Lucreti Cari De Rerum Natura Libri Sex*. Oxford: Clarendon Press.

Barchfeld, Wilhelm. 1880. "De comparationum usu apud Silium Italicum." Diss. University of Göttingen.

Barchiesi, Alessandro. 2001. "Genealogie letterarie nell' epica imperiale: Fondamentalismo e ironia." In *L'Histoire littéraire immanente dans la poésie latine* (Entretiens sur l'Antiquité classique 47), ed. E. A. Schmidt, 315–54. Geneva: Fondation Hardt.

Bassett, Edward L., Delz, Josef, and Dunston, A. J. 1976. "Silius Italicus." *Catalogus Translationum et Commentariorum* 3: 341–98.

Bauer, Ludwig. 1890–2. *Sili Italici Punica*. Leipzig: B. G. Teubner.

Bauer, Ludwig. 1893. *Handschriftliche und kritisch-exegetische Erörterungen zu den Punica des Silius Italicus*. Augsburg: P. J. Pfeiffer.

Bennardo, Lorenza. 2021. "Colour Terms and the Creation of Statius' Ekphrastic Style." *CQ* 71(1): 292–307.

Bernstein, Neil W. 2004. "*Auferte oculos*: Modes of Spectatorship in Statius, *Thebaid* 11." *Phoenix* 58: 62–85.

Bernstein, Neil W. 2008. *In the Image of the Ancestors: Narratives of Kinship in Flavian Epic*. Toronto: University of Toronto Press.

Bibliography

Bernstein, Neil W. 2009. "The White Doe of Capua (Silius Italicus, *Punica* 13.115–37)." *Scholia* 18: 89–106.

Bernstein, Neil W. 2010. "Family and State in the *Punica*." In *Brill's Companion to Silius Italicus*, ed. Antony Augoustakis, 377–97. Leiden: Brill.

Bernstein, Neil W. 2013. "*Distat opus nostrum, sed fontibus exit ab isdem:* Declamation and Flavian epic." In *Flavian Epic Interactions*, ed. Gesine Manuwald and Astrid Voigt, 139–56. Berlin: De Gruyter.

Bernstein, Neil W. 2014. "*Romanas ueluti saeuissima cum legiones Tisiphone regesque mouet:* Valerius Flaccus' Argonautica and the Flavian Era." In *Brill's Companion to Valerius Flaccus*, ed. Mark Heerink and Gesine Manuwald, 154–69. Leiden: Brill.

Bernstein, Neil W. 2017. *Silius Italicus: Punica 2.* Oxford: Oxford University Press.

Bernstein, Neil W. 2018. "Continuing the *Aeneid* in the First Century: Ovid's Little *Aeneid*, Lucan's *Bellum Civile*, and Silius' *Punica*." In *Brill's Companion to Prequels, Sequels, and Retellings of Classical Epic*, ed. Robert Simms, 248–66. Leiden: Brill.

Berti, Emanuele. 2000. *M. Annaei Lucani Bellum Civile Liber X.* Florence: Felice Le Monnier.

Biggs, Thomas. 2019. "Campania at War in the Punica." In *Campania in the Flavian Poetic Imagination*, ed. Antony Augoustakis and R. Joy Littlewood, 201–18. Oxford: Oxford University Press.

Billerbeck, Margarethe. 1985. "Aspects of Stoicism in Flavian Epic." *PLLS* 5: 341–56.

Blass, Hermann. 1867. "Emendationen zu Silius Italicus." *Jahresbericht über die Louisenstädtische Realschule*: 21–44.

Bleisch, P. 1999. "The Empty Tomb at Rhoeteum: Deiphobus and the Problem of the Past in *Aeneid* 6.494–547." *ClAnt* 18: 187–226.

Blomgren, Sven Åke. 1938. *Siliana: De Silii Italici Punicis Quaestiones Criticae et Interpretatoriae.* Uppsala: A.-b. Lundequistska bokhandeln.

Bömer, Franz. 1957. *Ovid: Die Fasten.* Heidelberg: C. Winter.

Bömer, Franz. 1969–86. *P. Ovidius Naso Metamorphosen: Kommentar.* Heidelberg: Carl Winter Universitätsverlag.

Bona, Isabella. 1998. *La visione geografica nei Punica di Silio Italico.* Genoa: Università di Genova.

Bothe, F. H. 1855–7. *Des Cajus Silius Italicus punischer Krieg: Oder, Hannibal.* Stuttgart: J. B. Metzler.

Brouwers, J. H. 1982. "Zur Lucan-Imitation bei Silius Italicus." In *Actus. Studies in Honour of H. L. W. Nelson*, ed. J. den Boeft and A. H. M. Kessels, 73–87. Utrecht: Inst. voor Klass. Talen.

Brown, Robert. 1991. "India's Ivory Palisade." *CPh* 86: 318–23.

Bruère, Richard T. 1958. "*Color Ovidianus* in Silius *Punica* 1–7." In *Ovidiana*, ed. N. Herescu, 475–99. Paris: Les Belles Lettres.

Bruère, Richard T. 1959. "*Color Ovidianus* in Silius *Punica* 8–17." *CPh* 54(4): 228–45.

Burck, Erich. 1984. *Historische und epische Tradition bei Silius Italicus.* Munich: C. H. Beck.

Burck, Erich. 1988. "*Fides* in den *Punica* des Silius Italicus." In *Munera philologica et historica Mariano Plezia oblata*, ed. J. Safarewicz and M. Plezia, 49–60. Wróclaw: Zaklad Narodowy im. Ossolinskich.

Burgeon, Christophe. 2016. "L'Éléphant carthaginois dans les 'Punica' de Silius Italicus: Un Symbole punique annonciateur de la victoire romaine." *Folia Electronica Classica* 32, http://bcs.fltr.ucl.ac.be/FE/32/TM32.html, accessed December 17, 2021.

266 *Bibliography*

Cameron, Alan. 1970. *Claudian: Poetry and Propaganda at the Court of Honorius*. Oxford: Clarendon Press.

Cameron, Alan. 2011. *The Last Pagans of Rome*. New York: Oxford University Press.

Ceccarelli, Lucio. 2008. *Contributi per la storia dell'esametro latino*. Rome: Herder.

Champion, Craige B. 2004. *Cultural Politics in Polybius's Histories*. Berkeley, CA: University of California Press.

Charles, Michael B. 2008. "African Forest Elephants and Turrets in the Ancient World." *Phoenix* 62: 338–62.

Chaudhuri, Pramit. 2014. *The War with God: Theomachy in Roman Imperial Poetry*. Oxford: Oxford University Press.

Ciocarlie, A. 2008. "Carthage et les Carthaginois dans l'épopée latine." *REA* 110: 541–68.

Clark, Jessica H. 2014. *Triumph in Defeat: Military Loss and the Roman Republic*. New York: Oxford University Press.

Clausen, Wendell. 1994. *A Commentary on Virgil: Eclogues*. Oxford: Clarendon Press.

Clayman, Dee L. 1987. "Sigmatism in Greek Poetry." *TAPhA* 117: 69–84.

Coffee, Neil. 2009. *The Commerce of War: Exchange and Social Order in Latin Epic*. Chicago: University of Chicago Press.

Coleman, Kathleen M. 1986. "The Emperor Domitian and Literature." *ANRW* 2.32.5: 3087–115.

Coleman, Kathleen M. 1988. *Statius: Silvae IV*. Oxford: Clarendon Press.

Coleman, R. G. G. 1999. "Poetic Diction, Poetic Discourse and the Poetic Register." In *Aspects of the Language of Latin Poetry*, ed. J. N. Adams and R. G. Mayer, 21–96. Oxford: Oxford University Press.

Collins, Suzanne. 2009. *The Hunger Games: Catching Fire*. New York: Scholastic.

Conte, Gian Biagio. 2007. *The Poetry of Pathos: Studies in Virgilian Epic*, ed. S. J. Harrison. Oxford: Oxford University Press.

Cosack, Wilhelm. 1844. "Quaestiones Silianae." Diss. University of Halle.

Courtney, Edward. 1980. *A Commentary on the Satires of Juvenal*. London: Athlone Press.

Courtney, Edward. 1989. "Some Problems in the Text of Silius Italicus." *RFIC* 117: 325–8.

Courtney, Edward. 2004. "The 'Greek' Accusative." *CJ* 99(4): 425–31.

Cowan, Robert. 2009. "Thrasymennus' Wanton Wedding: Etymology, Genre, and Virtus in Silius Italicus, *Punica*." *CQ* 59(1): 226–37.

Cowan, Robert. 2010. "Virtual Epic: Counterfactuals, Sideshadowing, and the Poetics of Contingency in the *Punica*." In *Brill's Companion to Silius Italicus*, ed. Antony Augoustakis, 323–51. Leiden: Brill.

Cowan, Robert. 2013. "Back Out of Hell: The Virtual Katabasis and Initiation of Silius' Minucius." In *Ritual and Religion in Flavian Epic*, ed. Antony Augoustakis, 217–32. Oxford: Oxford University Press.

D'Alessandro Behr, Francesca. 2007. *Feeling History: Lucan, Stoicism, and the Poetics of Passion*. Columbus, OH: Ohio State University Press.

Daly, Gregory. 2002. *Cannae: The Experience of Battle in the Second Punic War*. London: Routledge.

Damschen, Gregor. 2004. "Das lateinische Akrostichon: Neue Funde bei Ovid sowie Vergil, Grattius, Manilius und Silius Italicus." *Philologus* 148(1): 88–115.

Bibliography

Dausqueius, Claudius. 1618. *In C. Silii Italici viri consularis Punica seu de Bello Punico Secundo libros XVII*. Parisiis: Apud Davidem Douceur.

Delarue, Fernand. 1992. "Sur l'architecture des *Punica* de Silius Italicus." *REL* 70: 149–65.

Delz, Josef. 1987. *Sili Italici Punica*. Stuttgart: B. G. Teubner.

Delz, Josef. 1995. "Zur Neubewertung der lateinischer Epik flavischer Zeit." In *Aspetti della poesia epica latina*, ed. Giancarlo Reggi, 143–72. Lugano: Casagrande.

Delz, Josef. 1997. "Nachlese zu Silius Italicus." *MH* 54(3): 163–74.

Dewar, Michael J. 1994. "Hannibal and Alaric in the Later Poems of Claudian." *Mnemosyne* 47 (3): 349–72.

Dewar, Michael J. 1996. *Claudian: Panegyricus de Sexto Consulatu Honorii Augusti*. Oxford: Clarendon Press.

Dewar, Michael J. 2003. "Multi-Ethnic Armies in Virgil, Lucan, and Claudian: Intertextuality, War, and the Ideology of *Romanitas*." *SyllClass* 14: 143–59.

Diggle, James, and Goodyear, Francis Richard David, eds. 1972. *The Classical Papers of A. E. Housman*. Cambridge: Cambridge University Press.

Dinter, Martin. 2005. "Epic and Epigram: Minor Heroes in Virgil's *Aeneid*." *CQ* 55(1): 153–69.

Dinter, Martin. 2010. "…und es bewegt sich doch! Der Automatismus des abgehackten Gliedes." In *Lucan between Epic Tradition and Aesthetic Innovation*, ed. N. Hömke, and C. Reitz, 175–90. Berlin: De Gruyter.

Dinter, Martin. 2012. *Anatomizing Civil War: Studies in Lucan's Epic Technique*. Ann Arbor, MI: University of Michigan Press.

Dominik, William J. 2003. "Hannibal at the Gates: Programmatising Rome and Romanitas in Silius Italicus' *Punica* 1 and 2." In *Flavian Rome: Culture, Image, Text*, ed. A. J. Boyle and W. J. Dominik, 469–97. Leiden: Brill.

Dominik, William J. 2006. "Rome Then and Now: Linking the Saguntum and Cannae episodes in Silius Italicus' *Punica*." In *Flavian Poetry*, ed. R. R. Nauta, H.-J. van Dam and J. J. L. Smolenaars, 113–27. Leiden: Brill.

Dominik, William J. 2010. "The Reception of Silius Italicus in Modern Scholarship." In *Brill's Companion to Silius Italicus*, ed. Antony Augoustakis, 425–47. Leiden: Brill.

Dominik, William J. 2018. "Civil War, Parricide, and the Sword in Silius Italicus' *Punica*." In *After 69 CE: Writing Civil War in Flavian Rome*, ed. Lauren Donovan Ginsberg and Darcy Krasne, 271–94. Berlin: De Gruyter.

Dominik, William J., Newlands, Carole E., and Gervais, Kyle, eds. 2015. *Brill's Companion to Statius*. Leiden: Brill.

Drakenborch, Arnold. 1717. *Caji Silii Italici Punicorum Libri Septemdecim*. Trajecti ad Rhenum: Guilielmum Van de Water.

Duckworth, George E. 1967. "Five Centuries of Latin Hexameter Poetry: Silver Age and Late Empire." *TAPhA* 98: 77–150.

Duff, J. Wight, ed. 1934. *Silius Italicus: Punica*. Cambridge, MA: Harvard University Press.

Dyck, Andrew R. 1996. *A Commentary on Cicero, De Officiis*. Ann Arbor, MI: University of Michigan Press.

Endt, Johannes. 1905. "Die Gebrauch der Apostrophe bei den lateinischen Epikern." *WS* 27: 106–29.

Ernesti, J.C.T. 1791. *Caii Silii Italici Punicorum Libri Septemdecim*. Lipsiae: Weidmann.

268 *Bibliography*

Ernout, A. 1949. *Les Adjectifs latins en -osvs et en -vlentvs*. Paris: C. Klincksieck.

Esposito, Paolo. 2004. "Lucano e la negazione per antitesi." In *Lucano e la tradizione dell'epica latina*, ed. Paolo Esposito and E. M. Ariemma, 39–67. Naples: Guida.

Esposito, Paolo, and E. M. Ariemma, ed. 2004. *Lucano e la tradizione dell'epica latina*. Naples: Guida.

Fantham, Elaine. 1992. *Lucan De Bello Civili: Book II*. Cambridge: Cambridge University Press.

Farrell, Joseph. 2005. "Intention and Intertext." *Phoenix* 59: 98–111.

Feeney, D. C. 1982. "A Commentary on Silius Italicus Book 1." Diss. University of Oxford.

Feeney, D. C. 1991. *The Gods in Epic: Poets and Critics of the Classical Tradition*. Oxford: Clarendon Press.

Fernandelli, Marco. 2005–6. "La maniera classicistica di Silio: Tre esempi dal libro VII." *Incontri triestini di filologia classica* 5: 73–118.

Flammini, Giuseppe. 1983. "Tecnica e strutture del chiasmo in Silio Italico." *GIF* 14: 85–101.

Fowler, Don P. 1990. "Deviant Focalisation in Virgil's *Aeneid*." *PCPhS* 36: 42–63.

Fowler, Don P. 1996. "Even Better than the Real Thing: A Tale of Two Cities." In *Art and Text in Roman Culture*, ed. J. Elsner, 57–74. Cambridge: Cambridge University Press.

Fraenkel, Eduard. 1964. *Kleine Beiträge zur klassischen Philologie*. Rome: Edizione di storia e letteratura.

Fraenkel, Eduard. 2010 [1928]. "Lucan as the Transmitter of Ancient Pathos." In *Lucan*, ed. C. Tesoriero, 15–45. Oxford: Oxford University Press.

Franchet d'Espèrey, Sylvie. 1999. *Conflit, violence et non-violence dans la "Thébaïde" de Stace*. Paris: Les Belles Lettres.

Franke, Josephus. 1889. *De Tib. Silii Italici Punicorum tropis*. Münster: Ex typographia Aschendorffiana.

Frassinetti, Paolo. 1989. "Contributi al testo di Silio Italico." *Civiltà Classica e Cristiana* 9: 144–9.

Fratantuono, Lee M., and Smith, R. Alden. 2015. *Virgil, Aeneid 5: Text, Translation and Commentary*. Leiden: Brill.

Fröhlich, Uwe. 2000. *Regulus, Archetyp römischer fides: Das sechste Buch als Schlüssel zu den Punica des Silius Italicus: Interpretation, Kommentar und Übersetzung*. Tübingen: Stauffenburg.

Fucecchi, Marco. 1990. "Il declino di Annibale nei Punica." *Maia* 42: 151–66.

Fucecchi, Marco. 1999. "La vigilia di Canne nei *Punica* e un contributo allo studio dei rapporti fra Silio Italico e Lucano." In *Interpretare Lucano*, ed. Paolo Esposito and Luciano Nicastri, 305–42. Naples: Arte Tipographica.

Fucecchi, Marco. 2003. "I *Punica* e altre storie di Roma nell'epos di Silio Italico." In *Evento, racconto, scrittura nell'antichità classica*, ed. A. Casanova and P. Desideri, 269–92. Florence: Università degli studi di Firenze.

Fucecchi, Marco. 2010. "The Shield and the Sword: Q. Fabius Maximus and M. Claudius Marcellus as Models of Heroism in Silius' *Punica*." In *Brill's Companion to Silius Italicus*, ed. Antony Augoustakis, 219–40. Leiden: Brill.

Fucecchi, Marco. 2013. "With (a) God on Our Side: Ancient Ritual Practices and Imagery in Flavian Epic." In *Ritual and Religion in Flavian Epic*, ed. Antony Augoustakis, 17–32. Oxford: Oxford University Press.

Bibliography

Fucecchi, Marco. 2014. "The Philosophy of Power: Greek Literary Tradition and Silius' On Kingship." In *Flavian Poetry and its Greek Past*, ed. Antony Augoustakis, 305–24. Leiden: Brill.

Fucecchi, Marco. 2018. "Flavian Epic: Roman Ways of Metabolizing a Cultural Nightmare?" In *After 69 CE: Writing Civil War in Flavian Rome*, ed. Lauren Donovan Ginsberg and Darcy Krasne, 25–49. Berlin: De Gruyter.

Fucecchi, Marco. 2019. "Campania and the Punica." In *Campania in the Flavian Poetic Imagination*, ed. Antony Augoustakis and R. Joy Littlewood, 183–200. Oxford: Oxford University Press.

Gaertner, Jan Felix. 2005. *Ovid Epistulae Ex Ponto 1*. Oxford: Oxford University Press.

Gallia, Andrew B. 2012. *Remembering the Roman Republic: Culture, Politics and History under the Principate*. Cambridge: Cambridge University Press.

Ganiban, Randall Toth. 2007. *Statius and Virgil. The Thebaid and the Reinterpretation of the Aeneid*. Cambridge: Cambridge University Press.

Ganiban, Randall Toth. 2010. "Virgil's Dido and the Heroism of Hannibal in Silius' Punica." In *Brill's Companion to Silius Italicus*, ed. Antony Augoustakis, 73–98. Leiden: Brill.

Gantz, Timothy. 1993. *Early Greek Myth: A Guide to Literary and Artistic Sources*. Baltimore, MD: Johns Hopkins University Press.

García Amutxastegi, Iratxe. 2015. *Comentario y estudio literario de los relatos de derrota en la épica romana: El libro IX de los Punica de Silio Itálico*. Vitoria-Gasteiz: Universidad del País Vasco.

García Ruiz, M. Pilar. 2014. "*Aequor*: The Sea of Prophecies in Virgil's *Aeneid*." *CQ* 64(2): 694–706.

Gärtner, Thomas. 2009. "Kritische Bemerkungen zu den *Punica* des Silius Italicus." *Exemplaria Classica* 13: 71–94.

Gärtner, Thomas. 2010. "Überlegungen zur Makrostruktur der *Punica*." In *Silius Italicus: Akten der Innsbrucker Tagung vom 19.–21. Juni 2008*, ed. Florian Schaffenrath, 77–96. Frankfurt am Main: Lang.

Georgacopoulou, Sophia. 2005. *Aux frontières du récit épique: L'Emploi de l'apostrophe du narrateur dans la Thébaïde de Stace*. Brussels: Éditions Latomus.

Gervais, Kyle. 2017. *Statius, Thebaid 2*. Oxford: Oxford University Press.

Gibson, Bruce J. 2010. "Silius Italicus: A Consular Historian." In *Brill's Companion to Silius Italicus*, ed. Antony Augoustakis, 47–72. Leiden: Brill.

Ginsberg, Lauren Donovan. 2011. "*Ingens* as an Etymological Pun in the *Octavia*." *CPh* 106: 357–60.

Ginsberg, Lauren Donovan, and Krasne, Darcy, eds. 2018. *After 69 CE: Writing Civil War in Flavian Rome*. Berlin: De Gruyter.

Goldsworthy, Adrian. 2001. *Cannae*. London: Cassell.

Gowers, Emily. 2005. "Virgil's Sibyl and the 'Many Mouths' Cliché (*Aen*. 6.625–7)." *CQ* 55: 170–82.

Green, Steven J. 2004. *Ovid, Fasti 1: A Commentary*. Leiden: Brill.

Greene, Thomas M. 1982. *The Light in Troy: Imitation and Discovery in Renaissance Poetry*. New Haven, CT: Yale University Press.

Griffin, Jasper. 1980. *Homer on Life and Death*. Oxford: Clarendon Press.

Guastella, Gianni. 1985. "La rete del sangue: Simbologia delle relazioni e modelli dell'identità nella cultura romana." *MD* 15: 49–123.

Bibliography

Håkanson, L. 1976. *Silius Italicus: Kritische und exegetische Bemerkungen.* Lund: Gleerup.

Hampel, E. 1908. "De apostrophae apud Romanorum poetas usu." Diss. University of Jena.

Hardie, Philip R. 1993. *The Epic Successors of Virgil: A Study in the Dynamics of a Tradition.* Cambridge: Cambridge University Press.

Harrison, Stephen J., ed. 1991. *Vergil: Aeneid 10.* Oxford: Clarendon Press.

Haupt, Moritz. 1870. "Iohannis Schraderi emendationes *Punicorum* Silii Italici." *Hermes* 4: 345.

Haury, Auguste. 1984. "*Silius Italicus: La Guerre punique: Tome III: Livres IX–XIII.* Texte établi et trad., par Volpilhac-Lentheric, Martin, Miniconi et Devallet." *REA* 86(1): 374–5.

Heerink, Mark, and Manuwald, Gesine, eds. 2014. *Brill's Companion to Valerius Flaccus.* Leiden: Brill.

Hellegouarc'h, Joseph. 1964. *Le Monosyllabe dans l'hexamètre latin: Essai de métrique verbale.* Paris: C. Klincksieck.

Helzle, Martin. 1996. *Der Stil ist der Mensch: Redner und Reden im römischen Epos.* Stuttgart: B. G. Teubner.

Henry, James. 1873–92. *Aeneidea.* London: Williams and Norgate.

Hershkowitz, Debra. 1997. "'Parce Metu, Cytherea': 'Failed' Intertext Repetition in Statius' *Thebaid*, or, Don't Stop Me If You've Heard This One Before." *MD* 39: 35–52.

Hershkowitz, Debra. 1998. *The Madness of Epic: Reading Insanity from Homer to Statius.* Oxford: Oxford University Press.

Heyworth, S. J. 2009. *Cynthia: A Companion to the Text of Propertius.* Oxford: Oxford University Press.

Holder, Alfred. 1896. *Alt-celtischer Sprachschatz.* Leipzig: Teubner.

Horsfall, Nicholas M. 2000. *Virgil, Aeneid 7: A Commentary.* Leiden: Brill.

Housman, A. E. 1903. *M. Manilii Astronomicon Liber Primus.* London: Grant Richards.

Jacobs, John. 2010. "From Sallust to Silius Italicus: *Metus Hostilis* and the Fall of Rome in the *Punica.*" In *Latin Historiography and Poetry in the Early Empire*, ed. John Miller and Anthony Woodman, 123–39. Leiden: Brill.

Jones, Frederick. 2008. "Juvenal and the Hexameter." *Studies in Latin Literature and Roman History* 14: 348–64.

Jones, Prudence J. 2005. *Reading Rivers in Roman Literature and Culture.* Lanham, MD: Lexington Books.

Juhnke, Herbert. 1972. *Homerisches in römischer Epic flavischer Zeit: Untersuchungen zu Szenennachbildungen und Strukturentsprechungen in Statius' Thebais und Achilleis und in Silius' Punica.* Munich: C. H. Beck.

Keith, Alison M. 1991. "Etymological Play on *Ingens* in Ovid, Vergil, and *Octavia.*" *AJPh* 112: 73–6.

Keith, Alison M. 2000. *Engendering Rome: Women in Latin Epic.* Cambridge: Cambridge University Press.

Keith, Alison M. 2008. "Etymological Wordplay in Flavian Epic." *PLLS* 13: 231–53.

Keith, Alison M. 2010. "Engendering Orientalism in Silius' *Punica.*" In *Brill's Companion to Silius Italicus*, ed. Antony Augoustakis, 355–73. Leiden: Brill.

Kenney, E. J. 1996. *Ovid: Heroides XVI–XXI.* Cambridge: Cambridge University Press.

Bibliography

Kißel, Walter. 1979. *Das Geschichtsbild des Silius Italicus*. Frankfurt am Main: Peter Lang.

Klaassen, Elizabeth Kennedy. 2010. "Imitation and the Hero." In *Brill's Companion to Silius Italicus*, ed. Antony Augoustakis, 99–126. Leiden: Brill.

Klecka, Joseph. 1983. *Concordantia in Publium Papinium Statium*. Hildesheim: Georg Olms Verlag.

Knox, P. E. 1986a. "Adjectives in -osus and Latin Poetic Diction." *Glotta* 64: 90–101.

Knox, P. E. 1986b. *Ovid's Metamorphoses and the Traditions of Augustan Poetry*. Cambridge: Cambridge Philological Society.

Knox, P. E. 1995. *Ovid: Heroides: Select Epistles*. Cambridge: Cambridge University Press.

Kohl, Richard. 1915. *De scholasticarum declamationum argumentis ex historia petitis*. Paderborn: Ferdinand Schöningh.

Korn, M. 1989. *Valerius Flaccus, Argonautica 4, 1–343: Ein Kommentar*. Hildesheim: Olms.

Kösters, Heinrich. 1893. "Quaestiones metricae et prosodiacae ad Valerium Flaccum pertinentes." Diss. University of Münster.

Kühner, Raphael, and Stegmann, Karl. 1912. *Ausführliche Grammatik der lateinischen Sprache*. Hanover: Hahn.

Küppers, Joachim. 1986. *Tantarum Causas Irarum: Untersuchungen zur einleitenden Bücherdyade der Punica des Silius Italicus*. Berlin: De Gruyter.

Laird, Andrew. 1993. "Sounding Out Ecphrasis: Art and Text in Catullus 64." *JRS* 83: 18–30.

Lancel, Serge. 1998. *Hannibal*. Trans. Antonia Nevill. Oxford: Blackwell.

Landrey, Leo. 2014. "Skeletons in Armor: The *Aeneid's* Proem and Silius Italicus' *Punica.*" *AJPh* 135(4): 599–633.

Langen, Peter. 1896–7. *C. Valeri Flacci Setini Balbi Argonavticon libri octo*. Berlin: S. Calvary.

Lanzarone, Nicola. 2016. *M. Annaei Lucani Belli Civilis Liber VII*. Florence: Felice Le Monnier.

La Penna, Antonio. 1979. "*Sibila torquet* (Prop. IV, 8, 8): Storia (tentata) di una *callida iunctura.*" *Maia* 31: 135–7.

La Penna, Antonio. 1987. "*Vidi*: Per la storia di una formula poetica." In *Laurea Corona: Studies in Honour of Edward Coleiro*, ed. Anthony Bonanno, 99–119. Amsterdam: B. R. Grüner.

La Penna, Antonio. 1996. "Modelli efebici nella poesia di Stazio." In *Epicedion: Hommage à P. Papinius Statius 96–1996*, ed. F. Delarue, S. Georgacopoulou, P. Laurens, and A.-M. Taisne, 161–84. Poitiers: La Licorne.

Laudizi, Giovanni. 1989. *Silio Italico: Il passato tra mito e restaurazione etica*. Galatina: Congedo Editore.

Lausberg, H. 1998. *Handbook of Literary Rhetoric: A Foundation for Literary Study*. Leiden: Brill.

Lazenby, J. F. 1996. *The First Punic War: A Military History*. Stanford, CA: Stanford University Press.

Leigh, Matthew G. L. 1995. "Wounding and Popular Rhetoric at Rome." *BICS* 39: 195–212.

Bibliography

Leigh, Matthew G. L. 1997. *Lucan: Spectacle and Engagement.* Oxford: Oxford University Press.

Leumann, Manu. 1977. *Lateinische Laut- und Formenlehre.* Munich: C. H. Beck.

Levene, D. S. 2010. *Livy on the Hannibalic War.* Oxford: Oxford University Press.

Liberman, Gauthier. 2006. "What Future for the Text of Silius Italicus after Josef Delz?" *Aevum Antiquum* 6: 19–38.

Lindblom, A. T. 1906. "In Silii Italici Punica Quaestiones." Diss. University of Uppsala.

Littlewood, R. J. 2011. *A Commentary on Silius Italicus' Punica 7.* Oxford: Oxford University Press.

Littlewood, R. J. 2017. *A Commentary on Silius Italicus' Punica 10.* Oxford: Oxford University Press.

Lovano, Michael. 2002. *The Age of Cinna: Crucible of Late Republican Rome.* Stuttgart: Franz Steiner Verlag.

Lovatt, Helen V. 2005. *Statius and Epic Games: Sport, Politics, and Poetics in the Thebaid.* Cambridge: Cambridge University Press.

Lovatt, Helen V. 2010. "Interplay: Reading Backwards and Forwards in the Games of Statius *Thebaid* 6 and Silius *Punica* 16." In *Brill's Companion to Silius Italicus*, ed. Antony Augoustakis, 155–76. Leiden: Brill.

Lovatt, Helen V. 2013. *The Epic Gaze: Vision, Gender and Narrative in Ancient Epic.* Cambridge: Cambridge University Press.

Lyne, R. O. A. M. 1987. *Further Voices in Vergil's Aeneid.* Oxford: Clarendon Press.

Lyne, R. O. A. M. 2004. *Ciris: A Poem Attributed to Vergil.* Cambridge: Cambridge University Press.

McClellan, Andrew M. 2021. "Silius on Rome's 'Revivification' in the *Punica*." In *Roman Poetry, Republican and Imperial* (Papers of the Langford Latin Seminar 18), ed. Francis Cairns, 198–214. Leeds: Francis Cairns.

McClellan, Andrew M. 2019. *Abused Bodies in Roman Epic.* Cambridge: Cambridge University Press.

McDermott, W. C., and Orentzel, A. E. 1977. "Silius Italicus and Domitian." *AJPh* 98(1): 24–34.

McGuire, D. T. 1995. "History Compressed: The Roman Names of Silius' Cannae Episode." *Latomus* 54.1: 110–18.

McGuire, D. T. 1997. *Acts of Silence: Civil War, Tyranny, and Suicide in the Flavian Epics.* Hildesheim: Olms-Weidmann.

McGushin, Patrick. 1985. *The Transmission of the Punica of Silius Italicus.* Amsterdam: Adolf M. Hakkert.

McIntyre, Gwynaeth, and McCallum, Sarah, eds. 2019. *Uncovering Anna Perenna: A Focused Study of Roman Myth and Culture.* London: Bloomsbury Academic.

Mader, Gottfried. 1993. "Ἀννίβας ὑβριστής: Traces of a 'Tragic' Pattern in Livy's Hannibal Portrait in Book XXI?" *AncSoc* 24: 205–24.

Maltby, Robert. 1991. *A Lexicon of Ancient Latin Etymologies.* Leeds: Francis Cairns.

Manuwald, Gesine. 2006. "The Trojans, Dido, and the Punic War: Silius Italicus on the Causes of the Conflict between Romans and Carthaginians." *Aevum Antiquum* 6: 65–83.

Manuwald, Gesine. 2007. "Epic Poets as Characters: On Poetics and Multiple Intertextuality in Silius Italicus' *Punica*." *RFIC* 135(1): 71–90.

Bibliography

Manuwald, Gesine. 2014. "'Fact' and 'Fiction' In Roman Historical Epic." *G&R* 61(2): 204–21.

Manuwald, Gesine. 2015. *Valerius Flaccus: Argonautica 3*. Cambridge: Cambridge University Press.

Manuwald, Gesine, and Voigt Astrid, eds. 2013. *Flavian Epic Interactions*. Berlin: De Gruyter.

Marangoni, Claudio. 2007. *Supplementum etymologicum Latinum*. Trieste: Edizioni Università di Trieste.

Marks, Raymond. 2005a. *From Republic to Empire: Scipio Africanus in the Punica of Silius Italicus*. Frankfurt am Main: Peter Lang.

Marks, Raymond. 2005b. "*Per vulnera regnum*: Self-Destruction, Self-Sacrifice, and *devotio* in *Punica* 4–10." *Ramus* 34: 127–51.

Marks, Raymond. 2008. "Getting Ahead: Decapitation as Political Metaphor in Silius Italicus' *Punica*." *Mnemosyne* 61: 66–88.

Marks, Raymond. 2010a. "Silius and Lucan." In *Brill's Companion to Silius Italicus*, ed. Antony Augoustakis, 127–53. Leiden: Brill.

Marks, Raymond. 2010b. "Lucan's Curio in the *Punica*." In *Silius Italicus. Akten der Innsbrucker Tagung vom 19.–21. Juni 2008*, ed. Florian Schaffenrath, 29–46. Frankfurt am Main: Peter Lang.

Marks, Raymond. 2010c. "The Song and the Sword: Silius's Punica and the Crisis of Early Imperial Epic." In *Epic and History*, ed. D. Konstan and K. A. Raaflaub, 185–211. Malden, MA: Wiley-Blackwell.

Marks, Raymond. 2013. "Reconcilable Differences: Anna Perenna and the Battle of Cannae in the *Punica*." In *Ritual and Religion in Flavian Epic*, ed. Antony Augoustakis, 287–301. Oxford: Oxford University Press.

Marks, Raymond. 2014. "Statio-Silian Relations in the *Thebaid* and *Punica* 1–2." *CPh* 109: 130–9.

Marks, Raymond. 2019. "Searching for Ovid at Cannae: A Contribution to the Reception of Ovid in Silius Italicus' *Punica*." In *Intertextuality in Flavian Epic Poetry: Contemporary Approaches*, ed. Neil Coffee, Chris Forstall, Lavinia Galli Milić, and Damien Nelis, 87–106. Berlin: De Gruyter.

Masters, Jamie. 1992. *Poetry and Civil War in Lucan's Bellum Civile*. Cambridge: Cambridge University Press.

Mayer, Kenneth. 2002. "The Golden Line: Ancient and Medieval Lists of Special Hexameters and Modern Scholarship." In *Latin Grammar and Rhetoric: Classical Theory and Modern Practice*, ed. C. Lanham, 139–79. London: Continuum Press.

Mendell, C.W. 1924. "Silius the Reactionary." *PhQ* 3: 92–106.

Meurig Davies, E. L. B. 1951. "Elephant Tactics: Amm. Marc. 25.1.14; Sil. 9.581–3; Lucr. 2.537–9." *CQ* 1: 153–5.

Mezzanotte, Alessandro. 1995. "Echi del mondo contemporaneo in Silio Italico." *RIL* 129(2): 357–88.

Michalopoulos, Andreas. 2001. *Ancient Etymologies in Ovid's Metamorphoses: A Commented Lexicon*. Leeds: Francis Cairns.

Möhler, Gabriele. 1989. *Hexameterstudien zu Lukrez, Vergil, Horaz, Ovid, Lukan, Silius Italicus und der Ilias Latina*. Frankfurt am Main: Peter Lang.

Moore, Frank Gardner. 1940. *Livy: History of Rome, Vol. 6: Books 23–25*. Cambridge, MA: Harvard University Press.

274 *Bibliography*

Morgan, Llewellyn. 2010. *Musa Pedestris: Metre and Meaning in Roman Verse*. Oxford: Oxford University Press.

Muecke, Frances. 2005a. "Domizio Calderini's Lost 'Edition' of Silius Italicus." *Res Publica Litterarum* 28: 51–67.

Muecke, Frances. 2005b. "Pomponio Leto's Later Work on Silius Italicus: The Evidence of BAV, Vat. Inc. I 4." *RCCM* 47: 139–56.

Muecke, Frances. 2010. "Silius Italicus in the Italian Renaissance." In *Brill's Companion to Silius Italicus*, ed. Antony Augoustakis, 401–24. Leiden: Brill.

Mulder, H. M. 1954. *P. Papinii Statii Thebaidos Liber II commentario exegetico aestheticoque instructus*. Groningen: De Waal.

Müller, Lucian. 1861. *De re metrica poetarum latinorum praeter Plautum et Terentium libri septem*. Leipzig: B. G. Teubner.

Murgatroyd, Paul. 2009. *A Commentary on Book 4 of Valerius Flaccus' Argonautica*. Leiden: Brill.

Nesselrath, H.-G. 1986. "Zu den Quellen des Silius Italicus." *Hermes* 114: 203–30.

Neue, Christian Friedrich, and Wagener, Carl. 1892–1905. *Formenlehre der lateinischen Sprache*. Leipzig: O. R. Reisland.

Nicol, J. 1936. *The Historical and Geographical Sources Used by Silius Italicus*. Oxford: Basil Blackwell.

Niemann, Karl-Heinz. 1975. *Die Darstellung der römischen Niederlagen in den Punica des Silius Italicus*. Bonn: Rudolf Habelt.

Nisbet, Robin G. M., and Hubbard, Margaret. 1970. *A Commentary on Horace: Odes Book I*. Oxford: Clarendon Press.

Nisbet, Robin G. M., and Hubbard, Margaret. 1978. *A Commentary on Horace: Odes Book II*. Oxford: Clarendon Press.

Nolan, Cathal J. 2017. *The Allure of Battle: A History of How Wars Have Been Won and Lost*. Oxford: Oxford University Press.

Norden, Eduard. 1903. *P. Vergilius Maro Aeneis Buch VI*. Leipzig: B. G. Teubner.

Occioni, Onorato. 1871. *Cajo Silio Italico e il suo poema*. Florence: Le Monnier.

Ogilvie, R.M. 1970. *A Commentary on Livy Books 1–5*. Oxford: Clarendon Press.

O'Hara, James J. 1996. *True Names: Vergil and the Alexandrian Tradition of Etymological Wordplay*. Ann Arbor, MI: University of Michigan Press.

Otto, A. 1890. *Die Sprichwörter und sprichwörtlichen Redensarten der Römer*. Leipzig: B. G. Teubner.

Owen, S. G. 1909. "On Silius Italicus." *CQ* 3.4: 254–7.

Parkes, R. E. 2012. *Statius, Thebaid 4*. Oxford: Oxford University Press.

Paton, W. R. 2010. *Polybius: The Histories: Volume II: Books 3–4*. Cambridge, MA: Harvard University Press.

Pearce, T. E. V. 1966. "The Enclosing Word Order in the Latin Hexameter." *CQ* 16: 140–71, 298–320.

Pease, Arthur Stanley. 1935. *Publi Vergili Maronis Aeneidos liber quartus*. Cambridge, MA: Harvard University Press.

Perutelli, Alessandro. 1997a. *C. Valeri Flacci Argonauticon liber VII*. Florence: Le Monnier.

Perutelli, Alessandro. 1997b. "Sul manierismo di Silio Italico: Le ninfe interrogano Proteo (7,409–493)." *BStudLat* 27: 470–8.

Pianezzola, Emilio. 1965. *Gli aggettivi verbali in -bundus*. Florence: G. C. Sansoni.

Bibliography

Plessis, Frédéric Edouard. 1899. *Traité de métrique grecque et latine*. Paris: C. Klincksieck.

Pollmann, K. F. L. 2001. "Statius' *Thebaid* and the Legacy of Vergil's *Aeneid*." *Mnemosyne* 54(1): 10–30.

Pomeroy, Arthur J. 1990. "Silius Italicus as 'doctus poeta'." In *The Imperial Muse: Ramus Essays on Roman Literature of the Empire: Flavian Epicist to Claudian*, ed. A. J. Boyle, 119–39. Bentleigh, Victoria: Aureal Publications.

Pomeroy, Arthur J. 2000. "Silius' Rome: The Rewriting of Vergil's Vision." *Ramus* 29: 149–68.

Pomeroy, Arthur J. 2010a. "*Fides* in Silius Italicus' *Punica*." In *Silius Italicus: Akten der Innsbrucker Tagung vom 19.–21. Juni 2008*, ed. Florian Schaffenrath, 59–76. Frankfurt am Main: Lang.

Pomeroy, Arthur J. 2010b. "To Silius through Livy and his Predecessors." In *Brill's Companion to Silius Italicus*, ed. Antony Augoustakis, 27–45. Leiden: Brill.

Poortvliet, Harm Marien. 1991. *C. Valerius Flaccus Argonautica Book II: A Commentary*. Amsterdam: VU University Press.

Postgate, J. P. 1905. *Corpus Poetarum Latinorum: A Se Aliisque Denuo Recognitorum et Brevi Lectionum Varietate Instructorum*. London: G. Bell.

Quint, David. 1993. *Epic and Empire: Politics and Generic Form from Virgil to Milton*. Princeton, NJ: Princeton University Press.

Raabe, Hermann. 1974. *Plurima mortis imago: Vergleichende Interpretationen zur Bildersprache Vergils*. Munich: C. H. Beck.

Rance, Philip. 2009. "Hannibal, Elephants and Turrets in *Suda* Θ 438 [Polybius Fr. 162b]: An Unidentified Fragment of Diodorus." *CQ* 59.1: 91–111.

Rebeggiani, Stefano. 2013. "Reading the Republican Forum: Virgil's *Aeneid*, the Dioscuri, and the Battle of Lake Regillus." *CPh* 108.1: 53–69.

Rebischke, R. 1913. *De Silii Italici orationibus*. Gdańsk: Ex Officina Boenigiana.

Reed, J. D. 2007. *Virgil's Gaze: Nation and Poetry in the Aeneid*. Princeton, NJ: Princeton University Press.

Reeson, James. 2001. *Ovid Heroides 11, 13, and 14: A Commentary*. Leiden: Brill.

Reeve, M. D. 1989. "A New Edition of Silius Italicus." *CR* 39(2): 215–18.

Richardson, L. 1992. *A New Topographical Dictionary of Ancient Rome*. Baltimore, MD: Johns Hopkins University Press.

Richmond, J. A. 1965. "A Note on the Elision of final ĕ in Certain Particles used by Latin Poets." *Glotta* 43: 78–103.

Ripoll, François. 1998. *La Morale héroïque dans les épopées latines d'époque flavienne: Tradition et innovation*. Louvain: Éditions Peeters.

Ripoll, François. 2003. "Vieillesse et héroïsme dans les épopées flaviennes: Silius Italicus et Valerius Flaccus." In *L'Ancienneté chez les anciens*, vol. 2, ed. B. Bakhouche, 653–76. Montpellier: Université Paul-Valéry Montpellier III.

Ripoll, François. 2006. "Adaptations latines d'un thème homérique: La Théomachie." *Phoenix* 60(3–4): 236–58.

Ripoll, François. 2015. "Statius and Silius Italicus." In *Brill's Companion to Statius*, ed. William J. Dominik, Carole E. Newlands, and Kyle Gervais, 425–43. Leiden: Brill.

Robinson, Matthew. 2011. *Ovid Fasti, Book 2*. Oxford: Oxford University Press.

Roche, Paul. 2009. *Lucan De Bello Civili Book 1*. Oxford: Oxford University Press.

Rohde, Fridericus. 1911. *De interiectionum usu apud aetatis argenteae scriptores Latinos*. Königsberg: Ex officina Hartungiana.

276 Bibliography

Roosjen, P. P. K. 1996. *Silius Italicus Punica liber XIV: Een Commentaar.* Maastricht: UPM.

Rosenstein, Nathan Stewart. 1990. *Imperatores Victi: Military Defeat and Aristocratic Competition in the Middle and Late Republic.* Berkeley, CA: University of California Press.

Ross, Thomas. 1661/1672. *The Second Punick War between Hannibal, and the Romanes.* London: Thomas Roycroft.

Ruperti, G. A. 1795. *Caii Silii Italici Punicorum Libri Septemdecim.* Göttingen: J. C. Dieterich.

Rutledge, Steven H. 2009. "Writing Imperial Politics: The Social and Political Background". In *Writing Politics in Imperial Rome,* ed. W. J. Dominik, J. Garthwaite, and P. A. Roche, 23–61. Leiden: Brill.

Sacerdoti, Arianna. 2007. "L'area semantica di *squaleo* nell'epica latina imperiale." *Invigilata Lucernis* 29: 229–40.

Santini, Carlo. 2008. "La lingua di Silio Italico: Sette parametri di analisi." In *Amicitiae templa serena: studi in onore di Giuseppe Aricò,* ed. L. Castagna and C. Riboldi, 1459–79. Milan: Vita e Pensiero.

Schiesaro, Alessandro. 1984. "*Nonne vides* in Lucrezio." *MD* 13: 143–57.

Schlieffen, Alfred, Graf von. 1931. *Cannae.* Fort Leavenworth, KS: Command and General Staff School Press.

Schöffel, Christian. 2002. *Martial, Buch 8: Einleitung, Text, Übersetzung, Kommentar.* Stuttgart: F. Steiner.

Schrijvers, Piet H. 2006. "Silius Italicus and the Roman Sublime." In *Flavian Poetry,* ed. R. R. Nauta, H.-J. van Dam, and J. J. L. Smolenaars, 97–111. Leiden: Brill.

Schuster, Mauriz. 1942. "Neue kritische Beiträge zu Silius Italicus." *WS* 60: 98–105.

Scullard, H. H. 1974. *The Elephant in the Greek and Roman World.* London: Thames & Hudson.

Shackleton Bailey, D. R. 1994. *Homoeoteleuton in Latin Dactylic Verse.* Stuttgart: B. G. Teubner.

Shackleton Bailey, D. R. 1959. "Siliana." *CQ* 9: 173–80.

Sharrock, Alison. 2000. "Intratextuality: Texts, Parts, and (W)holes in Theory." In *Intratextuality: Greek and Roman Relations,* ed. Alison Sharrock and Helen Morales, 1–39. Oxford: Oxford University Press.

Shaw, Brent D. 2001. "Raising and Killing Children: Two Roman Myths." *Mnemosyne* 54(1): 31–77.

Sklenár, Robert. 2003. *The Taste for Nothingness: A Study of Virtus and Related Themes in Lucan's Bellum Civile.* Ann Arbor, MI: University of Michigan Press.

Smolenaars, J. J. L., ed. 1994. *Statius: Thebaid VII.* Leiden: Brill.

Soubiran, Jean. 1966. *L'Élision dans la poésie latine.* Paris: C. Klincksieck.

Spaltenstein, François. 1986. *Commentaire des Punica de Silius Italicus (livres 1 à 8).* Geneva: Droz.

Spaltenstein, François. 1990. *Commentaire des Punica de Silius Italicus (livres 9 à 17).* Geneva: Droz.

Star, Christopher. 2006. "Commanding *Constantia* in Senecan Tragedy." *TAPhA* 136(1): 207–44.

Starks, J. 1999. "*Fides Aeneia:* The Transference of Punic Stereotypes in the *Aeneid.*" *CJ* 94: 255–83.

Bibliography

Steele, R. B. 1930. "The Interrelation of the Latin Poets under Domitian." *CP* 25: 328–42.

Stevenson, T. R. 1992. "The Ideal Benefactor and the Father Analogy in Greek and Roman Thought." *CQ* 42: 421–36.

Stocks, Claire. 2014. *The Roman Hannibal: Remembering the Enemy in Silius Italicus' Punica*. Liverpool: Liverpool University Press.

Stover, Tim. 2012. *Epic and Empire in Vespasianic Rome: A New Reading of Valerius Flaccus' Argonautica*. Oxford: Oxford University Press.

Summers, W. C. 1907. "Lindblom on Silius Italicus." *CQ* 1: 231–3.

Summers, W. C. 1900. "Notes on Silius Italicus, IX.–XVII." *CR* 14.6: 305–9.

Syme, Ronald. 1929. "The Argonautica of Valerius Flaccus." *CQ* 23 (3–4) 129.

Talbert, Richard J. A., et al. 2000. *Barrington Atlas of the Greek and Roman World*. Princeton, NJ: Princeton University Press.

Tarrant, R. J., ed. 1976. *Seneca: Agamemnon*. Cambridge: Cambridge University Press.

Tarrant, R. J. 2012. *Virgil: Aeneid Book XII*. Cambridge: Cambridge University Press.

Testard, Maurice. 1988. "*Silius Italicus: La Guerre punique: Tome III: Livres IX–XIII*. Texte établi et trad., par Volpilhac-Lenthéric, Martin, Miniconi et Devallet." *Revue Belge de Philologie et d'Histoire* 66(1): 144–6.

Thilo, Georg. 1891. "Zu den *Punica* des Silius Italicus." *Jahrbücher für classische Philologie* 143: 589–624.

Thomas, J.-F. 2001. "Le Thème de la perfidie carthaginoise dans l'œuvre de Silius Italicus." *Vita Latina* 161: 2–14.

Thomas, Richard F. 1986. "Virgil's Georgics and the Art of Reference." *HSCP* 90: 171–98.

Thomas, Richard F. 1988. *Virgil: Georgics*. Cambridge: Cambridge University Press.

Tipping, Ben. 2010. *Exemplary Epic: Silius Italicus' Punica*. Oxford: Oxford University Press.

Tytler, Henry William. 1828. *The Punics of Caius Silius Italicus*. Calcutta: V. Holcroft, Asiatic Press.

Ussani, Vicenzo. 1950. "Imitazioni dell'*Appendix Vergiliana* nei *Punica* di Silio Italico." *Maia* 3: 117–31.

Väänänen, Veikko. 1963. *Introduction au latin vulgaire*. Paris: C. Klincksieck.

van Dam, Harm-Jan, ed. 1984. *P. Papinius Statius Silvae Book 2*. Leiden: Brill.

van der Keur, Michiel. 2015. "A Commentary on Silius Italicus' Punica 13: Intertextuality and Narrative Structure." Diss. University of Amsterdam.

Van Veen, J.S. 1893. "Notulae Criticae ad Silium Italicum." *Mnemosyne* 21: 264–7.

Venini, Paola. 1978. "La visione dell'Italia nel catalogo di Silio Italico (Pun. 8.316–616)." *MIL* 36: 123–227.

Venini, Paola. 1972. "Cronologia e composizione nei '*Punica*' di Silio Italico." *RIL* 106: 518–31.

Villalba Álvarez, Joaquín. 2005. *Silio Itálico: La guerra púnica*. Madrid: Ediciones Akal.

Villalba Álvarez, Joaquín. 2008. "Épica e historiografía: La arenga militar en los *Punica* de Silio Itálico y su relación con Tito Livio." In *Retórica e historiografía: El discurso militar en la historiografía desde la Antigüedad hasta el Renacimiento*, ed. Juan Carlos Iglesias Zoido, 341–66. Madrid: Clásicas.

Vinchesi, Maria Assunta. 2001. *Silio Italico: Le guerre puniche*. Milan: Rizzoli.

Vinchesi, Maria Assunta. 2005. "Tipologie femminili nei Punica di Silio Italico: La fida coniunx e la virgo belligera." In *Modelli letterari e ideologia nell'età flavia*, ed. F. Gasti and G. Mazzoli, 97–126. Pavia.

Volpilhac-Lenthéric, Josée, ed. 2003. *Silius Italicus: La Guerre punique: Tome III: Livres IX et X*. Paris: Les Belles Lettres. [Josée Volpilhac-Lenthéric, Livres IX–X; Michael Martin, Livres XI–XII; Pierre Miniconi et Georges Devallet, Livre XIII].

Wacht, Manfred. 1989. *Concordantia in Silii Italici Punica*. Hildesheim: Olms-Weidmann.

Wagner, G. P. E. 1832. *Publius Virgilius Maro varietate lectionis et perpetua adnotatione illustratus a Christ. Gottl. Heyne*. 4th edn. Leipzig: Hahn.

Wallace, M. T. V. 1968. "Some Aspects of Time in the *Punica* of Silius Italicus." *CW* 62: 83–93.

Watson, Patricia. 1985. "Axelson Revisited: The Selection of Vocabulary in Latin Poetry." *CQ* 35(2): 430–48.

Watt, W. S. 1984. "Notes on Latin Epic Poetry." *BICS* 31: 153–70.

Watt, W. S. 1985. "Siliana." *ICS* 10(2): 275–80.

Watt, W. S. 1988. "Siliana." *MH* 45(3): 170–81.

White, Peter. 1975. "The Friends of Martial, Statius, and Pliny, and the Dispersal of Patronage." *HSCP* 79: 265–300.

Wick, Claudia. 2004. *M. Annaeus Lucanus: Bellum Civile Liber IX: Kommentar*. Munich: K. G. Saur.

Wiedermann, M. 1898. *De elisione in carmine Punicorum Silii Italici*. Teschen: K. und K. Hofbuchdruckerei K. Prochaska.

Wijsman, H. J. W. 1996. *Valerius Flaccus, Argonautica, Book V: A Commentary*. Leiden: Brill.

Wijsman, H. J. W. 2000. *Valerius Flaccus, Argonautica, Book VI: A Commentary*. Leiden: Brill.

Wilkinson, L. P. 1963. *Golden Latin Artistry*. Cambridge: Cambridge University Press.

Wills, J. 1996. *Repetition in Latin Poetry: Figures of Allusion*. Oxford: Clarendon Press.

Yardley, J. C. 2019. *Livy: History of Rome, Vol. 5: Books 21–22*. Cambridge, MA: Harvard University Press.

Zaia, Silvia. 2016. "Sili Italici Punicorum Liber Nonus: Introduzione e commento." Diss. University of Padua.

Zwiener, Karl August. 1909. *De vocum Graecarum apud poetas Latinos ab Ovidi temporibus usque ad primi p. Chr. n. saeculi finem usu*. Bratislava: M. et H. Marcus.

Index Locorum

Apollonius Rhodius, *Argonautica*
1.609–26	126
4.1309–11	183

Appian, *Hannibalica*
7	20
22	19, 232
26	177

Catullus
64.65	257
64.340	128
64.397	174
66.23	222
68.92–3	142
76.18	214
101.6	212

Cicero
Acad. 1.29	126
Amic. 32	206
Arat. 114	127
Arat. 431	221
Att. 2.5.4	102
Balb. 28	122
Balb. 51	157
Brut. 54	120
Brut. 263	150
Carm. 23.1	144
De Orat. 3.102	153
De Orat. 3.167	156
Div. 2.85	208
Dom. 64	214
Fam. 7.13.2	97
Leg. 2.21	94
Leg. 3.9	97
Marcell. 13	173
Mil. 85	119
Mur. 1	94
Mur. 88	114
ND 1.42	129
Off. 3.47	7
Off. 3.116	244
Phil. 2.77	138
Phil. 3.5	135
Phil. 5.39	237
Phil. 12.8	113
Phil. 13.20	236
Phil. 14.26	211

Pis. 20	181
Planc. 5	209
Planc. 101	131
Prov. Cons. 23	213
Rab. 10	139
Scaur. 48	237
Sest. 7	109
Sest. 35	247
Sull. 91.8	97
TD 2.15	115
Tusc. 1.101	191
Tusc. 1.115	140
Verr. 2.5.103	248
Verr. 2.5.186	189

Quintus Cicero
Pet. 20, 57	175

Claudian
III Cos. Hon. 93–5	232
IV Cos. Hon. 630	152
VI Cos. Hon. 1	142
VI Cos. Hon. 182–3	157
VI Cos. Hon. 325	251
Carm. Min. 53.77–9	190
DRP 1.212	182
DRP 3.125–6	173
Eutr. 2.284	168
Eutr. 2.349	212
Goth. 469–70	109
Hon. nupt. 14	240
Ruf. 1.97	177
Ruf. 2 praef. 10	171
Ruf. 2.115	109
Stil. 1.162	164
Stil. 1.285	195
Stil. 1.343	239
Stil. 1.355–6	119
Stil. 2.47–8	115
Stil. 2.374	257
Theod. 262	243

Corippus
Ioh. 3.22	256
Ioh. 5.114	248
Ioh. 5.174	250
Ioh. 5.33	186
Ioh. 6.24	180
Ioh. 6.349	97
Ioh. 8.397	134

Index Locorum

Ennius
Ann. 26	151
Ann. 126	126
Ann. 234–5	157
Ann. 252	97
Ann. 258–60	100
Ann. 266	97, 187, 247
Ann. 292	170
Ann. 297	141
Ann. 319	186
Ann. 350	184
Ann. 353	132
Ann. 355	249
Ann. 363	113
Ann. 389	199
Ann. 428	178, 185
Ann. 431	253
Ann. 453	157
Ann. 469	194
Ann. 483–4	203
Ann. 484	133
Ann. 554	216
Ann. 557	193
Ann. 581	228
Ann. 584	189, 190
Ann. 618	124

Euripides
Frg. 449	140
Med. 476–7	174
Ion 871–2	183

Homer
Il. 1.148–71	155
Il. 1.475	149
Il. 2.145	229
Il. 2.147–9	197
Il. 2.153	185
Il. 2.162	203
Il. 2.204–5	105
Il. 2.225–42	155
Il. 2.257–64	129
Il. 2.417–18	202
Il. 2.484–93	193
Il. 2.488–92	194
Il. 2.529	249
Il. 2.638	126
Il. 2.786	225
Il. 2.793	126
Il. 3.381	227
Il. 4.20–4	236
Il. 4.50–67	238
Il. 4.104	191
Il. 4.105–13	253
Il. 4.164–5	242

Il. 4.422–8	179
Il. 4.442–3	219
Il. 4.515	183
Il. 4.527	126
Il. 5.302–10	205
Il. 5.846–63	18 (n. 56)
Il. 5.853–4	220
Il. 5.864–7	221
Il. 6.175	149
Il. 6.448–9	242
Il. 8.39	183
Il. 8.47–52	184
Il. 8.86	202
Il. 9.2	132
Il. 9.705	149
Il. 10.460–6	202
Il. 11.1–2	149
Il. 11.97–8	206
Il. 11.384–95	253
Il. 11.500	177
Il. 11.749	202
Il. 11.817	203
Il. 12.154–61	247
Il. 12.243	93
Il. 12.278–89	247
Il. 12.338	185
Il. 12.378–86	205
Il. 13.130–1	189
Il. 13.137–9	205
Il. 13.713	253
Il. 13.797–9	180
Il. 14.394–5	176, 178
Il. 14.398–401	179
Il. 15.157–67	224
Il. 15.618–19	188
Il. 15.694–5	227, 228
Il. 16.765–71	179
Il. 19.1–2	149
Il. 19.61	202
Il. 20.285–7	205
Il. 20.302	225
Il. 20.399–400	206
Il. 20.438–40	220
Il. 21.218–20	152
Il. 21.403–6	223
Il. 21.407	184
Il. 22.131–7	216
Il. 22.183	183
Il. 23.222–3	110
Il. 24.77	225
Il. 24.738	202
Od. 5.295–6	229
Od. 11.303–4	183
Od. 11.313–16	186
Od. 19.361–475	143

Index Locorum

Horace
- *AP* 408–11 — 4 (n. 9)
- *Carm.* 1.2.38 — 243
- *Carm.* 1.3.14 — 179
- *Carm.* 1.10.15 — 122
- *Carm.* 1.15.9–10 — 244
- *Carm.* 1.28.15 — 111
- *Carm.* 1.35.15 — 149
- *Carm.* 2.1.3 — 196
- *Carm.* 2.1.4–5 — 98, 99
- *Carm.* 3.1.3 — 193
- *Carm.* 3.7.4 — 95
- *Carm.* 3.25.9 — 95
- *Carm.* 3.27.15 — 171
- *Carm.* 3.27.75 — 156
- *Carm.* 4.1.2 — 133
- *Carm.* 4.4.12 — 108
- *Epist.* 1.6.14 — 172
- *Epist.* 1.14.37–8 — 223
- *Epist.* 1.17.41–2 — 201
- *Epist.* 1.19.9 — 143
- *Epist.* 2.1.5 — 183
- *Epist.* 2.2.70 — 198
- *Epod.* 1.2 — 167
- *Epod.* 16.19 — 122
- *Epod.* 17.31–2 — 141
- *Serm.* 1.2.41 — 254
- *Serm.* 1.3.104 — 226
- *Serm.* 1.5.39 — 153
- *Serm.* 1.9.28 — 125
- *Serm.* 1.9.59–60 — 140
- *Serm.* 2.1.47 — 102
- *Serm.* 2.2.124 — 156

Ilias Latina
- 248–9 — 129
- 356 — 109
- 398 — 123
- 530 — 196
- 543 — 127
- 562 — 136
- 777 — 134
- 893 — 201
- 955–6 — 190
- 1055 — 186

Livy
- 1.25.9 — 105
- 1.26.12 — 200
- 1.46.2 — 173
- 2.6.7 — 129
- 2.10.11 — 151
- 2.12 — 199
- 2.19.5 — 192
- 2.19.10 — 228
- 2.19–20 — 182
- 2.55.6 — 198
- 2.59.6 — 109
- 3.6.9 — 155
- 3.47.6 — 172
- 3.60.9 — 211
- 3.63.1 — 228
- 4.20.6 — 214
- 4.37.11 — 116
- 4.40.7 — 228
- 4.51.8 — 119
- 5.37.7 — 151
- 5.39.5 — 132
- 5.52.7 — 237
- 6.12.8 — 97
- 6.18.14 — 240
- 6.24.3 — 97
- 6.32.10 — 126
- 7.40.14 — 97
- 8.2.3 — 100
- 8.7.10 — 250
- 9.3.4 — 141
- 9.6.3 — 128
- 9.12.8 — 247
- 9.14.9 — 159
- 9.37.9 — 97
- 9.45.14 — 116
- 10.5.3 — 169
- 10.29.5 — 228
- 10.36.6 — 246
- 10.36.12 — 228
- 21.8.10–12 — 193
- 21.19.1 — 151
- 21.21.1 — 151
- 21.21.12 — 165
- 21.27.1 — 244
- 21.28.1 — 95
- 21.32.9 — 116
- 21.40.9 — 235
- 21.43.6 — 153
- 21.43.13 — 14, 150
- 21.43.17 — 170
- 21.45.5–6 — 14, 155
- 21.52–6 — 24 (n. 45)
- 21.56.6 — 20 (n. 43)
- 21.58.11 — 20 (n. 43)
- 22.2.10 — 20 (n. 43)
- 22.5.6 — 105
- 22.5.8 — 219
- 22.7.1 — 257
- 22.9.5 — 175
- 22.12.10 — 112
- 22.15.4 — 98
- 22.18.6–7 — 120
- 22.32.5 — 163

22.35.3	102
22.39	258
22.40.3	102
22.40.6	176
22.41.1	96, 97
22.41.1–3	10
22.41.2	99
22.41.5	112, 136
22.42.7	104
22.42.8	99
22.42.9	9
22.42.10–12	12
22.42.12	104
22.43.9	97, 117
22.43.10	230
22.43.10–11	18 (n.38)
22.44.5	95, 113
22.44.5–7	10
22.45.4	104
22.45.4–5	99
22.45.5	110
22.45.8	15 (n. 27), 174
22.46.2	160, 164
22.46.3	166
22.46.4	15
22.46.6	164
22.46.7	15, 163
22.46.9	18
22.47	188, 197
22.47.2	164, 190
22.47.4	188
22.47.5	17 (n. 35), 198
22.49.7	111
22.49.13	258
22.49.14	261
22.49.16	244
22.51	159
22.51.4	158
22.51.8	233
22.53.1–3	176
22.53.6	172
22.57.9	211
22.59.15	109
22.60.13	142
22.61.6–7	24 (n. 48)
22.61.11	175
22.61.11–13	174
23.13.7	20
23.15.13	232
23.17.9	208
23.21.7	24 (n. 48)
23.24.4	199
23.40–1	202
24.10.11	247
24.35.7	175
24.44.10	246

24.48.11	104
25.6.21	178
25.12.6	116
25.12.8	116
25.26.10	125
26.4.1	119
26.5.10–26	20 (n. 44)
26.27.14	237
26.34.5	157
27.18.17	198
27.34.3	102
28.11.2	119
28.17.7	197
28.45.19	175
29.37.13	102
30.10.20	257
30.18.15	228
30.30.1	215
30.31.8	97
30.45.6	240
32.37.5	100
33.4.4	165
33.15.11	123
34.14.11	127
34.36.6	109
35.11.3	109
37.19.5	228
37.59.3	248
38.17.5	178
38.21.9	141
39.15.9	210
40.8.17	131
41.19.4	192
44.5.2	231
44.15.5	100
44.42.6	257
Per. 79	12 (n. 23)
Per. 117	178

Lucan, *Bellum Civile*

1.28–9	152
1.68	194
1.129	216
1.137	202
1.150	98
1.154	222
1.168–9	152
1.207	226
1.208	150
1.228	28 (n. 54)
1.239–40	149
1.245	166
1.278	122
1.287	241
1.303–5	111
1.341	205

Index Locorum

1.341–2	119	4.155	149
1.371	180	4.174–5	246
1.373–4	158	4.259	174
1.391	228	4.286–7	235
1.397	160	4.370	252
1.420	160	4.472–3	139
1.470	93, 94	4.511	146
1.474	177	4.536	259
1.528–9	218	4.585	239
1.540–1	234	4.677	168
1.556	182	4.678–9	161
1.564–5	116	4.702	113
1.600	182	4.713–14	123, 127
1.638	116	4.746	177
1.667–8	201	4.781–2	190
2.9	166	4.785	198
2.21–8	108	5.14	142
2.41	197	5.41	137
2.116	155	5.82	239
2.184–5	206	5.118	247
2.187	232	5.330	119
2.201–4	190	5.349–51	103
2.203	190	5.375	158
2.209–20	152	5.406	122
2.261–2	98	5.461–2	215
2.297–304	108	5.567	180
2.453–4	210	5.608–9	229
2.525	160	5.660	137
2.532	189	5.737	104
2.625	224	6.103	125
2.682	177	6.184	167
3.16–17	170	6.184	198
3.17	171	6.198	193
3.71	155	6.225–6	219
3.142	129	6.269–70	177
3.203–4	166	6.290	159
3.278	150	6.293–7	230
3.316	186	6.296	231
3.350	136	6.351	255
3.350	151	6.417	109
3.385	97	6.621	110
3.469–73	205	6.625	165
3.479	253	6.631	173
3.498	176	6.631	27
3.501	252	6.773	133
3.521–2	106	6.800	171
3.579	251	7.1–2	26, 148
3.609–12	203	7.30–1	25, 100
3.627	152	7.47–8	25
3.697	101	7.52	26, 113
3.709–11	165	7.52–3	25, 95
3.739–40	140	7.58–9	26, 118
3.744–5	110	7.60	26
4.9	164	7.82	25, 95
4.19	243	7.82–3	26, 104
4.151–2	105	7.87–123	25, 26, 111

284 Index Locorum

7.105–7	26, 113
7.144–50	27
7.144–6	221
7.149	217
7.152	94
7.195	242
7.205–13	27, 195
7.214–34	26
7.232	165
7.272–3	26
7.287–9	27, 169
7.288–9	170
7.318–19	26, 158
7.326	27, 159
7.329–33	26, 104
7.339–40	173
7.342	246
7.367–8	27, 192
7.381	137
7.426–7	26, 148
7.475–84	178
7.487–8	27, 196
7.490–1	187
7.517	199
7.519–20	27, 191
7.520	191
7.527	121
7.552	147
7.573	27, 190
7.578	171
7.655	251
7.669–70	21
7.671	125
7.675–9	21
7.676	100
7.686	21
7.686–7	21
7.689	26, 147
7.701–2	21
7.729	133
7.795	123
8.14	236
8.314	137
8.314–16	137
8.332	100
8.332	26
8.506	213
8.568	225
8.608	194
8.658	100
8.669–70	133
9.11–12	237
9.66–7	258
9.127–8	146
9.133	172
9.304	227

9.350–4	183
9.439–41	160
9.470–5	187
9.491	258
9.514	183
9.588	144
9.720	193
9.735	150
9.881	144
9.891–3	161
10.131	162
10.144	248
10.203	168
10.203	171
10.334	174
10.400	104

Lucretius, *De Rerum Natura*

1.2	184
1.100	94
1.252	197
1.475	136
1.1107	229
2.40–1	168
2.136	127
2.144	106
2.343	246
2.537	256
2.537–8	247
2.914	143
2.922	246
3.544	144, 145
3.966	230
3.1034	177
4.843	136
4.978–9	109
4.1069	204
4.1197	246
5.246	94
5.313	205
5.564	96
5.631	159
5.632	201
5.795	143
5.887	144
5.1188	237
5.1230	233
5.1252–3	252
5.1289	236
5.1296	136
5.1302	167, 246
6.308	231
6.479–80	243
6.757–8	125
6.1011	132
6.1129	236

Index Locorum

6.1227	122
6.1251–2	110
6.1265	125

Manilius

Astr. 1.245	214
Astr. 1.391	187
Astr. 1.692	163
Astr. 1.783	130
Astr. 3.19	107
Astr. 3.629	156
Astr. 4.40	239
Astr. 4.187	129
Astr. 4.228	108
Astr. 4.315	113
Astr. 4.374	100
Astr. 4.558	197
Astr. 4.758–9	162

Martial

1.57.1	209
4.434	154
4.632	154
5.5.7	7
5.71.4	236
7.6.10	241
7.32.1	240
8.65	142
8.66	3 (n. 4)
9.20.7	178
9.30.5	135
11.91–6	206
14.179.1	221

Ovid

AA 2.669	144
AA 3.373	129
Am. 1.7.54–5	197
Am. 1.8.97	127
Am. 1.15.14	4 (n. 9)
Am. 2.8.21	102
Am. 2.12.1	241
Am. 2.13.18	177
Am. 3.1.59	170
Am. 3.8.12	172
Am. 3.8.14	183
Fasti 1.71	153
Fasti 1.501	164
Fasti 1.558	152
Fasti 1.623	127
Fasti 2.16	153
Fasti 2.75	145
Fasti 2.94	151
Fasti 2.211–12	199
Fasti 2.235–6	100
Fasti 2.502	223

Fasti 2.579	201
Fasti 2.734	150
Fasti 3.86	241
Fasti 3.259–60	244
Fasti 3.505	134
Fasti 3.568	180
Fasti 3.680	196
Fasti 4.79–80	120, 121
Fasti 4.157–8	116
Fasti 4.255–6	155
Fasti 4.463	204
Fasti 4.472	210
Fasti 4.481	141
Fasti 4.626	236
Fasti 4.675–6	153
Fasti 5.71	172
Fasti 5.299	144
Fasti 5.357	197
Fasti 5.426	125
Fasti 5.453	131
Fasti 5.640	157
Fasti 5.719	183
Fasti 6.45	239
Fasti 6.371	113
Her. 1.52	157
Her. 1.114	147
Her. 3.43	97
Her. 3.63	239
Her. 4.20	127
Her. 6.162	158
Her. 9.39	99
Her. 10.88	171
Her. 12.161–2	132
Her. 14.126	125
Her. 16.67	132
Her. 16.372	236
Her. 19.156	222
Her. 21.18	141
Ibis 137	97
Ibis 172	169
Ibis 243–8	115
Ibis 246–7	116
Ibis 625	46
Ibis. 644	228
Met. 1.143	178
Met. 1.175	130
Met. 1.202	251
Met. 1.234	226
Met. 1.268	191
Met. 1.325–6	100
Met. 1.423	151
Met. 1.452–3	126
Met. 1.484	222
Met. 1.527	124
Met. 1.602	98
Met. 1.623	196

Index Locorum

Met. 1.674	216	*Met.* 6.398	145
Met. 1.731	145	*Met.* 6.427	181
Met. 1.774	162	*Met.* 6.545	130
Met. 2.222–5	252	*Met.* 6.555–62	203
Met. 2.235–6	162	*Met.* 7.56	189
Met. 2.272	184	*Met.* 7.108	231
Met. 2.326	174	*Met.* 7.111	111
Met. 2.342	141	*Met.* 7.136	112
Met. 2.361	133	*Met.* 7.211	254
Met. 2.398–9	225	*Met.* 7.342	127
Met. 2.439	223	*Met.* 7.422–3	143
Met. 2.482	115	*Met.* 7.429	256
Met. 2.655–6	141	*Met.* 7.804	106
Met. 2.720–1	178	*Met.* 7.848–9	141
Met. 3.64	221	*Met.* 8.12	197
Met. 3.80	219	*Met.* 8.20	136
Met. 3.88	227	*Met.* 8.27	123
Met. 3.141–2	118	*Met.* 8.87	124
Met. 3.173	145	*Met.* 8.106	112
Met. 3.191	94	*Met.* 8.231	137
Met. 3.271–2	129	*Met.* 8.363–4	105
Met. 3.341	95	*Met.* 8.408	245
Met. 3.421	256	*Met.* 8.418	127
Met. 3.704	197	*Met.* 8.425	230
Met. 3.705	108	*Met.* 8.703	240
Met. 4.67	155	*Met.* 8.708–9	209
Met. 4.99	128	*Met.* 9.40–1	189
Met. 4.99–100	125	*Met.* 9.43–5	189
Met. 4.105	127	*Met.* 9.60	202
Met. 4.156–7	137	*Met.* 9.86	206
Met. 4.226	134	*Met.* 9.132	99
Met. 4.448	183	*Met.* 9.202	252
Met. 4.595	135	*Met.* 9.271	216
Met. 4.616	234	*Met.* 9.275	196
Met. 4.655–6	217	*Met.* 9.289	144
Met. 4.656	231	*Met.* 9.307	211
Met. 4.663	229	*Met.* 9.450	160
Met. 4.674	206	*Met.* 9.520	230
Met. 4.709–10	165	*Met.* 9.574	129
Met. 4.778	224	*Met.* 9.581	135
Met. 5.47	241	*Met.* 9.630	259
Met. 5.73	209	*Met.* 9.749–50	108
Met. 5.96	144	*Met.* 10.37	121
Met. 5.133	127	*Met.* 10.44	259
Met. 5.191–2	213	*Met.* 10.73	171
Met. 5.197–9	247	*Met.* 10.151	186
Met. 5.251–2	216, 228	*Met.* 10.256	138
Met. 5.293	174	*Met.* 10.366–7	149
Met. 5.325	186	*Met.* 10.399	112
Met. 5.328	183	*Met.* 10.611	144
Met. 5.345	256	*Met.* 10.634	100
Met. 5.655–6	156	*Met.* 10.664	242
Met. 6.118	211	*Met.* 10.683	129
Met. 6.218	243	*Met.* 11.138	167
Met. 6.242	256	*Met.* 11.139	254
Met. 6.257	230	*Met.* 11.177	122

Index Locorum

Met. 11.216–17	155	*Pont.* 4.9.17	164
Met. 11.411	94	*Rem.* 129	240
Met. 11.464	104	*Rem.* 797	155
Met. 11.490–1	179	*Rem.* 808	252
Met. 11.543	201	*Trist.* 1.6.9	187
Met. 11.553	163	*Trist.* 2.1.149–50	179
Met. 11.554	249	*Trist.* 2.424	4 (n. 9)
Met. 12.67–8	98	*Trist.* 3.2.27	144
Met. 12.79	95	*Trist.* 3.10.9	231
Met. 12.155	253	*Trist.* 3.11.34	118
Met. 12.172	249	*Trist.* 4.3.43–4	140
Met. 12.180	136	*Trist.* 4.6.15	225
Met. 12.223	246	*Trist.* 4.10.1–3	134
Met. 12.228	131	*Trist.* 5.7b.65	260
Met. 12.256	141	*Trist.* 5.8.2	129
Met. 12.291	165	*Trist.* 5.12.13	232
Met. 12.373–4	113	*Trist.* 5.12.36	256
Met. 12.469	145		
Met. 12.491	202	*Panegyricus Messallae*	
Met. 13.15	139	60	157
Met. 13.33	240		
Met. 13.91	235	Pliny the Elder	
Met. 13.241	100	*NH* 2.148	178
Met. 13.296	175	*NH* 3.22	165
Met. 13.485	258	*NH* 3.68	119
Met. 13.958–9	108	*NH* 3.152	224
Met. 14.51	163	*NH* 4.110	165
Met. 14.66	252	*NH* 5.24	156
Met. 14.181–4	223	*NH* 5.30	161
Met. 14.448	234	*NH* 5.34	97
Met. 14.495	150	*NH* 5.39	162
Met. 14.539	252	*NH* 5.39	162
Met. 14.541	252	*NH* 5.94	120
Met. 14.633	157	*NH* 7.24	231
Met. 14.734	104	*NH* 7.123	120
Met. 14.762	196	*NH* 7.143	120
Met. 14.800–1	125	*NH* 8.16	246
Met. 15.52	150	*NH* 8.27	167
Met. 15.174	174	*NH* 8.29	256
Met. 15.220	145	*NH* 11.150	140
Met. 15.296	126	*NH* 17.37	210
Met. 15.348	231	*NH* 17.41	156
Met. 15.409	196	*NH* 18.94	156
Met. 15.432	166		
Met. 15.446	155		
Met. 15.580	99	Pliny the Younger	
Met. 15.583	160	*Ep.* 2.3.2	126
Met. 15.806	213	*Ep.* 3.7.1	3
Met. 15.807–15	241	*Ep.* 3.7.2	3 (n. 4)
Met. 15.862	182	*Ep.* 3.7.3	3 (n. 2)
Pont. 1.2.3–4	100	*Ep.* 3.7.5	3 (n. 8)
Pont. 1.7.47	143	*Ep.* 3.7.8	3
Pont. 2.2.80	116	*Ep.* 6.20.15	200
Pont. 2.3.23	256	*Ep.* 8.6.10	120
Pont. 3.3.61	166	*Pan.* 6.1	139
Pont. 4.8.59	186	*Pan.* 24.2	138

288   Index Locorum

Polybius

Hist. 1.32	119
Hist. 3.19	102
Hist. 3.22.8–9	202
Hist. 3.23.2	156
Hist. 3.33.15	97
Hist. 3.71–4	24 (n. 49)
Hist. 3.72.10	168
Hist. 3.111.5	14
Hist. 3.113	15 (n. 27)
Hist. 3.115.11–12	17 (n. 35)
Hist. 7.9.2	183
Hist. 15.9.4	215

Propertius

2.7.16	137
2.8.10	151
2.10.3	236
2.13.8	129
2.13.25	137
2.18.13	144
2.34.33	128
3.7.47	235
3.21.6	95
3.21.14	233
3.21.31	198
3.22.8	217
3.24.7	149
3.24.14	257
4.2.55–6	186
4.7.54	135
4.8.8	218
4.9.38	134

Seneca the Elder

Contr. 2.3.14	138
Contr. 2.4.2	142
Contr. 7.1.4	226
Contr. 7.1.23	139
Contr. 7.3.8	214
Contr. 8.6	115
Contr. 9.4.5	140
Suas. 2.16	146

Seneca the Younger

Ag. 600	121
Ag. 754–5	162
Ag. 154	106
Ben. 3.28.6	259
Ben. 7.27.2	130
Ep. 16.2	150
Ep. 3.1.3	208
Epig. 18.7	197
HF 92	234
HF 240	124
HF 695	183

HF 699	197
HF 919	158
HF 1015	133
HF 1143–4	123
HF 1236	145
HF 1237	118
HF 1319	133
Ira 1.1.4	245
Ira 1.16.2	138
Ira 3.9.4	141
Marc. 18.5	168
Med. 42	174
Med. 74	106
Med. 256	174
Med. 376–7	243
Med. 552	110
Med. 793	128
NQ 2.34.2	94
NQ 3.pr.6	200
NQ 5.16.4	18 (n. 39), 229, 230
NQ 6.32.4	226
Oed. 31	261
Oed. 94	152
Oed. 202	247
Oed. 212	116
Oed. 357	99
Oed. 652	200
Oed. 712–14	127
Oed. 773	207
Oed. 976–7	146
Phaed. 69	164
Phaed. 117	254
Phaed. 352	246
Phaed. 545–7	247
Phaed. 724	139
Phaed. 1082	154
Phaed. 962	168
Phaed. 1159	181
Phoen. 36	147
Phoen. 38–9	107
Phoen. 279–80	171
Phoen. 280	94
Phoen. 404	99
Phoen. 530	223
Phoen. 575	157
Prov. 5.9	200
Thy. 530–1	102
Thy. 573	246
Thy. 763	124
Thy. 781–2	234
Thy. 795	146
Thy. 1057	139
Thy. 1085	107
Tro. 179–80	239
Tro. 446	237
Tro. 457	132

Index Locorum

Tro. 609	207
Tro. 1170	132

Silius Italicus, *Punica*

1.7–8	196
1.38–9	238
1.40–1	180
1.50–1	22, 152
1.59–60	222
1.68–9	94
1.72–3	156
1.141–2	150
1.190	164
1.211	166
1.218–19	161
1.237	156
1.244–5	95
1.245–6	94
1.249–50	166
1.267	253
1.280–1	215
1.314	165, 255
1.318	233
1.321	255
1.384–5	158
1.398–400	155
1.400–1	219
1.416	183
1.443–4	174, 245
1.507	95
1.514	109
1.515–16	202
1.550	139
1.551	228
1.592–3	180
1.607	157
1.681	135
2.38	247
2.51–3	155
2.54	114
2.66	121
2.79	164
2.145–6	148, 256
2.196	250
2.211	129
2.234	248
2.236	102
2.285	114
2.290	180
2.296	174, 245
2.304	116, 155
2.363	157
2.347	95
2.338–9	237
2.378	198
2.453–4	212

2.543–4	228
2.565	211
2.576	200
2.591	180
2.630–1	198
2.649	148
2.658–9	218
2.734	150
3.2	151
3.25	13
3.62	135
3.156	105
3.172	94
3.221	164
3.242–3	240
3.256–8	156
3.271–2	249
3.278–9	165
3.282–3	161
3.320–1	160
3.326–7	165
3.322–3	225
3.365	165, 255
3.366	121
3.373–4	195
3.389–90	154
3.405	241
3.425–6	237
3.450	151
3.463–4	246
3.495	151
3.509–10	158
3.564	151
3.565–6	181
3.580–1	194
3.584–5	195
3.588–90	196
3.607	169
3.619–20	194
3.620	114
3.658–9	229
3.687	116
3.707	22
3.714	107
4.35–7	200
4.53–5	215
4.63	105
4.79–80	239
4.98	149
4.134–5	245
4.162–3	191
4.207	256
4.234	222
4.242	206
4.275–6	185
4.277–8	218

290 Index Locorum

4.281–3	245		5.415	161
4.305	251		5.442–4	253
4.315	233		5.431–2	198
4.318	163		5.509	257
4.352–3	189		5.535	231
4.361–2	169		5.562–3	213
4.389–90	203		5.595–6	255
4.431–2	217		5.603	244
4.431–4	219		5.612–13	224
4.450	98		5.642–3	145
4.461–2	253		6.6–10	243
4.476–7	221, 259		6.50–1	209
4.481–2	149		6.101	145
4.496–7	153		6.110	114
4.516–17	211		6.129–30	237
4.549	164		6.143	219
4.550–1	98		6.169–70	132
4.553	190		6.223–5	168
4.582–3	105		6.226	163
4.584	232		6.246–7	246
4.599	167		6.321–2	231
4.601–2	250		6.335	107
4.603–4	249		6.439–40	122
4.605–6	234		6.466	145
4.610–11	249		6.476–8	134
4.621	152, 250		6.503	181
4.626	143		6.527–8	197
4.711	100		6.537–8	195
4.728	141		6.548–9	201
4.752–3	206		6.566	226
4.777	141		6.612–13	100
4.797	133		6.620–1	113
4.828	229		6.621	142
5.54	181, 259		6.625–6	98
5.71–2	186		6.644	147
5.76	240		6.665	123
5.92–3	238		7.26	149
5.100	257		7.51–2	250
5.160	151		7.101–2	159
5.167–8	214		7.106–7	177
5.172–3	237		7.155–6	125
5.174	250		7.160	121
5.191–2	149		7.217	139
5.197	165		7.228–9	117
5.198	255		7.230–1	105
5.204–5	181		7.232	99
5.214–15	187		7.248–9	114
5.240–1	176		7.280	151
5.255–6	146		7.294	128
5.275–6	222		7.295	147
5.328–30	188		7.316	253
5.373–4	188		7.325–7	95
5.387	184		7.329–30	102
5.393–4	219		7.360	253
5.395–6	188		7.364–6	252
5.406–7	242		7.383–4	104

Index Locorum

7.393	169	10.55–6	259
7.399	113	10.56	259, 261
7.459–61	217	10.62–3	199
7.480	224	10.89	163
7.483–4	114	10.107	218
7.491	240	10.151	193
7.493	241	10.188–90	177
7.528–9	159	10.203–4	230
7.539–41	259	10.209	234
7.549–50	109	10.222–3	154, 176
7.569–70	179	10.266–7	109
7.643–4	205	10.283–5	257
7.701–3	112	10.289–90	114
7.730	113	10.310–11	109
7.734–5	245	10.312–13	176
8.2–3	245	10.314–15	175
8.39	182	10.334	227
8.43	173	10.360–2	239
8.138	238	10.364	176
8.241	117	10.366	153
8.256–7	22	10.385–6	159
8.259–61	212	10.403–4	211, 234
8.263	95	10.405–6	108
8.276–7	257	10.434–5	222
8.286–7	257	10.455–6	144
8.299	141	10.468–9	153
8.301	23	10.476–7	103
8.310	8	10.511–12	245
8.309–10	212	10.514	10, 261
8.327	101	10.598–9	103
8.332–3	134, 258	10.604	124
8.352–3	215	10.608–14	9
8.364–5	208	10.627–9	261
8.367	166	10.657–8	22, 194
8.383	199	11.7–8	175
8.409–10	99	11.10	176
8.433	260	11.65	239
8.450–1	166	11.98	136
8.510	120	11.115–16	109
8.531	115	11.117	257
8.562–3	175	11.133	149
8.579	136	11.140	196
8.617–18	101	11.154	10
8.624–5	93	11.178–9	156
8.636–7	218	11.218–19	222
8.644–5	198	11.327–8	217
8.657–8	93	11.374–6	123
8.658–9	111	11.398	197
8.663–4	18	11.507–8	163, 164
8.670	20, 166	11.518	184
8.671–2	261	11.521–2	181
9.439	138	11.524	9
10.7–8	199	11.566	188
10.17–18	232	12.15–16	134
10.20	194	12.50	170
10.29–30	117	12.128	239

Index Locorum

12.133–5	251		15.135–6	250
12.168–9	149		15.140	115
12.188	229		15.246–7	257
12.232–3	164		15.340	188
12.267	105		15.377–8	132
12.329–30	114		15.378	112
12.343	166		15.451	215
12.358	121		15.471	96
12.388	194		15.508	241
12.406	220		15.508–9	168
12.431–2	151		15.516–17	187
12.472	105		15.532–3	152
12.512	238		15.554	96
12.549–50	109		15.604	175
12.574–5	106		15.621–3	163
12.613	139		15.686	248
12.621–2	219		15.691	187
12.643–4	139		15.697	124
12.647	191		15.716–17	198
12.672–3	109		16.30	178
12.687–8	165		16.66–7	204
12.719–21	236		16.73–4	237
13.41	155		16.133	119
13.59–60	158		16.149	150
13.65	131		16.277–8	164
13.129	111		16.412–13	109
13.158	231		16.428	156
13.209	258		16.515–16	122
13.217–18	176		16.590	116, 221
13.254	139		16.592–700	9
13.380	199		16.650–1	213
13.391–2	97		16.653	115
13.394	109		16.664–5	186
13.519–20	140		16.683–4	173
13.538–9	194		17.33	156
13.749	216		17.63–4	185
13.759–61	171		17.92–3	251
13.779–82	193		17.133–7	250
13.793–4	115		17.262–3	202
13.810	209		17.293–4	169
13.848–9	118		17.371	238
13.855–6	251		17.378	185
13.878	228		17.387–9	215
14.193	149		17.398	218
14.213	253		17.411	254
14.239	239		17.412	191
14.277–8	185		17.423	123
14.307	252		17.488–9	227
14.385–6	149		17.504–6	252
14.434	127		17.517	123
14.520–1	253		17.537	256
14.557–8	243		17.545–7	227
14.560	210		17.584	97
14.688	155		17.608	153
15.119–20	241		17.621	167
15.131	96		17.626	240

Index Locorum

17.649–50	185
17.650	219

Statius

Ach. 1.42	174
Ach. 1.115	252
Ach. 1.685	225
Ach. 1.791	103
Ach. 1.825–6	221
Ach. 1.926	149
Ach. 1.955	129
Ach. 2.132–4	192
Silv. 1.2.52–3	172
Silv. 1.4.79	151
Silv. 1.5.39	127
Silv. 1.6.1	194
Silv. 2.1.12–13	174
Silv. 2.1.229	111
Silv. 2.7.93	152
Silv. 3.2.45	229
Silv. 3.3.31	131
Silv. 3.3.101	167
Silv. 3.3.127	238
Silv. 3.4.24–5	141
Silv. 3.5.23	238
Silv. 3.5.35–6	238
Silv. 4.1.41	241
Silv. 4.3.4–6	19 (n. 42)
Silv. 4.3.32	178
Silv. 4.3.67	234
Silv. 4.3.90–1	19 (n. 42)
Silv. 4.4.61	211
Silv. 4.6.59	256
Silv. 4.6.83	151
Silv. 4.8.2	99
Silv. 4.8.19	184
Silv. 5.1.132	98
Theb. 1.184	239
Theb. 1.202	240
Theb. 1.309	216
Theb. 1.337	145
Theb. 1.395	230
Theb. 1.445–6	143
Theb. 1.490–1	172
Theb. 1.516	164
Theb. 1.652–4	156
Theb. 1.696	194
Theb. 2.3	171
Theb. 2.38	216
Theb. 2.74	95
Theb. 2.90	225
Theb. 2.94	28
Theb. 2.131	177
Theb. 2.187	153, 154
Theb. 2.225	171
Theb. 2,288	16 (n. 33)
Theb. 2.534	202
Theb. 2.559–69	205
Theb. 2.571	204
Theb. 2.642–3	209
Theb. 2.652–3	233
Theb. 2.707–12	202
Theb. 2.722–3	183
Theb. 2.733–4	131
Theb. 3.5–6	109
Theb. 3.17–18	95
Theb. 3.18	97
Theb. 3.92	259
Theb. 3.94	190
Theb. 3.115	110
Theb. 3.135	104
Theb. 3.175–6	139
Theb. 3.239–43	240
Theb. 3.314	168
Theb. 3.377	223
Theb. 3.423	212
Theb. 3.432	229
Theb. 3.456	99
Theb. 3.459	185
Theb. 4.33	201
Theb. 4.41	183
Theb. 4.47	167
Theb. 4.94	204
Theb. 4.111	184
Theb. 4.125	177
Theb. 4.146–7	149
Theb. 4.201–2	177
Theb. 4.211–13	171
Theb. 4.212	170
Theb. 4.302–3	193
Theb. 4.354–5	207
Theb. 4.394	127
Theb. 4.434	243
Theb. 4.488	116
Theb. 4.499	179
Theb. 4. 543–4	140
Theb. 4.638	176
Theb. 4.649	155
Theb. 4.730–1	256
Theb. 5.163	111
Theb. 5.227	173
Theb. 5.239–51	126
Theb. 5.348	164
Theb. 5.436	129
Theb. 5.685	210
Theb. 5.690	136
Theb. 5.722	183
Theb. 6.177	132
Theb. 6.211–12	141
Theb. 6.222	207
Theb. 6.295	250
Theb. 6.299–300	179

Index Locorum

Theb. 6.460	150	*Theb.* 10.391–2	125
Theb. 6.551	247	*Theb* 10.433	106
Theb. 6.715	232	*Theb.* 10.476	248
Theb. 6.734	100	*Theb.* 10.536	170
Theb. 6.766	169	*Theb.* 10.754–5	232
Theb. 6.772	176	*Theb.* 10.856–7	193
Theb. 6.793	199	*Theb.* 11.87–8	169
Theb. 6.935–6	93	*Theb.* 11.126	227
Theb. 7.11–12	232	*Theb.* 11.152	173
Theb. 7.52	232	*Theb.* 11.175	239
Theb. 7.128	100	*Theb.* 11.253	212
Theb. 7.155	186	*Theb.* 11.336–7	183
Theb. 7.196	113	*Theb.* 11.347	219
Theb. 7.354	143	*Theb.* 11.363	260
Theb. 7.379	102	*Theb.* 11.464	237
Theb. 7.589	178	*Theb.* 11.497	246
Theb. 7.591	152	*Theb.* 11.535–6	172
Theb. 7.673	98	*Theb.* 11.541–2	216
Theb. 7.682	113	*Theb.* 11.577–9	149
Theb. 7.744–9	205	*Theb.* 11.586	172
Theb. 8.19–20	239	*Theb.* 11.648	196
Theb. 8.78–9	123	*Theb.* 11.692	227
Theb. 8.138	147	*Theb.* 12.7	124
Theb. 8.173	134	*Theb.* 12.9–10	159
Theb. 8.373–4	193	*Theb.* 12.71	141
Theb. 8.398–9	189	*Theb.* 12.183	177
Theb. 8.421	250	*Theb.* 12.393	149
Theb. 8.496	147	*Theb.* 12.417–18	138
Theb. 8.531	240		
Theb. 8.638	101	**Suetonius**	
Theb. 8.657	96	*Claud.* 15.2	142
Theb. 8.669	207	*Dom.* 15.6	208
Theb. 8.711	141		
Theb. 8.754	221	**Tacitus**	
Theb. 9.50	102	*Agr.* 18.5	126
Theb. 9.91	188	*Ann.* 1.61	152
Theb. 9.110	176	*Ann.* 2.24	233
Theb. 9.111–12	125	*Ann.* 3.21	177
Theb. 9.126	249	*Ann.* 12.37	119
Theb. 9.155–6	217	*Ann.* 12.60.16	100
Theb. 9.241	249	*Germ.* 6.1	165
Theb. 9.268–9	203	*Germ.* 33.2	97
Theb. 9.273	212	*Germ.* 42	159
Theb. 9.453	145	*Hist.* 1.38.3	105
Theb. 9.484–5	238	*Hist.* 1.79	219
Theb. 9.506–10	234	*Hist.* 3.51	12 (n. 23)
Theb. 9.558	127	*Hist.* 3.51	12 (n. 24)
Theb. 9.569	131	*Hist.* 4.20.3	**197**
Theb. 9.621	186	*Hist.* 4.50.4	161, 163
Theb. 9.773–4	235		
Theb. 10.23–4	256	**Valerius Flaccus**	
Theb. 10.78	185	*Arg.* 1.48	231
Theb. 10.178	171	*Arg.* 1.73	236
Theb. 10.196–7	159	*Arg.* 1.99	194
Theb. 10.219	132	*Arg.* 1.164	113
Theb. 10.249–346	11	*Arg.* 1.177	119

Index Locorum

Arg. 1.251	95	*Arg.* 5.575	181
Arg. 1.602	229	*Arg.* 5.613	256
Arg. 1.613	234	*Arg.* 5.650	181
Arg. 1.615	206	*Arg.* 5.672	238
Arg. 1.850	119	*Arg.* 6.27–8	96
Arg. 2.26–7	256	*Arg.* 6.158–9	171
Arg. 2.86	230	*Arg.* 6.159	171
Arg. 2.114	119	*Arg.* 6.162	192
Arg. 2.170	122	*Arg.* 6.198	250
Arg. 2.184–5	222	*Arg.* 6.201–2	170
Arg. 2.198	216	*Arg.* 6.225	249
Arg. 2.261	149	*Arg.* 6.276	147
Arg. 2.410–13	126	*Arg.* 6.340	258
Arg. 2.482	183	*Arg.* 6.347	248
Arg. 2.516	98	*Arg.* 6.411–12	155
Arg. 2.522–4	188	*Arg.* 6.427	97
Arg. 2.541	112	*Arg.* 6.427–8	125
Arg. 2.544–5	130	*Arg.* 6.463	109
Arg. 2.655	221	*Arg.* 6.480–1	217
Arg. 2.664–5	141	*Arg.* 6.518	248
Arg. 3.9	228	*Arg.* 6.520–1	199
Arg. 3.18	95	*Arg.* 6.548	137
Arg. 3.84	243	*Arg.* 6.588	168
Arg. 3.96	193	*Arg.* 6.648–51	205
Arg. 3.123	97	*Arg.* 6.708	141
Arg. 3.179–80	144	*Arg.* 6.733–4	100
Arg. 3.191	163	*Arg.* 6.746	220
Arg. 3.211	148	*Arg.* 7.97	96
Arg. 3.251	204	*Arg.* 7.197	225
Arg. 3.257	106	*Arg.* 7.335	226
Arg. 3.276	152	*Arg.* 7.335	226
Arg. 3.309–10	140	*Arg.* 7.413	109
Arg. 3.330	183	*Arg.* 7.525–6	218
Arg. 3.442–3	250	*Arg.* 7.533	212
Arg. 3.451	226	*Arg.* 7.604	239
Arg. 3.509	141	*Arg.* 8.81	124
Arg. 3.550	169	*Arg.* 33.723	183
Arg. 3.507–8	219		
Arg. 4.77	224	**Valerius Maximus**	
Arg. 4.149	219	1.1.15–16	7 (n. 14)
Arg. 4.176	247	1.1.16	115
Arg. 4.184–5	206	3.2.*ext.* 4	146
Arg. 4.235	218	5.5.4	12
Arg. 4.373	137	5.5.4	12 (n. 23)
Arg. 4.602	181	5.8.4	237
Arg. 4.620	126	6.4.1	7 (n. 14)
Arg. 4.686	253	7.4.*ext.* 2	7 (n. 14)
Arg. 5.43	116	8.15.7	124
Arg. 5.95–6	172	9.11.*ext.* 1	142
Arg. 5.252	232	9.15.3	142
Arg. 5.288–9	174		
Arg. 5.321	153, 154	**Virgil**	
Arg. 5.331	106	*Aen.* 1.40	255
Arg. 5.339	213	*Aen.* 1.53–4	229
Arg. 5.520	222	*Aen.* 1.54	230
Arg. 5.521–2	180	*Aen.* 1.62	229, 230

Index Locorum

Aen. 1.65–75	229		*Aen.* 2.575	129
Aen. 1.66	122		*Aen.* 2.591–2	184
Aen. 1.69–70	240		*Aen.* 2.612–14	183
Aen. 1.83	231		*Aen.* 2.653	97
Aen. 1.85–6	229		*Aen.* 2.668	149
Aen. 1.88	107		*Aen.* 2.679	132
Aen. 1.88–9	231		*Aen.* 2.699	250
Aen. 1.91	213		*Aen.* 2.719–20	254
Aen. 1.102	231		*Aen.* 2.730	178
Aen. 1.102	235		*Aen.* 2.753–4	125
Aen. 1.129	229		*Aen.* 2.758	252
Aen. 1.162–3	187		*Aen.* 3.28	141
Aen. 1.209	203		*Aen.* 3.29–30	132
Aen. 1.215	237		*Aen.* 3.108	134
Aen. 1.247–8	237		*Aen.* 3.160	238
Aen. 1.248–9	131		*Aen.* 3.166	240
Aen. 1.254	186		*Aen.* 3.169–70	135
Aen. 1.255	240		*Aen.* 3.198–9	191
Aen. 1.262	241		*Aen.* 3.234	113
Aen. 1.263–4	240		*Aen.* 3.237	126
Aen. 1.371	140		*Aen.* 3.246	141
Aen. 1.377	155		*Aen.* 3.259–60	112
Aen. 1.378–80	134		*Aen.* 3.265	114
Aen. 1.397	234		*Aen.* 3.287	174
Aen. 1.471	158		*Aen.* 3.318	256
Aen. 1.523	211		*Aen.* 3.380	183
Aen. 1.533	240		*Aen.* 3.444	116
Aen. 1.566	250		*Aen.* 3.490	255
Aen. 1.567	180		*Aen.* 3.500	112
Aen. 2.6	188		*Aen.* 3.509	232
Aen. 2.14	28		*Aen.* 3.564	163
Aen. 2.14	28 (n. 54)		*Aen.* 3.573–4	231
Aen. 2.27	106		*Aen.* 3.578	133
Aen. 2.29	189		*Aen.* 3.578	137
Aen. 2.128–9	141		*Aen.* 3.588	149
Aen. 2.152	177		*Aen.* 3.614	208
Aen. 2.169	233		*Aen.* 3.622	141
Aen. 2.190–1	114		*Aen.* 3.627	110
Aen. 2.199–200	94		*Aen.* 4.8	207
Aen. 2.210	218		*Aen.* 4.64	241
Aen. 2.257	144		*Aen.* 4.114	238
Aen. 2.268–9	124		*Aen.* 4.206	255
Aen. 2.316	173		*Aen.* 4.233	225
Aen. 2.321	159		*Aen.* 4.327–8	143
Aen. 2.324–5	242		*Aen.* 4.368	261
Aen. 2.325	151		*Aen.* 4.484	161
Aen. 2.333–4	247		*Aen.* 4.544–5	127
Aen. 2.338	105		*Aen.* 4.567	253
Aen. 2.360	111		*Aen.* 4.569	160
Aen. 2.363	159		*Aen.* 4.584	106
Aen. 2.395	12		*Aen.* 4.625–6	230
Aen. 2.458	147		*Aen.* 4.628–9	190
Aen. 2.467–8	192		*Aen.* 4.684–5	137
Aen. 2.499	237		*Aen.* 4.687	141
Aen. 2.530	132		*Aen.* 4.687	141
Aen. 2.538–9	130		*Aen.* 4.700	224

Index Locorum

Aen. 5.7	173	*Aen.* 7.43	189
Aen. 5.159	178	*Aen.* 7.44–5	221
Aen. 5.208	191	*Aen.* 7.85	121, 225
Aen. 5.241–2	228	*Aen.* 7.126	122
Aen. 5.247–8	157	*Aen.* 7.148–9	106
Aen. 5.285	120	*Aen.* 7.160	150
Aen. 5.302	184	*Aen.* 7.166	246
Aen. 5.320	198	*Aen.* 7.274	227
Aen. 5.383	245	*Aen.* 7.281	256
Aen. 5.427	256	*Aen.* 7.330	225
Aen. 5.436	205	*Aen.* 7.340	95
Aen. 5.439–42	255	*Aen.* 7.397	193
Aen. 5.450	189	*Aen.* 7.437	113
Aen. 5.451	181	*Aen.* 7.448–9	222
Aen. 5.482	133	*Aen.* 7.461	187
Aen. 5.502	170	*Aen.* 7.461	246
Aen. 5.515	185	*Aen.* 7.528–30	179
Aen. 5.524	115	*Aen.* 7.528–30	180
Aen. 5.552	243	*Aen.* 7.551	177
Aen. 5.643	132	*Aen.* 7.551	97
Aen. 5.688–9	140	*Aen.* 7.554	126
Aen. 5.706–7	112	*Aen.* 7.575	135
Aen. 5.749	251	*Aen.* 7.586	189
Aen. 5.799	181	*Aen.* 7.620–2	106
Aen. 5.812	109	*Aen.* 7.623	94
Aen. 6.99	116	*Aen.* 7.632	147
Aen. 6.121	183	*Aen.* 7.689–90	204
Aen. 6.174	255	*Aen.* 7.691	181
Aen. 6.243	139	*Aen.* 7.713	224
Aen. 6.255	106	*Aen.* 7.728–9	162
Aen. 6.280–1	16 (n. 32)	*Aen.* 7.728–9	162
Aen. 6.313	171	*Aen.* 7.732	165
Aen. 6.315	171	*Aen.* 7.759	192
Aen. 6.434–6	111	*Aen.* 7.768	185
Aen. 6.491	105	*Aen.* 7.785	217
Aen. 6.528	198	*Aen.* 8.3	137
Aen. 6.535	141	*Aen.* 8.70	186
Aen. 6.535	149	*Aen.* 8.90	123
Aen. 6.556	95	*Aen.* 8.117	240
Aen. 6.574	106	*Aen.* 8.274	221
Aen. 6.591	178	*Aen.* 8.320	213
Aen. 6.625–7	194	*Aen.* 8.340	115
Aen. 6.686	172	*Aen.* 8.419	221
Aen. 6.687–8	142	*Aen.* 8.435–8	217
Aen. 6.697–8	139, 140	*Aen.* 8.438	222
Aen. 6.810–11	121	*Aen.* 8.445	219
Aen. 6.842	210	*Aen.* 8.476	126
Aen. 6.842–3	177	*Aen.* 8.478–9	121
Aen. 6.845–6	113	*Aen.* 8.527	169
Aen. 6.851–3	195	*Aen.* 8.537	237
Aen. 6.859	182	*Aen.* 8.698	184
Aen. 6.866	111	*Aen.* 8.702	98
Aen. 6.889	107	*Aen.* 8.706	105
Aen. 6.891	241	*Aen.* 8.728	151
Aen. 7.20	252	*Aen.* 9.27–8	166
Aen. 7.33	151	*Aen.* 9.33	141, 231

Aen. 9.37	235	*Aen.* 9.809	190
Aen. 9.51–3	187	*Aen.* 9.812	204
Aen. 9.53	107	*Aen.* 9.816–17	157
Aen. 9.56–7	176	*Aen.* 10.9	224
Aen. 9.57	107	*Aen.* 10.11–13	151
Aen. 9.63–4	226	*Aen.* 10.11–14	242
Aen. 9.66	222	*Aen.* 10.98–9	178
Aen. 9.131	109	*Aen.* 10.106	210
Aen. 9.143	159	*Aen.* 10.120	170
Aen. 9.144	241	*Aen.* 10.127–8	205
Aen. 9.159	125	*Aen.* 10.145	156
Aen. 9.166	96	*Aen.* 10.146	136
Aen. 9.184–5	220	*Aen.* 10.150	127
Aen. 9.186	98	*Aen.* 10.176	99
Aen. 9.194–5	153	*Aen.* 10.186	28 (n. 54)
Aen. 9.247–8	237	*Aen.* 10.249–50	172
Aen. 9.249	149	*Aen.* 10.270–1	218
Aen. 9.271	155	*Aen.* 10.270–5	217
Aen. 9.282	195	*Aen.* 10.353	195
Aen. 9.282	256	*Aen.* 10.361	189
Aen. 9.312	147	*Aen.* 10.361	190
Aen. 9.371	178	*Aen.* 10.362–3	205
Aen. 9.371–4	127	*Aen.* 10.364	176
Aen. 9.372	129	*Aen.* 10.395	204
Aen. 9.414	202	*Aen.* 10.395–6	203
Aen. 9.427	260	*Aen.* 10.415–16	206
Aen. 9.433	202	*Aen.* 10.430	143
Aen. 9.440	107	*Aen.* 10.432–3	190
Aen. 9.441	219	*Aen.* 10.438	214
Aen. 9.456	198	*Aen.* 10.445	228
Aen. 9.459	106	*Aen.* 10.467–9	201
Aen. 9.512	250	*Aen.* 10.489	202
Aen. 9.520	192	*Aen.* 10.489	203
Aen. 9.523	181	*Aen.* 10.513–14	253
Aen. 9.549	211	*Aen.* 10.514	201
Aen. 9.559–60	128	*Aen.* 10.525	101
Aen. 9.560–1	130	*Aen.* 10.532–3	154
Aen. 9.563	253	*Aen.* 10.536	201
Aen. 9.573	187	*Aen.* 10.558	126
Aen. 9.580	172	*Aen.* 10.564	151
Aen. 9.584	210	*Aen.* 10.590	202
Aen. 9.667	190	*Aen.* 10.599	255
Aen. 9.671	216	*Aen.* 10.602–3	251
Aen. 9.692–3	227	*Aen.* 10.616	158
Aen. 9.705	193	*Aen.* 10.650	155
Aen. 9.736	172	*Aen.* 10.651–2	131
Aen. 9.745–6	220	*Aen.* 10.682	249
Aen. 9.748	127	*Aen.* 10.693–4	188
Aen. 9.762–3	238	*Aen.* 10.712–13	253
Aen. 9.773	98	*Aen.* 10.733	127
Aen. 9.786–7	95	*Aen.* 10.746	111
Aen. 9.791	197	*Aen.* 10.753	163
Aen. 9.797	223	*Aen.* 10.760	219
Aen. 9.797–8	125	*Aen.* 10.770	111
Aen. 9.803–4	224	*Aen.* 10.794	223
Aen. 9.808–9	178	Aen. 10.801	219

Index Locorum

Aen. 10.803–4	247		*Aen.* 12.83	241
Aen. 10.829	213		*Aen.* 12.101–2	244
Aen. 10.892–4	250		*Aen.* 12.109	98
Aen. 11.1	149		*Aen.* 12.113	106
Aen. 11.5–6	201		*Aen.* 12.128	181
Aen. 11.5–8	202		*Aen.* 12.167	197
Aen. 11.6	135		*Aen.* 12.216–18	216
Aen. 11.62	131		*Aen.* 12.225–6	121
Aen. 11.78	205		*Aen.* 12.242	95
Aen. 11.78	205		*Aen.* 12.246	94
Aen. 11.130	168		*Aen.* 12.260–1	260
Aen. 11.187	233		*Aen.* 12.264	207
Aen. 11.225–42	117		*Aen.* 12.266	245
Aen. 11.233	112		*Aen.* 12.271	188
Aen. 11.233	112		*Aen.* 12.284	98
Aen. 11.244	150		*Aen.* 12.373	221
Aen. 11.247	106		*Aen.* 12.437	119
Aen. 11.247	150		*Aen.* 12.444	231
Aen. 11.265	154		*Aen.* 12.456	120
Aen. 11.290	125		*Aen.* 12.457–8	198
Aen. 11.291–2	215		*Aen.* 12.460–1	98
Aen. 11.291–2	216		*Aen.* 12.462	185
Aen. 11.296–7	178		*Aen.* 12.500–4	193
Aen. 11.373	109		*Aen.* 12.546	242
Aen. 11.377	141		*Aen.* 12.578	191
Aen. 11.385–6	117		*Aen.* 12.584	106
Aen. 11.424	113		*Aen.* 12.589	248
Aen. 11.427	196		*Aen.* 12.591	179
Aen. 11.455	250		*Aen.* 12.599	204
Aen. 11.536	123		*Aen.* 12.614	243
Aen. 11.553	161		*Aen.* 12.672–3	218
Aen. 11.561	233		*Aen.* 12.684–5	205
Aen. 11.612–13	256		*Aen.* 12.707–9	215
Aen. 11.617	144		*Aen.* 12.708	215
Aen. 11.617	145		*Aen.* 12.710	243
Aen. 11.624	189		*Aen.* 12.712	98
Aen. 11.639–40	250		*Aen.* 12.790	136
Aen. 11.640	202		*Aen.* 12.792	184
Aen. 11.646	141		*Aen.* 12.855	201
Aen. 11.688–9	213		*Aen.* 12.868	217
Aen. 11.700	166		*Aen.* 12.896–902	205
Aen. 11.745	185		*Aen.* 12.919	204
Aen. 11.749	172		*Aen.* 12.921–3	245
Aen. 11.780	136		*Aen.* 12.942–3	128
Aen. 11.790–2	191		*Aen.* 12.946–7	129
Aen. 11.793	192		*Aen.* 12.947–8	130
Aen. 11.795	145		*Ecl.* 3.94	111
Aen. 11.809	240		*Ecl.* 6.16	128
Aen. 11.823	131		*Geo.* 1.7	184
Aen. 11.832–3	185		*Geo.* 1.40	194
Aen. 11.850–1	126		*Geo.* 1.200	233
Aen. 12.9	205		*Geo.* 1.208	95
Aen. 12.10	101		*Geo.* 1.214	191
Aen. 12.36	152		*Geo.* 1.281	186
Aen. 12.66	178		*Geo.* 1.283	186
Aen. 12.73	136		*Geo.* 1.308–9	165

Geo. 1.318	179		*Geo.* 2.531	124
Geo. 1.320	198		*Geo.* 3.10	133
Geo. 1.331–3	239		*Geo.* 3.109	145
Geo. 1.348	197		*Geo.* 3.143	157
Geo. 1.364	243		*Geo.* 3.239	246
Geo. 1.390	96		*Geo.* 3.310	206
Geo. 1.482	151		*Geo.* 3.350	233
Geo. 1.498	182		*Geo.* 3.498	256
Geo. 1.506–7	152		*Geo.* 3.518	172
Geo. 2.114	155		*Geo.* 4.77	243
Geo. 2.146–7	166		*Geo.* 4.240	200
Geo. 2.282–3	179		*Geo.* 4.287–8	162
Geo. 2.385	121		*Geo.* 4.293	154
Geo. 2.405	240		*Geo.* 4.369	151
Geo. 2.462	235		*Geo.* 4.486	256
Geo. 2.475–7	193		*Geo.* 4.502	171
Geo. 2.475–7	194		*Geo.* 4.529	180
Geo. 2.506	156			

General Index

ablative 96, 97, 108, 124, 143, 157, 199, 206, 226, 255
abundance 28, 228, 243, 255, 258
Acca 46, 47, 131, 134
Achilles 103, 110, 128, 155, 216, 220
acrostic 131, 135
Actium 6, 16, 18, 180, 181, 184
accusative 95, 103, 124, 157, 161, 165, 181, 183, 199, 211, 220, 234, 257, 261
adjective 28–30, 94, 97, 98, 101, 108, 116, 124, 131, 138, 148, 169, 172, 207, 212, 223, 226, 234, 253, 254, 256
Adrastus 143, 147
Adyrmachidae 29, 55, 160, 162, 164
Aeneadae *see* Aeneas
Aeneas 22, 43, 94, 107, 110, 125, 128, 130, 132, 134, 139, 140, 147, 172, 181, 182, 184, 190, 201, 213, 216, 219, 225, 227, 229, 237, 242, 245, 247
Aeolus 18, 75, 229, 231, 240
Aetna 18, 73, 77, 128, 154, 171, 179, 219, 221, 230, 231, 234, 251
Aetolia 22, 45, 77, 117, 126, 230
Alexander 214
alliteration 29, 122, 124–126, 129, 141, 157, 168, 171, 174, 176, 221, 226, 228, 251
allusion 12, 100, 102, 113, 137, 142, 143, 147, 178, 179, 190, 201, 228, 237
Alps 5, 14, 19, 53, 81, 96, 150–152, 158, 181, 194, 195, 200, 240, 242
anachronism 211, 244, 246
anaphora 29, 103, 193
anastrophe 125, 177, 214
Anchises 102, 107, 139, 140, 142, 172, 195
Anna Perenna 22, 104, 136
Apollo 18, 43, 60, 61, 65, 115, 181, 194, 220, 227, 238
apostrophe 8, 194–196
apposition 162, 167, 182
Apulia 5, 106, 158, 227
Araxes 151
Argonaut 4, 11, 118, 140
asyndeton 139
Athene 18, 191, 220–223, 236; *see also* Minerva, Pallas
Atreus 107, 124, 143
Aufidus 15, 19, 54, 55, 160, 163, 164, 167, 180, 234, 254

augury 49, 136
Ausonia 28, 38, 54, 78, 94, 157, 181, 202, 235, 258
Autololes 43, 117–119, 121, 122

Baetis 57, 163, 165
Bagrada 168, 246, 249, 254
Balearic 57, 163, 165
ballista 81, 245
Brutus 23, 68, 69, 199, 205, 206, 210, 211
Byrsa 54, 55, 157

Cadmus 205
Caesar 8, 15, 21, 24–27, 93, 97, 103, 104, 111, 121, 137, 146, 158, 159, 166, 169, 170, 182, 195, 200, 212, 222, 230
caesura 98, 99, 108, 138, 162, 172, 228, 240
Camilla 131, 191, 213, 227
Cantabrians 57, 163, 165
Capaneus 169
Capua 9, 20, 100, 105, 106, 109, 158, 160, 230, 257
Cato 8, 9, 108, 110, 146
Celts 15, 57, 166, 198, 199, 203
Ceres 156, 184
Charon 29, 57, 111, 170, 171
chiasmus 29, 97, 111, 124, 129, 140, 158, 165, 178, 183, 186, 212, 213, 215, 244, 248, 251, 256
Cinyps 19, 135, 163
citizenship 14, 26, 55, 102, 110, 150, 155, 158
civil war 3, 4, 6, 7, 10, 12, 13, 16, 17, 21, 23, 24, 108, 113, 116, 146, 152, 170, 181, 184, 207, 259
clausula 31, 93, 94, 97, 100–102, 107, 111, 113, 119, 124, 129, 131, 134, 136, 140, 142, 167, 172, 174, 183, 186, 187, 189, 191–193, 196, 198, 201, 209, 226, 232, 236, 237, 239–241, 245, 246, 248, 250–256
conjecture 128, 135, 152, 177, 186, 195, 203, 213, 232, 235, 236, 241, 247, 248, 256, 260
consolation 20, 49, 51, 131, 136–138, 143, 153, 195, 213, 226
correption 154
corruption 17, 94, 122, 144, 173, 194, 213, 214, 256
Corvinus 93, 110, 257
Crista 72, 78, 204, 207, 208, 218, 219, 236
Curio 23, 24, 68, 69, 200, 210, 211, 234
Cyclops 60, 61, 72, 73, 186, 219, 221
Cyrene 161, 162
Cyzicus 11, 95, 118, 140

General Index

dactyl 30, 98, 105, 210, 254
Dardanian 42, 52, 62, 84, 117, 121, 122, 134, 155, 189, 195, 230, 242, 251
dative 102, 135, 138, 154, 181, 198, 199, 216, 226, 237, 241
Daunus, Daunia 55, 76, 77, 158, 174, 189, 231, 245
Decius 134, 140, 160, 222
Deianira 133, 134
Dido 22, 23, 102, 107, 110, 140, 143, 157, 173, 190, 218, 230, 238, 261
Diomedes 22, 43, 117, 126, 215, 220, 221, 230
discipline 5, 103, 104, 175
Domitian 3, 7, 19, 142, 160, 169, 192, 194, 195, 208
doublets 124, 127, 129, 130, 234, 246
duel 17, 71, 73, 94, 146, 149, 215, 216, 220, 226, 235, 236, 245

Ebro 53, 154, 165
ekphrasis 217, 218, 244
elegy 29, 94, 114, 134, 137, 139, 149, 199, 212, 238
elephant 20, 21, 29, 32, 57, 81, 83, 84, 85, 87, 166–168, 244, 246–257
elision 96, 107, 121, 169
enclosure 108, 148
enjambement 30, 116, 137, 138, 161, 175, 199, 204, 205, 214, 221, 230
Ennius 4, 16, 30, 115, 157, 158, 170, 181, 193, 220
Eteocles 143, 256
ethnography 160
ethnonym 97, 160, 189, 199, 246
etymology, *figura etymologica* 29, 119, 120, 121, 150, 162, 168, 171, 182, 184, 186, 235, 248–250
Eurus 75, 179, 229, 234
Euryalus 11, 123, 125, 127, 145, 147, 202, 206, 209, 220, 237, 260

Fabius 7–10, 13, 20, 23, 26, 42, 43, 80, 81, 87, 93, 94, 95, 96, 99, 101, 102, 105, 106, 107, 110, 112, 113–117, 134, 135, 142, 195, 196, 204, 207, 217, 218, 244, 245, 259, 261
Fate 13, 18, 21, 6, 39, 41, 63, 65, 75, 81, 97, 99, 100, 105, 137, 148, 150, 12, 204, 225, 239, 240, 241, 242, 259, 260, 269
Faunus 61, 182,
Fibrenus 234, 249, 250
First Punic War 116–19, 154, 202, 239
Flaminius 7–10, 14, 23, 42, 43, 53, 70, 71, 93, 99, 100, 101, 105, 110, 113, 114, 152, 169, 176, 181, 211, 212, 214, 244, 259
focalization 108

Fortuna 26, 27, 39, 41, 51, 63, 65, 69, 87, 96, 97, 142, 196, 259
four-word line 182, 244
Fury, Furies 59, 81, 174, 227, 245

Gaetulia 45, 119, 122
Galba 12, 13, 23, 105, 177, 187
Garamantia 55, 160, 161
Garganus 55, 75, 158, 223, 227
Gaul 15, 166, 214
gemination 29, 99, 132, 193, 235
gender (grammatical) 100, 107, 151, 182
genitive 95, 102, 119, 121, 124, 127, 153, 172, 175, 183, 186, 192, 193, 195, 196, 211, 255, 256, 257
geography 161, 162, 167, 252
Gerunium 244, 245, 252, 253
Gestar 95, 103, 130, 173
Giant 61, 161, 185, 186, 219
Gigantomachy 27, 185, 186, 219, 221
glory 12, 14, 53, 63, 65, 83, 96, 153, 154, 192, 213
gloss 156, 230
golden line, "near-golden" line 30, 126, 185, 186
Gorgon 70–73, 217, 222

Hamilcar 156, 216
Hammon 16, 60, 61, 183, 184
Hannibal 3–9, 11, 13, 14, 15, 17, 18, 19, 20, 22, 23, 26, 27, 36, 39, 40, 41, 49, 53, 55, 57, 59, 69, 70, 73, 75, 78, 79, 81, 86, 87, 88, 89, 93, 94, 95, 97, 100, 102, 103, 110, 112, 117, 120, 123, 129, 135
Hanno 13, 103, 114, 115, 116, 163
haruspicy 99
Hasdrubal 124, 160, 163, 165, 167, 202, 255
Hebrus 163
Hector 188, 205, 216, 220, 227, 242
hendiadys 105, 123, 177, 216
Hercules 11, 53, 61, 95, 102, 112, 131, 133, 145, 182, 183, 185, 188, 189, 201, 206, 212, 219
Hesperides 161
Hunger Games 146
hypallage 10, 254
hyperbaton 29, 30, 116, 138, 161
hyperbole 152

Iapygia 53, 59, 174, 176
Iberia, Iberian 154, 160, 162 166
Imilce 133, 135, 260
imperative 106, 107, 140
infinitive 111, 123, 125, 135, 138, 143, 157, 162, 171, 192, 213, 220, 221, 227, 237, 253
initial word of line 253
interlaced 99, 160, 168, 202, 209
intertextuality 21
intratextuality 21, 218, 231, 244

General Index

Iris 18, 56, 58, 73, 79, 81, 82, 123, 138, 170, 211, 224, 225, 237, 240, 242–244, 247
irony 32, 93, 123, 126, 127, 130, 135, 136, 241

Juno 16–19, 22, 61, 75, 79, 106, 111, 114, 132, 182–185, 199, 215, 219, 220, 224–230, 236, 238, 241, 242, 259
Jupiter 3, 4, 18, 22, 61, 75, 79, 81, 116, 151, 153, 169, 181, 183, 185, 186, 194, 195, 196, 201, 214, 215, 216, 224, 225, 226, 227, 228, 238–243

Latins 94, 127, 231, 268
Latinus 101, 182, 189, 215
Lemnian 173, 222
lengthening (syllabic) 241, 246
Lentulus 23, 26, 100, 111, 137, 146
litotes 96, 127, 249
locative 173

Macae 38, 39, 160, 161
Mago 9, 15, 20, 54, 102, 109, 150, 159, 163, 164, 184, 237, 247
Maharbal 15, 158, 160, 163
Mancinus 11, 38, 39, 42, 43, 45, 47, 57, 98, 117, 120, 122, 124, 127
"many mouths" topos 193, 194
Maraxes 95, 102
Marcellus 101, 106, 132, 196, 214
Marcius 115, 116, 241
Marius 12, 17, 23, 68, 69, 203, 206–210
Marmarica 55, 160, 161
Marsi 15, 59, 175
Massylia 22, 55, 114, 152, 160, 161, 214
Medea 112, 128
Metaurus 163, 198, 199
Metellus 183, 199, 259
metonymy 94, 117, 119, 121, 127, 147, 154, 156, 158, 161, 164, 193, 202, 227, 232, 243
Mezentius 188, 201, 219
Mincius 20, 86, 87, 256
Minerva 16, 18, 217, 218, 220, 221, 228, 238; see also Athene, Pallas
Minucius 7, 23, 81, 111, 113, 117, 176, 204, 244, 245, 259
Moor 13, 55, 83, 85, 160, 161, 255
Mopsus 133, 148, 172, 208, 209
multiethnic 15, 26, 160, 164
Muse 65, 174, 193, 194

Nasamon 54, 55, 97, 160
Nealces 15, 17, 54, 55, 58, 59, 64, 65, 67, 69, 160, 162, 172, 174, 175
Neptune 19, 114, 181, 256
Nile, Nilotic 55, 94, 128, 162

Nisus 11, 124, 125, 145–47, 206, 209, 220, 237
nominative 98, 124, 216, 220, 241
Numidia 57, 59, 98, 104, 160, 163, 168, 176, 177

Oedipus 12,146, 147
Olympus 81, 180, 184, 185, 186, 216, 221, 225
omens, portents 8, 93, 94, 99, 110, 119, 136, 148, 173, 202, 207
Oscan 78, 165, 238
oxymoron 141, 167, 247

Pallas (Minerva) 17–19, 60, 61, 70–75, 79, 170, 181, 183, 184, 205, 216–227, 236–238, 240, 242–244
Pallas, son of Evander 128, 129, 131, 142, 201–203, 205, 252
parenthesis 97, 113, 231, 237
Paulus 8–11, 13–15, 20, 21, 23, 25, 26, 30, 32, 39–43, 49, 58, 59, 71, 86, 87, 94, 95, 99–104, 107–117, 135–137, 173, 174, 176, 183, 196, 198, 199, 206, 211, 212, 235, 241, 244, 257–259, 261
periphrasis 122, 159, 177, 181, 195, 238, 252
Pharsalus 6, 15, 21, 23–27, 93, 95, 100, 103, 111, 113, 118, 147–149, 158, 159, 169, 170, 173, 190–192, 195, 196, 221, 242, 259
Philip 101, 165, 183
Picentine, Picenum 59, 176, 207, 211
pietas 11, 12, 118, 128, 134, 139, 140, 142, 148, 174
pleonasm 147, 159
Po 57
Polynices 11, 143, 216
polyptoton 17, 27, 30, 189, 190
polysyndeton 229, 243, 244
Pompey 21, 25, 26, 93, 95, 100, 103, 104, 111, 113, 118, 137, 146, 147, 158, 174, 230, 259
Porsenna 199
Poseidon 224, 225, 227
Priam 130
Procris 12, 141, 144
prolepsis 126, 223
prophecy 4, 8, 9, 18, 20, 22, 43, 93, 110–112, 114–116, 136, 151, 152, 169, 174, 187, 194–196, 240–242, 261
prosaic usage 94, 98, 101, 113, 126, 141, 149, 197, 198, 223, 231, 238, 247, 257
Proteus 22, 114, 116, 224, 240, 241
Pyramus 12, 126–128, 137
Pyrenees 55, 163–165
Pyrrhus 130, 246, 247, 251

quantity (syllabic) 99, 182, 186
Quirinus 60, 61, 182

redditio 212, 256
Regulus 107, 118–120, 134, 146, 195, 201, 237, 246, 257

General Index

repetition 28, 101, 102, 105, 108, 109, 123, 125, 140–142, 145, 149, 153, 154, 157, 167, 169, 180, 186, 188, 196, 197, 200, 206, 218, 221, 223, 224, 226, 236–238, 241, 244, 247, 255, 256, 260, 261
Romulus 131, 182, 183, 236
Rutulian 22, 130, 182, 216

Saguntum 11–14, 21, 53, 61, 95, 101, 103, 106, 112, 129, 132, 133, 136, 147, 148, 150, 151, 155, 158, 171, 174, 182, 198, 201, 211, 217, 218, 227, 229, 242, 245, 247
Samnite 15, 59, 128, 159, 174–176
Sarranus 156
Satricus 10–14, 26, 29, 30, 32, 42–47, 49, 99, 117–127, 132–140, 144, 145, 148, 171, 172, 174, 213
Scaevola 17, 67, 69, 199–203, 205, 210, 211, 223
Scipio Africanus 4, 8, 9, 16–20, 24, 59, 68–71, 73, 94, 115, 116, 123, 131, 140, 169, 176, 177, 182, 185, 186, 206, 207, 210–216, 219–222, 225–227, 235, 236, 240–242, 245, 258
Scipio the Elder 215, 222
Senate 9, 20, 23, 24, 103, 114, 115, 173, 174, 184, 200, 208, 213, 257
Serranus 114, 120, 135, 145, 195
Sibyl 43, 93, 110, 114–116, 140, 171
Sicily 53, 154, 210
Sidon, Sidonian 79, 257
simile 8, 9, 16, 19, 27, 37, 58, 108, 110, 149, 166, 173, 178–180, 185, 188, 189, 197, 205, 221, 224, 230, 252
simplex pro composito 95, 129, 196, 235, 240
Solymus 8, 10–14, 23, 26, 29, 30, 32, 42–45, 47, 51, 57, 94, 110, 117, 118, 120, 122, 124–133, 135–148, 171–174, 258, 261
spondee 30, 31, 98, 105, 108, 116, 121, 181, 199, 204, 225, 240, 254
Steigerung 17–19, 170, 220, 222, 235, 246
Stoic 200, 250
storm 16, 19, 75, 83, 107, 112, 142, 178, 179, 186, 187, 191, 224, 226, 229, 231, 234, 235, 247
sublime 19, 82, 179, 191, 249
substantive 126, 161
suicide 8, 12, 13, 20, 23, 101, 111, 117, 118, 123, 133, 136, 137, 140, 143, 145–148, 150, 173, 208, 214, 233, 258–260
Sulla 190, 251
Sulmo 29, 43–45, 47, 117, 120–122, 134
synaloepha 129
syncopation 133, 147
synonym 4, 28, 94, 150, 156, 157, 160, 173, 178, 206, 235

Syphax 101, 104, 161, 207
Syracuse 12, 101, 106, 233, 234, 243, 249
Syrtis 156, 160, 180

Tellus 5, 52, 60, 70, 121, 125, 152, 155, 156, 158, 161, 164, 166, 173, 174, 184, 191, 215, 231, 243, 247
Thebes 7, 16, 110, 159, 188, 256
theomachy 17, 18, 32, 170, 181, 220, 221, 223, 224, 238
Thisbe 12, 125, 126, 128, 137
Thoas 45, 126, 206
Thyestes 107, 143, 146
Tiber 53, 151, 152, 157
Ticinus 5, 14, 17, 71, 131, 150, 151, 155, 170, 187, 189, 214, 215–222, 231, 245, 258
toponym 122, 202, 210, 248
tragedy 8, 11, 12, 17, 32, 98, 99, 118, 128, 130, 131, 140, 142, 147, 148
transferred epithet 96, 125, 131
Trasimene 5–7, 14, 23, 53, 93, 99, 105, 110, 113, 114, 150, 152, 161, 169, 176, 181, 182, 184, 187–189, 193, 202, 211, 212, 214, 224, 226, 229, 259
Trebia 5, 6, 19, 20, 24, 52, 53, 105, 152, 158, 190, 193, 218, 229, 234, 239, 248–250
tricolon abundans 241, 255
Tritonia 18, 61, 70, 74, 138, 183, 216, 225, 237
Troy 12, 22, 43, 53, 65, 93, 120, 125, 130, 179–181, 183, 224, 225, 227, 238, 242, 255
Turnus 93, 94, 101, 107, 128, 130, 132, 154, 155, 158, 166, 187, 201, 202, 205, 215, 216, 217, 220, 224, 244
Tydeus 11, 22, 110, 131, 169, 204
Tyre 47, 156

Umbria 59, 176

Varro 7–10, 14, 20, 21, 26, 39, 49, 56, 57, 59, 68, 71, 85, 87, 89, 93–95, 99, 100–108, 113, 115, 118, 134–136, 147, 168–176, 181, 210–214, 244, 248, 251, 253, 257–261
Vascones 57, 165
Venus 19, 29, 31, 60, 61, 100, 157, 172, 181, 183, 184, 194, 196, 216, 219, 222, 227
Vulturnus 16–19, 32, 76, 77, 79, 98, 179, 219, 229–236, 240, 242, 252, 254

wall 111, 158, 168, 193

Xanthippus 43, 107, 118–120, 153, 169

Zama 19, 21, 123, 153, 159, 185, 214–217, 219, 221, 225–227, 229, 242, 245, 250

Latin Words

adimere 143, 211, 213
agger 56, 167, 247, 255
ante oculos, ante ora 40, 46, 86, 109, 128, 130, 131, 142, 258
arma uirumque 44, 111, 126

bellator, bellatrix 29, 30, 54, 66, 82, 160, 161, 164, 183, 199, 225, 234, 243, 247
-bundus, adjectives in 138, 224

Concordia 17, 68, 203, 206, 207, 209
cruor 99, 141, 144, 191, 227, 235
cuneus, cunei 64, 167, 198

dies 100, 107
Discordia 10, 16, 60, 88, 98, 101, 181, 207, 224, 231, 259, 260
ductor 28, 40, 50, 52, 68, 70, 84, 102, 120, 149, 155, 166, 204, 211, 216, 217, 251

error 26, 118, 134, 139, 145, 173, 174

-fer, adjectives in 107, 225
fraus 46, 88, 118, 134, 259, 260

-ger, adjectives in 107, 225

induere 66, 202, 240

moenia 40, 95, 111, 120, 125, 158, 195, 209
moru 54, 76, 84, 101, 159, 160, 240, 251

pariter 54, 60, 108, 128, 162, 182, 185, 255
properus 96, 106

sanguis 42, 80, 112, 132, 134, 141, 143, 222, 243
sator 31, 60, 182, 186
scelus, sceleratus 13, 26, 42, 118, 133, 145, 148, 149, 174
segnis, segnitia 25, 26, 42, 95, 102, 113
sensim 72, 80, 82, 148, 222–224, 234, 243, 244, 249
signum 25, 26, 28, 40, 93, 94, 96, 103–105, 113, 116, 137, 143, 157, 161, 171, 175, 176, 185, 228
stare 145, 171, 173, 176, 200, 215, 248

turbidus 8, 101, 102, 107, 108, 205, 248

uallum 8, 38, 40, 68, 101, 102, 107, 108, 205, 248
uariatio 17, 20, 28, 29, 124, 126, 127, 135–137, 142, 146, 149, 157, 158, 166, 170, 173, 175, 176, 178, 196, 203, 228, 240
uates 9, 42, 114–116, 221
uirgo 72, 74, 78, 149, 157, 172, 183, 217, 221, 222, 225, 226, 236
unanimus 207
uirtus 20, 66, 82, 84, 94, 153, 194, 201, 225, 241, 249, 250, 253